ISAIAH IN THE
BOOK OF MORMON

FARMS Publications

Teachings of the Book of Mormon

The Geography of Book of Mormon Events: A Source Book

The Book of Mormon Text Reformatted according to Parallelistic Patterns

Eldin Ricks's Thorough Concordance of the LDS Standard Works

A Guide to Publications on the Book of Mormon: A Selected Annotated Bibliography

Book of Mormon Authorship Revisited: The Evidences for Ancient Origins

Ancient Scrolls from the Dead Sea: Photographs and Commentary on a Unique Collection of Scrolls

LDS Perspectives on the Dead Sea Scrolls

Periodicals

Insights: An Ancient Window

FARMS Review of Books

Journal of Book of Mormon Studies

FARMS Reprint Series

Book of Mormon Authorship: New Light on Ancient Origins

The Doctrine and Covenants by Themes

Copublished with Deseret Book Company

An Ancient American Setting for the Book of Mormon

Warfare in the Book of Mormon

By Study and Also by Faith: Essays in Honor of Hugh W. Nibley

The Sermon at the Temple and the Sermon on the Mount

Rediscovering the Book of Mormon

Reexploring the Book of Mormon

Of All Things Classic Quotations from Hugh Nibley

The Allegory of the Olive Tree

Temples of the Ancient World

Expressions of Faith: Testimonies from LDS Scholars

Feasting on the Word: The Literary Testimony of the Book of Mormon

The Collected Works of Hugh Nibley

Old Testament and Related Studies

Enoch the Prophet

The World and the Prophets

Mormonism and Early Christianity

Lehi in the Desert; The World of the Jaredites; There Were Jaredites

An Approach to the Book of Mormon

Since Cumorah

The Prophetic Book of Mormon

Approaching Zion

The Ancient State

Tinkling Cymbals and Sounding Brass

Temple and Cosmos

Brother Brigham Challenges the Saints

Published through Research Press

Pre-Columbian Contact with the Americas across the Oceans: An Annotated Bibliography

New World Figurine Project, vol. 1

A Comprehensive Annotated Book of Mormon Bibliography

ISAIAH IN THE
BOOK OF MORMON

Edited by
Donald W. Parry and John W. Welch

Foundation for Ancient Research and Mormon Studies
Provo, Utah

Foundation for Ancient Research and Mormon Studies
The Neal A. Maxwell Institute for Religious Scholarship
Brigham Young University

Printed in the United States of America
12 11 10 09 08 07   6 5 4 3 2

Library of Congress Cataloguing-in-Publication Data

Isaiah in the Book of Mormon / edited by Donald W. Parry and
John W. Welch
    p.   cm.
  Book originated from an address delivered at the FARMS
Symposium in 1995.
   Includes bibliographical references and indexes.
   ISBN 0-934893-29-2
   1. Bible. O.T. Isaiah—Criticism, interpretation, etc. 2. Book
of Mormon—Criticism, interpretation, etc. 3. Book of Mormon—
Relation to the Bible. 4. Isaiah (Biblical prophet) I. Parry, Donald W.
II. Welch, John W. (John Woodland)
BS1515.2.I76   1998
289.3'22—dc21   97-39238
                                                CIP

Table of Contents

Introduction

No chapters in the Book of Mormon are more formidable to readers than are the Isaiah passages quoted by Nephi, Jacob, Abinadi, and the resurrected Lord. Recognizing this challenge, the purpose of this book is to help readers get through the Isaiah barrier in the Book of Mormon. We hope that readers will not only get through Isaiah, but will get much out of this great and marvelous book of prophecy.

Obviously, Isaiah is difficult to understand. In fact, Isaiah was specifically commanded by the Lord to speak precisely in such a way that his recalcitrant audience would "hear . . . but understand *not*" and would "see . . . but perceive *not*" (Isaiah 6:9). God wanted Isaiah to tell the people enough to warn them, but not to tell them enough to let them comprehend what was really going on (see Isaiah 6:10–11). Isaiah carried out this assignment masterfully, making it hard for almost everyone to understand what he was talking about.

In the face of this difficulty, our objective in this book is to make Isaiah as plain as possible. To do this, we turn primarily to the Book of Mormon itself. Each time Isaiah is quoted in the Book of Mormon, it is for a specific, intentional purpose. The use of Isaiah in the Book of Mormon is not a shallow or superficial importing of extraneous material into an illogical context. In each case, it is clear that the Book of Mormon teachers were intimately, deeply, and profoundly immersed in the meanings of these Isaiah texts. If modern readers can only understand why and how Nephi, Jacob, Abinadi, and Jesus interpreted and used Isaiah, the insights in the Book of Mormon will do much to clarify what those Isaiah chapters are all about. Intriguingly, Nephi rejoiced in the "plainness" of Isaiah (2 Nephi 25:4) and knew that Isaiah possessed great knowledge of the Messiah, for he had seen the Redeemer as had Nephi (see 2 Nephi 11:2). By using Nephi, his fellow prophets, and the words of Christ as our guide, hopefully the writings of Isaiah can become plainer and simpler to us.

To this end, we have amassed a large amount of interesting information, analyzed quantities of data, pursued various approaches, and utilized several tools. Hopefully, all of this will promote a clearer understanding of Isaiah and a greater appreciation for the Book of Mormon.

In the first part of this book, we offer four introductory chapters: the keynote address delivered by Elder Jeffrey R. Holland at the FARMS Symposium, held 20 May 1995 at Brigham Young University, from which this volume originated; an overview by John W. Welch, discussing the Nephite view of the future and how that prophetic outlook derived from and gave structure to their understanding of Isaiah; an analysis by John Gee of factors involved in the selection of the Isaiah passages included in the Book of Mormon; and an explanation by Donald W. Parry of the keys offered by Nephi to understand Isaiah.

In part two, we study the main blocks of Isaiah quoted in the Book of Mormon. In each case, the authors ask such questions as these: Why did Nephi or Jacob quote this particular Isaiah passage? Does the Book of Mormon context shed light on the meaning of the passage? or How do the Book of Mormon authors understand or interpret that Isaiah text? To shed light on helpful questions such as these, Andrew C. Skinner explains Nephi's use of Isaiah 48–49 in 1 Nephi 19–22; John S. Thompson explores Jacob's use of Isaiah 50–51 in 2 Nephi 6–10; David R. Seely focuses on the theme of pride drawn by Nephi out of Isaiah 2–14 in 2 Nephi 12–30; Stephen D. Ricks clarifies the vision and calling of the prophet in Isaiah 6 as a prototypical heavenly commission; Robert A. Cloward explicates the relevance of Isaiah 29 to the Book of Mormon, especially in 2 Nephi 27; Dana M. Pike interprets Isaiah 52 historically, linguistically and religiously; John W. Welch surveys the use of Isaiah 53, which together with Isaiah 52 figures prominently in the trial of Abinadi; and Cynthia L. Hallen shows why and how Jesus turned to Isaiah 54 to introduce his covenant of kindness in 3 Nephi 22.

In part three, we provide three additional studies that cover subjects relevant to Isaiah and the Restoration. Ann N. Madsen traces the powerful Isaiah threads that run through the life and teachings of Joseph Smith. Royal Skousen tells what we can learn from the original 1829 manuscripts of the Book of Mormon and the textual variants that exist between the King James Version and the translation of the Book of Mormon. Andrew H. Hedges looks into the status of Isaiah in America during the century before the time of Joseph Smith and concludes that the Book of Mormon makes much more of Isaiah than did the predecessors and contemporaries of Joseph Smith.

Finally, in part 4, we offer several resources concerning the ancient words of Isaiah and modern LDS writings regarding his fascinating texts. Donald W. Parry and Janet L. Garrard Willis offer a glossary to help modern readers understand the meanings of some of Isaiah's obscure vocabulary; John W. Welch summarizes LDS thought concerning the question of authorship of Isaiah and explores that issue in light of Book of Mormon perspectives; John L. Hilton reports on the latest attempts to determine by wordprinting analysis whether the book of Isaiah was written by one author or several; and John S. Thompson and Eric Smith supply a comprehensive bibliographic survey of LDS literature about Isaiah to help diligent students pursue their studies further.

We hope that these materials will help average but diligent readers find their way through the Isaiah sections in the Book of Mormon. While we do not imagine that we have attained the same plane of understanding of Isaiah that Nephi enjoyed, we feel confident that Nephi's example in reaching a degree of simple clarity is at least possible for all those who seek it. If we have supplied answers to even a few of the many questions that confront readers as they encounter the words of Isaiah in the Book of Mormon, we will consider the time and toil of all involved to have been worthwhile.

We are indebted to many for the creation of this volume. We have received every possible assistance from FARMS, including encouragement, editorial and research support, and a multitude of other resources. We appreciate Brent Hall and his team for assistance with our 1995 conference on Isaiah. We thank the editorial staff who worked under the direction of Mel Thorne, including Claire Foley, Mary Mahan, Jessica Taylor, and Stephanie Terry, for their excellent service. We are grateful to the research efforts of Jeanette Miller, Becky Schultheis, David Geilman, and others who tracked down obscure details, bibliographic materials, checked a host of sources for accuracy, and proofread the manuscript. A score of scholars examined the articles in this volume, adding insights and improvements. We appreciate their professionalism and scholarship. We gratefully recognize that all author and editor royalties from this book have been dedicated to FARMS for future Book of Mormon research.

PART ONE

Overviews

"More Fully Persuaded"
Isaiah's Witness of Christ's Ministry

Elder Jeffrey R. Holland

As a testament of Jesus Christ, the Book of Mormon centers on the Redeemer's ministry and, to this end, uses Isaiah as a witness of Christ's past, present, and future loving and saving acts.

I am honored to speak of Isaiah's witness of the Lord Jesus Christ. In doing so I acknowledge on the one hand my great inadequacy and on the other the grandeur of the Savior as subject and Isaiah as writer. Nevertheless, I am determined to proceed, if only because of my love for this magnificent messianic message and the texts that bring it to us.[1]

I have taken my title from 1 Nephi 19. In that chapter Nephi says he read and taught his brethren many things, "that they might know concerning the doings of the Lord in other lands, among people of old" (1 Nephi 19:22). Citing several of the ancient prophets from the engraved plates carrying such information, Nephi then says, "that I might more fully persuade them to believe in the Lord their Redeemer I did read unto them that which was written by the prophet Isaiah" (1 Nephi 19:23).

Although for the most part I use the King James rendering of the Isaiah passages in this paper, nevertheless I have (with just two exceptions) used only those verses that also appear in the Book of Mormon. I do that, first, because the Book of Mormon does such a marvelous job of focusing Isaiah's witness for Christ, and second, because this will remind us all of the grand purpose of the Book of Mormon: to convince "the Jew and Gentile that Jesus is the Christ, the Eternal God, manifesting himself unto all nations" (Book of

Mormon, title page). Isaiah's words fulfill this purpose in a singular and inspiring way, and no other textual source in all the world makes the contribution to understanding Isaiah that the Book of Mormon makes. Its impact is still not fully recognized and its depths are still not fully plumbed. We can help the whole world be "more fully persuaded" of Christ's divinity because of our Latter-day Saint view of him as seen through the eyes of Isaiah.

In a helpful footnote to 2 Nephi 12:2, our current edition of the LDS scriptures notes that there are some 433 verses of Isaiah quoted in the Book of Mormon. According to Monte Nyman, of those 433 (or so) verses of Isaiah, some 391 of them refer to the attributes or mission of Christ.[2] In that same vein, Donald Parry pointed out to me that Isaiah provides 61 names and titles of deity in his writings. Those names and titles are found 708 times in the book of Isaiah, giving us an average appearance of one every 1.9 verses.

Surely it is because of this messianic focus in Isaiah—a messianic preoccupation, we might say—that Nephi feels so strongly about his writings:

> Wherefore, hearken, O my people, which are of the house of Israel, and give ear unto my words; for because the words of Isaiah are not plain unto you, nevertheless they are plain unto all those that are filled with the spirit of prophecy. . . . Yea, and my soul delighteth in the words of Isaiah. . . . [and] they are of worth unto the children of men, and he that supposeth that they are not, unto them will I speak particularly, . . . for I know that they shall be of great worth unto them in the last days; for in that day shall they understand them; wherefore, for their good have I written them. (2 Nephi 25:4, 5, 8)

In our own time Elder Bruce R. McConkie has said:

> If our eternal salvation depends upon our ability to understand the writings of Isaiah as fully and truly as

Nephi understood them—and who shall say such is not the case!—how shall we fare in that great day when with Nephi we shall stand before the pleasing bar of Him who said: "great are the words of Isaiah"? . . .

It just may be that my salvation (and yours also!) does in fact depend upon our ability to understand the writings of Isaiah as fully and truly as Nephi understood them. . . .

Isaiah is everywhere known as the messianic prophet because of the abundance, beauty, and perfection of his prophetic utterances foretelling the first coming of our Lord. And truly such he is. No old world prophet, whose inspired sayings have come down to us, can compare with him in this respect. Moreover, the first coming of the Messiah is past, and so even those among us who are not overly endowed with spiritual insight can look back and see in the birth, ministry, and death of our Lord the fulfillment of Isaiah's forecasts.[3]

It was, after all, the Savior of the world himself who said, after quoting to the Nephites chapter 54 of Isaiah, "And now, behold, I say unto you, that ye ought to search these things. [By "these things" I presume he means all the writings of Isaiah generally and not just chapter 54.] Yea, a commandment I give unto you that ye search these things diligently; for great are the words of Isaiah. For surely he spake as touching all things concerning my people which are of the house of Israel" (3 Nephi 23:1–2).

One of the reasons Nephi feels so strongly about Isaiah and, as I have said elsewhere,[4] one of the reasons Isaiah is so conspicuous at the outset of the Book of Mormon is that Isaiah and Nephi (along with Nephi's younger brother Jacob) constitute the original "three witnesses" of the Book of Mormon—or more precisely the original three Book of Mormon witnesses of the Lord Jesus Christ and his divinity.

Nephi wrote:

> And now I, Nephi, write more of the words of Isaiah,
> for my soul delighteth in his words. For I will liken his
> words unto my people, and I will send them forth unto
> all my children, for he verily saw my Redeemer, even as I
> have seen him. And my brother, Jacob, also has seen him
> as I have seen him; wherefore, I will send their words
> forth unto my children to prove unto them that my
> words are true. Wherefore, by the words of three, God
> hath said, I will establish my word. Nevertheless, God
> sendeth more witnesses, and he proveth all his
> words. . . . And now I write some of the words of Isaiah,
> that whoso of my people shall see these words may lift
> up their hearts and rejoice for all men. Now these are the
> words, and ye may liken them unto you and unto all
> men. (2 Nephi 11:2, 3, 8)

It would seem, even in Isaiah's very name, which in
Hebrew means "Jehovah saves" or "the Lord is salvation,"
that Isaiah was prepared from birth—and of course we
would say from before birth—to testify of the Messiah and
bear such witness of the divinity of Christ's coming.

It is, of course, important to remember that many of
Isaiah's prophecies can be or have been or will be fulfilled
in more than one way and in more than one dispensation.[5]
Obviously, we have material in Isaiah's writings that applies to a whole range of experiences, including that of the
premortal Christ, of his first mortal advent in the meridian
of time, and of his Second Coming in the latter days.

New Testament contemporaries struggled with the du-
ality of Isaiah's prophecies a bit, perhaps too eagerly taking
a passage clearly applying to Christ's Second Coming and
forcing it to represent his appearance in the meridian of
time. Of course, when Christ refused to proclaim himself
the messiah of the last days in his first advent, some were
disappointed. But everyone should learn a little patience in

all of this: many of those prophecies have since then been fulfilled, and they will all be fulfilled in time.

Let me leave these introductory comments and turn to five aspects of Christ's divine mission that are testified of and outlined by Isaiah. As all of you know, there is much messianic material from Isaiah that could be included. Nevertheless, I will limit my categories to five. Even with that small number I can give only a few "headlines"—or, if you prefer, "heads," as Jacob calls them in the Book of Mormon (Jacob 1:4).

Christ's Birth, Mortal Ministry, and Atonement

I begin with the great Immanuel prophecy of Isaiah 7 and 2 Nephi 17:

> Therefore the Lord himself shall give you a sign; Behold, a virgin shall conceive, and bear a son, and shall call his name Immanuel. Butter and honey shall he eat, that he may know to refuse the evil, and choose the good. For before the child shall know to refuse the evil, and choose the good, the land that thou abhorrest shall be forsaken of both her kings. The Lord shall bring upon thee, and upon thy people, and upon thy father's house, days that have not come, from the day that Ephraim departed from Judah; even the king of Assyria. (Isaiah 7:14–17, parallel to 2 Nephi 17:14–17)

As given in the Old Testament, this passage was intended to be a sign to King Ahaz, encouraging him to take his strength from the Lord and put his faith in the power of heaven, rather than in the military might of Damascus or Samaria or other militant camps in the neighborhood. Ahaz was not particularly interested in this sign, but the Lord gave it to him anyway, specifying that a virgin would conceive and bring forth a son whose name would be called Immanuel.

The dual or parallel fulfillment of this prophecy comes in the realization that Isaiah's wife, a pure and good young woman—symbolically representing another pure young woman—did bring forth a son. This boy's birth was a type and shadow of the greater and later fulfillment of that prophecy, the virgin birth of the Lord Jesus Christ. The dual fulfillment here is particularly interesting in light of the fact that Isaiah's wife apparently was of royal blood, and therefore her son was of the royal line of David. Isaiah's son is thus the type, the prefiguring, of the greater Immanuel, Jesus Christ, the ultimate King who would be born of a literal virgin. His title Immanuel would be carried forward to latter days, being applied to the Savior in Doctrine and Covenants 128:22.

Turning to Isaiah 9 and 2 Nephi 19, there are many ways to use this famous passage, including as the coronation of a King/Messiah, but let me refer to it here for its references to Christ's birth. We all love and respond to these lines perhaps made more famous by George F. Handel than by Isaiah himself: "For unto us a child is born, unto us a son is given: and the government shall be upon his shoulder: and his name shall be called Wonderful, Counsellor, The mighty God, The everlasting Father, The Prince of Peace" (Isaiah 9:6, parallel to 2 Nephi 19:6).

One of the things I love most about this magnificent passage, even with its splendor and royalty and culmination, is the reminder that through it all Christ is still the son. "For unto us a child is born, unto us a son is given." He is the child of heaven, the Son of God, of whom the Prophet Joseph Smith said, "When still a boy He had all the intelligence necessary to enable Him to rule and govern the kingdom of the Jews, and could reason with the wisest and most profound doctors of law and divinity, and make their theories and practice to appear like folly compared with the wisdom He possessed."[6]

The fact that the government will eventually be upon his shoulder affirms what all Latter-day Saints clearly understand—that he is Lord of Lords and King of Kings and will one day rule over his kingdom in person, with all of the majesty and sacred vestments that belong to a high priest and to a holy sovereign. And we all take great comfort from the fact that because the government—and its burdens—will be upon his shoulders, such concerns will therefore be lifted in great measure from ours.

This idea of the Messiah bearing the burden of the government seems to me yet another not-so-oblique reference in Isaiah to the atonement. Bearing that burden refers to Christ's bearing away our sins—or at the very least our temporal, telestial problems—on his shoulders. As Wonderful Counselor he will be our mediator, our intercessor, defending our case in the courts of heaven. "The Lord standeth up to plead, and standeth to judge the people," Isaiah had written earlier (Isaiah 3:13, parallel to 2 Nephi 13:13).

From latter-day scripture comes this affirmation:

> Listen to him who is the advocate with the Father, who is pleading your cause before him—Saying: Father, behold the sufferings and death of him who did no sin, in whom thou wast well pleased; behold the blood of thy Son which was shed, the blood of him whom thou gavest that thyself might be glorified; Wherefore, Father, spare these my brethren that believe on my name, that they may come unto me and have everlasting life. (D&C 45:3–5)

As Isaiah notes, Christ is not only a mediator but also a judge (see Mosiah 3:10; Moroni 10:34; Moses 6:57). In fact, it is in Christ's role of judge that I find even greater meaning in Abinadi's repeated references to the fact that "God himself" shall come down to redeem his people. In that great courtroom in heaven I see the judge, as it were, unwilling to ask anyone but himself to bear the burdens of all the guilty people standing in the dock, so he himself takes off his judicial robes and comes down to bear their stripes. I love the merciful imagery of this kind of mediator and judge.

"Mighty God" conveys something of the power of God, his strength and omnipotence and unconquerable influence. Isaiah sees him as always able to overcome the effects of sin and transgression in his people and to forever triumph over those would-be oppressors of the children of Israel.

"Everlasting Father" suggests one of those very special Book of Mormon doctrines regarding the several ways in which Christ is the father—the Creator of worlds without number (Mosiah 3:8), the Father of restored physical life through the resurrection (Mosiah 15:8), the Father of eternal life for his spiritually begotten sons and daughters (Mosiah 5:7), and representative of the Father (3 Nephi 11:36) acting through divine investiture of authority. We should all want to be born of him and become new sons and daughters of this "Father" (see Mosiah 5:7).

Lastly, with the phrase "Prince of Peace," we rejoice that when the King shall come there shall be no more war in the human heart or among the nations of the world, for Satan shall be bound. This is a peaceful king, the king of Salem (Salem meaning "peace" in Hebrew; compare Alma 13:18). Christ will bring peace to those who accept him in mortality, and he will also bring peace to those in the millennial and postmillennial realms of his glory.

Christ Visits the Spirits in Prison

In Isaiah 49:8–9, we read: "Thus saith the Lord, In an acceptable time have I heard thee, and in a day of salvation have I helped thee: and I will preserve thee, and give thee for a covenant of the people, to establish the earth, to cause to inherit the desolate heritages; That thou mayest say to the prisoners, Go forth; to them that are in darkness, Shew yourselves." The Prophet Joseph Smith, commenting on this passage and others like it, said,

> Peter, also, in speaking concerning our Savior, says, that "He went and preached unto the spirits in prison, which sometimes were disobedient, when once the long-suffering of God waited in the days of Noah." (1 Peter 3:19, 20.) Here then we have an account of our Savior preaching to the spirits in prison, to spirits that had been imprisoned from the days of Noah; and what did He preach to them? That they were to stay there? Certainly not! Let His own declaration testify. "He hath sent me to heal the broken-hearted, to preach deliverance to the captives, and recovering of sight of the blind, to set at liberty them that are bruised." (Luke 4:18.) Isaiah has it—"To bring out the prisoners from the prison, and them that sit in darkness from the prison house." (Isaiah 42:7.) It is very evident from this that He not only went to preach to them, but to deliver, or bring them out of the prison house.[7]

In teaching this doctrine, the Prophet Joseph might well have used the other magnificent passage from Isaiah 61 that so eloquently and lyrically refers to Christ's freeing the bands of physical and spiritual death: "The Spirit of the Lord God is upon me; because the Lord hath anointed me to preach good tidings unto the meek; he hath sent me to bind up the brokenhearted, to proclaim liberty to the captives, and the opening of the prison to them that are bound" (Isaiah 61:1). On both sides of the veil, we rejoice as Christ throws wide the prison doors.

Christ Shows Kindness and Preserves Latter-day Zion

Isaiah 49:13–16 contains a beautiful reference—also in the first block of Isaiah's passages used in the Book of Mormon as we now have it (1 Nephi 21:13–16)—regarding Christ's care for Zion, both ancient and latter day. That care is conveyed through moving images of the crucifixion and atonement of Jesus Christ:

> Sing, O heavens; and be joyful, O earth; and break forth into singing, O mountains: for the Lord hath comforted his people, and will have mercy upon his afflicted. But Zion said, The Lord hath forsaken me, and my Lord hath forgotten me. Can a woman forget her sucking child, that she should not have compassion on the son of her womb? yea, they may forget, yet will I not forget thee. Behold, I have graven thee upon the palms of my hands; thy walls are continually before me.

Graven upon the palms of his hands are those marks of the crucifiers' nails, a sign to his disciples in the Old World, to his Nephite congregation in the New World, and to us in latter-day appearances that he is the Savior of the world and was crucified in "the house of [his] friends" (Luke 24:39; 3 Nephi 11:14; D&C 45:52).

The beautiful imagery in Isaiah 49 provides another reminder of Christ's saving role—that of a protecting, redeeming parent to Zion's children. He comforts his people and shows mercy when they are afflicted very much as any loving father or mother would show toward a child—but, as Isaiah records, the intensity and extent of his care is much greater than that of any other loving father and mother. Although we parents may think it unlikely that a mother could forget her sucking child, yet that could happen. But what cannot ever happen and will not ever happen is that Christ would forget his children or his covenant made with them in Zion.

This image of Christ as a protective, redemptive, loving father is carried over to Isaiah 50, in which Christ speaks to the children of Israel—as his children:

> Thus saith the Lord, Where is the bill of your mother's divorcement, . . . or which of my creditors is it to whom I have sold you? Behold, for your iniquities have ye sold yourselves, and for your transgressions is your mother put away. Wherefore, when I came, was there no man? when I called, was there none to answer? Is my hand shortened at all, that it cannot redeem? or have I no power to deliver?" (Isaiah 50:1–2; compare 2 Nephi 7:1–2)

These children will yet have a happy home and sealed parents. In the last days, that bill of divorcement against their mother will be set aside and so will the demands of any creditors against their transgressions. The Lord is in debt to no one, so neither will his children be. He alone can pay the price for the salvation of Israel and the establishment of Zion. His wrath is turned away, and he has not cast off the bride or sold her children into slavery.

As far as the shortening of hands, the scriptures repeatedly testify that the reach of God's arm is more than adequate. He can always claim and embrace the Israel that he loves. In spite of his family's faithlessness, his hand remains constant, not shortened or slackened or withheld. "In a little wrath I hid my face from thee for a moment; but with everlasting kindness will I have mercy on thee, saith the Lord thy Redeemer" (Isaiah 54:8, parallel to 3 Nephi 22:8).

The Millennial Christ

One of the most important passages in all of Isaiah is rich with nuances of the Restoration and is a favorite of Latter-day Saints:

> And there shall come forth a rod out of the stem of Jesse, and a Branch shall grow out of his roots: And the spirit of the Lord shall rest upon him, the spirit of wisdom and understanding, the spirit of counsel and might, the spirit of knowledge and of the fear of the Lord; And shall make him of quick understanding in the fear of the Lord: and he shall not judge after the sight of his eyes, neither reprove after the hearing of his ears: But with righteousness shall he judge the poor, and reprove with equity for the meek of the earth: and he shall smite the earth with the rod of his mouth, and with the breath of his lips shall he slay the wicked. And righteousness shall be the girdle of his loins, and faithfulness the girdle of his reins. (Isaiah 11:1–5, parallel to 2 Nephi 21:1–5)

It is clear from the Book of Mormon (see especially 2 Nephi 30:9) and from the Doctrine and Covenants (section 113) that the main character in this passage is Jesus Christ. Joseph Smith, recalling the visit of the angel Moroni on the night of 21 September 1823, wrote that Moroni "quoted the eleventh chapter of Isaiah, saying that it was about to be fulfilled."[8]

The discussion of the tree in Isaiah 11:1 is a natural continuation of the prophecy through that portion of Isaiah in which the Lord is cutting down boughs, hewing the particularly lofty and arrogant ones, leveling thickets of the forest in every direction (see Isaiah 10). Israel's history, as is so often the case, is compared to a tree. At this point in Isaiah 11, all that remains of it is a stump. Heaven's forester carefully trims his trees—Latter-day Saints think instantly of Jacob 5 in the Book of Mormon—and in this manner he clears out the evil trees of his forest and prepares the way for flourishing new shoots to come out of the stump of Jesse. (Donald Parry tells me that "shoot" is a better translation from the Hebrew than "rod," and "stump" is better than "stem.")

So it is with the restoration of the gospel. It is like the new shoot out of the old stump, and we see the fruits of those labors in—and with—Zion. Note this statement from Elder McConkie about the "branch." He says:

> The king who shall reign personally upon the earth during the Millennium shall be the Branch who grew out of the house of David. He shall execute judgment and justice in all the earth because he is the Lord Jehovah, even him whom we call Christ.[9]

Through Zechariah the Lord spoke similarly: "Thus saith the Lord of Hosts: . . . I will bring forth my servant the Branch. . . . I will remove the iniquity of the land in one day. . . . In that day, saith the Lord of hosts, shall ye call every man his neighbour under the vine and under the fig tree" (Zechariah 3:7–10). Of that glorious millennial day the Lord says also: "Behold the man whose name is The Branch; and he shall grow up out of his place, and he shall build the temple of the Lord: Even he shall build the temple of the Lord; and he shall bear the glory and shall sit and rule upon his throne" (Zechariah 6:12–13).

Brother McConkie concludes:

> That the Branch of David is Christ is perfectly clear. . . . He is a new David, an Eternal David, who shall reign forever on the throne of his ancient ancestor. . . .
>
> . . . David's temporal throne fell long centuries before our Lord was born, and that portion of Israel which had

not been scattered to the ends of the earth was in bondage to the iron yoke of Rome. But the promises remain.
The eternal throne shall be restored in due course with a
new David sitting thereon, and he shall reign forever
and ever. . . .

How glorious shall be the coming day when the
second David, who is Christ, reigns on the throne of
the first David; when all men shall dwell safely; when
the earth shall be dotted with temples; and when the
gospel covenant shall have full force and validity in all
the earth![10]

There is a warning in all of this as we note the need for
appropriate fear of the Lord and the reproof that will accompany his coming: "He shall smite the earth with the rod
of his mouth; and with the breath of his lips shall he slay the
wicked" (Isaiah 11:4, parallel to 2 Nephi 21:4). Nephi repeats this sentiment in almost identical language when he
says near the end of his life,

And with righteousness shall the Lord God judge
the poor, and reprove with equity for the meek of the
earth. And he shall smite the earth with the rod of his
mouth; and with the breath of his lips shall he slay the
wicked. For the time speedily cometh that the Lord
God shall cause a great division among the people,
and the wicked will he destroy; and he will spare his
people, yea, even if it so be that he must destroy the
wicked by fire. (2 Nephi 30:9–10)

This doctrine evoked the following declaration from the
Prophet Joseph Smith: "Behold, He will not fail you! He will
come with ten thousand of His Saints, and all His adversaries
shall be destroyed with the breath of His lips!"[11] In that day the
word will come with power, yea with power in his word, and
Christ's judgment will be the truth he speaks and the acknowledgment of that truth extracted from those who hear him.

In this millennial moment the Messiah will usher in the long-sought-for peace all have anticipated:

> The wolf also shall dwell with the lamb, and the leopard shall lie down with the kid; and the calf and the young lion and the fatling together; and a little child shall lead them. And the cow and the bear shall feed; their young ones shall lie down together: and the lion shall eat straw like the ox. And the sucking child shall play on the hole of the asp, and the weaned child shall put his hand on the cockatrice' den. They shall not hurt nor destroy in all my holy mountain: for the earth shall be full of the knowledge of the Lord, as the waters cover the sea. And in that day there shall be a root of Jesse, which shall stand for an ensign of the people; to it shall the Gentiles seek: and his rest shall be glorious. (Isaiah 11:6–10, parallel to 2 Nephi 21:6–10)

In equally triumphant language, referring to the temples of the last days as well as the headquarters of the Kingdom of God on earth, Isaiah prophesied:

> And it shall come to pass in the last days, that the mountain of the Lord's house shall be established in the top of the mountains, and shall be exalted above the hills; and all nations shall flow unto it. And many people shall go and say, Come ye, and let us go up to the mountain of the Lord, to the house of the God of Jacob; and he will teach us of his ways, and we will walk in his paths: for out of Zion shall go forth the law, and the word of the Lord from Jerusalem. And he shall judge among the nations, and shall rebuke many people: and they shall beat their swords into plowshares, and their spears into pruninghooks: nation shall not lift up sword against nation, neither shall they learn war any more. O house of Jacob, come ye, and let us walk in the light of the Lord. (Isaiah 2:2–5, parallel to 2 Nephi 12:2–5)

Images of the Crucifixion and Atonement

I conclude with a point of personal privilege. I wish to share three passages from Isaiah's text. More beautiful passages do not exist regarding the Savior's atonement and crucifixion. I provide no commentary but invite you to enjoy the poetic eloquence of a prophet's testimony.

First I cite the messianic declaration Christ gave that day to those startled rabbis in the synagogue of Nazareth when he began his ministry:

> The Spirit of the Lord God is upon me; because the Lord hath anointed me to preach good tidings unto the meek; he hath sent me to bind up the brokenhearted, to proclaim liberty to the captives, and the opening of the prison to them that are bound; To proclaim the acceptable year of the Lord, and the day of vengeance of our God; to comfort all that mourn; To appoint unto them that mourn in Zion, to give unto them beauty for ashes, the oil of joy for mourning, the garment of praise for the spirit of heaviness; that they might be called trees of righteousness, the planting of the Lord, that he might be glorified. (Isaiah 61:1–3; see also Luke 4:17–19)

I add to that Isaiah 50:5–7:

> The Lord God hath opened mine ear, and I was not rebellious, neither turned away back. I gave my back to the smiters, and my cheeks to them that plucked off the hair: I hid not my face from shame and spitting. For the Lord God will help me; therefore shall I not be confounded: therefore have I set my face like a flint, and I know that I shall not be ashamed.

And lastly Isaiah 53, one of my favorite chapters in all of Holy Writ:

> Who hath believed our report? and to whom is the arm of the Lord revealed?

For he shall grow up before him as a tender plant, and as a root out of a dry ground: he hath no form nor comeliness; and when we shall see him, there is no beauty that we should desire him.

He is despised and rejected of men; a man of sorrows, and acquainted with grief: and we hid as it were our faces from him; he was despised, and we esteemed him not.

Surely he hath borne our griefs, and carried our sorrows: yet we did esteem him stricken, smitten of God, and afflicted.

But he was wounded for our transgressions, he was bruised for our iniquities: the chastisement of our peace was upon him; and with his stripes we are healed.

All we like sheep have gone astray; we have turned every one to his own way; and the Lord hath laid on him the iniquity of us all.

He was oppressed, and he was afflicted, yet he opened not his mouth: he is brought as a lamb to the slaughter, and as a sheep before her shearers is dumb, so he openeth not his mouth.

He was taken from prison and from judgment: and who shall declare his generation? for he was cut off out of the land of the living: for the transgression of my people was he stricken.

And he made his grave with the wicked, and with the rich in his death; because he had done no violence, neither was any deceit in his mouth.

Yet it pleased the Lord to bruise him; he hath put him to grief: when thou shalt make his soul an offering for sin, he shall see his seed, he shall prolong his days, and the pleasure of the Lord shall prosper in his hand.

He shall see of the travail of his soul, and shall be satisfied: by his knowledge shall my righteous servant justify many; for he shall bear their iniquities.

Therefore will I divide him a portion with the great, and he shall divide the spoil with the strong; because he hath poured out his soul unto death: and he was numbered with the transgressors; and he bare the sin of many, and made intercession for the transgressors. (Isaiah 53:1–12, parallel to Mosiah 14:1–12)

May we too set our faces like flints and bear our own powerful witnesses of Christ as Isaiah has done, I pray in the name of Jesus Christ.

Notes

1. I note the help of many who have shaped my thinking on this subject, particularly Donald W. Parry. He and my Salt Lake colleague Hoyt Brewster have been more than generous in sharing ideas, refining points of view, and helping me select salient elements for this paper from the near-endless array of options and possibilities inherent in such a topic.

2. Monte S. Nyman, *Great Are the Words of Isaiah* (Salt Lake City: Bookcraft, 1980), 7.

3. Bruce R. McConkie, "The Keys of Understanding Isaiah," *Ensign* (October 1973): 78, 81.

4. Church Educational System Symposium, August 9, 1994.

5. Dallin H. Oaks, "Scripture Reading and Revelation," *Ensign* (January 1995): 7–9.

6. Joseph Fielding Smith, comp., *Teachings of the Prophet Joseph Smith* (Salt Lake City: Deseret Book, 1976), 392.

7. Ibid., 219.

8. Joseph Smith, *History of the Church of Jesus Christ of Latter-day Saints*, ed. B. H. Roberts (Salt Lake City: Deseret Book, 1976), 1:12.

9. Bruce R. McConkie, *The Promised Messiah* (Salt Lake City: Deseret Book, 1978), 193–5.

10. Ibid.

11. Smith, comp., *Teachings of the Prophet Joseph Smith*, 36.

Getting through Isaiah with the Help of the Nephite Prophetic View

John W. Welch

Nephi's prophetic view foresaw the future in four distinct stages, and each time he quoted a section from Isaiah it was because it contained words relevant to one of those stages.

Getting through Isaiah is not easy. Virtually all readers of the Book of Mormon get bogged down at the end of 1 Nephi, and many simply ignore the Isaiah chapters in 2 Nephi. Yet it is hard to imagine comprehending the full message of the Book of Mormon without grasping the main concepts taught by Isaiah. To put Isaiah's historical prominence and stature somewhat into perspective, it helps readers of the Book of Mormon to realize that he lived about as many years before Nephi and Jacob as Joseph Smith lived before the present day. In many ways, Isaiah was "the Prophet" in ancient Israel, and so it is no surprise that his revelations set much of the stage for the religious and social outlook of Lehi and the Nephite prophets who followed him.

Of all the writers of the Book of Mormon, Nephi and Jacob were the most prone to quote or paraphrase Isaiah. Because of the great interest Nephi and Jacob had in reading and citing Isaiah, the more we perceive how these two prophets understood and used Isaiah, the better off we will be in getting through the words of Isaiah quoted in the Book of Mormon. One key to comprehending how Nephi and Jacob understood and used Isaiah is to grasp the basic "prophetic worldview" that is found repeatedly in the Book of Mormon, particularly on the small plates of Nephi. Because most of the Isaiah materials that are quoted in the Book of

Mormon (namely, Isaiah 2–14, 29, and 48–51) are included by Nephi and Jacob as they state and explain their prophetic worldview, tuning in to that worldview greatly helps modern readers in orienting and guiding themselves through the Isaiah chapters in the Book of Mormon.

Accordingly, this paper first asks, How did the Nephite prophets understand the future? It then shows that the answers to that question explain why and how the Nephite prophets used certain texts of Isaiah as they did. Specifically, we will see that the prophetic writings of Nephi and Jacob consistently chart the main events of the future by casting world history into four distinct stages. They selected, used, and interpreted certain Isaiah texts because those texts served within a particular prophetic view.

The Nephite Prophetic View in 1 Nephi 11–14

The four stages or phases in the Nephite prophetic view are visible in several texts, but never more clearly than in Nephi's vision in 1 Nephi 11–14, which divides naturally into four sections that correspond to chapters 11, 12, 13, and 14. This influential text seems to have set the basic prophetic frame of reference for the Nephites who followed Nephi.

In general, the pattern begins with revelations that look forward to the coming of Jesus Christ to the Jews in Jerusalem—the easily recognized and well-known theme of the condescension of God in 1 Nephi 11. Here and elsewhere, the first stage of Nephite prophecy begins with the prophet foretelling how and when Jesus would come down in the flesh, as God, to preach and to work miracles in the midst of the Jews, and how the Jews would reject him and, through priestcraft, crucify him. In connection with this stage, the Nephite prophets also explain that the suffering of the Messiah would bring about the atonement and the resurrection, but that his rejection would further spell disaster and dispersion for the Jews and would complete the scattering of Israel.

In the second phase of the Nephite prophetic view, the Book of Mormon prophets turn their attention to scattered Israel—those scattered both before and after the coming of Christ. Thus, in 1 Nephi 12, Nephi describes the conditions of Lehi's posterity after they scatter abroad and eventually dwindle in unbelief and darkness. In this phase, the Nephite prophets typically explain how all Israel, dispersed among the lands of the earth, would languish in disbelief, be subjected to conflict, and grow in spiritual darkness and wickedness. Although they would be scourged for having fought against the Son of God or for having rejected their covenants, the house of Israel would not be forgotten by God. He would remember the covenants he had made to their forefathers, and he would remember his covenant people wherever they might be scattered, even in the most remote areas of the world. For obvious reasons, the Nephite prophets took a special personal interest in the Lord's promises that he would remember the house of Israel even upon "the isles of the sea" (2 Nephi 10:8).

The third stage in Nephi's formative text comes in 1 Nephi 13. This stage envisions the day of the Gentiles, or the working of the Lord through the non-Israelite nations. In an unexpected turn of irony, God would begin to reconstitute the house of Israel by commencing a great and marvelous work among the godless. In wondrous and miraculous ways, the Gentiles would become the conveyors of the word of God, nursing fathers and nursing mothers through whom the gathering and rebuilding of Israel would begin. The Gentiles would be the medium through which the ancient stock would be preserved as the words and records of ancient Israel come forth "out of the dust" and "out of obscurity" (2 Nephi 26:16; 27:29). While that day of the Gentiles would be crucial, it would not be the final, everlasting day. Eventually the fruit of this day would begin to turn bitter, setting the stage for the ultimate conflict between good and evil.

The fourth stage (found in 1 Nephi 14, the final chapter of Nephi's vision), discloses the events and conditions that will prevail at the end of times. In the end, God will be victorious over the powers of evil. The great and abominable kingdom of the devil, the harlot of all the earth, will be made to drink blood, and all punishments that are due and owing to the evil ones will be exacted. In this day, righteousness will be established and peace and harmony will eventually prevail, with the covenant people being armed "with the power of God in great glory" (1 Nephi 14:14).

This four-staged pattern comprises the Nephite prophetic view. Over and over in the writings on the small plates of Nephi, these four elements provide the outline for Nephite prophecy. In short, the four phases cover

1. Christ's coming;
2. his rejection and the scattering of the Jews;
3. the day of the Gentiles; and
4. the restoration of Israel and the ultimate victory of good over evil.

Before addressing the roles played by the Isaiah texts in connection with this pattern, it is important to realize the significance of this prophetic view to the Nephites. This set of four specific stages of expectation for the future was more than just a social perspective or a political outlook: it constituted a full worldview that shaped and controlled other interpretations and opinions about various scriptures, religious questions, personal and group identity, and the very purpose of life among the Nephites. To the righteous Nephites, this sequence of truths and values explained the big questions of their group's existence: where they as a people had come from, why they had left the Old World, what they were doing in a remote corner of the world, and where their extraordinary journey would eventually take them and their posterity. Thus, this prophetic expectation constituted a richly developed and actualized worldview, not merely an abstract hypothesis.

Moreover, this worldview saw the world particularly from the viewpoint of the Nephites. Its specific formulation seems to have originated in the vision shared by Lehi and Nephi, especially in the writings of Nephi. Because Lehi and Nephi saw the same vision (see 1 Nephi 11:3; 14:29), many elements in Lehi's dream (see 1 Nephi 8, 10) are also present in Nephi's prophecy (see 1 Nephi 11–14).[1] But Nephi's explanation is more systematic and more definitive than Lehi's, for Nephi sought and obtained specific information about the chronological and historical meaning of the things he and his father were shown. Thus it appears that the Nephite prophetic view crystallized when Nephi wrote his seminal text now found in 1 Nephi 11–14. That prophetic view significantly centered on Nephite concerns (such as whether God would remember people scattered upon the islands of the sea), and thus it did not focus in any detail on several themes that figure much more saliently in the modern LDS worldview. For instance, the Nephite prophets were greatly concerned about the first coming of Christ; they had less concern about his second coming; indeed, the early Nephites were still looking forward to and mustering faith in Jesus' first advent, and even that event was so remote and incomprehensible from their frame of reference that people who prophesied of the distant first coming of Christ were regularly accused of blasphemy and false prophecy (see, for example, Jacob 7:7; Mosiah 17:7–8; Alma 14:5). While all true prophets testify of the same ultimate realities, each works from his own distinctive perspective.

The four-part pattern established in Nephi's main vision in 1 Nephi 11–14 constitutes the basic outline for most of the other prophetic texts in the small plates. Three of those texts, namely, 1 Nephi 19–22, 2 Nephi 6–10, and 2 Nephi 12–30, extensively involve the writings of Isaiah. In fact, they contain almost all the Isaiah materials quoted in the Book of Mormon. By understanding these three Nephite texts, one will be a long way toward the goal of understanding the use of Isaiah in the Book of Mormon.

The Role of Isaiah in Nephi's View in 1 Nephi 19–22

The last four chapters of 1 Nephi deal with the future of Nephi's people in their new land of promise. Their topics follow in order the same four stages found in 1 Nephi 11–14 and described above.

First, chapter 19 clearly discusses Christ's coming. For example, Nephi prophesies: "And the world, because of their iniquity, shall judge him to be a thing of naught; wherefore they scourge him, and he suffereth it; and they smite him, and he suffereth it. Yea, they spit upon him, and he suffereth it, because of his loving kindness and his long-suffering towards the children of men" (1 Nephi 19:9). Throughout the chapter are found the elements of stage one, which describes the coming of Christ, his mission, his suffering, his rejection, and its consequences.

Second, in 1 Nephi 20, Nephi quotes Isaiah 48. This chapter describes the rejection of Christ by the Jews and their scattering, the elements of stage two. The text begins by affirming that Israel is in apostasy: "They swear not in truth nor in righteousness" (verse 1) and "do not stay themselves upon the God of Israel" (verse 2) because of their stiffneckedness (verse 4), even after having been shown the truth. Nevertheless, Isaiah says, God will "defer [his] anger" for His name's sake (verse 9) and refrain from cutting Israel off, but will refine them in a "furnace of affliction" (verse 10) and lead them "through the deserts" (verse 21). Although the promise still stands that Israel will come forth out of the world (see verse 20), the chapter ends by seeing no peace for the wicked (see verse 22). When one reads Isaiah 48 in connection with stage two of the Nephite worldview, one readily sees many points of contact between the two. Indeed, as a modern reader stands in Nephi's place and strives to see things through Nephi's eyes, it becomes quite evident why Nephi would have found in Isaiah a soul mate and how he would have seized upon many words and phrases in Isaiah 48 as having a direct bearing upon the themes of stage two in his worldview.

Third, in chapter 21, Nephi goes on to quote Isaiah 49. This chapter contains several passages that pertain directly to the central theme of Nephi's stage three, the day of the Gentiles. For example, a key verse reads, "Thus saith the Lord God: Behold, I will lift up mine hand to the Gentiles, and set up my standard to the people; and they shall bring thy sons in their arms, and thy daughters shall be carried upon their shoulders" (1 Nephi 21:22). In addition, this chapter calls for Israel to "listen, O isles" (verse 1), tells how a servant will be raised up "for a light to the Gentiles" (verse 6), that "kings shall see and arise" (verse 7) while messengers will be sent "to them that sit in darkness" (verse 9), and that the Lord will comfort and not forget his people (see verses 13 and 15). These and several other elements in Isaiah 49 relate and apply directly to Nephi's stage three.

Finally, Nephi concludes his prophecy in 1 Nephi 22 by discussing the restoration of Israel and the victory of God over evil, declaring that there will be "one shepherd" who will "reign in dominion, and might, and power, and great glory" (1 Nephi 22:24–25; see also verse 26). This theme was already introduced, at the end of 1 Nephi 21 (which quotes Isaiah 49). There Isaiah prophesies that Israel will be restored, and that they who oppress the righteous "shall be drunken with their own blood," and that "all flesh shall know that I, the Lord, am thy Savior" (1 Nephi 21:26). Isaiah 49 served Nephi's purposes not only by declaring stage three, but also by leading directly into his concluding comments on stage four in 1 Nephi 22.

The Role of Isaiah in Jacob's View in 2 Nephi 6–10

The second Nephite text that uses Isaiah in conjunction with the Nephite prophetic view is Jacob's covenant speech in 2 Nephi 6–10. This speech is built around the theme, "Behold, I will lift up mine hand to the Gentiles, . . . and they shall bring thy sons in their arms" (2 Nephi 6:6), which will usher in the victorious day of the Lord. After summarizing the basic Nephite prophetic view, Jacob uses two chapters from Isaiah to establish and expound upon stage four of that view, which deals with the theme of the day of the Lord.

Jacob begins his speech by summarizing the four stages in seven verses. First, he states, "Nevertheless, the Lord . . . has shown unto me that the Lord God, the Holy One of Israel, should manifest himself unto them in the flesh; and after he should manifest himself they should scourge him and crucify him, according to the words of the angel who spake it unto me" (2 Nephi 6:9)—stage one.

In the next verse, he turns immediately to the fact that because "they [the Jews] have hardened their hearts and stiffened their necks . . . , the judgments of the Holy One of Israel shall come upon them" (2 Nephi 6:10)—stage two.

Jacob then promises that "nevertheless, the Lord will be merciful unto them [the Jews]. . . . And blessed are the Gentiles

. . . and the people of the Lord . . . who wait for him" (2 Nephi 6:11–13)—themes regarding stage three, the day of the Gentiles.

He concludes his overview by prophesying that "the Messiah will set himself again the second time to recover them . . . unto the destruction of their enemies. . . . And they shall know that the Lord is God, the Holy One of Israel" (2 Nephi 6:14–15)—in other words, stage four.

At this point in stage four (at the end of 2 Nephi 6), Jacob begins quoting the last verses of Isaiah 49, the same text that Nephi had used to introduce stage four in 1 Nephi 21; then Jacob continues on, quoting Isaiah 50 and 51. He turns to these texts to reinforce the points he had made in chapter 6, especially regarding stage four, for in Isaiah 50, God declares his "power to deliver" (Isaiah 50:2, parallel to 2 Nephi 7:2) and to help (see Isaiah 50:9, parallel to 2 Nephi 7:9) those who obey "the voice of his servant" (Isaiah 50:10, parallel to 2 Nephi 7:10), but those who walk in the light of their own fire "shall lie down in sorrow" (Isaiah 50:11, parallel to 2 Nephi 7:11). In Isaiah 51, which is thoroughly relevant to stage four, a law proceeds forth from God, who makes a judgment (see Isaiah 51:4, parallel to 2 Nephi 8:4), the righteous awake and "the dragon" is wounded (Isaiah 51:9, parallel to 2 Nephi 8:9), the redeemed return singing unto Zion with everlasting joy (see Isaiah 51:11, parallel to 2 Nephi 8:11), and the fury of the oppressor is gone (see Isaiah 51:13, parallel to 2 Nephi 8:13).

In 2 Nephi 9, Jacob continues his development of the themes of stage four, as he discusses the rejoicing that will occur when the Jews "shall be restored to the true church and fold of God" (verse 2). He then gives his famous extended discourse on God's ultimate victory over sin and death and on the glorious resurrection and day of the Lord's judgment. Whereas Isaiah 50 and 51 seem to prophesy primarily that the righteous will prevail in this world, Jacob extends Isaiah's field of vision to include not only the dragon of wicked oppression but the ultimate enemies, death and hell.

Jacob concludes his covenant speech in 2 Nephi 10 by briefly revisiting all four of the basic stages: He assures his people that they are "this righteous branch" (2 Nephi 10:1), preserved even though others will reject Christ when he will come among them (see verse 3). Those who reject Christ will thus be "scattered among all nations" (verse 6), but they will be remembered and gathered "from the isles of the sea" (verse 8). This promise of restoration deftly brings Jacob back to the point where he began, with the kings of the gentiles being his people's "nursing fathers" (verse 9; see also verse 18) so that the righteous may inherit this land (see verse 19). Although Jacob covers all four phases in giving his audience a basic frame of reference, he spends most of his time in this speech focusing on stage four, which he elaborates with the aid of Isaiah's writings.

The Role of Isaiah in Nephi's View in 2 Nephi 25–30

Nephi's extensive quotation of the prophecies of Isaiah 2–14 appears in 2 Nephi 12–24; these Isaiah chapters are then interpreted by Nephi in 2 Nephi 25–30. In this block of texts, Nephi begins by quoting thirteen chapters of Isaiah in one continuous stretch. He does this to supply Isaiah as a third witness to the things that he and Jacob have said (see 2 Nephi 11:3). After quoting those chapters, Nephi draws individual words and phrases from Isaiah 2–14 to corroborate and substantiate his now familiar four-phased prophetic view as he follows the pattern again in 2 Nephi 25–30.

First, Nephi begins again at the standard Nephite point of departure: "Behold, they will crucify him; and after he is laid in a sepulchre for the space of three days he shall rise from the dead, with healing in his wings" (2 Nephi 25:13). Most of chapter 25 deals with Christ.

Second, after discussing the scattering of the Jews (see 2 Nephi 25:14–16), Nephi explains in chapter 26 how Lehi's posterity will be afflicted with internal contention (see 2 Nephi 26:1–7) and will eventually be smitten by the Gentiles (see 2 Nephi 26:8–15). Here Nephi draws expressly on words and phrases from Isaiah 5:24–30, which he quoted in 2 Nephi 15, regarding earthquakes, blood, anger, pain, sorrow, and burning as stubble. In this section, Nephi also quotes or paraphrases Isaiah 3:15 (see 2 Nephi 26:20); 29:3–5 (see 2 Nephi 26:15–18); 52:3; and 55:1 (see 2 Nephi 26:25).

Third, the theme of the day of the Gentiles is treated extensively from the end of 2 Nephi 26–27. In these chapters Nephi talks about the conditions during the days of the Gentiles, the convincing of the Gentiles that Jesus is the Christ, the stumbling of the Gentiles (see 2 Nephi 26:20), and the latter-day coming forth of the book from the dust (see 2 Nephi 27:6–19). In this iteration of stage three, Nephi draws heavily on Isaiah 29 (see 2 Nephi 27:2–4, 7, 12, 15, 25–34), and also on passages from Isaiah 2:12; 3:15 (see 2 Nephi 28:12–13); 8:14 (see 2 Nephi 26:20); 9:16 (see 2 Nephi 26:20); and 10:25 (see 2 Nephi 28:16).

Finally, the opening of the sealed book (see 2 Nephi 27:11) will commence the day of woe and judgment upon the wicked (see 2 Nephi 27:27, 31), leading to the fall of the great and abominable enemy of God (see 2 Nephi 28:18). But the words of the Lord shall be gathered into one, as will all his faithful (see 2 Nephi 29:14), and "the wolf [shall] dwell with the lamb" (2 Nephi 30:12) and "Satan shall have power over the hearts of the children of men no more" (2 Nephi 30:18). Here, in this stage four, Nephi quotes heavily from Isaiah 11 and also from several other verses in

Isaiah 2–14. For example, Nephi's words in 2 Nephi 29:1–2 about the Lord setting his hand a second time and an ensign being raised come from Isaiah 11:10–11, and Nephi's lesson that God shall "judge the poor" in righteousness (2 Nephi 30:9) comes straight from Isaiah 11:4. Isaiah 14:19 talks of an "abominable branch," a phrase that likely resonated in Nephi's mind as he wrote his expression "great and abominable" (2 Nephi 28:18).

Much more could be said about these four stages of the Nephite prophetic view and the ways in which that view governed or influenced how the Nephites read their sacred texts (such as those of Zenos and Zenock, in addition to Isaiah's) and how they understood their religious heritage and tradition. For example, one could show how, in teaching Zenos' allegory of the olive tree, Jacob places that prophecy into this prophetic framework [in Jacob 4–6; see table 3]. Many more details about these Isaiah texts are discussed in other chapters in this volume, but the concept is illustrated clearly enough by the texts of 1 Nephi 19–22, 2 Nephi 6–10, and 2 Nephi 12–30 that one may see how that prophetic view gives structure to the use of Isaiah by Nephi and Jacob.

Conclusion

With these examples of the stages of the Nephite prophetic view in mind, I offer a few concluding observations. As a practical recommendation, I would hope that a reader who gets lost in the middle of an Isaiah text in the Book of Mormon might stop and ask, "Which of the four stages in the Nephite prophetic view does this passage support or substantiate?" By answering that question, the reader will generally be able to understand why the passage was inserted by the Nephite writers into their text and how the Isaiah text is relevant to the Nephite message at hand. Each segment of material quoted from Isaiah almost always pertains, at least in broad terms, to one of the four Nephite themes: the coming of Christ, the scattering of Israel, the restoring of Israel through the Gentiles, or God's ultimate victory over evil. (Table 1 describes how each chapter of the book of Isaiah quoted in the Book of Mormon relates to these four themes.) Each Isaiah segment that is quoted, except for Isaiah 7:1–9 (which prophesies that Syria will not capture Jerusalem) and Isaiah 48:3–8 (which explains why God reveals the future to obstinate people), can be fairly easily classified under at least one of the four main headings. The possibility that a scripture may have multiple meanings and the fact that two themes may partially overlap allows some room for interpretation and ambiguity in this process of classification, but for the most part, these problems are small and generally unproblematic for those readers who are trying to grasp Isaiah's general message.

Moreover, as an evaluative observation, I would hope that readers might pause and realize how impressive it is that Isaiah's words were not just quoted arbitrarily in the Book of Mormon. Chapters like Isaiah 48 and 49 are quoted purposefully and intelligently within the guiding sequence and framework of the Nephite prophetic view. (Table 2 lists the themes of each of the four stages of the Nephite prophetic view and the Isaiah passages pertinent to each of those themes.) To accomplish this meaningful integration of the complex Isaiah texts into the literary context of the Book of Mormon, Nephi and Jacob needed to be thoroughly conversant with the writings of Isaiah as well as fully immersed in the Nephite worldview. Such an impressive feat of meaningful integration and extensive utilization of Isaiah required much more than a casual or random association of one text with the other.

The presence of this underlying consistency in the Nephite texts should not be particularly surprising to us. Indeed, the Nephite prophets claimed that all prophets prophesied essentially the same word of Christ (see Jacob 4:13). Thus, the Nephite prophets all sought to convey essentially the same vision and the same story. The same main themes come through again and again, but they are told in different ways and approached through different settings and purposes. (Table 3 shows how and where the Nephite prophetic view appears in at least six texts on the small plates of Nephi in addition to Jacob 4–6.) Accordingly, although all four stages are present in each of the prophetic texts in the small plates, equal time and attention are not given to each stage in each passage. For example, in 2 Nephi, Jacob emphasizes stage four (in 2 Nephi 7–9), while Nephi spends more time on stage three (in 2 Nephi 26–29). Still, all four phases are present in each of these cases.

The Nephite prophetic view supplies modern readers with the big picture in understanding Isaiah. The lines and images in the prophetic poetry of Isaiah are like puzzle pieces in a large jigsaw puzzle, and the Nephite prophetic view is the picture on the box. With that picture, we can put the puzzle of Isaiah's words together.

I have always been amazed at Nephi's claim that he saw Isaiah as being "plain" (2 Nephi 25:4), an astonishing assertion to most people who knock their heads and hearts against these rich but difficult texts. But now, in light of the Nephite prophetic view, the meaning that Nephi saw in these Isaiah texts truly does become plainer and clearer. As Nephi states, "They are plain unto all those that are filled with the spirit of prophecy" (2 Nephi 25:4), by which one can conclude that he means to include all those who share and comprehend the spirit and understanding of the Nephite prophetic view.

Note

1. See "Connections between the Visions of Lehi and Nephi," FARMS Update, *Insights* (July 1993): 2. Nephi's and Lehi's visions both embrace the same prophetic elements, but while Lehi's dream is intimate and symbolic, focusing on his family, Nephi's dream is collective and historic, applying to all humankind. Nephi and Lehi view the same elements with different perspectives and purposes.

Table 1

The Isaiah Chapters in the Book of Mormon Classified by the Four Stages of the Nephite Prophetic View

• Isaiah 2–4 (parallel to 2 Nephi 12–14), *stage 4*—Speaks concerning the day of the Lord, the law going forth, the vanquishing of evil, and the defeat of the mighty men of war.
• Isaiah 5 (parallel to 2 Nephi 15), *stage 2*—"My people are gone into captivity, because they have no knowledge" (v. 13, parallel to 2 Nephi 15:3), but "for all this his anger is not turned away" (v. 25); and *stage 3*, "And he will lift up an ensign to the nations" (v. 26).
• Isaiah 6 (parallel to 2 Nephi 16), *stage 3*—How long the people will remain in darkness (see v. 11), as the Lord has "removed men far away" (v. 12).
• Isaiah 7 (parallel to 2 Nephi 17), *stage 1*—"A virgin shall conceive, and bear a son, and shall call his name Immanuel" (v. 7:14), but the land will become desolate, with briers and thorns (see 7:23).
• Isaiah 8 (parallel to 2 Nephi 18), *stage 3*—"Give ear, all ye of far countries" (v. 9), "I should not walk in the way of this people" (v. 11) but "let [the Lord of Hosts] be your fear" (v. 13). They will "be driven to darkness" (v. 22).
• Isaiah 9 (parallel to 2 Nephi 19), *stage 1*—But those of the nations "that walked in darkness have seen a great light" (v. 2), "for unto us a child is born" (v. 6).

- Isaiah 10–14 (parallel to 2 Nephi 20–24), *stage 4*—"The remnant shall return" (10:21), the Lord will judge, and "the wolf also shall dwell with the lamb" (11:6); God will set his hand a "second time to recover the remnant of his people" (11:11), and all will praise God's name in that day (see 12:4); Babylon, on the other hand, will be destroyed in the day of "wrath and fierce anger" (13:9), and Lucifer will be "cut down" (14:12); people will say that "the Lord hath founded Zion, and the poor of his people shall trust in it" (14:32).
- Isaiah 48 (parallel to 1 Nephi 20), *stage 2*—Israel will be in apostasy because of stiffneckedness (vv. 2–4); they are to be refined in a "furnace of affliction" (v. 10); there is no peace for the wicked (see v. 22).
- Isaiah 49 (parallel to 1 Nephi 21), *stage 3*—God will lift up his hand to the Gentiles (see v. 22), those on the isles of the sea will hear (see v. 1), and messengers will be sent "to them that are in darkness" (v. 9).
- Isaiah 50 (parallel to 2 Nephi 7), *stage 4*—God's power to deliver and to help; the wicked to be destroyed.
- Isaiah 51 (parallel to 2 Nephi 8), *stage 4*—Law and judgment come forth from God, the righteous awake, and the dragon is wounded (see v. 9); the redeemed have "everlasting joy" (v. 11).
- Isaiah 52, *stage 4*—"The Lord shall bring again Zion" (v. 8) and will redeem Jerusalem (see v. 9); all the world will see the salvation of the Lord (see v. 10).
- Isaiah 53 (Mosiah 14), quoted by Abinadi, relates to *stage 1*—The suffering and death of Christ (see vv. 2–4); he is "taken from prison" and bruised (vv. 8–10), to make "intercession for the transgressors" (v. 12).
- Isaiah 54 (3 Nephi 22), quoted by the resurrected Christ, relates to *stage 3*—Speaks of God's "everlasting kindness" (v. 8) and assurance that he will remember his people and that "no weapon . . . formed against [them] will prosper" (v. 17).

Table 2

The Four Stages of the Nephite Prophetic View Supported by the Isaiah Texts in the Book of Mormon

The following table takes the four stages of the Nephite prophetic view and arranges each Isaiah passage in the Book of Mormon under one of those stages.

Stage 1. The coming of Jesus Christ among the Jews and his rejection because of priestcrafts.

Isaiah

7:10–16	a sign is given of the birth of Immanuel (see also 1 Nephi 11:13–18), but the land will be forsaken
7:17–25	the land of Judah will be desolate, filled with briers
8:1–8	"as this people refuseth the waters of Shiloah" (v. 6), they will be overrun
8:9–10	those who counsel against God will come to naught
8:11–18	the Lord will be a "sanctuary" for some, but "a stone of stumbling" for others (v. 14); "I will look for [the Lord]" (v. 17)
9:1–7	a "great light" has shined, "for unto us a son is given" (v. 6)
9:8–17	but the proud will be devoured, for they do not seek the Lord; their leaders "cause them to err" (v. 16; see also 2 Nephi 10:5; Isaiah 3:12), and they that follow them are destroyed (cf. 2 Nephi 10:6)
48:12–22	"I am he," "the first [and] the last" (v. 12); God "hath sent me, . . . thy Redeemer" (v. 16–17); if thou "hadst hearkened to my commandments" "then had thy peace been as a river" (v. 18); "the Lord hath redeemed his servant" (v. 20)
53:1–12	"He is despised and rejected of men" (v. 3); "he hath borne our griefs" (v. 4), and is smitten, afflicted, judged, killed as an offering for sin; he intercedes for the transgressors

Stage 2. Jews will be scattered and smitten, will suffer in contention and darkness, but the Lord will not forget them.

3:1–4:1	the stay will be taken away from Judah; Jerusalem will be ruined; proud men and women will fall
5:1–25	"What could I have done more [for] my vineyard?" (v. 4); "my people are gone into captivity" (v. 13); the anger of the Lord is against his people, but he will still lift up an ensign for them (see v. 25–26)
6:1–12	how long will they not understand? until the land is "utterly desolate" (v. 11)
8:18–22	those with no light in them will be driven to darkness
9:18–21	"no man shall spare his brother" (v. 19); all will be against each other (see also 1 Nephi 12:21); but the Lord's "hand is stretched out still" (v. 21)
48:1–2	Judah will not swear by the Lord in righteousness
48:9–11	God will refine Judah in the fire of affliction
50:1–11	Even though none answered when the Lord came, he will not put Israel away; he did not turn away when he was rejected; but those who kindle a fire other than the light of the Lord will stay in darkness and sorrow

Stage 3. In the day of the Gentiles, a remnant will be summoned and gathered again.

5:26–30	he will "lift up an ensign to the nations" (v. 26); "they shall come with speed" (v. 26)
6:13	a portion will return
10:20–23	the remnant of Israel will return
11:10–16	an ensign will stand for the Gentiles; the Lord will recover the remnant a second time from the islands of the sea and from all the nations
49:1–26	the islands hearken; the Gentiles will see and arise "to restore the preserved of Israel," from afar (v. 6); the Lord will not forget his people (see v. 15); God will lift up his hand to the Gentiles (see v. 22), and their kings and queens will help Israel, and all flesh will know that the Lord is the Redeemer
51:1–23	the Lord will comfort his people (see v. 3); the isles will wait upon the Lord (see v. 5), and the redeemed of the

drunk the dregs of trembling (v. 16); and God pleads the cause of his people (see v. 23)

54:1–17 God will keep his covenant of kindness; he will be called "the God of the whole earth" (v. 5); he calls Israel to enlarge the tent and strengthen the stakes (see v. 2); the posterity of Israel will "inherit the Gentiles" (v. 3) and "remember the reproach" no more (v. 4)

Stage 4. In the day of God's judgment, the wicked will be destroyed and God's righteousness will be victorious.

2:6–9, 11 idolatry in the land will be destroyed

2:12–22 the lofty "shall be brought low" (v. 12)

10:1–19 in the day of visitation, God will punish the wicked and will "burn and devour [them] in one day" (v. 17)

10:24–34 the Lord will "stir up a scourge" (v. 26) and lop off the haughty bough with terror (see v. 33)

13:1–22 "the day of the Lord is at hand" (v. 6); he will destroy the sinners and cause arrogance to cease (see v. 11); God will destroy the wicked speedily

14:9–28 "Hell . . . is moved" (v. 9); Lucifer is fallen, cast out like an "abominable branch" (v. 19)

2:1–5 the Lord's house and peace will be established

2:10–11 "the Lord alone shall be exalted" (v. 11)

4:2–6 the branch of the Lord will be beautiful; a tabernacle will be in Jerusalem, "cloud . . . by day" and a "fire by night"

11:1–9 "a rod [will grow] out of the stem of Jesse" (v. 1) and will judge the earth with righteousness; the wolf and the lamb shall dwell in peace, and "the earth shall be full of the knowledge of the Lord" (v. 9)

12:1–6 righteous will be comforted; "God is my salvation"; "with joy shall ye draw water out of the wells of salvation"

14:1–8 "the Lord will have mercy" and choose Israel, and they will return to their lands (v. 1); "The whole earth is at rest" (v. 7)

14:29–32 Zion is established

52:1–15 "How beautiful upon the mountains are the feet of him that bringeth good tidings, that publisheth peace" (v. 7); all the ends of the earth will see the salvation of God when he "shall bring again Zion" (v. 8)

Table 3
The Nephite Prophetic World View

Stage 1. The Coming of Jesus Christ

	1 Nephi 11–14	1 Nephi 19–21	1 Nephi 22	2 Nephi 6–10	2 Nephi 25	2 Nephi 26–30	Jacob 4–6
at Jerusalem	11:13			6:8	25:11		
600 years after Lehi left Jerusalem		19:8			25:19		
after the return from captivity				6:8	25:11		
his name Jesus Christ, the Son of God					25:19		
born to Mary of Nazareth	11:13–21						
will come	11:13–21	19:8		6:9	25:12		4:11
in the flesh				6:9	25:12		
with love	11:22	19:9					4:10
many worship him	11:24						
baptism by the prophet	11:27						
minister with power and glory	11:28	19:13					4:11
will suffer		19:9, 12					

will be cast out	11:28							
perform miracles	11:31							
be judged and rejected	11:32	19:9	22:5		25:12		4:15	
scourged		19:9		6:9				
smitten, spat on		19:9						
will die on the cross	11:33	19:10		6:9	25:13		4:14	
sign of his death especially to those of the house of Israel		19:10–12				26:3		
fulfill law					25:24, 27			
atonement, infinite atonement for all mankind	11:33				25:16		4:11–12	
resurrection					25:13–14	26:1	4:11–12	
twelve rejected by house of Israel	11:34–35							
all who reject the twelve will fall	11:36							
wo unto them that fight against God and the people of his church					25:14			
they perish who cast out the prophets and slay the saints						26:3		
the tree began to decay								5:3

Stage 2. The Scattering of the Jews

	1 Nephi 11–14	1 Nephi 19–21	1 Nephi 22	2 Nephi 6–10	2 Nephi 25	2 Nephi 26–30	Jacob 4–6
scourged, destroyed	11:36	19:13		6:10	25:14–16		
scattered, confounded			22:3, 4				
because they:							
• fight against the twelve in pride	11:36						
• are proud and wicked						26:4	
• fight against God and the people of his church					25:14	26:3	
• turn hearts aside		19:13–14					
• harden hearts and stiffen necks		20:4		6:10			4:14
• do iniquities and harden their hearts			22:5		25:12		
• looking beyond the mark they stumble							4:14
multitude in the promised land as sand of sea, thy seed as the sand	12:1	20:19					
God led them through the deserts		20:21					

wars and contentions	12:2–3		25:12	26:2
I knew you would deal treacherously		20:8		
depths swallow and buildings fall on them, signs of death				26:4–6
he will remember the isles of the sea, gather		19:16, 21:1		
all the earth shall see the salvation of the Lord		19:17		
for I am he, all ye assemble		20:12, 14		
Christ to appear in New World	12:4–6			26:1, 9
righteous perish not				26:8
twelve disciples in New World and four righteous generations	12:7–12			26:9
destruction of Nephites • by Lamanites	12:13–23			26:10
• in darkness	12:23	21:9		26:10
• no peace unto wicked		20:22		
Lord will not suffer the Gentiles to destroy the seed of Lehi	13:31			

Stage 3. The Day of the Gentiles

	1 Nephi 11–14	1 Nephi 19–21	1 Nephi 22	2 Nephi 6–10	2 Nephi 25	2 Nephi 26–30	Jacob 4–6
Many Gentile nations and kingdoms and church of the devil	13:1–10					27:1	
many churches and the methods of the devil						26:20–33	
Israel scattered among Gentile nations			22:3–4		25:15–16		
Gentiles come to smite the Lamanites	13:11–15					26:15	
our seed brought low in dust						26:15	
dwindle in unbelief						26:17	
by the Gentiles shall our seed be scattered			22:7				
one Gentile group delivered from nations	13:16–19						
raise up a mighty nation among the Gentiles even upon face of this land		21:6	22:7				
wild branches grafted in							5:7

the Gentiles must be convinced					26:12
convincing them of the true Messiah	13:41			25:18	
book to come forth	13:20–29				26:16, 27:6
standard set up		21:22	22:6		29:3
restore the preserved of Israel; for a light to the Gentiles		21:6		25:17	
marvelous work among Gentiles	14:7		22:8	25:17	27:6–35
of worth to the Gentiles and also to all Israel			22:9		28:2
kings shall see and arise		21:7			
false teachings in the latter days, wo to Gentiles					28:3–32
after Gentiles stumble and Lamanites smitten, Lord is merciful to bring forth the gospel to	13:30–42	21:10			26:20
last and first		20:12			
first and last					5:63
O isles I have heard thee I have helped thee and I will preserve thee		21:8			

Stage 4. The Reestablishment of Israel and the Judgment of the World

	1 Nephi 11–14	1 Nephi 19–21	1 Nephi 22	2 Nephi 6–10	2 Nephi 25	2 Nephi 26–30	Jacob 4–6
numbered among seed	14:1					30:2	
gathered from afar		21:12					
gathered together			22:12				
confounded no more	14:2						
smitten no more		21:13				30:3	
out of darkness			22:12			30:6	
I will not forget thee		21:15					
Father will fulfill covenants	14:17						
all the children back		21:18–22			25:21	28:1	
Gentiles bring them back		21:22–23				30:8	
Gentiles will forget the Jews						29:5	
all people commanded to write						29:11–13	
words shall judge them					25:18, 22		
they that oppress the righteous shall be drunken with own blood		21:26					

blood of great and abominable upon their own head, drunken with own blood		22:13		27:3	
pit digged by great and abominable	14:3	22:14			
only two churches	14:10			30:10	
all that fight against Zion shall be destroyed		22:14, 22–23		27:3	
wars on all earth	14:15				
wicked burn as stubble		22:15			
wicked destroyed by fire				30:10	5:77, 6:3
righteous shall not perish		22:19, 24		30:10–11	
prophet like Moses is Holy One of Israel		22:21			
Christ is the Holy One of Israel			25:29		
all people shall dwell safely in the Holy One		22:28		30:12–15	
all flesh shall know that I am thy Savior, Redeemer	21:26	22:12			
no other Messiah or name			25:23–27		
all things shall be made known				30:16–18	

Nephi's Keys to Understanding Isaiah (2 Nephi 25:1–8)

Donald W. Parry

Unlocking Isaiah's prophecies requires a knowledge of their literary and geographical settings, being in tune with the Spirit, and acknowledging in hindsight their fulfillment.

After Nephi recorded Isaiah chapters 2–14 (see 2 Nephi 12–24) on the plates, he authored eight verses, 2 Nephi 25:1–8, that pertain directly to the large Isaiah quotation. The verses make up a significant literary unit and serve as a transitional link between the Isaianic quotation and the remainder of 2 Nephi 25. In these eight verses, Nephi provides keys to understanding Isaiah's words, because, as Nephi explains and as students of Isaiah's writings know, "Isaiah spake many things which were hard for many . . . people to understand" (2 Nephi 25:1). This chapter briefly examines each of the following five keys given in 2 Nephi 25:

1. Understand the "manner of prophesying among the Jews" (verse 1).

2. Do not do "works of darkness" or "doings of abominations" (verse 2).

3. Be filled with the spirit of prophecy (verse 4).

4. Be familiar with the regions around Jerusalem (verse 6).

5. Live during the days that the prophecies of Isaiah are fulfilled (verse 7).

Let us briefly examine each of these five keys.

1. Understand How the Jews Prophesied
(see 2 Nephi 25:1)

Nephi explains, "Isaiah spake many things which were hard for many of my people to understand; for they know not concerning the manner of prophesying among the Jews" (2 Nephi 25:1). The concept of understanding the "manner of prophesying among the Jews" was of sufficient import that Nephi used it as a theme throughout 2 Nephi 25:1–8. He includes the expressions "the manner of the Jews" (verse 2), "the things of the Jews" (verse 5), "the things of the prophets" (verse 5), "the things which were spoken unto the Jews" (verse 5), "the manner of the things of the Jews" (verse 5), and "the manner of the Jews" (verse 6). Joining all of these statements together into a composite statement creates the following summary: Isaiah spake many things that are hard for many people to understand because they do not know concerning the manner of prophesying among the Jews, the things of the prophets, or the things of the Jews.

What are the "things of the prophets"? Or, what is the "manner of prophesying among the Jews"? Exactly what Nephi had in mind with these statements is unclear, but perhaps he was referring to several literary devices or figures—symbolic language, poetic parallelism, and prophetic speech forms—that composed the prophetic approach in that period.

Symbolism

One prominent literary device connected to the manner of prophesying among the Jews deals with symbols and symbolic language. "Symbols are the timeless and universal language in which God, in his wisdom, has chosen to teach his gospel and bear witness of his Son. They are the language of the scriptures, the language of revelation, the language of the Spirit, the language of faith. . . . They are a means whereby we enrich, deepen, and enhance understanding and expression. They enable us to give visual and conceptual form to ideas and feelings that may otherwise defy the power of words."[1] Symbols "gain richness in their variety of meanings and purposes, which range from revealing to concealing great gospel truths."[2] For these reasons, Isaiah and most of the prophets used symbols throughout their poetic writings, symbols whose meanings elude many readers.

Symbolism is an integral part of the Isaianic text. Isaiah drew upon his familial, social, cultural, religious, and political backgrounds for scores of different metaphors. He used common aspects of everyday life—geography, plants, animals, insects, rocks, minerals, atmospheric conditions, heavenly bodies and objects, famous persons, dress, common occupations, ecclesiastical offices, social callings, human anatomy, architecture, numbers, colors, various foods, and sacral and common actions—as symbols.

Isaianic symbols may be classified into twenty-one major categories. These are listed below with a sampling of symbols from Isaiah found in these categories.

- Persons—Abraham, Sarah, Jesse, David, Cyrus
- Actions—
  (a) Sacral actions: anointings, sacrifices, ordinations, spreading forth the hands
  (b) Common actions: drinking, eating, falling down, fornicating, shaving the hair, singing, sitting, childbirth
- Human Anatomy—arms, heart, eyes, face, beard, belly, blood, bones, cheeks, ears, feet, fingers
- Animals—ass, bear, beast, bird, bittern, bullock, calf, camel, cattle, crane

- Objects—
  - (a) Sacred objects: incense, drink offering, temple, altar, burnt offering
  - (b) Common objects: ax, bed, bill of divorcement, book, chains, chariots, cup, idol
- Ecclesiastical Offices—prophet, priest
- Occupations—carpenter, creditor, fisherman, harvestman, king, officer, seller, servant
- Places—Assyria, Babylon, Sodom, Gomorrah, Egypt, Edom, Ariel, Jerusalem, Tarshish
- Plants—fig tree, cedar tree, flower, grass, groves, leaf, oak tree, olive tree, orchard, root, seed
- Elements/Rocks/Minerals—ashes, tin, iron, clay, clods, gold, light, rock, silver, dirt
- Foods—bread, barley, berries, butter, corn, fruit, grapes, honey, wine, milk, wheat
- Numbers—one, thousand
- Celestial Orbs/Objects—clouds, constellations, heaven, sun, moon, stars
- Time—day, daytime, night, noonday, winter, summer
- Colors—red, white, crimson, scarlet
- Atmospheric Conditions—storm, earthquake, flood, hail, tempest, wind, whirlwind
- Social Status—bridegroom, brother, children, daughter, father, firstborn, handmaid, slave, princess, queen, king
- Armor—armor, arrow, shield, sword, weapon, bow
- Geography—brook, river, cities, deep, desert, dry ground, field, highway, hill, mountain

- Names and Titles—
  (a) Of deity: Jehovah, Wonderful, Immanuel
  (b) Of persons: Beulah, Cyrus, Lucifer
  (c) Of places: Edom, Israel
- Architectural items—gate, foundation, house, wall, pillar, watchtower, windows, bulwarks

In order to understand the writings of Isaiah, one must first become familiar with the symbolism, parallelistic structures, and prophetic and revelatory language Isaiah uses in his writings, which give clues to the prophet's intended meanings.[3]

Poetic Parallelism

A second literary device that may be connected to the "manner of prophesying among the Jews" is poetic parallelism. Poetic parallelism may be defined as two short, balanced lines (phrases or sentences), with line one featuring words that are paralleled by the words of line two. Line two is a repetition, echo, or symmetrical counterpart of line one. Parallelisms rarely feature rhymes of assonance or consonance; rather, they present a harmonious construction of two expressions. Other parallel words may be synonymous or antithetical, or they may correspond in a number of other ways, including the following:

- Synonyms (or near synonyms), such as "heart–soul" and "statutes–commandments";
- Identical words or phrases, such as "light–light" and "cry unto him–cry unto him";
- Antonyms, such as "holy–unholy" and "poor–rich";
- Complementaries, such as "bows–arrows" and "river–sea";

- Different inflections of the same root, such as "to judge," "a judge," "judgment," and "judgment-seat";
- Gradations (an increase or decrease of the sense or idea), such as "the prince became king" and "forget God–sin against the Lord";
- Superordinates, such as "breastplates–shields," "wine–drink," and "gold–metal";
- Reciprocals, such as "to retire–to sleep," "to eat–to be full," and "to sin–pain of conscience"

Poetic parallelisms are poetic units often used in the book of Isaiah; they are found in almost every chapter. A preliminary count reveals more than one thousand parallelisms in Isaiah's writings, indicating that Isaiah used the poetry as a major means of presenting his prophecies to the world. Poetic parallelism "can verify or confirm the interpretations of scriptural symbols."[4] For example, the poetic parallel in 2 Nephi 8:24 (parallel to Isaiah 52:1: "Awake, awake, put on thy strength, O Zion; put on thy beautiful garments, O Jerusalem") confirms the symbolic meaning of Zion as Jerusalem.

The following examples of parallelisms are from Isaiah 2:1–5 (parallel to 2 Nephi 12:1–5), where Isaiah prophesies concerning the mountain (temple) of the Lord. Here each parallel is arranged as a two-line unit; the underlined terms in each parallel unit correspond with one another, as do the bold terms.

Isaiah prophesied that in the last days the mountain of the Lord's house

> shall be <u>established</u> in the top of the **mountains**,
> and shall be <u>exalted</u> above the **hills**;
>
> and all <u>nations</u> **shall flow** unto it.
> And many <u>people</u> **shall go** and say,

Come <u>ye</u>,
and let **us** <u>go</u> up

to the <u>mountain</u> of the **Lord**,
to the <u>house</u> of the **God of Jacob**;

and he will <u>teach us</u> of **his ways**,
and <u>we will walk</u> in **his paths**:

for <u>out of Zion</u> shall go forth the **law**,
and the **word** of the Lord <u>from Jerusalem</u>.

And he shall <u>judge</u> among the **nations**,
and shall <u>rebuke</u> many **people**:

and they shall beat <u>their swords</u> into **plowshares**,
and <u>their spears</u> into **pruninghooks**:

<u>nation</u> shall not lift up **sword** against <u>nation</u>,
neither shall <u>they</u> learn **war** any more.

By way of example, the following remarks explain the first parallelistic unit shown above. Many elements in the two lines of the first parallel unit correspond in one way or another. Both lines feature the verb *shall be*. The verb *established* in line one is synonymous with the verb *exalted* in line two. The prepositional phrase in line one, *in the top of*, correlates with the preposition in line two, *above:* both refer to height, elevation, or eminence. Line one presents the term *mountains*, which harmonizes with the word *hills* of line two: they are virtual synonyms, and both are preceded with the definite article *the*. In several aspects, these parallelisms possess corresponding elements; line two represents a counterpart or near mirror-image of line one. The parallel units in the book of Isaiah, when similarly examined, can be found to possess analogous features.

Prophetic Speech Forms

A third literary device found in Isaiah's writings pertains to the so-called prophetic speech forms,[5] which are directly connected to the prophetic approach ("manner of prophesying" or "things of the prophets"). They belong to the world of prophets and prophecy and are well-attested in the writings of Isaiah, Hosea, Ezekiel, Helaman, Joseph Smith, and many other prophets. By definition, prophetic speech forms are brief revelatory statements that (1) are attached to speeches, prophecies, or other revelations from God; (2) frequently contain the name of God; and (3) are often located at the beginning or end of a revelation or both. Prophetic speech forms have a significant function in prophetic writings: they indicate prophetic authority and prerogative. Nonprophets may not use the forms with power, because the power attached to the forms originates from God. Nor may nonprophets use the forms with authority; any attempt to do so would be met with disaster.[6]

The following five prophetic speech forms are found in the book of Isaiah. The form is identified first, followed by an example or explanation or both.

Messenger Formula—"Thus saith the Lord." (See, for example, Isaiah 7:7.) The messenger formula, used forty-six times in the writings of Isaiah, introduces prophetic language, and so it is often located at the beginning of a revelatory unit. God, through his prophet, is the ultimate source of the formula; hence its purpose is to announce both the divine authority and the origin of the revelation.

Proclamation Formula—"Hearken unto me" or "Hear the word of the Lord." (See, for example, Isaiah 48:1, parallel to 1 Nephi 20:1.) The proclamation formula is frequently located at the beginning of a revelatory pronouncement. Its primary function is to serve as a summons to hearken to God's word as it is revealed through the prophets.

Oath Formula—"As the Lord liveth" or "The Lord of hosts hath sworn." (See, for example, Isaiah 14:24.) This declaration, a solemn promise or oath that calls upon the existence of the Lord, is added to a revelation to accentuate it.

Woe Oracle—"Wo unto them that" or a similar accusation form that comprises the term "woe" one or more times in the oracle and is located within a judgment speech. (See, for example, Isaiah 5:8, 11, 20–22, parallel to 2 Nephi 15:8, 11, 20–22.) "The characteristic woe oracle consists of the accusation, the addressee, the intent of the accusation, and the promise of judgment."[7]

Revelation Formula—"The word that Isaiah the son of Amoz saw" (Isaiah 2:1, parallel to 2 Nephi 12:1; see also Isaiah 1:1) and "The Lord spake also unto me, again, saying" (Isaiah 8:5, 11, parallel to 2 Nephi 18:5, 11). The revelation formula consists of phrases that indicate prophetic authority and often provide the source of the revelation.

2. Do Not Commit Works of Darkness or Abomination (see 2 Nephi 25:2)

"Works of darkness" and "doings of abominations" (2 Nephi 25:2) conceal the meaning of prophetic speech from the one committing evil acts. When Laman and Lemuel complained that Lehi had taught things that were "hard to be understood" (1 Nephi 15:3), Nephi asked them, "Have ye inquired of the Lord?" (1 Nephi 15:8). He then provided a formula for understanding the prophetic word, including Isaiah's teachings: "If ye will not harden your hearts, and ask [the Lord] in faith, believing that ye shall receive, with diligence in keeping [his] commandments, surely these things shall be known unto you" (1 Nephi 15:11). Those who are involved in works of darkness and who break the commandments never understand the revelations of God or the things of the prophets.

3. Have the Spirit of Prophecy (See 2 Nephi 25:4)

A third vital key to understanding the writings of Isaiah is set forth by Nephi, who taught that the "words of Isaiah . . . are plain unto all those that are filled with the spirit of prophecy" (2 Nephi 25:4). It is natural that the reader be required to possess the spirit of prophecy in order to understand Isaiah's words, because the same spirit of prophecy provided or prompted the words of revelation to Isaiah; subsequently, it can provide those who diligently search Isaiah's prophecies with the interpretation of Isaiah's words. Nephi told his brethren that the prophecies of Isaiah "were manifest unto the prophet [Isaiah] by the voice of the Spirit; for by the Spirit are all things made known unto the prophets, which shall come upon the children of men according to the flesh" (1 Nephi 22:2).

Within scripture, the expression *spirit of prophecy* belongs almost exclusively to the Book of Mormon. It appears there more than twenty times, compared to only one occurrence in the Bible. This phrase as defined in scripture refers to the testimony of Jesus (see Revelation 19:10; see also Alma 6:8).[8] Joseph Smith understood this well and made frequent reference to it in his sermons.[9] On one occasion he explained, "No man can be a minister of Jesus Christ except he has the testimony of Jesus; and this is the spirit of prophecy. Whenever salvation has been administered, it has been by testimony."[10]

Several ancient prophets have connected the spirit of prophecy to the Holy Ghost or the Spirit of God (see Alma

5:47), to truth (see Alma 5:47; 6:8; 43:2), and to the gifts of the Holy Ghost, including the gift of tongues and the gift of translation (see Alma 9:21). Modern prophets view the spirit of prophecy and the Holy Ghost as virtually equivalent. Elder Delbert Stapley stated, "The Holy Ghost is the spirit of prophecy."[11] Similarly, President Wilford Woodruff wrote, "It is the privilege of every man and woman in this kingdom to enjoy the spirit of prophecy, which is the Spirit of God."[12]

The spirit of prophecy is intimately bound to the concept of revelation; the two are frequently presented as a pair (see, for example, the Book of Mormon title page; Jacob 4:6; Alma 6:8; 9:21; 17:3). Furthermore, the expression *the spirit of revelation and prophecy* (see Alma 4:20; 8:24; see also Alma 23:6 and 3 Nephi 3:19) is a common formula in the Book of Mormon.

Individuals who possess the spirit of prophecy, or the testimony of Jesus, are, in a sense, prophets—not in terms of having the high calling of members of the First Presidency and Quorum of the Twelve Apostles as prophets, seers, and revelators, but in terms of possessing a personal, revealed testimony of Jesus Christ.[13] If a person has the spirit of prophecy, he or she is a prophet—that is, on the same level of understanding as a prophet—and can therefore understand the writings of the prophets, such as Isaiah, who wrote by the spirit of prophecy. The fruits of the spirit of prophecy are many: besides being able to understand the writings of the prophets, one who possesses the spirit of prophecy may also have the gifts of discernment, revelation, translation of inspired scripture, and prophecy.[14]

The formula for receiving the spirit of prophecy is presented in Alma 17:2–3, where three key themes—diligent scriptural search, much prayer, and fasting—are set forth:

> Now these sons of Mosiah . . . had waxed strong in
> the knowledge of the truth; for they were men of a sound
> understanding and they had searched the scriptures dili-
> gently, that they might know the word of God. But this is
> not all; they had given themselves to much prayer, and
> fasting; therefore they had the spirit of prophecy, and the
> spirit of revelation.

4. Become Familiar with the Regions around Jerusalem (see 2 Nephi 25:6)

Nephi writes, "But behold, I, Nephi, have not taught my
children after the manner of the Jews; but behold, I, of myself, have dwelt at Jerusalem, wherefore I know concerning
the regions round about" (2 Nephi 25:6). In the context of
2 Nephi 25:1–8, this statement indicates that diligent search-
ers will more readily understand the book of Isaiah if they
comprehend things pertaining to the "regions round about"
Jerusalem.

Isaiah's prophecies frequently mention geographical
place-names and physical features connected with the ancient
Near East. There are more than 100 different geographical place-
names in the book of Isaiah (see chart 1), including cities
(e.g., Jerusalem, Sodom, Bozrah), lands (e.g., Egypt, Israel),
regions (e.g., Bashan, Galilee, Naphtali), valleys (e.g., Achor,
Rephaim), mountains (e.g., Carmel, Lebanon), and oases
(e.g., Nimrim, Tema). Many place-names appear more than
once: for example, Jerusalem is mentioned forty-eight times;
Egypt, forty-one; Moab, twenty-one; Ethiopia, six; Samaria,
eight; and Damascus, seven.

Understanding aspects of the place-names may explain
the meaning behind Isaiah's use of the name. At times, when
Isaiah refers to a place-name, he makes an actual reference
to that city, territory, or country; on other occasions, Isaiah

Chart 1

Place-Names in the Book of Isaiah

A representative list of place-names in the book of Isaiah. (Numbers in parentheses indicate how often the name appears in the book of Isaiah. The names in italics also appear in the Book of Mormon.)

Achor (1)	Dimon (2)	*Jerusalem* (48)	Perazim (1)
Aiath (1)	Dumah (1)	Jerusalem's (1)	Pul (1)
Ammon (1)	*Eden* (2)	Jesurun (1)	Ramah (1)
Anathoth (1)	*Edom* (2)	*Jordan* (1)	*Ramath* (1)
Ar (1)	Eglaim (1)	*Judah* (29)	Rephaim (1)
Arabia (1)	*Egypt* (41)	Kedar (4)	Rezeph (1)
Ariel (5)	*Elam* (3)	Kir (2)	*Samaria* (8)
Armenia (1)	Elealeh (2)	Kir-hareseth (1)	Seir (1)
Arnon (1)	*Ephraim* (9)	Kir-haresh (1)	Seba (1)
Arpad (1)	Ethiopia (6)	Lachish (2)	Sela (1)
Arphad (1)	Ethiopians (1)	*Laish* (1)	Sepharvaim
Aroer (1)	*Galilee* (1)	*Lebanon* (9)	(2)
Ashdod (2)	*Gallim* (1)	Libna (1)	Sharon (3)
Assyria (34)	*Geba* (1)	Lud (1)	Sheba (1)
Babylon (13)	*Gebim* (1)	Luhith (2)	*Shiloah* (1)
Bajith (1)	Gibeon (1)	*Madmenah* (1)	*Shinar* (1)
Bashan (2)	*Gibeah* (1)	Medeba (1)	Sibmah (2)
Beerelim (1)	*Gomorrah* (3)	Medes (1)	*Sinim* (1)
Bozrah (2)	Gozan (1)	Media (1)	*Sodom* (4)
Calno (1)	*Hamath* (4)	*Michmash* (1)	*Syria* (7)
Canaan (1)	Hanes (1)	*Midian* (1)	*Syrians* (1)
Carchemish (1)	Haran (1)	*Migron* (1)	*Tarshish* (7)
Carmel (3)	Hena (1)	*Moab* (21)	Telassar (1)
Chaldea (1)	Hephzi-bah (1)	*Naphtali* (1)	Tema (1)
Chaldees (1)	Heshbon (3)	Nebo (2)	Topheth (1)
Chittim (2)	Horonaim (1)	Nimrim (1)	Tubal (1)
City of David	Idumea (2)	Nineveh (1)	Tyre (7)
(1)	*Israel* (5)	*Nob* (1)	*Zebulun* (1)
Cush (1)	Ivah (1)	Noph (1)	Zidon (3)
Damascus (7)	Jahaz (1)	*Oreb* (1)	*Zion* (43)
Dedan(im)	Javan (1)	*Palestina* (2)	Zoan (3)
Dibon (1)	Jazer (2)	*Pathros* (1)	Zoar (1)

attaches a symbolic meaning to the place-name. The follow-ing are some examples of symbolic references to place-names:

Sodom—(see Isaiah 3:9; 13:19, parallel to 2 Nephi 13:9; 23:19). Inhabitants of the ancient cities of Sodom (with Gomorrah) committed enormous sins (see Ezekiel 16:49–50). Besides being lazy, prideful, and neglecting the poor, Sodom's inhabitants committed "fornication, and [went] after strange flesh" (Jude 1:7). Isaiah used Sodom as an example of a wicked city that was judged and destroyed by the power of God, never to be rebuilt, and he prophesied that other cities would be similarly destroyed by God's power around the time of the second coming of Christ. Hence, Sodom symbolizes all wicked cities of the last days that will suffer the judgments of God.

Assyria—(see Isaiah 7:17–18, 20; 10:12; 11:11, 16, parallel to 2 Nephi 17:17–18, 20; 18:7; 20:12; 21:11, 16). As the scriptures indicate, Assyria represents warring nations of the last days. "The great eastern empire of Assyria of biblical days, with its appalling cruel monarchs and its seemingly invincible armies, is a type of the warring nations of the latter days who will fight against Israel. However, although they suc-ceeded then in deporting the northern tribes of Israel from the Israelite homeland, the God of Israel will prevail against the modern Assyrian nations and they will be burned as 'thorns and briers' (See Isaiah 10)."[15]

Jerusalem—(see Isaiah 2:3; 3:1; 4:3–4; 5:3; 10:12, 32, parallel to 2 Nephi 12:3; 13:1; 14:3–4; 15:3; 20:12, 32). Isaiah's titles for Jerusalem point out her sacred mission and prophetic calling as the place where the infinite atonement of Jesus Christ would take place. Isaiah calls Jerusalem "the holy city" (Isaiah 52:1), "the city of righteousness" (Isaiah 1:26), "the faithful city" (Isaiah 1:26), and "the city of the Lord" (Isaiah 60:14).

Tarshish, ships of—(see Isaiah 2:16, parallel to 2 Nephi 12:16; see also Isaiah 23:1). Tarshish was a famous commercial port perhaps located on the Mediterranean Sea. Its exact location is presently unknown. Its ships carried riches and exotic materials of all sorts, including gold, silver, ivory, apes, and peacocks (see 1 Kings 10:22). Ancient Tarshish and its ships symbolize the materialism and worldliness during the time of the "day of the Lord" (Isaiah 2:12), or the last days (see Isaiah 2), and Isaiah's prophecy thus speaks of the eventual destruction of cities that traffic in worldliness.

In addition to place-names, Isaiah speaks of various physical features of the ancient Near East (see Chart 2).

In many instances, Isaiah uses these terms literally to denote a geographical item, while on other occasions he uses them symbolically to point to some deeper truth. Being aware that a place-name may have symbolic meaning aids a reader in that he or she can look for the deeper meaning intended by the prophet, applying Nephi's other keys when appropriate.[16]

Chart 2
Geographical Features in Isaiah's Prophecies

A selected list of bodies of water, places of human habitation, cardinal directions, and physical features found in Isaiah's prophecies. (Numbers in parentheses indicate how often the word appears in the book of Isaiah. Words in italics appear in the Book of Mormon.)

brook(s) (6)	*fountain*(s) (1)	*river(s)* (26)
caves (1)	*ground* (15)	*sea(s)* (29)
channel(s) (2)	*hill(s)* (16)	sluices (1)
city/cities (60)	*island(s)* (7)	*south* (3)
clefts (1)	*isle(s)* (12)	*springs* (8)
clifts (1)	*land(s)* (83)	*stream(s)* (10)
country/countries (7)	*mount/moun-*	*valley(s)* (13)
desert(s) (12)	*tain(s)* (58)	*villages* (1)
east (6)	*north* (5)	*waves* (2)
field(s) (18)	*place(s)* (54)	*west* (5)
flood(s) (3)	ponds (1)	*wilderness* (21)
fords (1)	*pool(s)* (8)	

5. Live during the Days in Which the Prophecies of Isaiah Are Fulfilled (See 2 Nephi 25:7)

Nephi prophesies, "In the days that the prophecies of Isaiah shall be fulfilled men shall know of a surety, at the times when they shall come to pass. . . . For I know that [Isaiah's prophecies] shall be of great worth unto them in the last days; for in that day shall they understand them" (2 Nephi 25:7–8). Nephi specifically identifies the "last days" as the time when many of Isaiah's prophecies will be fulfilled. Simply observing this prophet's prophecies being fulfilled helps readers recognize and understand Isaiah's words.

In my view, several of Isaiah's prophecies are presently being fulfilled, at least in a partial manner. These include the invitation for Israel to repent and cleanse themselves (see Isaiah 1:16–20), the building of temples (see Isaiah 2:1–5), the lifting of the ensign to the nations for Israel's gathering (see Isaiah 5:26–30; 11:11–16; see also Isaiah 10:20–27; 14:1–3; 49:8–26; 55:12–13), the Lord calling forth his armies (see Isaiah 13:1–5; compare D&C 105, especially verses 26 and 31), the coming forth of the Book of Mormon (see JST Isaiah 29:11–14), the welcoming of the Gentiles to the covenant (see Isaiah 56:1–8), and the restoration of Zion (see Isaiah 33:17–24; see also Isaiah 35:5–10; 54:1–3), and Israel's flight from Babylon (see Isaiah 48:20–22). Many other prophecies are also being fulfilled, as discerning members of the church will note, particularly with the aid of Nephi's interpretations.

Conclusion

Nephi provides two keys dealing with temporal or mechanical approaches to Isaiah. These include understanding the area in and around Jerusalem (see 2 Nephi 25:6) and comprehending the "manner of prophesying among the Jews" (2 Nephi 25:1), including symbols. Nephi also sets forth two keys that are connected with spiritual things: possessing the "spirit of prophecy" (2 Nephi 25:4) and avoiding "works of darkness" (2 Nephi 25:2). Nephi's fifth key deals with living during the days when the prophecies of Isaiah are fulfilled (see 2 Nephi 25:7).

I do not believe that anyone can fully understand Isaiah's prophecies without taking the time and effort to examine them thoroughly, or in scriptural terms, *search*. Jesus declared, "Behold they [the words of Isaiah] are written, ye have them before you, therefore *search* them" (3 Nephi 20:11). Later, Jesus commanded: "And now, behold, I say unto you, that ye ought to *search* these things. Yea, a commandment I give unto you that ye *search* these things diligently; for great are the words of Isaiah" (3 Nephi 23:1). Moroni set forth the imperative "*Search* the prophecies of Isaiah" (Mormon 8:23). Using the keys given by Nephi, we can search the words of Isaiah and truly come to understand them, thereby drawing closer to the Lord and gaining a fuller knowledge of the events of the last days.

Notes

1. Joseph Fielding McConkie, *Gospel Symbolism* (Salt Lake City: Bookcraft, 1985), 1.

2. Ibid., ix.

3. Those interested in learning more about scriptural symbolism will benefit from learning about the eight different types of symbolism, discussed in Joseph Fielding McConkie and Donald W. Parry, *A Guide to Scriptural Symbols* (Salt Lake City: Bookcraft, 1990), and from learning to use an exhaustive concordance of scriptural terms. See also McConkie, *Gospel Symbolism*.

4. McConkie and Parry, *A Guide to Scriptural Symbols*, 10.

5. For a study on the subject, see David E. Aune, *Prophecy in Early Christianity and the Ancient Mediterranean World* (Grand Rapids, Mich.: Eerdmans, 1983), 88–100.

6. The scriptures record instances of two false prophets who attempted to use the messenger formula, discussed below, in their prophecies. Both false prophets (see Zedekiah in 1 Kings 22:11 and 2 Chronicles 18:10; and Hananiah in Jeremiah 28:10–11) were severely dealt with by God.

7. See Donald W. Parry, "'Thus Saith the Lord': Prophetic Language in Samuel's Speech," in *Journal of Book of Mormon Studies* 1 / 1 (1992): 182. This article also contains examples of the woe oracle from the Book of Mormon.

8. President John Taylor explained, "These scriptures evidently show that the testimony of Jesus was the very principle, essence, and power of the spirit of prophecy whereby the ancient prophets were inspired" (John Taylor, *The Gospel Kingdom*, comp. G. Homer Durham [Salt Lake City: Bookcraft, 1964], 120). See also JST 1 Corinthians 2:11.

9. See, for example, Joseph Fielding Smith, comp., *Teachings of the Prophet Joseph Smith* (Salt Lake City: Deseret Book, 1976), 300, 312, 314.

10. Ibid., 160.

11. Delbert L. Stapley, untitled address, *Conference Report* (October 1966): 113.

12. Wilford Woodruff, *The Discourses of Wilford Woodruff*, comp. G. Homer Durham (Salt Lake City: Bookcraft, 1969), 61.

13. Joseph Smith presented the basic definition of a prophet:

> If any person should ask me if I were a prophet, I should not deny it, as that would give me the lie; for, according to John, the testimony of Jesus is the spirit of prophecy; therefore, if I profess to be a witness or teacher, and have not the spirit of prophecy, which is the testimony of Jesus, I must be a false witness; but if I be a true teacher and witness, I must possess the spirit of prophecy, and that constitutes a prophet. (Smith, *Teachings,* 269)

Wilford Woodruff similarly taught that Brigham Young "is a prophet, I am a prophet, you are, and anybody is a prophet who has the testimony of Jesus Christ, for that is the spirit of prophecy" (Woodruff, *Discourses*, 90).

14. See Book of Mormon title page; Jacob 1:6; Alma 12:7; 16:5–6; 25:16; 37:15; Joseph Smith–History 1:73. See also Smith, *Teachings*, 259; and Brigham Young, *Discourses of Brigham Young*, comp. John A. Widtsoe (Salt Lake City: Deseret Book, 1971), 131.

15. Joseph Fielding McConkie and Donald W. Parry, *A Guide to Scripture Symbols* (Salt Lake City: Bookcraft, 1990), 18.

16. To understand the symbolic meaning of a place-name, a reader may refer to scholarly commentary, such as that given in McConkie and Parry, *A Guide to Scriptural Symbols* and McConkie, *Gospel Symbolism*.

"Choose the Things That Please Me": On the Selection of the Isaiah Sections in the Book of Mormon

John Gee

Verbal markers, interpretive patterns, and explicit statements of purpose help modern readers appreciate why the Nephites included certain precise passages in their writings.

Moroni exhorts his readers to "search the prophecies of Isaiah" (Mormon 8:23). "And behold, I would write it also if I had room upon the plates" (Mormon 8:5), he says, telling us that had he had the time and the room, he would have written and expounded all the prophecies of Isaiah. Anytime everything is not or cannot be included in a record, the writer must choose[1] what to include and what to exclude (see 3 Nephi 7:17). That the choice of Isaiah selections in the Book of Mormon was deliberate is shown by Jacob's statement in 2 Nephi 6:4: "I will read you the words of Isaiah. And they are the words which my brother has desired that I should speak unto you." Not all the chapters of Isaiah are included in the Book of Mormon, and certainly not all are explained. But "the Lord had a purpose in preserving the prophecies of Isaiah in the Book of Mormon, notwithstanding they become a barrier to the casual reader."[2] Perhaps understanding why certain Isaiah passages have been chosen rather than others may prevent the prophecies of the Old Testament prophet Isaiah from looming "as a barrier, like a roadblock or a checkpoint beyond which the casual reader, one with idle curiosity, generally will not go."[3]

Our purpose in this chapter is to explain four points: first, how the text of Isaiah is divided into blocks; second, why certain blocks of text are chosen over others; third, how the Nephite prophets used and interpreted these blocks of text in their discourses; and fourth, how the Nephite writers signaled to readers their main reason for quoting a particular Isaiah passage. General guidelines to recognizing textual divisions are given, along with distinctive illustrations, to aid readers with their own analyses of the remaining quoted texts.

Textual Divisions

It should hardly surprise us that Nephi's and Jacob's quotations of Isaiah in the ancient text of the Book of Mormon do not break at our current chapter and verse designations. The Isaiah Scroll of the Dead Sea Scrolls, as well as Greek and other ancient biblical manuscripts, show that chapter and verse breaks were not present in ancient manuscripts.[4] More recent hands, following the traditions of the rabbis and doctors, placed artificial divisions into the texts of these ancient scriptures. The division into chapters and verses that we now employ can be a subtle impediment to understanding the scriptures. A close examination of the Book of Mormon reveals the section divisions of the Nephite version of Isaiah.

Phrasal Markers Using Verbs

When quoting lengthy passages, Book of Mormon prophets intentionally start and stop in certain specific places, reflecting natural breaks in Isaiah's text. Nephite writers normally marked breaks in passages through a syntactic or phrasal marker at the beginning of a new section.[5] One of these is a statement of acknowledging the presence of a quotation; such statements are common in ancient authors and we will refer to them as "inquit" statements, after the most common Latin phrase *inquit,* "he said." The most common inquit statement in Isaiah (occurring 66 times) is "(Thus) saith the Lord." A rhetorical question or an exclamation may also mark a section division (for example, see Mosiah 12:21; 14:1; 2 Nephi 27:25–35), as might other constructions, such as a simple noun phrase. Let us now examine how these syntactic and phrasal markers show how Nephite writers divided the text of Isaiah into sections.

Inquit Statements. Jacob chose with care the long Isaiah passage that he quotes in 2 Nephi 6:6–8:25 (see 2 Nephi 6:4); he is not simply rambling on until he gets tired. Inquit statements mark the boundaries of the passage he quotes. The selection Jacob quotes from Isaiah contains four sections, each of which begins with the phrase "Thus saith the Lord" (Isaiah 49:22, 25; 50:1; 51:22, parallel to 2 Nephi 6:6, 17; 7:1; 8:22), and the final section ends just before a fifth "Thus saith the Lord" (Isaiah 52:3).

Imperative with Vocative (Change of Addressee). Nephi also quotes part of this passage (1 Nephi 21:22–26, parallel to Isaiah 49:22–26), but he stops earlier. The words immediately after his stopping point are "Thus saith the Lord" (Isaiah 50:1, parallel to 2 Nephi 7:1), and he began with a phrase just as distinctive: "Hear ye this, O house of Jacob" (Isaiah 48:1, parallel to 1 Nephi 20:1). This phrase includes the imperative (command) "Hear" and its accompanying vocative (addressee) "ye"—and more specifically the "house of Jacob." The phrase indicates a shift to direct speech and a shift in the subject addressed; it also serves to mark the beginning of a new section. The same construction also applies to a passage from Isaiah that Jesus quotes, which begins "Sing, O barren" (Isaiah 54:1, parallel to 3 Nephi 22:1) and ends just before "Ho, every one that thirsteth, come ye to the waters" (Isaiah 55:1). Other relevant passages that use an imperative to mark the beginning of a section are given in Table 1.

Table 1

Selection of Isaiah Passages: Beginning and Ending Statements

Passages marked as follows: *Imperative with vocative*, INQUIT STATEMENT, **noun phrase**, exclamation, rhetorical question

Book of Mormon reference	Isaiah reference	End of previous Isaiah passage	Beginning of quotation	End of quotation	Beginning of following Isaiah passage
1 Nephi 20–1	48–9	... none shall save thee.	*Hearken and hear this, O house of Jacob* . . .	. . . I, the Lord am thy Savior and thy Redeemer, the Mighty One of Jacob.	THUS SAITH THE LORD, . . .
2 Nephi 6:6b–7, 16–8:25	49:22–52:2	. . . Behold, I was left alone; these, where had they been?	THUS SAITH THE LORD GOD: . . .	. . . loose thyself from the bands of thy neck, O captive daughter of Zion.	FOR THUS SAITH THE LORD, . . .
2 Nephi 9:50–1	55:1–2	. . . and their righteousness is of me, SAITH THE LORD.	*Come, my brethren, every one that thirsteth* . . .	. . . and let your soul delight in fatness.	*Incline your ear, and come unto me:* . . .
2 Nephi 12–24	2–14	. . . and none shall quench them.	**The word that Isaiah, the son of Amos, saw concerning Judah and Jerusalem:** . . .	. . . and poor of his people shall trust in it.	**The burden of Moab** . . .
2 Nephi 27:2–9, 15–19, 25–35	29:6–24	. . . it shall be at an instant suddenly.	they shall be visited of the Lord of Hosts, . . .	. . . and they that murmured shall learn doctrine.	Woe to the rebellious children, SAITH THE LORD, . . .

Book of Mormon reference	Isaiah reference	End of previous Isaiah passage	Beginning of quotation	End of quotation	Beginning of following Isaiah passage
Mosiah 12:21–4	52:7–10	. . . in that day that I am he that doth speak: behold, it is I.	How beautiful upon the mountains are the feet of him that bringeth good tidings; . . .	. . . and all the ends of the earth shall see the salvation of our God.	*Depart ye, depart ye, go ye out from thence, . . .*
Mosiah 14	53:1–12	. . . that which they had not heard shall they consider.	Who hath believed our report? . . .	. . . and made intercession for the transgressors.	*Sing, O barren, thou that didst not bear; . . .*
3 Nephi 16:18–20	52:8–10	. . . Thy God reigneth!	Thy watchmen shall lift up the voice; . . .	. . . and all the ends of the earth shall see the salvation of God.	*Depart ye, depart ye, go ye out from thence, . . .*
3 Nephi 20:32–46	52:1–3, 6–15	. . . and thou hast laid thy body as the ground, and as the street, to them then went over.	*Awake, awake, put on thy strength, O Zion; . . .*	. . . and that which they had not heard shall they consider.	Who hath believed our report? . . .
3 Nephi 22	54	. . . and made intercession for the transgressors.	*Sing, O barren, thou that didst not bear . . .*	. . . and their righteousness is of me, saith the Lord.	*Ho, every one that thirsteth, come ye to the waters, . . .*

Phrasal Markers Using Nouns

Similar markers are found in the longest of the passages of Isaiah quoted in the Book of Mormon (Isaiah 2–14, parallel to 2 Nephi 12–24). In these chapters, simple noun phrases mark section boundaries. The list of these phrases forms an almost complete atlas of Isaiah's world (collecting prophecies against various nations is a common feature of the preexilic prophets): "The word that Isaiah the son of Amoz saw concerning Judah and Jerusalem" (Isaiah 2:1); "the burden of Babylon, which Isaiah the son of Amoz did see" (Isaiah 13:1); "the burden of Moab" (Isaiah 15:1); "the burden of Damascus" (Isaiah 17:1); "the burden of Egypt" (Isaiah 19:1); "the burden of the desert of the sea" (Isaiah 21:1); "the burden of Dumah" (Isaiah 21:11); "the burden upon Arabia" (Isaiah 21:13); "the burden of the valley of vision," or the Hizayon valley (Isaiah 22:1); "the burden of Tyre" (Isaiah 23:1); and "the beasts of the south" (Isaiah 30:6). All these phrases are designated burdens (*maśśā'*), with the exception of the first phrase, which is designated a word (*dāḇār*). This word, however, is also linked with the other phrases because it and the next one are modified by the phrase "that Isaiah the son of Amoz saw."[6] These phrases should thus be grouped together. These then are the major divisions in the first part of Isaiah (chapters 1–35). Each of these textual divisions in Isaiah discusses the word of the Lord to the various nations in question. The approach is tailored specifically to the nation in question: Judah receives a "word" while the rest receive "burdens," and Assyria is omitted because the Assyrians are going to conquer or destroy all the kingdoms with burdens (Isaiah 13:19–22; 15:1; 17:1; 19:2–4; 20:4; 21:2–3; 21:15–17; 22:4; 23:1). Jerusalem, which received a "word" rather than a "burden," is the exception; she is told that she will ultimately be spared (Isaiah 8:7–8). The entire book of

Isaiah is divided into three sections by a historical passage in the center of the book (Isaiah chapters 36–39).

Nephi's Selection of Sections

Nephi seems to indicate that he is aware of the narrative structure of Isaiah as well as its content when he says that he understands Isaiah because "I, of myself, have dwelt at Jerusalem, wherefore I know concerning the regions round about; and I have made mention unto my children concerning the judgments of God, which hath come to pass among the Jews, unto my children, according to all that which Isaiah hath spoken, and I do not write them" (2 Nephi 25:6). But the question of why Isaiah 2–14 is quoted in particular remains unanswered. Of all the quotations Nephi could have used, he purposefully gave us what Isaiah saw of Jerusalem, or Zion (2 Nephi 12–22, parallel to Isaiah 2–12) and Babylon (2 Nephi 23–24, parallel to Isaiah 13–14). These chapters are impressively relevant to Nephi's main messages.

In his long explanation in 2 Nephi 25–30, Nephi notes that "Jerusalem shall be destroyed again; for wo unto them that fight against God and the people of his church. Wherefore, the Jews shall be scattered among all nations; yea, and also Babylon shall be destroyed" (2 Nephi 25:14–15), but he mainly discusses the contrast between Zion and the churches that fight against Zion. The contrast between Zion and Babylon mirrors Nephi's angelic guide's statement that there are "two churches only; the one is the church of the Lamb of God, and the other is the church of the devil . . . which is the mother of abominations; and she is the whore of all the earth" (1 Nephi 14:10).

Babylon is a fitting symbol for the great and abominable church. The angel tells Nephi that "the gold, and the silver, and the silks, and the scarlets, and the fine-twined linen, and the precious clothing, and the harlots, are the desires of this great and abominable church" (1 Nephi 13:8). In a parallel revelation to John (see also 1 Nephi 14:18–28), when "Babylon the great, the mother of harlots and abominations of the earth" falls (Revelation 17:5), it is "the kings of the earth" (Revelation 18:9) and "the merchants of the earth" who "weep and mourn over her" (Revelation 18:11). Thanks to the thousands of tablets unearthed in the last century or so, we now have a better idea of what that civilization was like. John Oates explains that "by far the greatest number of these documents are economic in content, dealing with such mundane transactions as sales of land and loans."[7]

Knowing that the Babylonians were astronomers who dreaded eclipses because of their dire indications—usually the death of the king[8]—helps us better understand Isaiah 13:10, parallel to 2 Nephi 23:10: "For the stars of heaven and the constellations thereof shall not give their light: the sun shall be darkened in his going forth, and the moon shall not cause her light to shine." Isaiah, in his Babylonian prophecies, makes two clear allusions to two well-known pieces of Babylonian literature, the *Gilgamesh Epic* and the *Descent of Ishtar*. His statement that "the fir trees rejoice at thee, and the cedars of Lebanon, saying, Since thou art laid down, no feller is come up against us" (Isaiah 14:8, parallel to 2 Nephi 24:8) recalls the expedition to the cedar forests in *Gilgamesh* tablets II–V,[9] only in Isaiah's case it is the Babylonian king, not Humbaba, who is felled. Isaiah's comparison of the king of Babylon with the morning star descending into hell (Isaiah 14:12–16, parallel to 2 Nephi 24:12–16) compares well to the *Descent of Ishtar,* in which Ishtar, the morning star, descends to the netherworld.[10] In the Babylonian version, however, Ishtar emerges from the netherworld, while in Isaiah the king is brought down to hell, where he remains.

In two sections (Isaiah 2–12 and 13–14, parallel to 2 Nephi 12–22 and 23–24) Isaiah contrasts Judah and Babylon. One is interested in "the mountain of the Lord's house" (Isaiah 2:2; 11:9, parallel to 2 Nephi 12:2; 21:9), while the other is interested in the "mount of the congregation, in the sides of the north" (Isaiah 14:13, parallel to 2 Nephi 24:13). Judah has "the Holy One of Israel in the midst of thee" (Isaiah 12:6, parallel to 2 Nephi 22:6), while in the midst of Babylon reigns "Lucifer, son of the morning" (Isaiah 14:12, parallel to 2 Nephi 24:12). The "remnant of Israel" shall return to Jerusalem (Isaiah 10:20–22; 49:18–25, parallel to 2 Nephi 20:20–22; 1 Nephi 21:18–25), but the Lord shall "cut off from Babylon the name, and remnant, and son, and nephew" (Isaiah 14:22, parallel to 2 Nephi 24:22). The two countries have different reactions to the banner lifted "upon the high mountain" (Isaiah 2:2–5; 11:10–14; 13:2–5, parallel to 2 Nephi 12:2–5; 21:10–14; 23:2–5); the "day of the Lord of hosts" befalls each, but for one it is great and the other it is dreadful (Isaiah 2:10–22; 13:6–22, parallel to 2 Nephi 12:10–22; 23:6–22). Like the Gadianton robbers, the guerrilla warriors of the Book of Mormon,[11] Marduk-apla-iddina II (Merodach-baladin), a crafty and cunning guerrilla warrior, ruled Babylon in Isaiah's day (Isaiah 39:1–2, parallel to 2 Kings 20:12–13).[12] Nephi's division of the world into two camps is not unusual, although the lines upon which he divides them are. The division is the burden of Nephi's quotation of Isaiah and his explanation of the passages he quotes.

Interpretation of Passages

When Nephite prophets quoted Isaiah, they followed a regular pattern. The pattern they used in citing and interpreting Isaiah in the Book of Mormon (see 1 Nephi 19–22;

Table 2
Outlines of Passages Quoting Isaiah

Nephi addresses his brethren	"The words of Jacob, which he spake unto the people of Nephi"	Nephi writes more of the words of Isaiah	Abinadi's discourse
Introduction 1 Nephi 19:22–4 Quotation of Isaiah 48:1–49:26 1 Nephi 20:1–21:26	**Introduction** 2 Nephi 6:1–5 Quotation of Isaiah 49:22–3 2 Nephi 6:6–7	**Introduction** 2 Nephi 11:1–8 Quotation of Isaiah 2:1–14:32 2 Nephi 12:1–24:32	**Question** on Isaiah 52:7–10 Mosiah 12:20–4 **Question and answer** Mosiah 12:25–32 **Quotation** of Exodus 20:2–4 Mosiah 12:34–6 **Explanation** of Exodus 20:2–17
Explanation 1 Nephi 22:1–31	**Explanation** 2 Nephi 6:8–15	**Explanation** 2 Nephi 25:1–27:2 Quotation of Isaiah 29:7–11 2 Nephi 27:3–6 **Explanation** 2 Nephi 27:7–16 Quotation of Isaiah 29:11–12 2 Nephi 27:17–19 **Explanation** 2 Nephi 27:20–24 Quotation of Isaiah 29:13–24 2 Nephi 27:25–35	Mosiah 13:25–35 Quotation of Isaiah 53:1–12 Mosiah 14:1–12 **Explanation** Mosiah 15:1–28
	Quotation of Isaiah 49:24–52:2 2 Nephi 6:16–8:25 **Conclusion of discourse** 2 Nephi 9:1–54	**Conclusion of discourse** 2 Nephi 28:1–30:10 Quotation of Isaiah 11:5–9 2 Nephi 30:11–5 **The End** 2 Nephi 30:16–8	**Quotation** of Isaiah 52:8–10 Mosiah 15:29–31 **Conclusion** Mosiah 16:1–15

2 Nephi 6–8; 2 Nephi 11–30; Mosiah 12–15) may be standard-ized as follows:

(A)   Introduction

(B)   Citation of a passage of scripture

(C)   Quotation of parts of the text and interpretation of the passage by explaining and defining terms

(D)   Conclusion by quoting the closing verses of the section

This pattern is a general working paradigm; like any other verbal paradigm, there are lots of individual exceptions to the general paradigm. Table 2 shows the full pattern.

Jacob's Interpretation: Substitution of Phrases

Jacob illustrates this interpretive pattern in 2 Nephi 6. Isaiah passages are in quotation marks, with square brackets mark-ing variations between the Masoretic text and the Book of Mormon; underlined passages of the Isaiah text (part B) cor-respond to *italicized* quotations of those passages in the text (part C). Verses have been kept standard for reference purposes.

A. Introduction

5. And now, the words which I shall read are they which Isaiah spake concerning all the house of Israel; wherefore, they may be likened unto you, for ye are of the house of Israel. And there are many things which have been spoken by Isaiah which may be likened unto you, because ye are of the house of Israel.

B. Quotation

6. And now, these are the words: "Thus saith the Lord God: Behold, I will lift up mine hand to the Gentiles, and set up my standard to the people; and they shall bring thy sons in their arms, and thy daughters shall be carried upon their shoulders.

7. And kings shall be thy nursing fathers, and their queens thy nursing mothers; they shall bow down to thee with their faces towards the earth, and <u>lick up the dust of</u> thy <u>feet</u>; and thou <u>shalt know that</u> I am <u>the Lord</u>; for they <u>shall not be ashamed</u> that <u>wait for</u> me."

C. Explanation

8. And now I, Jacob, would speak somewhat concerning these words. For behold, the Lord has shown me that those who were at Jerusalem, from whence we came, have been slain and carried away captive.

9. Nevertheless, the Lord has shown unto me that they should return again. And he also has shown unto me that the Lord God, the Holy One of Israel, should manifest himself unto them in the flesh; and after he should manifest himself they should scourge him and crucify him, according to the words of the angel who spake it unto me.

10. And after they have hardened their hearts and stiffened their necks against the Holy One of Israel, behold, the judgments of the Holy One of Israel shall come upon them. And the day cometh that they shall be smitten and afflicted.

11. Wherefore, after they are driven to and fro, for thus saith the angel, many shall be afflicted in the flesh, and shall not be suffered to perish, because of the prayers of the faithful; they shall be scattered, and smitten, and hated; nevertheless, the Lord will be merciful unto them, that when they shall come to the knowledge of their Redeemer, they shall be gathered together again to the lands of their inheritance.

12. And blessed are *the Gentiles*, they of whom the prophet has written; for behold, if it so be that they shall repent and fight not against Zion, and do not unite themselves to that great and abominable church, they shall be saved; for the Lord God will fulfil his covenants which he

has made unto his children; and for this cause the prophet has written these things.

13. Wherefore, they that fight against Zion and the covenant people of the Lord shall *lick up the dust of* their *feet*; and the people of the Lord *shall not be ashamed*. For the people of the Lord are they who *wait for* him; for they still *wait for* the coming of the Messiah.

14. And behold, according to the words of the prophet, the Messiah will *set* himself again the second time to recover them; wherefore, he will manifest himself unto them in power and great glory, unto the destruction of their enemies, when that day cometh when they shall believe in him; and none will he destroy that believe in him.

15. And they that believe not in him shall be destroyed, both by fire, and by tempest, and by earthquakes, and by bloodsheds, and by pestilence, and by famine. And they *shall know that the Lord* is God, the Holy One of Israel.

D. Conclusion

16. For "shall the prey be taken from the mighty, or the lawful captive delivered?

17. But thus saith the Lord: Even the captives of the mighty shall be taken away, and the prey of the terrible shall be delivered; for [the Mighty God shall deliver his covenant people. For thus saith the Lord]: I will contend with them that contendeth with thee—

18. And I will feed them that oppress thee, with their own flesh; and they shall be drunken with their own blood as with sweet wine; and all flesh shall know that I the Lord am thy Savior and thy Redeemer, the Mighty One of Jacob." (2 Nephi 6:6–18)

The Book of Mormon offers glosses on various phrases from Isaiah, interpreting the phrases by requoting them and replacing certain terms with equivalent terms. This is a venerable Jewish interpretive practice[13] that can be used to understand the book of Isaiah as the Nephites understood it. Isaiah 49:22–23 contains the following pronouns: "I" = "the Lord God"; "they" = "the Gentiles" / "kings and their queens"; "thou" = undefined. The Book of Mormon reuses these phrases from Isaiah (see the quotation section of 2 Nephi 6, above), defining them more specifically and thus giving them more meaning: "I" = "the Lord God, the Holy One of Israel," "the Messiah"; "they" = "they that fight against Zion and the covenant people of the Lord"; "thou" = "the people of the Lord." Furthermore, the "Standard to the people" that the Lord sets up is "the Messiah . . . himself." The Book of Mormon's interpretation is self-consistent and makes sense of the Isaiah passage. In the concluding passage, it is difficult to determine whether the bracketed words that differ from those of Isaiah in the Masoretic text reflect an earlier text or an interpretation by the Book of Mormon.

Nephi's Interpretation: Adding Explanations

Different parts of this same Isaiah section (Isaiah 49:22–23) are also explained in 1 Nephi 22, which uses several other techniques besides substitution of key phrases. In addition to requoting the phrase, the Nephite interpreter might provide an explanation: "they shall be nursed by the Gentiles . . . and it meaneth us in the days to come, and also all our brethren who are of the house of Israel" (1 Nephi 22:6). Also a verbal phrase might be added in order to define the previous phrase: "The Lord God will proceed to make bare his arm in the eyes of all nations, in bringing about his covenants and his gospel unto those who are of the house of Israel" (1 Nephi 22:11). To Nephi, for the Lord "to make bare his arm" means that he brings his covenants and his gospel to the Nephites.

Abinadi's Interpretation: Definition of Terms

In other places, a term might simply be defined. Abinadi explains to king Noah and his priests the meaning of Isaiah 53:10, which reads "when thou shalt make his soul an offering for sin, he shall see *his seed*, he shall prolong his days, and the pleasure of the Lord shall prosper in his hand" (emphasis added):

> whosoever has heard the words of the prophets, yea, all the holy prophets who have prophesied concerning the coming of the Lord—I say unto you, that all those who have hearkened unto their words, and believed that the Lord would redeem his people, and have looked forward to that day for a remission of their sins, I say unto you, that these are *his seed*, or they are the heirs of the kingdom of God. (Mosiah 15:11, emphasis added)

New Covenant, New Interpretive Pattern: Jesus on Isaiah

Interestingly, when Jesus visits the Nephites, he uses another pattern of interpretation of the scriptures. Christ's quotations on the second day of his visit (3 Nephi 19–26) do not follow the general Nephite pattern of quotation and interpretation of Isaiah that exists in the previous quotations in the Book of Mormon. An examination of the material quoted and its context shows how the Savior's purpose differs. After the people were baptized, and during the ministration of angels, "Jesus came and stood in the midst and ministered unto them" (3 Nephi 19:15). After prayers (3 Nephi 19:16–20:1), the Nephites partook of the sacrament (3 Nephi 20:3–9) and then Jesus proceeded to "finish the commandment which the Father hath commanded me concerning this people" (3 Nephi 20:10). The Savior reminded the Nephites that he had quoted Isaiah 52:8–10 the day before (3 Nephi 20:11),[14] then, picking up where he had left off in his discourse of the day before, he began to quote passages relating to the gathering of Israel and the part the Western Hemisphere plays in it, interspersed with his own comments and clarifications (see Table 3).

Christ uses a series of basic texts with slight changes to clarify his intent, continually alluding to these texts in his explanations by picking up the wording from the passages. He also introduces the writings of prophets that were not part of the Nephite canon (3 Nephi 23:6, 13; 26:2). In this fashion, Jesus "expounded all the scriptures in one" (3 Nephi 23:14; see also 26:1, 3–4), but because he said so much, Mormon was

Table 3	
Passages Quoted by Jesus in 3 Nephi	
Isaiah 52:8–10	3 Nephi 16:18–20
Micah 5:8–9	3 Nephi 20:16–17
Micah 4:12–13	3 Nephi 20:18–19
Deuteronomy 18:15–19	3 Nephi 20:23
Genesis 12:3	3 Nephi 20:25, 27
Isaiah 52:8	3 Nephi 20:32
Isaiah 52:9–10	3 Nephi 20:34–35
Isaiah 52:1–3	3 Nephi 20:36–38
Isaiah 52:6–7	3 Nephi 20:39–40
Isaiah 52:11–15	3 Nephi 20:41–45
Isaiah 52:15	3 Nephi 21:8
Isaiah 29:14	3 Nephi 21:9
Habakkuk 1:5	3 Nephi 21:9
Deuteronomy 18:19	3 Nephi 21:11 (allusion)
Micah 5:8–15	3 Nephi 21:12–18, 21
Deuteronomy 18:19	3 Nephi 21:20 (allusion)
Isaiah 52:12	3 Nephi 21:29
Isaiah 54:1–17	3 Nephi 22:1–17
Malachi 3:1–4:6	3 Nephi 24:1–25:6

unable to copy all the material into his abridgement (3 Nephi 26:6–8). We are fortunate to have what he was able to give us, however, because the New Testament reduces the resurrected Christ's scriptural sermon to a single statement: "Then opened [Jesus] their understanding, that they might understand the scriptures" (Luke 24:45) "which were written in the law of Moses, and in the prophets, and in the psalms" (Luke 24:44).[15] It is clear that Jesus' way of interpreting the scriptures left an impression on the Nephites; Moroni seems to have used the same method of interpreting scripture when he opened this dispensation.[16]

Statements of Intent

Fortunately, in many cases, the Book of Mormon prophets tell us why they choose to quote the passages they do. These statements of intent are often found in the introductions to the Isaiah quotations, and phrases in the statements are reflected in the passages they quote. These introductory remarks help the modern reader to understand the significance of these quoted passages in the Book of Mormon.

Nephi's Directives

For example, Nephi writes that in order to "more fully persuade them to believe in the *Lord their Redeemer* [he] did read unto them that which was written by the prophet Isaiah" (1 Nephi 19:23). In the Isaiah passage he then quotes the phrases "the Lord, thy Redeemer, the Holy One of Israel" (1 Nephi 20:17), "the Lord, the Redeemer of Israel, his Holy One" (1 Nephi 21:7), and "I, the Lord, am thy Savior and thy Redeemer, the Mighty One of Jacob" (1 Nephi 21:26). In the introduction to the passage, Nephi tells us what he wants his readers to look for in the passage and expands this in the following commentary: "Hear ye the words of the prophet, which were written unto all the *house of Israel*, and liken them unto yourselves, that ye may have hope as well as your brethren" (1 Nephi 19:24). The Isaiah passage begins with the phrase "hear this, O house of Jacob" (1 Nephi 20:1) and addresses Israel six times (1 Nephi 20:1, 12; 21:1, 3, 12, 15), thrice explicitly as the "house of Israel" (1 Nephi 21:1, 12, 15) (the phrase *house of Israel* does not occur in the corresponding passages as they have been preserved in the Masoretic text of the Bible [Isaiah 49:1, 12, 15]). Nephi ends the passage that discusses the restoration of the house of Israel through the Gentiles with a statement of intent: "that ye may have hope as well as your brethren" (1 Nephi 19:24).

"For He Verily Saw My Redeemer" (2 Nephi 11:2)

In order to appreciate the clarity of these statements of intent, readers need to follow the complex structure of Isaiah and think about how the Isaiah passage functions in its original context. For example, Isaiah chapters 7–12 are one succinct unit, a prophecy given to king Ahaz sometime in the first three years of his reign (see Isaiah 7:1, parallel to 2 Nephi 17:1; compare 2 Kings 15:27; 16:1). The dialogue can be confusing unless we keep track of who is speaking. The entire prophecy in Isaiah 7–12 is given to the faithless and vacillating king Ahaz.[17]

The first person to speak is the Lord, who tells Isaiah to tell Ahaz that impending war with Syria and Israel will not occur (see Isaiah 7:3–9). No record indicates that Isaiah said this directly to Ahaz; we are to assume that the message was delivered. The Lord then tells Ahaz to ask for a sign (see Isaiah 7:10–11), but Ahaz refuses (see Isaiah 7:12). Isaiah then tells Ahaz that the Lord will give him a sign: Immanuel, meaning "God with us," will be born of a virgin,[18] and before Immanuel knows good from evil, Syria and Israel will have been destroyed by the Assyrians (see Isaiah 7:13–25). Isaiah then recounts how the birth of his son Maher-shalal-hash-baz was prophesied, and how the Lord foretold that Judah's enemies would be conquered before the child could speak. Maher-shalal-hash-baz thus is a type of Immanuel (see Isaiah 8:1–4); his birth is an indication of God's love, a sign that God is protecting His people. Isaiah quotes the Lord about the coming of Assyria (see Isaiah 8:5–8) and tells Ahaz that joining a confederacy would be a disastrous mistake (see Isaiah 8:9–16). Isaiah again points to the sign of the children, noting that "I and the children whom the Lord hath given me are for signs and for wonders in Israel" (Isaiah 8:18), and Ahaz should therefore turn to the Lord instead of to the wisdom of men (see Isaiah 8:17–10:4). Isaiah points out that although the Assyrians are coming, they are a tool of the Lord and will be brought down by their own hubris. God will provide his people a righteous ruler (see Isaiah 10:5–34) who will usher in an era of peace (see Isaiah 11:1–16), "and in that day" even Ahaz will acknowledge, "God is my salvation" (Isaiah 12:1–2). The key figure in this prophecy is Immanuel, the babe born of a virgin (see Isaiah 7:14). This babe shall have the government; he is "The mighty God, The everlasting Father, The Prince of Peace" (Isaiah 9:6), and the stem of Jesse (see Isaiah 11:1), and "Of the increase of his government and peace there shall be no end" (Isaiah 9:7). All this explains why Nephi quotes this passage, and why he says that Isaiah "saw my Redeemer, even as I have seen him" (2 Nephi 11:2). Nephi, living after the Assyrians had destroyed both Israel and Syria and later destroyed themselves, knew that this child had yet to be born, and he thus introduces this passage: "There is a God, and he is Christ, and he cometh in the fulness of his own time. And now I write some of the words of Isaiah, that whoso of my people shall see these words may lift up their hearts and rejoice for all men" (2 Nephi 11:7–8).

Similarly, to show "that God himself should come down among the children of men, and take upon him the form of man, and . . . he, himself, should be oppressed and afflicted" (Mosiah 13:34–35), Abinadi also quotes Isaiah, saying that the Savior "was oppressed, and he was afflicted, yet he opened not his mouth" (Mosiah 14:7, parallel to Isaiah 53:7). Abinadi explains that he quoted this passage "that ye should understand that God himself shall come down among the children of men, and shall redeem his people" (Mosiah 15:1).[19]

Conclusion

Examining how and why the Book of Mormon prophets used Isaiah reveals that the Nephites explained scripture using a basic pattern[20] that they developed gradually over time. It also shows that the Isaiah selections are not simple filler,[21] but an integral part of Nephi's, Jacob's, Abinadi's, and Christ's discourses, which all serve to fulfill the Book of Mormon's stated purpose: "to show unto the remnant of the House of Israel what great things the Lord hath done for their fathers; and that they may know the covenants of the Lord, that they are not cast off forever—and also to the convincing of the Jew and Gentile that Jesus is the Christ, the Eternal God, manifesting himself unto all nations" (Book of Mormon title page). The Nephite prophets chose sections of Isaiah that would underscore their conviction that Jesus is the Christ.

Notes

1. The quotation in the title comes from Isaiah 56:4 and was suggested to me indirectly by Glen Cooper.

2. Boyd K. Packer, "The Things of My Soul," *Ensign* (May 1986): 61.

3. Ibid.

4. The Isaiah Scroll in the Dead Sea Scrolls uses indents and paragraphing to mark different sections. These sections are independent of our chapter and verse divisions. They are sometimes consistent with the divisions of the Book of Mormon, and they sometimes are not. See Millar Burrows, *The Dead Sea Scrolls of St. Mark's Monastery* (New Haven: American Schools of Oriental Research, 1950).

5. There are also subdivisions within these sections: Isaiah 2–12 seems to be broken into the following prophecies: Isaiah 2–4, 5, 6, and 7–12, with the last two sections being separately dated. Isaiah 13–14 is also divided into at least two separate prophecies (13:1–14:27 and 14:28–32), the last of which is dated.

6. Amos prophesied against Damascus (Amos 1:3–5), the Philistine cities (1:6–8), Tyre (1:9–10), Edom (1:11–12), the children of Ammon (1:13–15), Moab (2:1–3), Judah (2:4–5), and Israel (2:6–8). The last to do this is Zephaniah, who prophesied against the land of the Philistines (Zephaniah 2:4–7), Moab and the children of Ammon (2:8–11), the Nubian kings of Egypt (2:12), Assyria (2:13–15), and Jerusalem (3:1–20).

7. Joan Oates, *Babylon*, 2nd ed. (London: Thames and Hudson, 1986), 15; compare Seton Lloyd, *The Archaeology of Mesopotamia: From the Old Stone Age to the Persian Conquest*, 2nd ed. (London: Thames and Hudson, 1984), 90–1.

8. Usually a solar eclipse signified the death of the king, but sometimes other catastrophes could be involved. For a general discussion see Oates, *Babylon*, 187–90. The basic texts are available in Ch. Virolleaud, *L'Astrologie Chaldéenne*, 14 fascicles (Paris: Paul Geuthner, 1908–12); Hermann Hunger and David Pingree,

MUL.APIN: An Astronomical Compendium in Cuneiform, Beiheft 24 of Archiv für Orientforschung (Horn, Austria: Ferdinand Berger & Söhne, 1989); these might now be read in the light of Johannes Koch, *Neue Untersuchungen zur Topographie des babylonischen Fixsternhimmels* (Wiesbaden: Otto Harrassowitz, 1989). Other implications (disturbance, grief, fright, apprehensiveness, fear, awe) can be found in *The Assyrian Dictionary* (Chicago: Oriental Institute of the University of Chicago, 1954–present), s.v. "adāru." For example, "If on the first of the month of Nisan the sun is darkened the king of Akkad will die" (Virolleaud, *L'Astrologie Chaldéenne*, 2:24; compare 6:15).

9. Translations available in Maureen Gallery Kovacs, *The Epic of Gilgamesh* (Stanford: Stanford University Press, 1989), 19–47; and Stephanie Dalley, *Myths from Mesopotamia: Creation, The Flood, Gilgamesh, and Others* (Oxford: Oxford University Press, 1991), 61–77.

10. Translations in Benjamin R. Foster, *Before the Muses: An Anthology of Akkadian Literature* (Bethesda, Maryland: CDL, 1993), 1:403–9; Dalley, *Myths from Mesopotamia*, 154–62; and E. A. Speiser, "Descent of Ishtar to the Nether World," in *Ancient Near Eastern Texts Relating to the Old Testament*, ed. James B. Pritchard, 3rd ed. (Princeton: Princeton University Press, 1969), 106–9. For Ishtar as the morning star, see Foster, *Before the Muses*, 2:505.

11. See Daniel C. Peterson, "The Gadianton Robbers as Guerrilla Warriors," in *Warfare in the Book of Mormon*, ed. Stephen D. Ricks and William J. Hamblin (Salt Lake City: Deseret Book and FARMS, 1990), 146–73.

12. The standard account is J. A. Brinkman, "Merodach-Baladan II," in *Studies Presented to A. Leo Oppenheim* (Chicago: Oriental Institute of the University of Chicago, 1964), 6–53; a popular account may be found in Oates, *Babylon*, 115–7. Merodach-baladan earns the epithet of guerrilla warrior by fitting the following points of Peterson's essay: a religiously motivated (Brinkman, "Merodach-Baladan II," 14–7; Oates, *Babylon*, 115; compare 3 Nephi 3:9–10; Hugh W. Nibley, *Since Cumorah* [Salt Lake City: Deseret Book and FARMS, 1988], 365–6) political revolutionary (Brinkman, "Merodach-Baladan II," 12–4, 18–27; Oates, *Babylon*, 115; Peterson,

"Gadianton Robbers as Guerrilla Warriors," 147–9) who uses conscious retreat into the wilderness (Brinkman, "Merodach-Baladan II," 19–21, 26–7; Oates, *Babylon*, 116–17; Peterson, "Gadianton Robbers as Guerrilla Warriors," 149–54) and hit-and-run tactics (Brinkman, "Merodach-Baladan II," 12–3, 19; Oates, *Babylon*, 116; Peterson, "Gadianton Robbers as Guerilla Warriors," 154–8) until he can take over at the proper time (Oates, *Babylon*, 117; Peterson, "Gadianton Robbers as Guerilla Warriors," 159–66).

13. See Peder Borgen, *Bread from Heaven: An Exegetical Study of the Concept of Manna in the Gospel of John and the Writings of Philo*, Supplements to *Novum Testamentum*, vol. 10 (Leiden: Brill, 1965).

14. Referring to 3 Nephi 16:16–20, with the last three verses quoting Isaiah 52:8–10. He had to stop his discourse because "my time is at hand. I perceive that ye are weak, that ye cannot understand all my words which I am commanded of the Father to speak unto you at this time" (3 Nephi 17:1–2). For further discussion, see Dana M. Pike, " 'How Beautiful upon the Mountains': The Imagery of Isaiah 52:7–10 and Its Occurrences in the Book of Mormon," in this book.

15. The parallel is implicit but not explicit in John Gee, "Jesus Christ, Forty-Day Ministry and Other Post-Resurrection Appearances of," in *Encyclopedia of Mormonism*, ed. Daniel H. Ludlow (New York: Macmillan, 1992), 2:734–6.

16. Joseph Smith—History 1:34–49. See also *The Papers of Joseph Smith*, ed. Dean C. Jessee (Salt Lake City: Deseret Book, 1989–92), 1:52–4, 56–60, 62–70, 127, 277–81, 412–5, 429–31; 2:70; *The Personal Writings of Joseph Smith*, ed. Dean C. Jessee (Salt Lake City: Deseret Book, 1984), 76, 203–5, 213–5; and Smith, *History of the Church*, 1:11–3. See also Joseph Smith, "Church History," *Times and Seasons* 3 (1842): 706–7. For further discussion, see Ann N. Madsen, "Joseph Smith and the Words of Isaiah," in this volume.

17. One indication that the entire section is one prophecy is Isaiah's statement in Isaiah 8:18 (compare 2 Nephi 18:18): "I and the children whom the Lord hath given me are for signs and for wonders in Israel." Isaiah has been accompanied by his son Shearjashub (see Isaiah 7:3, parallel to 2 Nephi 17:3), whose name

means "a remnant shall return." He puns off his son's name in Isaiah 10:19–22 (compare 2 Nephi 20:19–22) and alludes again to it in Isaiah 11:16 (compare 2 Nephi 21:16). He puns off his son Maher-shalal-hash-baz's name, meaning "he has hastened the spoil, he has hurried the prey" (Isaiah 8:1, 3, parallel to 2 Nephi 18:1, 3), in Isaiah 8:4 (compare 2 Nephi 18:4) and alludes to it in Isaiah 10:2, 6 (compare 2 Nephi 20:2, 6). Immanuel is referred to in both Isaiah 7:14 and 8:8 (compare 2 Nephi 17:14; 18:8).

Another indication of the unity of these sections is that they are a single chapter in the 1830 Book of Mormon. See Thomas W. Mackay, "Mormon as Editor: A Study in Colophons, Headers and Source Indicators," *Journal of Book of Mormon Studies* 2/2 (Fall 1993): 92–5, 104–5; Royal Skousen, "Critical Methodology and the Text of the Book of Mormon," *Review of Books on the Book of Mormon* 6/1 (1994): 137–9.

18. Both George D. Smith and Avraham Gileadi have taken this as a prophecy of the birth of Hezekiah, not Jesus (George D. Smith, "Isaiah Updated," in *The Word of God: Essays on Mormon Scripture,* ed. Dan Vogel [Salt Lake City: Signature Books, 1990], 115–9; Avraham Gileadi, "A Holistic Structure of the Book of Isaiah," [Ph.D. diss., Brigham Young University, 1981], 37). This is impossible. Ahaz reigned sixteen years (2 Kings 16:2; compare 2 Chronicles 28:1) to be succeeded by his son Hezekiah who began ruling at the age of twenty-five (2 Kings 18:1–2; compare 2 Chronicles 29:1). The date of the prophecy to "the days of Ahaz . . . king of Judah" (Isaiah 7:1) presents a major chronological problem for this hypothesis. Even though Pekah was in the last three years of his reign when Ahaz took over the Judean kingdom (see 2 Kings 15:27; 16:1), Hezekiah would have been somewhere between nine and twelve years old; it would have been too late for Isaiah to have prophesied his birth or when he would start talking.

19. For further discussion, see Jennifer Clark Lane, "The Lord Will Redeem His People: Adoptive Covenant and Redemption in the Old Testament and Book of Mormon," *Journal of Book of Mormon Studies* 2/2 (Fall 1993): 53–6; compare Jennifer Clark Lane, "The Lord Will Redeem His People: 'Adoptive' Covenant and

Redemption in the Old Testament," in *Thy People Shall Be My People and Thy God My God, The Twenty-second Annual Sidney B. Sperry Symposium,* ed. Paul Y. Hoskisson (Salt Lake City: Deseret Book, 1994), 58.

20. Exegetical patterns tend to remain constant as long as the tradition and basic assumptions are intact; for example, see the exhaustive documentation in Thomas Mackay, "Early Christian Millenarianist Interpretation of the Two Witnesses in John's Apocalypse 11:3–13," in *By Study and Also by Faith,* ed. John M. Lundquist and Stephen D. Ricks (Salt Lake City: Deseret Book and FARMS, 1990), 1:222–331.

21. Harold Bloom insists that Joseph "Smith's insight could have come only from a remarkably apt reading of the Bible" (*The American Religion: The Emergence of the Post-Christian Nation* [New York: Simon & Schuster, 1992], 84). It takes a more sophisticated reading of both the Bible and the Book of Mormon, however, to catch what the Book of Mormon does with the Isaiah material; compare Alan Goff, "Reduction and Enlargement: Harold Bloom's Mormons," *Review of Books on the Book of Mormon* 5 (1993): 96–108.

PART TWO

Section by Section Explanations

Nephi's Lessons to His People
The Messiah, the Land, and Isaiah 48–49
in 1 Nephi 19–22

Andrew C. Skinner

Nephi used Isaiah to teach his people faith in the future Redeemer who will reject the rebellious, save the righteous from sins, suffering, and scattering, and redeem them to their land.

The first of the Book of Mormon chapters that quote extensively or entirely from the great prophet Isaiah are 1 Nephi 20–21, in which Nephi quotes Isaiah 48–49 from the brass plates brought from Jerusalem. That Nephi begins his expansive recitations of Isaiah with chapters 48 and 49 and not with other chapters of that prophet's book shows that, as a prophet to his family, to his descendants, and to the Gentiles and Jews of the latter days, Nephi first offers Isaiah's message of hope and redemption in Christ.

Nephi's Text of Isaiah

The Isaiah text that Nephi possessed was somewhat different from that found in the King James Version of the Bible (KJV).[1] This is not surprising, however, because Nephi's version came from the brass plates, which seem to have contained a Northern Kingdom version of the Old Testament.[2] The Old Testament text of Isaiah found on the brass plates was apparently more expansive and expressive than the Masoretic text that originated in the Southern Kingdom of Judah. Sidney B. Sperry suggests that "From the time of the division [of the twelve tribes] until the fall of the Northern Kingdom in 722 B.C., the Brass Plates may well have been the official scripture of the Ten Tribes."[3] In proposing how

the brass plates were transferred from the Northern Kingdom to Jerusalem in Judea, Sperry further notes:

> The Northern Kingdom of Israel fell to the Assyrians
> when its capital of Samaria capitulated to Sargon II in 722
> B.C. The forebears of Laban may have fled to Jerusalem to
> prevent the sacred records from falling into alien hands.
> Lehi's grandfather or great-grandfather may have left his
> northern home for Jerusalem in order to prevent his chil-
> dren from intermarrying and making religious compro-
> mises with the foreigners brought into the land by the
> Assyrians.[4]

The following example that compares the King James
Version with 1 Nephi shows that there are small but significant differences between the two versions:

Isaiah 48:1	1 Nephi 20:1
Hear ye this, O house of Jacob, which are called by the name of Israel, and are come forth out of the waters of Judah, which swear by the name of the LORD, and make mention of the God of Israel, but not in truth, nor in righteousness.	Hearken and hear this, O house of Jacob, who are called by the name of Israel, and are come forth out of the waters of Judah, or out of the waters of baptism, who swear by the name of the Lord, and make mention of the God of Israel, yet they swear not in truth nor in righteousness.

The first words in Nephi's version of Isaiah are not "Hear
ye this" but *"Hearken and hear this,"* a phrase that conveys a
sense of immediacy, action, and seriousness. While some
suggest that this addition may reflect Nephi's own bridge
to the Isaiah passages, it seems more likely from the structure of the Book of Mormon narrative that the original Isaiah
text uses this parallel phraseology to secure the attention of
the ancient audience. The more complete phrase, *Hearken and
hear this,* implores its listeners to engage in a more serious

level of interaction with the text. Also, the repetition of the verb *to swear*, in parallel antithetical clauses ("who swear" / "yet they swear not") appears to be more consistent with Isaiah's Hebrew literary style than the abbreviated phrasing of the King James Version.

Nephi's version of Isaiah 48 and 49 was also apparently slightly different from the text that appears in the current edition of the Book of Mormon. The phrase *out of the waters of baptism* was added to 1 Nephi 20:1 by Joseph Smith, presumably to explain the previous phrase, *out of the waters of Judah*. It first appeared in the 1840 and 1842 editions of the Book of Mormon and was eventually adopted by Elder James E. Talmage in the 1920 edition of the Book of Mormon.[5] It has appeared in all subsequent editions. If the phrase were part of the original brass plates version of Isaiah, it would likely have been in the 1830 edition of the Book of Mormon, but it was not. Thus, with the Book of Mormon version of Isaiah, modern readers are blessed to have not only a brass plates edition of Isaiah but also the added inspired commentary of a modern prophet.

Nephi's Context for Isaiah 48 and 49

In chapter 19 of 1 Nephi[6]—the chapter immediately preceding his quotations of Isaiah 48 and 49—Nephi teaches the things he deems *most* sacred, namely, the coming of Christ and Christ's relationship to the house of Israel. Nephi speaks of the Messiah's mortal ministry, including the hardships he would endure as the Redeemer come to earth. Nephi cites the prophecies of Zenock, Neum, and Zenos (prophecies not mentioned in our modern versions of the Old Testament).[7] These powerful preachers revealed in detail to their own ancient groups of people the signs and scenes that would accompany the crucifixion and burial of the God of nature (see 1 Nephi 19:10–12). Quoting and paraphrasing the prophet Zenos, Nephi describes the fate of Jerusalem's inhabitants after the crucifixion, as well as the fate of those who reject the Holy One of Israel: "And because they turn their hearts aside, saith the prophet, and have despised the Holy One of Israel, they shall wander in the flesh, and perish, and become a hiss and a byword, and be hated among all nations" (1 Nephi 19:14).

The record of Israelite and Jewish history reveals that these predictions of the ancient prophets have indeed come to pass; we see an instant, significant, and uncomfortable parallel—uncomfortable because of the accuracy of the prophecies when seen in light of centuries of inhuman, unconscionable cruelties heaped upon the different branches of the house of Israel, including the Jews and Lamanites.

But Nephi does not leave the story of scattered Israel at its lowest ebb. He explains that all their difficulties notwithstanding, the battered and scattered house of Israel ultimately does have a bright future. The Lord will remember the covenants he made with Israel and bring about the spiritual and temporal salvation of those who initially rejected his atonement. When Israel no more turns aside from their Holy One, they will be gathered in. Continuing to quote Zenos, Nephi says, "Yea, and all the earth shall see the salvation of the Lord, saith the prophet; every nation, kindred, tongue and people shall be blessed" (1 Nephi 19:17).

After quoting to his brothers the testimonies of the prophets Zenock, Neum, and Zenos, Nephi reads to them many things found in the books of Moses, as written on the brass plates. He then does something that, in his view, is even more important:

> [B]ut that I might more fully persuade them to believe in the Lord their Redeemer I did read unto them that which was written by the prophet Isaiah; for I did liken all scrip-

tures unto us, that it might be for our profit and learning. Wherefore I spake unto them, saying: . . . hear ye the words of the prophet, which were written unto all the house of Israel, and liken them unto *yourselves*, that *ye* may have hope as well as your brethren from whom ye have been broken off. (1 Nephi 19:23–24)

Nephi then reads chapters 48 and 49 of Isaiah to his little gathering, bearing powerful testimony of Isaiah's ability to do three things: first, to help all people believe in the Lord as their ultimate Redeemer (see 1 Nephi 19:23); second, to address their personal circumstances (see 1 Nephi 19:24); and third, to provide a profound hope in the future for all the house of Israel, including Nephi's own family (see 1 Nephi 19:24).

These three purposes, then, provide the context for Nephi's first recitation of Isaiah's words. Nephi's concerns give full meaning to and applicability of Isaiah's preexilic prophecies in chapters 48 and 49. Nephi establishes his family on the cutting edge, so to speak, of the scattering of Judah that Isaiah prophesied. Those people were alone in a strange land, bereft of their familiar surroundings and struggling to forge a new life. Nephi envisions how an understanding of Christ's redemptive power, including the specific promises made to the house of Israel of a physical, geographical redemption, could buoy up and strengthen his family as well as future generations.

To teach about Christ, Nephi does not rely only on his personal testimony, which his older brothers have scorned; rather, he invokes the powerful witness of one of the greatest prophets of Israel—Isaiah. Isaiah was, after all, the prophet of Nephi's hometown, Jerusalem. He was an educated and articulate man who would have understood the social and economic circumstances of Nephi's people. Isaiah himself lived during a difficult time; he witnessed the destruction of the Northern Kingdom of Israel in the eighth century B.C. Isaiah was a respected spokesman for the Lord both in his day and in Nephi's. But above everything else, Isaiah knew of Christ's coming and of Christ's power to ransom all mankind not only from sin and suffering but also from scattering. As Isaiah taught, the power of the Messiah is the power of restoration—the power to restore people to their lands of promise and ultimately to the presence of God.

Fall of Judah Foreshadowed

Chapter 48 of Isaiah (parallel to 1 Nephi 20) begins by summoning the religious hypocrites of Israel to heed God's message for them; those summoned are they who talk about God and consider themselves holy, but who act duplicitously toward God.

> Hearken and hear this, O house of Jacob . . . who swear by the name of the Lord, and make mention of the God of Israel, yet they swear not in truth nor in righteousness. Nevertheless, they call themselves of the holy city, but they do not stay themselves upon the God of Israel, who is the Lord of Hosts; yea, the Lord of Hosts is his name. (1 Nephi 20:1–2, parallel to Isaiah 48:1–2)

These introductory words of Isaiah apply so well to Laman and Lemuel, who often act wickedly but consider themselves righteous. Indeed, Isaiah's opening comments in chapter 48, though addressed to all Israel, seem to speak directly to the rebellious and stubborn members of Nephi's family. Isaiah's description of Israel—"thou art obstinate, and thy neck is an iron sinew, and thy brow brass" (Isaiah 48:4, parallel to 1 Nephi 20:4)—fits Nephi's older brothers Laman and Lemuel perfectly.

After his initial call to hearken, Isaiah continues for several verses to remind Israel how its constant rebellion against

God began right at the time of its birth as a nation at Sinai. Speaking for the Lord, Isaiah says, "Yea, and thou heardest not; yea, thou knewest not; yea, from that time thine ear was not opened; for I knew that thou wouldst deal very treacherously, and wast called a transgressor *from the womb*" (1 Nephi 20:8).

The Lord revealed many great future events to his wayward people long before they could claim that idols possessed the power to prophesy about or bring to pass the great events associated with Israel's salvation history (1 Nephi 20:3–9, parallel to Isaiah 48:3–9). But the chosen people ignored their living God. God deferred the fulness of his wrath and judgments so that the priesthood and the covenant he made with Abraham could be solidly established in Israel, but Israel encountered hardships as a result of its rebellion: "For, behold, I have refined thee, I have chosen thee in the furnace of affliction" (1 Nephi 20:10, parallel to Isaiah 20:10). The Lord implies that Israel will suffer even more because he will not allow his "name to be polluted" by his chosen people (1 Nephi 20:11), and this greater affliction will include Judah's deportation at the hands of the king of Babylon. At the same time, however, Jehovah will not "give [his] glory unto another" (1 Nephi 20:11, parallel to Isaiah 48:11). In other words, regardless of Israel's transgressions, God will not select another group to be his "chosen" people.

But why not? Continuing to speak the words of Jehovah, Isaiah decrees that Israel is God's chosen people because they were called and foreordained by him in premortality to be such (see 1 Nephi 20:12, parallel to Isaiah 48:12)—a doctrine reminiscent of instruction given to Israel through Moses in an earlier day (see, for example, Exodus 4:22). Isaiah reminds his listeners that the Lord governs the whole universe, all creation obeys him, and it is his plan and purposes that are carried out: "Hearken unto me, O Jacob, and Israel my called, for I am he; I am the first, and I am also the last. Mine hand hath also laid the foundation of the earth, and my right hand hath spanned the heavens. I call unto them and they stand up together" (1 Nephi 20:12–13, parallel to Isaiah 48:12–13).

Good News about Israel's Future

Isaiah next turns to God's panoramic and prophetic perspective of Israel's destiny. He reveals, through prophecies that carry double meanings, the many redemptive events that will occur in Israel's future, as well as the several redeemers who will be raised up to help bring about God's desires and purposes for his chosen people (see 1 Nephi 20:14–21, parallel to Isaiah 48:14–21).

Isaiah seems to be alluding to a specific historical episode when he proclaims that one will come along who will "do his pleasure on Babylon," and whose "arm [will] come upon the Chaldeans" (1 Nephi 20:14, parallel to Isaiah 48:14). Surely this is a prophetic reference to Cyrus the Great, king of Persia, whom the Lord raised up to conquer the very kingdom responsible for the fall of Jerusalem in 586 B.C.—Babylon. History shows that Cyrus was indeed a redeemer to Israel who did "his pleasure on Babylon" and afterwards sponsored the return of Israel's remnant to their homeland. He even financially supported the reconstruction of Jerusalem and the holy temple. But this prophecy also points to the Lord himself, who, as scripture teaches, stands behind those whom he raises up and who guides the destinies of nations (see, for example, 2 Kings 17). Just a few verses after the mention of Babylon's fate at the hands of Cyrus, Isaiah declares:

> And thus saith the Lord, thy Redeemer, the Holy One
> of Israel; I have sent him [Cyrus], the Lord thy God who
> teacheth thee to profit, who leadeth thee by the way thou

shouldst go, hath done it. . . . Go ye forth of Babylon, flee
ye from the Chaldeans, with a voice of singing declare ye,
tell this, utter to the end of the earth; say ye: The Lord
hath redeemed his servant Jacob. (1 Nephi 20:17, 20; parallel to Isaiah 48:17, 20)

Verse 20 also seems to hold a double meaning. Israel was
commanded to go forth from Babylon in a literal sense, and
this they did when they returned to Jerusalem in 538 B.C.
Through Cyrus, the Lord redeemed his people and brought
them out of Babylon after they had endured fifty years of
captivity. But Israel was also commanded to go forth or flee
from Babylon in a spiritual sense. In a revelation given to
the Prophet Joseph Smith in 1831, when the church was still
young, the Lord issued a similar command, adding a few
words of clarification: "Go ye out from among the nations,
even from Babylon, from the midst of wickedness, which is
spiritual Babylon" (D&C 133:14). Thus ancient Israel was to
go forth from the literal place called Babylon as well as to
flee from the wickedness and spiritual corruption that existed in their world—just as modern Israel has been commanded to do.

In whatever ways Israel is commanded to flee Babylon,
the Lord makes clear through his prophets that he can assist
his people. Isaiah reinforces the idea of God's power to save
and redeem Israel by reminding his audience of the great
miracles Jehovah performed during an earlier but defining
moment in Israel's redemptive history—the time when they
were brought forth out of Egypt: "And they thirsted not; he
led them through the deserts; he caused the waters to flow
out of the rock for them; he clave the rock also and the waters
gushed out" (1 Nephi 20:21, parallel to Isaiah 48:21). Yet,
despite all that the Lord has done and will continue to do in
behalf of his people, they will enjoy no lasting peace or geographical redemption while they remain wicked: "And

notwithstanding he hath done all this, and greater also, there is no peace, saith the Lord, unto the wicked" (1 Nephi 20:22, parallel to Isaiah 48:22).

These verses are especially well suited to Nephi's family, particularly to the rebellious and spiritually impoverished brothers. Though Isaiah's words seem to have made little sense to many in Nephi's audience (see 2 Nephi 25:1–2), there were some gathered in the group to whom the Spirit of the Lord testified of the truthfulness of Isaiah's words. Father Lehi and his younger son Jacob seem to have been forcefully affected by Isaiah's message of hope and redemption for a broken-off branch of Israel (see 2 Nephi 1:1 and 10:7–9, respectively), even if Laman and Lemuel and their followers continued to waver. It would be but a few short years before Lehi's family learned that Jerusalem's destruction had occurred according to the promise of the Lord (see 2 Nephi 1:4).

Redemption in the Latter Days

At the beginning of Isaiah 49 (parallel to 1 Nephi 21), Isaiah advances to scenes of the latter days as he further prophesies of Israel's redemption and restoration. Chapter 49 refers to our modern dispensation—the dispensation of the fulness of times—as latter-day prophets have indicated. Wilford Woodruff said, "The revelations that are in the Bible, the predictions of the patriarchs and prophets who saw by vision and revelation the last dispensation and fulness of times plainly tell us what is to come to pass. The 49th chapter of Isaiah is having its fulfillment."[8]

Isaiah 49 opens with another summons for all Israel to pay strict attention to what is about to be revealed to them. Isaiah describes the life and work of another redeemer who will be raised up by the Lord in the latter days to bring salvation to Israel. As was the case with chapter 48, the introductory statements of chapter 49 also point out the completeness of Nephi's text of Isaiah compared with the KJV Isaiah:

Isaiah 49:1	1 Nephi 21:1
	And again: Hearken, O ye house of Israel, all ye that are broken off and are driven out, because of the wickedness of the pastors of my people; yea, all ye that are broken off, that are scattered abroad, who are of my people, O house of Israel.
Listen, O isles, unto me; and hearken, ye people, from far; The Lord hath called me from the womb; from the bowels of my mother hath he made mention of my name.	Listen, O isles, unto me, and hearken ye people from far; the Lord hath called me from the womb; from the bowels of my mother hath he made mention of my name.

Nephi's Isaiah text helps form in Nephi and other listeners a consciousness of their own identity as a remnant of Israel—a remnant broken off and separate from the rest of their people in the Old World. No wonder Nephi loves the words of Isaiah: he views them as being pointed directly at his people. Jeremiah, who prophesies and writes to Old World Israel during Nephi's own era, also knows that there will be a remnant scattered, and, like Isaiah, he understands that the scattering will be caused by the corrupt leaders of the Israelite community: "Woe be unto the pastors that destroy and scatter the sheep of my pasture! saith the Lord" (Jeremiah 23:1). Unlike Isaiah, however, Jeremiah does not boldly announce the appearance of a deliverer who will be raised up in the latter days to help bring about the final spiritual and geographical redemption of God's chosen people.

Who is this servant whom Isaiah announces in Isaiah 49:1, which Nephi quotes in 1 Nephi 21? Isaiah provides us with important clues as he describes this servant's life and work. The servant would be someone

- whom "the Lord hath called . . . from the womb" (1 Nephi 21:1, parallel to Isaiah 49:1);

- whose "mouth [was] like a sharp sword," or, in other words, someone who spoke with authority (1 Nephi 21:2, parallel to Isaiah 49:2);

- who was hidden "in the shadow of [the Lord's] hand" (1 Nephi 21:2, parallel to Isaiah 49:2);

- who was "made . . . a polished shaft; in his quiver hath he [the Lord] hid [the servant]" (1 Nephi 21:2, parallel to Isaiah 49:2);

- who would say, "I have labored in vain" (1 Nephi 21:4, parallel to Isaiah 49:4);

- who would authoritatively say, "And now, saith the Lord" (1 Nephi 21:5, parallel to Isaiah 49:5);

- who would say that the Lord "formed me from the womb" to do a special work, or, in other words, someone who *knew* he was foreordained (1 Nephi 21:5, parallel to Isaiah 49:5);

- whose life's work would be "to bring Jacob again to [the Lord]—though Israel be not gathered" (1 Nephi 21:5, parallel to Isaiah 49:5);

- who would be the Lord's "servant to raise up the tribes of Jacob, and to restore the preserved of Israel" (1 Nephi 21:6, parallel to Isaiah 49:6);

- whom the Lord would "give . . . for a light to the Gentiles" (1 Nephi 21:6, parallel to Isaiah 49:6);

- "whom man despiseth," but, at the same time, someone whom "Kings shall see and arise, princes also shall worship" (1 Nephi 21:7, parallel to Isaiah 49:7); and

- who will be given to Israel "for a covenant of the people, to establish the earth, to cause to inherit the desolate heritages," who will free the prisoners and enlighten those who sit in darkness, and who will shepherd the chosen people (1 Nephi 21:8–9, parallel to Isaiah 49:8–9).

Various aspects of these characteristics could probably be applied to several different individuals. Jewish theology maintains that this prophecy of the "suffering servant" depicts the Jewish nation,[9] but, taken together, the words Isaiah uses to describe this helper of Israel in the latter days apply only to two beings: the Messiah and the Prophet Joseph Smith. Nephi and Lehi seem to know not only that Isaiah intended to prophesy of Jesus *and* Joseph Smith (see 2 Nephi 3), but also that the latter-day restoration of the gospel would help bring about the final redemption of Israel.[10]

That these characteristics refer primarily to the Savior is probably obvious to many Christians, but Joseph Smith also fits many of the qualifications of that special servant. After all, every true prophet is a type, a foreshadowing, or a symbol of the Lord Jesus Christ. Consider that Joseph Smith

- was called "from the womb," or foreordained (2 Nephi 3:7–9, 14–15);

- knew through revelation, now recorded as Doctrine and Covenants 127:2, that he had been chosen to be the prophet of the restoration. On another occasion he said:

  > Every man who has a calling to minister to the inhabitants of the world was ordained to that very purpose in the Grand Council of heaven before this world was. I suppose I was ordained to this very office in that

Grand Council. It is the testimony that I want that I
am God's servant, and this people His people.[11]

- spoke as a "sharp sword" (1 Nephi 21:2, parallel to Isaiah
  49:2) because he spoke the words of the Lord (see D&C
  18:35–36; 21:5), which are described in modern revelation as "quick and powerful, sharper than a two-edged
  sword, to the dividing asunder of both joints and mar-
  row" (D&C 6:2);

- was "hid" by the Lord (D&C 86:9);

- became a polished shaft in the quiver of the Almighty,
  as his own characterization of himself testifies:

  > I am like a huge, rough stone rolling down from a
  > high mountain; and the only polishing I get is when
  > some corner gets rubbed off by coming in contact with
  > something else, striking with accelerated force against
  > religious bigotry, priestcraft, lawyer-craft, doctor-craft,
  > lying editors, suborned judges and jurors, and the
  > authority of perjured executives, backed by mobs,
  > blasphemers, licentious and corrupt men and
  > women—all hell knocking off a corner here and a cor-
  > ner there. Thus I will become a smooth and polished
  > shaft in the quiver of the Almighty, who will give me
  > dominion over all and every one of them, when their
  > refuge of lies shall fail, and their hiding place shall be
  > destroyed, while these smooth-polished stones with
  > which I come in contact become marred.[12]

- at times became discouraged and felt that he labored in
  vain (see D&C 121:2);

- not only had the authority to speak for God but on numerous occasions validated his messages by uttering the
  very words Isaiah predicted he would: "Thus saith the

Lord" (D&C 52:1; 54:1; 55:1; 60:1; and 87:1, to name a few references);

- spent his life working to bring the house of Israel again to the Lord by bringing forth the Book of Mormon and restoring the gospel (see Mormon 8:16; D&C 5:9–10; 6:6; 109:67);

- was also commissioned to "raise up the tribes of Jacob" (1 Nephi 21:6) and restore them by overseeing the latter-day gathering of Israel (see D&C 110:11, 16);

- is spoken of in the scriptures as "a light unto the Gentiles" (D&C 86:11). Only one other person can claim that distinction—the Lord himself (see Isaiah 42:6);

- was both despised and revered, just as the Lord had said he would be (see Joseph Smith—History 1:33). Joseph was also promised that the gospel he restored would be preached before "kings and rulers" (D&C 1:23);

- was the servant through whom the eternal gospel covenant was reestablished (see D&C 1:17–22). Surely it is not mere coincidence that this same section of the Doctrine and Covenants, the revelation in which the Lord introduces Joseph Smith to the world, begins with the same language as Isaiah 49:1. And just as Isaiah foretold, Joseph was commanded to "proclaim the acceptable year of the Lord, and the gospel of salvation" (D&C 93:51).

Redemptive Events of the Latter Days

Having described the special latter-day servant, the one who would be instrumental in bringing about the restoration and eventual redemption of Israel, Isaiah reveals the events associated with that restoration and redemption. He first asks Israel a rhetorical question: Is it really possible that the Lord can forget his people? Absolutely not. The Lord proclaims, "Yea, they [Israel, typified as a woman] may forget [the Lord], yet will I *not forget thee,* O house of Israel" (1 Nephi 21:15, parallel to Isaiah 49:15). Isaiah then describes how the Lord of the universe will bring about this redemption from sin, suffering, and scattering. It will be through the gentiles. He explains:

> Thus saith the Lord God: Behold, I will lift up mine hand to the Gentiles, and set up my standard to the people; and they shall bring thy sons in their arms, and thy daughters shall be carried upon their shoulders. And kings shall be thy nursing fathers, and their queens thy nursing mothers; they shall bow down to thee with their face towards the earth, and lick up the dust of thy feet; and thou shalt know that I am the Lord; for they shall not be ashamed that wait for me. (1 Nephi 21:22–23, parallel to Isaiah 49:22–23)

Nephi explains in his prophetic commentary on Isaiah 49 (found in 1 Nephi 22:7–14) that this work among the gentiles constitutes the raising up of "a mighty nation among the Gentiles, yea, even upon the face of *this* land; and by them shall [his] seed be scattered" (1 Nephi 22:7). The Lord will then deliver his covenant people:

> And after our seed is scattered the Lord God will proceed to do a marvelous work among the Gentiles, which shall be of great worth unto our seed; wherefore, it is likened unto their being nourished by the Gentiles and being carried in their arms and upon their shoulders. And it shall also be of worth unto the Gentiles; and not only unto the Gentiles but unto all the house of Israel, unto the making known of the covenants of the Father of heaven

> unto Abraham, saying: In thy seed shall all the kindreds
> of the earth be blessed. . . . Wherefore, he will bring them
> again out of captivity, and they shall be gathered together
> to the lands of their inheritance; and they shall be brought
> out of obscurity and out of darkness; and they shall know
> that the Lord is their Savior and their Redeemer, the
> Mighty One of Israel. (1 Nephi 22:8, 9, 12)

This inspired interpretation by Nephi is the key to understanding Isaiah 49.

The modern reader ought to consider four questions
when reading 1 Nephi 22:7–14:

1. Who are the gentiles of the "mighty nation" to which
    Isaiah and Nephi refer?

2. What is the "mighty nation" Nephi mentions?

3. Which land is "this land" upon which the mighty
    nation will be established?

4. What is the marvelous work that the Lord will pro-
    ceed to do among the gentiles of the mighty nation?

The answers to these questions explain *why* Nephi is so
excited about the message of Isaiah 48 and 49 and *how* Nephi
connects the Messiah's redemptive powers to Israel's restoration to its land of promise.

Significant help to understanding these questions is
found in 3 Nephi 21:1–4, which contains words that the
Savior speaks to the Nephites when he appears to them after his resurrection. The Savior speaks not only about the
same scattering of Israel that Nephi discusses but also about
the divine timetable for the gathering of scattered Israel:

> And verily I say unto you, I give unto you a sign, that
> ye may know the time when these things shall be about
> to take place—that I shall gather in, from their long dis-
> persion, my people, O house of Israel, and shall establish

again among them my Zion; And behold, this is the
thing which I will give unto you for a sign—for verily I
say unto you that when these things . . . shall be made
known unto the Gentiles that they may know concerning
this people who are a remnant of the house of Jacob, and
concerning this my people who shall be scattered by
them. . . . For it is wisdom in the Father that they [these
gentiles] should be established in this land, and be set up
as a free people by the power of the Father, that these
things [the gospel truths] might come forth from them
unto a remnant of your seed, that the covenant of the Father may be fulfilled which he hath covenanted with his
people, O house of Israel. (3 Nephi 21:1–2, 4)

These verses indicate that the Savior will gather his people,
the house of Israel, through the same gentiles of whom Nephi
spoke. Nephi explains in his inspired interpretation of Isaiah
49 that the Lord will "raise up a mighty nation among the
Gentiles . . . upon the face of *this* land" (1 Nephi 22:7) and
that the gentiles would be responsible for scattering Nephi's
descendants. The Lord will then "do a marvelous work"
(1 Nephi 22:8) among these gentiles, and this marvelous
work will then bless Nephi's descendants by "making known
[unto them] the covenants of the Father of heaven" (1 Nephi
22:9). In 3 Nephi, the Savior says much the same thing in a
slightly different way: the gentiles will be set up by the power
of the Father as a free people "in *this* land," and through
these gentiles will the covenants of the Father to Israel be
fulfilled, especially the branch of Israel already in "this land"
(see 3 Nephi 16:8; 20:22, 28).

The "mighty nation among the Gentiles," spoken of by
Nephi, and the gentiles "set up as a free people by the power
of the Father," spoken of by the Savior, appear to be one and
the same. Both would be established "in this land," and both
would bring forth the covenants of the Father that would

benefit the house of Israel. This gentile nation would also fulfill Isaiah's prophecies about the restoration of the rest of the house of Israel to its land of promise, acting, as it were, like nursing fathers and mothers (see 1 Nephi 21:22–23, parallel to Isaiah 49:22–23; 2 Nephi 10:8–9).

Let us now discuss each of the four questions posed above. First, who are these gentiles to whom both Nephi and, later on, the Savior refer? "We are," says Elder Mark E. Petersen, a modern prophet, seer, and revelator, referring to the members of the church. He declares:

> We are referred to in this prophecy [3 Nephi 21:1–4] as Gentiles, but we are the "believing Gentiles" because we have the "believing blood" of Ephraim in our veins as well as the blood of the Gentiles. Our pedigrees show that we come from many nationalities. In the revealed dedicatory prayer for the Kirtland Temple, the Prophet used this expression: "Concerning the revelations and commandments which thou hast given unto us, who are identified with the Gentiles" (D&C 109:60).
>
> It is inspiring indeed to realize that we who live now and have received this restored gospel are the very ones to whom Nephi and the Christ referred some two thousand years ago. We have lived in prophecy!
>
> "These things . . . shall be made known unto the Gentiles. . . . [T]hese things shall be made known unto them of the Father, and shall come forth of the Father from them unto you."
>
> When we consider that "these things shall be made known unto them of the Father," let us keep in mind that it was the Father who appeared to Joseph Smith in the first vision, together with the Savior, and it was He who directed Joseph to "Hear ye Him," referring to the Christ. The Father definitely was in charge, and truly enough the gospel came by his direction. Indeed it was made known "of the Father."[13]

Second, what is the "mighty nation"? According to Elder Peterson's interpretation of the term *gentiles*, the identification of the "mighty nation" to which Nephi also refers seems to be America, especially considering that Elder Petersen's statement describes the prophetic history of the United States.[14] Does this interpretation fit the descriptions presented by both Nephi and the Savior in their commentaries on Isaiah? Which nation most resembles a mighty country of free people, one that provides the setting for the establishment of a "marvelous work" that promotes and defines the covenants of the Father of heaven but at the same time is responsible for scattering the descendants of Nephi's family? In addition, which nation meets the following specific qualification mentioned by Nephi's brother Jacob:

> But behold, this land, said God, shall be a land of thine inheritance, and the Gentiles shall be blessed upon the land. And this land shall be a land of liberty unto the Gentiles, and there shall be no kings upon the land, who shall raise up unto the Gentiles. And I will fortify this land against all other nations. (2 Nephi 10:10–12)

No nation but America so completely fits the prophetic descriptions. Years ago President Ezra Taft Benson, student of the Book of Mormon and prophet of God, made various statements about America that correspond to the specific scriptural descriptions of the mighty nation that will be instrumental in gathering Israel:

> Our Heavenly Father raised up the men who founded this government (see D&C 101:80), thereby fulfilling the prophecy of His Beloved Son that the people "should be established in this land and be set up as a free people by the power of the Father." (3 Nephi 21:4)[15]

> In the scriptures there are set forth three phases of the gathering of Israel. One, the gathering of Israel to the land

of Zion which is America, this land. That is under way and has been under way since the Church was established and our missions abroad inaugurated. Then two, the return of the lost tribes, the ten lost tribes, from the land of the north (see D&C 133). And the third phase is the reestablishment of the Jews in Palestine as one of the events to precede the second coming of the Master. Isaiah said they will be gathered together.[16]

God revealed over twenty-five hundred years ago that the kingdoms of Europe would try to exercise dominion over the colonists who had fled to America, that this would lead to a struggle for independence, and that the colonists would win (1 Nephi 13:17–19). The Book of Mormon foretold the time when the colonists would establish this land of liberty which would not be governed by kings. The Lord declared that He would protect the land and whoever would attempt to establish kings from within or without would perish. (2 Nephi 10:11–14)[17]

This is a great country and certainly this greatness was foreshadowed and foreseen by ancient prophets who lived here, prophecies made by the brother of Jared (Ether 13:8), by Lehi, by Jacob (2 Nephi 10:18–19), and by Nephi of old (1 Nephi 13:13–20). It is enough to know that this nation has a prophetic history.[18]

It was here under a free government and a strong nation that protection was provided for His restored Church. Now God will not permit America, His base of operations, to be destroyed. He has promised protection to this land if we will but serve the God of the land (see Ether 2:12). He has also promised protection to the righteous even, if necessary, to send fire from heaven to destroy their enemies (1 Nephi 22:17).[19]

Third, to which land is the prophecy of Isaiah and the commentary of Nephi referring? In his last statement quoted above, President Benson links Nephi's commentary on Isaiah (in 1 Nephi 22) with America. While we cannot say with exactness where Nephi was actually standing when he used the phrase *this land,* there is little doubt that the mighty nation that would rise upon it would be located in North America—more particularly, the United States of America. Apparently President Benson thought so, and so did Elder Petersen.

Fourth, what is the marvelous work? There is hardly any question that the marvelous work to come forth in association with the mighty nation upon the land, as noted in Nephi's commentary on Isaiah, is the restoration of the gospel. In Isaiah's vision of the future, the believing gentiles would nurse the house of Israel by giving them both the milk and the meat of the gospel that would be restored in America. President Joseph F. Smith said:

> This great American nation the Almighty raised up by the power of his omnipotent hand, that it might be possible in the latter days for the kingdom of God to be established in the earth. If the Lord had not prepared the way by laying the foundations of this glorious nation, it would have been impossible (under the stringent laws and bigotry of the monarchical governments of the world) to have laid the foundations for the coming of his great kingdom. The Lord has done this. His hand has been over this nation, and it is his purpose and design to enlarge it, make it glorious above all others, and to give it dominion, and power over the earth, to the end that those who are kept in bondage and serfdom may be brought to the enjoyment of the fullest freedom and liberty of conscience possible for intelligent men to exercise in the earth.[20]

But there is another way in which the believing gentiles would fulfill the prophecy of Isaiah and "bring [the sons of

Israel] in their arms, and [the] daughters . . . upon their shoulders" (1 Nephi 21:22, parallel to Isaiah 49:22). This likely refers to the tangible assistance (economic, military, political, and so forth) that will be given to Israel as they begin to reestablish themselves in their lands of promise. Such help is reminiscent of that provided by Cyrus the Great in ancient times:

> When Israel's chief rabbi paid President Truman a visit in early 1949 and told him, "God put you in your mother's womb so you would be the instrument to bring about the rebirth of Israel after two thousand years," tears rose to the president's eyes. The rabbi then opened the Bible he was carrying with him and read the words of King Cyrus from the book of Ezra: "The Lord God of heaven hath given me all the kingdoms of the earth; and He hath charged me to build Him an house at Jerusalem, which is in Judah" (Ezra 1:2). . . .
>
> "The Jews who wish for a State shall have it," wrote Theodor Herzl in the summer of 1895, over a half-century after Orson Hyde's prophetic prayer offered from the Mount of Olives on October 21, 1841. And while Elder Hyde would probably never have thought that someone like the irascible "Man from Missouri" would someday help realize the petition that God "inspire the hearts of kings and the powers of the earth," history has confirmed that Harry S. Truman truly was a modern Cyrus.[21]

Nephi's message to his brothers is that the Lord will redeem Israel by restoring the gospel covenant on the land that they, the family of Lehi, already inhabit. In other words, the new land on which they are living is the choicest of the promised lands to be possessed by Israel, and it is *their* land of promise. Their land would be instrumental in redeeming the rest of Israel in the latter days.

Results of Nephi's Use of Isaiah 48 and 49

What were the results of Nephi's efforts to teach his brethren by reciting Isaiah 48 and 49? Nephi's brothers were too spiritually immature to understand the teachings of Isaiah; they asked Nephi what it all meant. In response to this query, Nephi gave the profound interpretations found in 1 Nephi 22, showing just how extensive his intimate relationship with the spirit of prophecy is. Nephi demonstrated his knowledge of future events, including the restoration of the gospel in the latter days and the role of America in the redemption of all Israel. Father Lehi was apparently present to hear Nephi's instruction, for Nephi says, "After I, Nephi, had made an end of teaching my brethren, our father, Lehi, also spake many things unto them, and rehearsed unto them, how great things the Lord had done for them in bringing them out of the land of Jerusalem" (2 Nephi 1:1). Lehi clearly understood the message of Isaiah, as did Nephi's brother Jacob, who was profoundly affected by Nephi's and Isaiah's message. When Jacob bore his testimony of the Messiah and his atoning power, he quoted Isaiah 49:22 and reiterated Nephi's (and the Savior's) panoramic perspective of the destiny of America, the promised land. That Jacob was in perfect harmony with Nephi's interpretation of Isaiah is evident in Jacob 6:4, which explains that it was Nephi who "desired" that Jacob speak to the people of Nephi. In fact, Jacob added some significant details to Nephi's interpretation of Isaiah 49 that indicate that Lehi's, Nephi's, and Jacob's appreciation for and understanding of Isaiah 48 and 49 was without parallel in all Israel:

> Yea, the kings of the Gentiles shall be nursing fathers unto them, and their queens shall become nursing mothers; wherefore, the promises of the Lord are great unto

the Gentiles, for he hath spoken it, and who can dispute? But behold, this land, said God, shall be a land of thine inheritance, and the Gentiles shall be blessed upon the land. And this land shall be a land of liberty unto the Gentiles, and there shall be no kings upon the land, who shall raise up unto the Gentiles. And I will fortify this land against all other nations. And he that fighteth against Zion shall perish, saith God. For he that raiseth up a king against me shall perish, for I, the Lord, the king of heaven, will be their king, and I will be a light unto them forever, that hear my words. (2 Nephi 10:9–14)

Conclusion

Nephi's hope for a bright future is grounded in the panoramic perspective of Isaiah's prophecy. No chapters in all of scripture teach this faith and hope in Israel's future redemption better than Isaiah 48 and 49. Similarly, no chapters more forcefully address Israel's rebellious hypocrites, including Laman and Lemuel, than do Isaiah 48 and 49. Isaiah's words teach powerfully about the Father's work and the Messiah's mission to redeem and restore the house of Israel first to their lands of promise and, more important, to the presence of the Father.

Thanks to Isaiah, and Nephi's and Jacob's usage and interpretation of the great eighth-century B.C. prophet, the modern reader can gain a greater appreciation for how lands of inheritance and messianic redemption are linked. These Isaiah passages and scriptural commentaries show how God used the gentiles as instruments to bring about the physical and spiritual redemption of Israel. The restoration of the gospel will ultimately redeem Israel from sin, suffering, and scattering. The fuller text found in the Book of Mormon helps us see that deliverance is both restoration to land and the removal of the debilitating effects of sin.

Related to these doctrines is the concept of the role of America in God's plan to redeem and restore Israel. The phrase *mighty nation* refers to the United States of America as the place of the restoration of the gospel covenants, as indicated in the interpretive pronouncements on Isaiah uttered by Nephi, Jacob, and the Savior, as well as by modern prophets.

The textual variants of Nephi's version of the book of Isaiah, which he took from the brass plates, contain important words and meanings long lost to modern readers of the Masoretic version found in the King James Version of the Bible. These restorations are sometimes only a word or two, but sometimes they restore entire sentences. They show that Isaiah 48 and 49 were intended for the remnant of Israel that would be broken off and taken to other lands.

Studying Nephi's use of Isaiah 48 and 49 also provides a valuable lesson to modern readers on how to teach from the scriptures, how to select the most appropriate and applicable passages to enhance the messages one wants to teach, and how better to engage the specific audiences one addresses. On a different level, however, the message of Isaiah 48 and 49 that Nephi transmits has great personal application. Just as Nephi's family found themselves struggling with new challenges and new surroundings, so too will many of us find ourselves in new places (both physically and spiritually) struggling and unsure and perhaps lacking hope in the future. Isaiah's message can help us in this case as well. The God who gave hope and promised redemption to the scattered remnant of Israel is the same Messiah who promises us all redemption from sin, suffering, and scattering. That is guaranteed if we look to him and remain faithful.

Notes

1. Not discussed in this essay but important to mention are previous studies that compare the textual variants of Isaiah in the Book of Mormon with other ancient versions or text-types of the prophet's book. The studies conclude that pre-1830 evidence among the other text-types of the Old Testament supports the textual variants in the Isaiah passages of the Book of Mormon. These other text-types include the Septuagint, Syriac, and Dead Sea Scrolls versions of the Old Testament. See John A. Tvedtnes, "Isaiah Variants in the Book of Mormon," in *Isaiah and the Prophets,* ed. Monte S. Nyman (Provo, Utah: BYU Religious Studies Center, 1984), 169, 174–5.

2. Nephi explains earlier in the Book of Mormon that "Laban also was a descendant of Joseph, wherefore he and his fathers had kept the records [that is, the brass plates]" (1 Nephi 5:16). Joseph's son Ephraim was a leader among the tribes of the Northern Kingdom of Israel, also called the Kingdom of Ephraim.

3. Sidney B. Sperry, *Answers to Book of Mormon Questions* (Salt Lake City: Bookcraft, 1967), 43–4.

4. Ibid.

5. See Sperry, *Compendium,* 127–8; see also Royal Skousen's discussion of this topic in his chapter, "Textual Variants in the Isaiah Quotations in the Book of Mormon," in this volume.

6. Chapter 18 of 1 Nephi concludes with Nephi's account of his family's long-awaited arrival in the land of promise in the Western Hemisphere. Nephi records in 1 Nephi 19 that the Lord commanded him to make a set of metal plates, which were the large plates upon which Nephi recorded the genealogy of his ancestors and his family's activities in the wilderness (see 1 Nephi 19:2), as well as the contentions of his people (see 1 Nephi 19:4). Perhaps twenty or thirty years later, God commanded Nephi to make another set of plates (see Sidney B. Sperry, *Book of Mormon Compendium* [Salt Lake City: Bookcraft, 1968], 127), and the actual manufacture of the small plates is mentioned in 2 Nephi 5:30. On the small plates, Nephi records the events of his ministry, the

prophecies, and the sacred truths that would be used to fulfill the Lord's wise purposes. Among those purposes is the instruction of not only Nephi's people but also the whole house of Israel (see 1 Nephi 19:3, 19). What we read today in 1 Nephi 19–22 (including the quotations from Isaiah) is from the small plates of Nephi.

7. The writings and prophecies of Zenock, Neum, and Zenos were more than likely recorded on the brass plates—the Northern Kingdom's version of the Old Testament—but not on the version of the Old Testament produced in the Southern Kingdom of Judah.

8. Quoted in Joseph Fielding Smith, *The Signs of the Times* (Salt Lake City: Deseret Book, 1964), 112.

9. See Theodore Friedman, "Isaiah," *Encyclopedia Judaica* (Jerusalem: Keter, 1972), 9:49. See also Joseph F. McConkie, "Joseph Smith as Found in Ancient Manuscripts," in *Isaiah and the Prophets,* Monte S. Nyman, ed. (Provo: BYU Religious Studies Center, 1984), 19.

10. Verse 3 refers to "my servant, O Israel," but this phrase might be regarded as a symbolic name for the corporate church body of the faithful, functioning under the direction of the Messiah and Joseph Smith to help restore scattered Israel.

11. Joseph Fielding Smith, comp., *Teachings of the Prophet Joseph Smith* (Salt Lake City: Deseret Book, 1970), 365.

12. Ibid., 304.

13. Mark E. Petersen, *The Great Prologue* (Salt Lake City: Deseret Book, 1975), 5–6.

14. Ibid. See the entire work.

15. Ezra Taft Benson, *The Teachings of Ezra Taft Benson* (Salt Lake City: Bookcraft, 1988), 594.

16. Ibid., 91.

17. Ibid., 578.

18. Ibid., 575.

19. Ibid., 571–2.

20. Joseph F. Smith, *Gospel Doctrine* (Salt Lake City: Deseret Book, 1968), 409.

21. Michael T. Benson, "Harry S. Truman as a Modern Cyrus," *BYU Studies* 34/1 (1994): 21–2.

Isaiah 50–51, the Israelite Autumn Festivals, and the Covenant Speech of Jacob in 2 Nephi 6–10

John S. Thompson

The structure and themes of Jacob's covenant speech show that he probably spoke in connection with a religious royal festival, to which these words of Isaiah were especially well suited.

An important element in understanding any text is establishing some idea of the historical or traditional setting in which its words were formulated. In recent years, scholarly research has focused on establishing such settings for various sermons in the Book of Mormon. For example, some scholars have shown that it is likely that King Benjamin's speech in Mosiah 1–6 was given sometime during the Israelite autumn festivals.[1] Viewing Benjamin's speech in this context gives new meaning to its passages about coronation, kingship, care for the poor, sacrifice of animals, covenant renewal, and other elements central to the autumn festivals' tradition. Similarly, understanding the setting for Jacob's sermon to the Nephites in 2 Nephi 6–10 will provide great insight into the speech as a whole and will also illuminate his use of Isaiah.

Unlike Benjamin's speech, the Book of Mormon gives no background for Jacob's sermon. While Nephi provides a fairly smooth historical narrative from Lehi's departure out of Jerusalem in 1 Nephi 1 to the establishment of the Nephite state in 2 Nephi 5, he provides no historical context from 2 Nephi 6 to the end of his record. Instead, he simply records the sermon of his brother Jacob (see 2 Nephi 6–10), the lengthy quotation from Isaiah (see 2 Nephi 12–24), and his own thoughts and feelings (see 2 Nephi 11, 25–33) without any mention of time or place.[2] Therefore, in order to determine a setting for Jacob's speech, one needs to turn to the sermon itself, hoping that something within it will reveal the context in which the speech was given.

Biblical scholars have developed various techniques for determining the setting of a text. Although these methods do not provide infallible or irrefutable results, they can add to the understanding of a text's meaning and history. Form criticism and its complement, tradition criticism, are two such techniques. Scholars use comparative studies to uncover forms or patterns within a text and then try to identify the traditional occasions in a culture's history when such forms or patterns were used.[3]

When these comparative methods are applied to Jacob's sermon, a form known as the covenant/treaty pattern emerges. The presence of this pattern, coupled with Jacob's statement in 2 Nephi 9:1—"I have read these things [i.e., the words of Isaiah] that ye might know concerning the covenants of the Lord"—make it fairly certain that this sermon was given in connection with covenant making or covenant renewal. This conclusion, as will be shown, connects Jacob's sermon with the Israelite autumn festivals, which in turn links much of the imagery in the Isaiah portions of Jacob's speech to several ritual and enthronement themes.

The Covenant/Treaty Pattern in Jacob's Sermon

The covenant/treaty pattern is found throughout much of the ancient Near East and has been the focus of numerous studies.[4] Though this pattern can vary in content and order,[5] it typically follows a basic six-part form:

(1) *Preamble and Titulary.* In its preamble, the covenant text names the king, suzerain, or overlord (or his official representative) who is making the covenant or treaty.

(2) *Historical Overview and Covenant Speech Proper.* The text then gives a historical overview and the covenant speech proper, usually reciting the ruler's acts of kindness and mercy (or, in the case of Israel, God's infinite might and power to save) in order to place the people under obligation to enter into the covenant or treaty.

(3) *Stipulations of the Covenant or Treaty.* The stipulations or requirements of the covenant or treaty are enumerated.

(4) *Cursings and Blessings.* Cursings and blessings are promised for those who respectively break or keep the covenant or treaty.

(5) *Witness Formula.* Witnesses to the contract are then identified.

(6) *Recording of the Contract.* The agreement is recorded to provide a permanent record for the parties.

Biblical scholars have found this pattern in many ancient Near Eastern texts, as well as in such places as Joshua 24, Exodus 19–24, and the entire book of Deuteronomy. The pattern also appears in the Book of Mormon.[6] It appears that Jacob's sermon also follows this pattern.

Preamble and Titulary: 2 Nephi 6:1–4

In the opening verses, Jacob is identified as the authorized representative of God and the king (Nephi). His audience, the people of Nephi, is also identified. Jacob begins his sermon in verse 2 by establishing his authority: "having been called of God, and ordained after the manner of his holy order, and having been consecrated by my brother Nephi, unto whom ye look as a king or a protector, and on whom ye depend for safety." Jacob indicates that his "anxiety is great," and verifies that he has previously exhorted the people "with all diligence," having taught them the words of Lehi and "concerning all things which are written, from the creation of the world." But now he speaks "concerning things which are, and which are to come." Accordingly, he explains that he will read "the words of Isaiah," which Nephi wanted Jacob to speak, so that the people "may learn and glorify the name of [their] God."

Historical Overview and Covenant Speech Proper: 2 Nephi 6:5–9:22

In the main body of his speech, Jacob dwells on God's promise and mighty ability to gather and save Israel. Using Isaiah, he exhorts his audience: "Look unto Abraham, your father, and unto Sarah, she that bare you; for I called him alone, and blessed him" (2 Nephi 8:2, parallel to Isaiah 51:2), reminding them that God covenanted with Abraham to bless his seed (i.e., to gather and save Israel). This covenant promise, Jacob assures his listeners, will be fulfilled by means of God's promised Messiah.[7]

Stipulations of the Covenant or Treaty: 2 Nephi 9:23–26

Here Jacob explains the obligations of those who would have the benefit of the covenant: "And he commandeth all men that they must repent, and be baptized in his name, having perfect faith in the Holy One of Israel." If they will not, "they must be damned," for God "has given a law," and anyone who is under the law is subject to its punishments.

Cursings and Blessings: 2 Nephi 9:27–43

In these verses, Jacob clearly enumerates ten "woes" for those who do not keep the law (see verses 27–38).[8] The blessings include "life eternal" (verse 39), "whoso knocketh, to him will [the Holy One of Israel] open" (verse 42), and "happiness" (verse 43).

Witness Formula: 2 Nephi 9:44

Jacob then invokes a witness clause: "O, my beloved brethren, remember my words. Behold, I take off my garments, and I shake them before you; I pray the God of my salvation that he view me with his all-searching eye; wherefore, ye shall know at the last day, when all men shall be judged of their works, that the God of Israel did witness that I shook your iniquities from my soul, and that I stand with brightness before him, and am rid of your blood."

Recording of the Contract: 2 Nephi 9:52

Although Jacob does not mention recording this covenant in writing, he admonishes the people to record it well in their memories: "Behold, my beloved brethren, remember the words of your God; pray unto him continually by day, and give thanks unto his holy name by night."[9]

Covenant-Renewal Ceremony

The presence of the covenant pattern in Jacob's sermon raises the question, Under what circumstance would Jacob have made such a speech and used this particular pattern to do so? Basing their arguments on covenant/treaty forms found in the biblical text, Gerhard von Rad and others have concluded that the Israelites periodically held a covenant-renewal ceremony during the Feast of Tabernacles (Sukkot).[10] Hence, the presence of this structure in Jacob's sermon may also suggest the possibility that he gave his covenant speech during this festival as well.[11]

The Israelite Autumn Festivals and Jacob's Sermon

Although many questions remain about the nature of the Feast of Tabernacles and the closely related holy days of the Blowing of the Trumpets (the Jewish New Year, Rosh Hashanah) and the Day of Atonement (Yom Kippur), all of which occur during the seventh month of the ancient Israelite calendar (Leviticus 23:23–43; Numbers 29), the following conclusions put forth by various scholars will be assumed here in order to analyze Jacob's covenant speech: (1) In preexilic times, a New Year's Day festival was observed on the first day of the seventh month;[12] (2) celebrations of the New Year, the Day of Atonement, and the Feast of Tabernacles were most likely connected as a single autumn festival conglomerate before the Babylonian Exile;[13] and (3) after the return of the Jews from Babylon, the traditions surrounding these celebrations may have continued to reflect earlier understandings.[14] With these assumptions in place, many of the topics Jacob chooses to address can be seen to reflect various elements of the ancient Israelite autumn festival tradition.

Judgment

One of the principal themes surrounding the New Year in postexilic Jewish tradition, as well as in the preexilic ancient Near East,[15] is God's judgment of his people. Louis Jacobs observes:

> In Talmudic times there were a number of periods of Rosh Hashanah ("New Year"), each for a specific purpose. . . . In the Jewish calendar, *Nissan* is the New Year for counting the months. And according to the Talmud, the first day of the month of Tishri [the seventh month] is the New Year for God's judgment of the world. . . . Rosh

Hashanah is a festival, with festive meals and an atmosphere of joyousness, yet at the same time it is a judgment day, demanding a much more serious mood.[16]

Similarly, Jacob addresses the theme of God's judgment as he invites his people to look forward:

Prepare your souls for that glorious day when justice shall be administered unto the righteous, even the day of judgment, that ye may not shrink with awful fear; that ye may not remember your awful guilt in perfectness, and be constrained to exclaim: Holy, holy are thy judgments, O Lord God Almighty—but I know my guilt; I transgressed thy law, and my transgressions are mine; and the devil hath obtained me, that I am a prey to his awful misery. (2 Nephi 9:46)

Many other references to judgment are found in Jacob's sermon: "Behold, the judgments of the Holy One of Israel shall come upon them" (2 Nephi 6:10). "I will make my judgment to rest for a light for the people" (2 Nephi 8:4, parallel to Isaiah 51:4). "Mine arm shall judge the people." (2 Nephi 8:5, parallel to Isaiah 51:5). "Save it should be an infinite atonement this corruption could not put on incorruption. Wherefore, the first judgment which came upon man must needs have remained to an endless duration" (2 Nephi 9:7). "When all men shall have passed from this first death unto life, insomuch as they have become immortal, they must appear before the judgment-seat of the Holy One of Israel; and then cometh the judgment, and then must they be judged according to the holy judgment of God" (2 Nephi 9:15). "And he suffereth this that the resurrection might pass upon all men, that all might stand before him at the great and judgment day" (2 Nephi 9:22). "All men shall be judged of their works" (2 Nephi 9:44).

Remembrance

In the Israelite calendar outlined in Leviticus 23, the first day of the seventh month is a day of *zikron*, which can be rendered "remembrance" or "memorial." Jacob's sermon emphasizes the theme of remembrance: "O, my beloved brethren, remember the awfulness in transgressing against that Holy God. . . . Remember, to be carnally-minded is death, and to be spiritually-minded is life eternal" (2 Nephi 9:39). "Remember the greatness of the Holy One of Israel" (2 Nephi 9:40). "Come unto the Lord, the Holy One. Remember that his paths are righteous" (2 Nephi 9:41). "O, my beloved brethren, remember my words" (2 Nephi 9:44; see also 9:51). "Behold, my beloved brethren, remember the words of your God" (2 Nephi 9:52). "Let us remember him" (2 Nephi 10:20). "Remember that ye are free to act for yourselves" (2 Nephi 10:23). "Remember, after ye are reconciled unto God, that it is only in and through the grace of God that ye are saved" (2 Nephi 10:24).

Creation

Throughout the ancient Near East and in many traditions around the world, New Year's Day is closely associated with the creation of the world.[17] For example, during the Mesopotamian New Year festival (the *akītu*), the *Enuma Elish*, an epic poem recounting the creation of the world, was read.[18] E. O. James postulates that the biblical creation account was used by the Israelites as preexilic temple liturgy during New Year festivals.[19] As far as postexilic Jewish tradition is concerned, Louis Jacobs notes that "there is an opinion in the talmudic literature that the world was created in Tishri . . . . This explains why there has been introduced into the Rosh Hashanah liturgy the tremendous theme of creation."[20]

In Jacob's speech, he begins by reminding the people that he has previously spoken to them "concerning all things which are written, from the creation of the world" (2 Nephi 6:3). He also refers to Christ as the "great Creator" (2 Nephi 9:5–6). These points may be echoes of a traditional New Year setting. This creation theme is further emphasized in an Isaiah passage quoted by Jacob: "And forgettest the Lord thy maker, that hath stretched forth the heavens, and laid the foundations of the earth?" (2 Nephi 8:13, parallel to Isaiah 51:13).

Garments

According to the Lord's instruction in Leviticus concerning the Day of Atonement, the high priest was to "wash his flesh in water" and then to "put on the holy linen coat," "linen breeches," "a linen girdle," and a "linen mitre" (Leviticus 16:4). While wearing these garments, the high priest was to make atonement for himself, the temple, and the people by sacrifice (see Leviticus 16:33). During this ceremony, the high priest and priests were instructed on numerous occasions to remove their garments, wash themselves, and wash their clothes (see Leviticus 16:23–24, 26, 28).[21]

Such emphasis on garments being kept clean (for example, from the blood of the sacrifices) in connection with the temple and the Day of Atonement may have inspired Jacob to take off his garments and display them before the Nephites, saying, "I pray the God of my salvation that he view me with his all-searching eye; . . . that the God of Israel did witness that I shook your iniquities from my soul, and that I stand with brightness before him, and am rid of your blood" (2 Nephi 9:44). This theme is further supported by Jacob's reference to "being clothed with purity, yea, even with the robe of righteousness" (2 Nephi 9:14) and by an Isaiah passage Jacob quotes: "Awake, awake, put on thy strength, O Zion; put on thy beautiful garments, O Jerusalem, the holy city; for henceforth there shall no more come into thee the uncircumcised and the unclean" (2 Nephi 8:24, parallel to Isaiah 52:1).[22]

The Name of God

According to the Babylonian Talmud, speaking the sacred name of God was allowed only on the Day of Atonement and even then only by the high priest in the Holy of Holies.[23] It is difficult to determine the basis for this tradition; however, it may have arisen from earlier associations of the secret name of God with creation or from other ancient traditions concerning the secrecy of names.[24] Regardless, it is interesting that Jacob begins his sermon by stating: "And I speak unto you for your sakes, that ye may learn and glorify the name of your God" (2 Nephi 6:4). Further, the rest of his sermon contains numerous references to the "name" of God: "The Lord of Hosts is my name" (2 Nephi 8:15, parallel to Isaiah 51:15). "And he commandeth all men that they must repent, and be baptized in his name" (2 Nephi 9:23). "And if they will not repent and believe in his name, and be baptized in his name, and endure to the end, they must be damned" (2 Nephi 9:24). "For he cannot be deceived, for the Lord God is his name" (2 Nephi 9:41). "I will praise the holy name of my God" (2 Nephi 9:49). "Give thanks unto his holy name by night" (2 Nephi 9:52). "For in the last night the angel spake unto me that this should be his name" (2 Nephi 10:3).

Sacrifice

As mentioned above, on the Day of Atonement a special sacrificial service was held in order to cleanse the priests, people, and temple from sin (see Leviticus 16). However, the animal sacrifices were to atone for sins committed in ignorance: those who sinned by rebellion against the law were simply "cut off" (Numbers 15:24–31). Jacob seems to have this in mind when he states:

> Where there is no law given there is no punishment; and where there is no punishment there is no condemnation; and where there is no condemnation the mercies of the Holy One of Israel have claim upon them, because of the atonement; for they are delivered by the power of him. For the atonement satisfieth the demands of his justice upon all those who have not the law given to them, . . . and they are restored to that God who gave them breath, which is the Holy One of Israel. But wo unto him that has the law given, yea, that has all the commandments of God, like unto us, and that transgresseth them, and that wasteth the days of his probation, for awful is his state! (2 Nephi 9:25–27)

However, there is hope for the rebellious who repent, for the sacrifice of "the great Creator" is an "infinite atonement—save it should be an infinite atonement this corruption could not put on incorruption" (2 Nephi 9:6–7). How fitting that Jacob would speak so much concerning the sacrifice and atonement of Christ (2 Nephi 9:4–22) if his speech was given during the autumn festivals that included the Day of Atonement.

Fasting

The Day of Atonement was the only fast prescribed by the law of Moses (Leviticus 16:29, 31; 23:27, 32—the word "afflict" parallels the word "fast" in Isaiah 58:3 and is typically understood to mean to "deny oneself"). Louis Jacobs describes this day as "a day of feasting without eating or drinking; the nourishment provided is for the soul."[25] Isaiah promises that those who fast properly by dealing "thy bread to the hungry" and bringing the "poor that are cast out to thy house" will be blessed, for the Lord will "satisfy thy soul in drought, and make fat thy bones" (Isaiah 58:7, 11; see also Isaiah 58:3–12). A similar allusion to fasting can be seen in the prophet Jacob's words:

> Come, my brethren, every one that thirsteth, come ye to the waters; and he that hath no money, come buy and eat; yea, come buy wine and milk without money and without price. Wherefore, do not spend money for that which is of no worth, nor your labor for that which cannot satisfy. Hearken diligently unto me, and remember the words which I have spoken; and come unto the Holy One of Israel, and feast upon that which perisheth not, neither can be corrupted, and let your soul delight in fatness. (2 Nephi 9:50–51, parallel to Isaiah 55:1–2)

Confession and Repentance

Louis Jacobs notes that "during the services on Yom Kippur the standard confession of sin is repeated a number of times." This confession is done as a group—that is, "*we* have sinned"—but it is also expected of each individual—"*I* have sinned."[26] The confession is simply to acknowledge one's sins,[27] but the purpose of the confession is to lead one to remorseful repentance. The repentant soul is atoned for through the sacrifice of the Lord's goat and the release of the "scapegoat" into the wilderness (Leviticus 16:7–10, 15–22).

Jacob addresses the idea of confession in 2 Nephi 9:46:

> Prepare your souls for that glorious day when justice
> shall be administered unto the righteous, even the day of
> judgment, that ye may not shrink with awful fear; that ye
> may not remember your awful guilt in perfectness, and
> be constrained to exclaim: Holy, holy are thy judgments,
> O Lord God Almighty—but *I know my guilt; I transgressed
> thy law, and my transgressions are mine;* and the devil hath
> obtained me, that I am a prey to his awful misery.

He takes the confession to the extreme by placing the specific confession formula in the setting of judgment. He does this in order to inspire his people to repent—to "turn away from [their] sins" (2 Nephi 9:45).

The Law

Simhat Torah "rejoicing of the Torah/Law," the last day of the Feast of Tabernacles in postexilic Jewish tradition, commemorated the giving of the law to Israel at Sinai. This idea is closely connected with the concept that the Feast of Tabernacles was a time of renewing covenants, specifically the Sinai covenant.[28] The Sinai covenant is renewed by participating vicariously in the events of the wilderness, such as dwelling in *sukkot*—"booths" or "tents"—and reading the law to commemorate the giving of the law.[29] In fact, the book of Deuteronomy provides a biblical example of the injunction to read the law during *Sukkot:*

> And Moses wrote this law, and delivered it unto the
> priests the sons of Levi, which bare the ark of the covenant
> of the Lord, and unto all the elders of Israel. And Moses
> commanded them, saying, At the end of every seven years,
> in the solemnity of the year of release, in the feast of taber-
> nacles, when all Israel is come to appear before the Lord thy
> God in the place which he shall choose, thou shalt read this
> law before all Israel in their hearing. Gather the people to-
> gether, men, and women, and children, and thy stranger

that is within thy gates, that they may hear, and that they
may learn, and fear the Lord your God, and observe to do
all the words of this law: And that their children, which
have not known any thing, may hear, and learn to fear the
Lord your God, as long as ye live in the land whither ye go
over Jordan to possess it. (Deuteronomy 31:9–13).

The fact that Jacob often refers to the law both in his
own words as well as in the passages quoted from Isaiah
may reflect this tradition surrounding the Feast of Tabernacles: "Hearken unto me, my people; and give ear unto
me, O my nation; for a law shall proceed from me, and I will
make my judgment to rest for a light for the people"
(2 Nephi 8:4, parallel to Isaiah 51:4). "Hearken unto me, ye
that know righteousness, the people in whose heart I have
written my law" (2 Nephi 8:7, parallel to Isaiah 51:7). "O the
greatness and the justice of our God! For he executeth all his
words, and they have gone forth out of his mouth, and his
law must be fulfilled" (2 Nephi 9:17). "Wherefore, he has
given a law; and where there is no law given there is no
punishment" (2 Nephi 9:25). "Wo unto him that has the law
given, yea, that has all the commandments of God, like unto
us, and that transgresseth them, and that wasteth the days
of his probation, for awful is his state!" (2 Nephi 9:27).

Isaiah and the Israelite Autumn Festivals

Of all the elements associated with the Israelite autumn
festivals, kingship figures most prominently. In the ancient
Near East, the New Year (including, in Israel, the Feast of
Tabernacles) was the time to celebrate, crown, and renew
the earthly king.[30] Some scholars also believe it was a time
to celebrate the kingship of God. For example, Sigmund
Mowinckel calls this time of year in Israel the "festival of
Yahweh's enthronement."[31] It is likely that because of this

aspect of the autumn festivals Jacob uses the writings of Isaiah.

Form-critical and tradition-critical methods in past decades have been used to analyze Isaiah's words, and the results are interesting in connection with Jacob's sermon. Most biblical scholars divide Isaiah into three literary sections, composed of chapters 1–39, 40–55, and 56–66.[32] Regardless of any uncertainties in the dating and authorship of these sections,[33] the divisions help identify certain themes in Isaiah and allow form-critical and tradition-critical scholars to draw certain conclusions.

Isaiah 40–55, from which Jacob quotes his Isaiah passages, have often been analyzed with form-critical methods; but because many units or forms within the text have little or no comparative material (for instance, the Servant Songs),[34] solid conclusions have been difficult to achieve. However, J. H. Eaton feels that there is enough evidence "to guide us to the decisive factors of tradition behind Isa. 40–55."[35] J. Begrich points out as early as 1938 that many of the forms in this section resemble materials from earlier services in the temple, such as hymns, laments, and prophetic oracles of assurance.[36] Mowinckel took this connection a step further, noting that there seems to be an association between the second division of Isaiah and the preexilic autumn festivals—namely the Feast of Tabernacles.[37] However, Mowinckel, who does not understand how the Servant Songs fit into the picture, stopped short of completely relating chapters 40–55 to *Sukkot*. It was I. Engnell and Eaton who completed the correspondence between the second division of Isaiah, including the Servant Songs, and the Feast of Tabernacles.[38] Engnell concluded that Isaiah 40–55 "is a prophetic collection of traditions" that may be called *"liturgy, . . .* not a cult liturgy but a prophetic imitation thereof."[39]

The conclusions of these scholars are significant in light of the possible setting of Jacob's sermon, for if the second division of Isaiah, from which Jacob obtained his quotes, is a prophetic imitation of *Sukkot* liturgy, then it is possible that Nephi instructed Jacob to use Isaiah not only for the prophetic teachings and elevated language, but because Isaiah's words reflect the very festival in which they, the Nephites, were participating.

As shown above, the main Isaiah portions of Jacob's address fall within the covenant speech proper of the covenant/treaty pattern. The purpose of that section of the speech is to give the people a reason or obligation to enter into the covenant. Jacob accomplished this by appealing to the prophetic future and the hope that it inspires. He explained that he was quoting Isaiah so "that ye may *rejoice*, and *lift up your heads forever* [that is, have hope], because of the blessings which the Lord God shall bestow upon your children. For I know that ye have searched much, many of you, *to know of things to come*" (2 Nephi 9:3–4). But what is this hope of things to come?

Mowinckel, in his book entitled *He That Cometh*, declared that the Israelite festivals were a factor in forming the basis of a "future hope" for the Messiah, who is characterized as the "ideal" king.[40] Further, he stated that the Messianic faith was "from the first, associated with the Jewish hope of a future restoration [of Israel]."[41] More precisely, it was associated with "the restoration of Israel from the grave misfortune which had befallen her, a hope of the national and political deliverance of the people from oppression and distress, and for a moral and religious purification and consummation."[42] These two hopes—the Messiah and the restoration of Israel—are the very things that Jacob emphasizes in his sermon.

The main passages concerning the restoration of Israel begin in 2 Nephi 6:6–7, parallel to Isaiah 49:22–23:

> And now, these are the words: Thus saith the Lord God: Behold, I will lift up mine hand to the Gentiles, and set up my standard to the people; and they shall bring thy sons in their arms, and thy daughters shall be carried upon their shoulders. And kings shall be thy nursing fathers, and their queens thy nursing mothers; they shall bow down to thee with their faces towards the earth, and lick up the dust of thy feet; and thou shalt know that I am the Lord; for they shall not be ashamed that wait for me.

Following this quotation, Jacob testified that this prophecy will come true, for the "Lord has shown me that those who were at Jerusalem, from whence we came, have been slain and carried away captive. Nevertheless, the Lord has shown unto me that they should return again. . . . [W]hen they shall come to the knowledge of their Redeemer, they shall be gathered together again to the lands of their inheritance" (2 Nephi 6:8–11). Jacob elaborated this theme further on the second day of his sermon (see 2 Nephi 9:53–10:22).[43]

The bulk of the Isaiah passages and commentary in Jacob's sermon, however, focused on the role of the Messiah, the ideal king. This brings us again to the central element of the autumn festivals—the celebration and renewal of kingship, specifically the enthronement of Yahweh.

Isaiah and the Enthronement of Yahweh

It was typical of ancient Near Eastern societies to renew or reenthrone their kings during New Year celebrations. However, in many societies, before the actual reenthronement ceremony, the king was ritually humiliated or sacrificed (or a proxy would be sacrificed). For example, in the *akītu* festival of ancient Mesopotamia, the king was ritually humiliated before being allowed to enter the inner sanctuary and sit upon his throne. The high priest would strip him of any royal insignia; he was then slapped on the cheek and his ears were pulled; and then he was to bow down and confess before the god Marduk that "he had not committed any sins or neglected Esagila and Babylon."[44] In the *sed*—a festival of ancient Egypt—the king (or his proxy) was sacrificed and then "buried," ritually reenacting the mythical defeat and death of Osiris by his evil brother Seth. While the king was in his tomb, Anubis, the jackal-headed priest, in conjunction with Isis and Nephtys, used magic to resuscitate the king while the priests and the people outside the tomb called to the king: "Awake! Arise and live!" Afterwards, the king, fully justified after having conquered his enemies, including death, assumed his position on the throne.[45]

Israelite parallels to the chain of events in these re-enthronement rituals can be seen in Eaton's discussion of Yahweh's kingship as reflected in the Psalms:

> The form of worship attested by the Psalms apparently did not present an idea of Yahweh having been seasonally deprived of his kingship, now to be won back. The tradition of lamentation . . . thinks of Yahweh as holding himself far off, as seeming inactive or indifferent for a while. . . . *Admittedly there are traces that in some periods the worship may have envisaged Yahweh as held awhile by enemies and affected by the drowsiness of death* (Ps. 78:61–6; 1 Sam. 4–6). *But the great majority of our texts concentrate on his victory, . . . his ascension to his throne-centre* on Mount Zion and in heaven.[46]

Like the Psalms, the Isaiah portions in Jacob's sermon reflect much of this traditional scenario as well. For instance, the Isaiah passages refer to the fact that Yahweh "gave [his] back to the smiter, and [his] cheeks to them that plucked off the hair. [He] hid not [his] face from shame and spitting" (2 Nephi 7:6, parallel to Isaiah 50:6). In spite of Yahweh's humiliation, the people of Israel call to Yahweh: "Awake, awake! Put on strength, O arm of the Lord; awake as in the ancient days. Art thou not he that hath cut Rahab, and wounded the dragon? Art thou not he who hath dried the sea, the waters of the great deep; that hath made the depths of the sea a way for the ransomed to pass over?" (2 Nephi 8:9–10, parallel to Isaiah 51:9–10).[47]

The humiliation and apparent dormancy are not permanent, however, for Yahweh triumphs over his enemies and his might is extolled: "Behold, at my rebuke I dry up the sea, I make their rivers a wilderness and their fish to stink because the waters are dried up, and they die because of thirst" (2 Nephi 7:2, parallel to Isaiah 50:2). "I set my face like a flint, and I know that I shall not be ashamed. And the Lord is near, and he justifieth me. Who will contend with me? Let us stand together. Who is mine adversary? Let him come near me, and I will smite him with the strength of my mouth" (2 Nephi 7:7–8, parallel to Isaiah 50:7–8).

According to Eaton's reconstruction of the enthronement of Yahweh at the Feast of Tabernacles, once Yahweh's enemies are conquered, he makes a procession to his throne on Mount Zion and takes his seat.[48] This may be reflected in 2 Nephi 8:3, parallel to Isaiah 51:3: "The Lord shall comfort Zion. . . . Joy and gladness shall be found therein, thanksgiving and the voice of melody." The Hebrew word *qøl* "voice" may refer to the sounding of a shofar horn, which was traditionally blown at the coronation of a king in Israel and at the New Year (see Leviticus 23:24).[49]

Once enthroned, Yahweh sits in judgment and promises his people ample provisions and safety from enemies.[50] The Isaiah passages in Jacob's sermon address these points as well: "I will make my judgment to rest for a light for the people. My righteousness is near; my salvation is gone forth, and mine arm shall judge the people. The isles shall wait upon me, and on mine arm shall they trust" (2 Nephi 8:4–5, parallel to Isaiah 51:4–5). "Fear ye not the reproach of men, neither be ye afraid of their revilings" (2 Nephi 8:7, parallel to Isaiah 51:7). "I am he; yea, I am he that comforteth you. Behold, who art thou, that thou shouldst be afraid of man, who shall die, and of the son of man, who shall be made like unto grass?" (2 Nephi 8:12, parallel to Isaiah 51:12). "I have covered thee in the shadow of mine hand, that I may plant the heavens and lay the foundations of the earth, and say unto Zion: Behold, thou art my people" (2 Nephi 8:16, parallel to Isaiah 51:16). "I have taken out of thine hand the cup of trembling, the dregs of the cup of my fury; thou shalt no more drink it again. But I will put it into the hand of them that afflict thee" (2 Nephi 8:22–23, parallel to Isaiah 51:22–23).

Yahweh's restoration to the throne also ensures that nature will function properly, bringing forth good things.[51] This element is also present in Jacob's sermon: "He will comfort all her waste places; and he will make her wilderness like Eden, and her desert like the garden of the Lord" (2 Nephi 8:3, parallel to Isaiah 51:3).

A prophecy by Zechariah provides one final note on Yahweh's kingship: "And it shall come to pass, that every one that is left of all the nations which came against Jerusalem shall even go up from year to year to worship the King, the Lord of hosts, and to keep the feast of tabernacles" (Zechariah 14:16). Though the setting of this prophecy is the last days, it is interesting to note that keeping the Feast of Tabernacles is mentioned in connection with going up to Jerusalem to worship Yahweh as king.

Conclusions

From the structure and themes of 2 Nephi 6–10, one may conclude that Jacob's speech was given in connection with a covenant-renewal celebration that was most likely performed as part of the traditional Israelite autumn festivals required by the law of Moses. Moreover, Jacob seems to use certain Isaiah passages as part of his speech in order to encourage the Nephites to renew their covenants by reminding them of the Lord's promises, giving them a hope in their salvation and future restoration. These blessings are made possible because of the Messiah, who is characterized as the ideal king, suffering humiliation, even death, but eventually triumphing over all.

Concerning Christ and the requirements of the law of Moses, Nephi states, "And, notwithstanding we believe in Christ, we keep the law of Moses, and look forward with steadfastness unto Christ, until the law shall be fulfilled. For, for this end was the law given; wherefore the law hath become dead unto us, and we are made alive in Christ because of our faith; yet we keep the law because of the commandments" (2 Nephi 25:24–25). This statement and others like it[52] indicate that the law of Moses was understood and observed among the Nephites, and that they had hope in the fact that it pointed to Christ and would have its fulfillment in him at some future day. With this in mind, it is interesting that immediately following Jacob's sermon Nephi states, "Behold, my soul delighteth in proving unto my people the truth of the coming of Christ; for, for this end hath the law of Moses been given; and all things which have been given of God from the beginning of the world, unto man, are the typifying of him" (2 Nephi 11:4). This statement makes perfect sense in the context of Jacob's words about Christ's coming (see 2 Nephi 9:4–5; 10:3) and especially if Jacob was indeed participating in a festival that was required by the law. Since the Israelite festivals were included in the law of Moses, the Nephites likely carried them out with full understanding that the elements of the festival all typify Christ and point to his coming. In support of that realization, Nephi and Jacob could have drawn on no prophet more appropriately than the great seer Isaiah.

Notes

1. Hugh Nibley, "Old World Ritual in the New World," in *An Approach to the Book of Mormon* (Salt Lake City: Deseret Book and FARMS, 1988), 295–310. See also John A. Tvedtnes, "King Benjamin and the Feast of Tabernacles," in *By Study and Also by Faith*, ed. John M. Lundquist and Stephen D. Ricks (Salt Lake City: Deseret Book and FARMS, 1990), 2:197–237; and Terrence Szink and John W. Welch, "King Benjamin's Speech in the Context of Ancient Israelite Festivals," *King Benjamin's Speech* (Provo, Utah: FARMS, 1998).

2. John W. Welch, in his article "The Temple in the Book of Mormon: The Temples at the Cities of Nephi, Zarahemla, and Bountiful," in *Temples of the Ancient World*, ed. Donald W. Parry (Salt Lake City: Deseret Book and FARMS, 1994), 297–387, attempts to establish a historical context for the sermon by connecting Jacob's speech in 2 Nephi 6–10 with the events found in 2 Nephi 5, namely, Nephi's coronation and the establishment of the Nephite state. Welch concludes that (1) Jacob's speech is a covenant speech (this conclusion is based primarily upon Jacob's statement in 2 Nephi 9:1: "I have read these things that ye might know concerning the covenants of the Lord"), (2) the speech was probably delivered at the temple in the city of Nephi at or around the coronation of Nephi, and (3) it was given to the people in order to establish their acceptance of Nephi as king and of the new Nephite state and law. However, an obstacle to Welch's thesis arises in the final verses of chapter 5, wherein Nephi records a

ten-year time span (see verses 28 and 34), preventing any positive connection between the events of chapter 5 and Jacob's sermon starting in chapter 6. I hastily add that this does not eliminate the possibility that Jacob's speech was in fact used for the purposes Welch claims; however, I feel a safer conclusion can be drawn by placing Jacob's sermon in a specific tradition rather than at a specific moment in time.

3. A modern example of form-criticism and tradition-criticism can be seen in the following scenario: A form-critical scholar who studied the words spoken at an LDS sacrament meeting or even in a home of LDS members would discover that, in general, a set pattern reoccurs time and time again: (1) Often the phrase "Our Father in Heaven" or some variation of those words is used at the beginning of this pattern; (2) following this, words denoting thanksgiving to God are used; (3) after giving thanks, the speaker begins to supplicate or ask for blessings; (4) finally, the phrase "In the name of Jesus Christ, Amen" consistently provides a closing statement. This has a specific "form," although there are variables, and it is possible that the form-critic would call this pattern a "prayer." A tradition-critical scholar would seek to establish the traditional "setting" for such forms, possibly recognizing that prayers are most often spoken at the beginning and ending of the day or meeting, and even occur at the beginning of meals.

4. See, for example, Kenneth A. Kitchen, "The Fall and Rise of Covenant, Law, and Treaty," *Tyndale Bulletin* 40 (1989): 118–35; Dennis J. McCarthy, *Treaty and Covenant,* rev. ed. (Rome: Biblical Institute, 1978); Klaus Baltzer, *The Covenant Formulary,* trans. David E. Green (Philadelphia: Fortress Press, 1971); and George E. Mendenhall, "Covenant Forms in Israelite Tradition," *Biblical Archaeologist* 17 (1954): 50–76.

5. See Kitchen, "The Patriarchal Age: Myth or History?" *Biblical Archaeology Review* 21 (March/April 1995): 48–57, 88–95, for a chart and brief discussion of these variables over the millennia.

6. See Stephen D. Ricks, "The Treaty/Covenant Pattern in King Benjamin's Address (Mosiah 1–6)," *BYU Studies* 24 (1984):

151–62; and Blake T. Ostler, "The Covenant Tradition in the Book of Mormon," in *Rediscovering the Book of Mormon*, ed. John L. Sorenson and Melvin J. Thorne (Salt Lake City: Deseret Book and FARMS, 1991), 230–40.

7. In regard to historical overview, note the allusion to the Exodus in an Isaiah passage Jacob quotes: "Art thou not he who hath dried the sea, the waters of the great deep; that hath made the depths of the sea a way for the ransomed to pass over?" (2 Nephi 8:10, parallel to Isaiah 51:10).

8. John W. Welch's "Jacob's Ten Commandments," in *Reexploring the Book of Mormon*, ed. John W. Welch (Salt Lake City: Deseret Book and FARMS, 1992), 69–72, provides another link to the covenant theme by showing that these ten woes echo the ten commandments, which are part of the Sinai covenant.

9. We must concede the fact, however, that this covenant was literally recorded as well. The mere appearance of it in Nephi's record attests to this fact and causes one to wonder from what written source Nephi obtained it.

10. Gerhard von Rad, "The Form–Critical Problem of the Hexateuch," in *The Problem of the Hexateuch and Other Essays*, trans. E. W. Trueman Dicken (New York: McGraw-Hill, 1966), 33–40; compare Deuteronomy 31:10–13. See also John Bright, *A History of Israel*, 3rd ed. (Philadelphia: Westminster, 1981), 171; and Artur Weiser, *The Psalms*, trans. H. Hartwell (Philadelphia: Westminster, 1962), 35–52.

11. Regarding the extent to which the Nephites participated in the law of Moses, including sacrifices and festivals, see John W. Welch, "The Temple in the Book of Mormon," 301–19, in which he concludes that "we are not at liberty to assume . . . that the Nephites could freely ignore certain provisions of the law of Moses as they had it, on the grounds that those requirements were beneath their religious dignity or station" (317–8).

12. For discussion on the Israelite New Year see Johannes C. de Moor, *New Year with Canaanites and Israelites*, 2 vols., Serie Kamper Caheirs, nos. 21–2 (Kampen: Kok, 1972); D. J. A. Clines, "The Evidence for an Autumnal New Year in Preexilic Israel

Reconsidered," *Journal of Biblical Literature* 93 (1974): 22–40; James C. Vanderkam, s.v. "Calendars, Ancient Israelite and Early Jewish," *Anchor Bible Dictionary* (New York: Doubleday, 1992), 1:814–20; and Robert F. Smith and Stephen D. Ricks, "New Year's Celebrations," in *Reexploring the Book of Mormon*, ed. Welch, 209–11.

13. See de Moor, *New Year*, 1:24–5; H. J. Kraus, *Worship in Israel: A Cultic History of the Old Testament*, trans. Geoffrey Buswell (Richmond: John Knox, 1966), 208.

14. It is recognized that this assumption is speculative; it would require a great deal of research and writing beyond the scope of this paper to address each tradition in postexilic Judaism to see if it indeed reflects earlier Israelite understanding. Where possible I have tried to include both preexilic and postexilic examples of each topic below, but all conclusions, as in any field of science or the arts, are tentative and subject to verification or dismissal.

15. For a discussion of the New Year and judgment as understood in ancient Mesopotamia, see Jacob Klein, s.v. "Akītu," in *Anchor Bible Dictionary*.

16. Louis Jacobs, *The Book of Jewish Practice* (New Jersey: Behrman House, 1987), 109–10.

17. For a general discussion of creation and New Year traditions see Mircea Eliade, *The Myth of the Eternal Return*, trans. Willard R. Trask (Princeton: Princeton University Press, 1954), 51–92.

18. W. G. Lambert, "Myth and Ritual as Conceived by the Babylonians," *Journal of Semitic Studies* 13 (1968): 107–8; compare Stephen D. Ricks, "Liturgy and Cosmogony: The Ritual Use of Creation Accounts in the Ancient Near East," in *Temples*, ed. Parry, 118–25.

19. E. O. James, *Creation and Cosmology: A Historical and Comparative Inquiry* (Leiden: E. J. Brill, 1969), 29.

20. Jacobs, *Jewish Practice*, 110; compare Babylonian Talmud, *Rosh Hashanah*, 10b.

21. See John A. Tvedtnes, "Priestly Clothing in Bible Times," in *Temples*, ed. Parry, 649–704, for discussion on the garments of the priests and their significance.

22. In light of the possible Day of Atonement tradition surrounding Jacob's sermon, it is of further interest to note that the word *atonement* appears only nine times in the small plates of Nephi. Four of the nine are spoken in this sermon. No other derivative of the word *atone* is found in the small plates.

23. Babylonian Talmud, *Kiddushin* 71a.

24. For brief discussions of this, see William J. Hamblin, "Temple Motifs in Jewish Mysticism," in *Temples*, ed. Parry, 454–5; and Hugh Nibley, "On the Sacred and the Symbolic," in *Temples*, ed. Parry, 558–9.

25. Jacobs, *Jewish Practice*, 113.

26. Ibid., 116.

27. Babylonian Talmud, *Yoma*, 87b.

28. Tvedtnes, "King Benjamin," 199–201 outlines the events of Exodus 24 (the giving of the law to Israel at Sinai), calling it the "first Sukkot."

29. See ibid., 207–9, for a discussion of *Sukkot* liturgy.

30. For Near Eastern examples in general see Samuel H. Hooke, ed., *Myth, Ritual, and Kingship* (Oxford: Clarendon, 1958); and Stephen D. Ricks and John J. Sroka, "King, Coronation, and Temple: Enthronement Ceremonies in History," in *Temples*, ed. Parry, 246–50. For kingship connections to cultic festivals in Israel see Sigmund Mowinckel, *Psalmenstudien*, book 2, *Das Thronbesteigungsfest Jahwäs und der Ursprung der Eschatologie* (Oslo: Christiania, 1922); also J. H. Eaton, *Kingship and Psalms* (London: SCM Press, 1976). Problems concerning cultic renewal of kingship in Israel are outlined in Tryggve N. D. Mettinger, *King and Messiah: The Civil and Sacral Legitimation of the Israelite Kings*, Coniectanea Biblica Old Testament Series 8 (Lund: CWK Gleerup, 1976), 304–8, in which he states that "there is no conclusive evidence to prove this theory. Thus, in the final analysis the question must be left open" (308).

31. Mowinckel, *He That Cometh,* trans. G. W. Anderson (New York: Abingdon Press, 1954), 139.

32. These divisions are based upon historical, political, and social elements: Chapters 1–39 deal primarily with the events contemporary with the Assyrian invasion of the Northern Kingdom of Israel, while in chapters 40–55, Babylon is the enemy. In chapters 1–39, Israel is subject to the Assyrian king, while Cyrus of Persia is the gentile king in chapters 40–55. In chapters 1–39 the people in Jerusalem are threatened by an Assyrian invasion, while chapters 40–55 are directed at Israel in Babylonian exile. Chapters 56–66 are typically offset from the rest since they portray the Jewish community founded once again, Jerusalem inhabited, and the temple rebuilt. For further information see Richard Clifford, s.v. "Isaiah, Book of (Second Isaiah)," in *Anchor Bible Dictionary.*

33. The dating and authorship of these units is a subject of debate, partly because of the "prophetic" content of Isaiah's words. For example, since the primary theme of Isaiah 40–55 is the deliverance of Israel out of Babylonian exile by the hand of Cyrus (all of which are events in the future to Isaiah), then it is generally concluded among biblical scholars that Isaiah could not have written this section. However, such issues as these would not be obstacles to those who believe in prophetic vision.

34. A title coined by B. Duhm for those poetic passages in Isaiah that refer to a servant (e.g., Isaiah 42:1–4; 49:1–6; 50:4–9; and 52:13–53:12). Scholars are divided as to the identity of the servant. Moses, other Old Testament prophets or kings, Cyrus, Isaiah himself, and the nation of Israel are some of the interpretations put forth. Many Christians see Christ as fulfilling the role of the servant.

35. J. H. Eaton, *Festal Drama in Deutero-Isaiah* (London: SPCK, 1979), 4.

36. J. Begrich, Studien zu Dueterojesaja (Munich: 1963).

37. Mowinckel, *He That Cometh,* 139.

38. See I. Engnell, "The ʿEbed Yahweh Songs and the Suffering Messiah in 'Deutero-Isaiah,'" *Bulletin of the John Rylands Library* 31 (1948): 54–93; Eaton, *Festal Drama.*

39. Engnell, "ʿEbed Yahweh Songs," 64.

40. Mowinckel, *He That Cometh,* 97–8.

41. Ibid., 125.

42. Ibid., 133.

43. The fact that Jacob's speech was spread out over two days is another strong indicator that this is a festival setting.

44. Joan Oates, *Babylon* (London: Thames and Hudson, 1986), 176.

45. For an outline and discussion of this ceremony, see Hugh W. Nibley, "A New Look at the Pearl of Great Price: Part 7, The Unknown Abraham," *Improvement Era,* June 1969, 126–32, and July 1969, 97–101. Ricks and Sroka in "King," 249–53, discuss elements of ritual combat in connection with enthronement ceremonies, wherein the king and his subjects engage in mock battles with the forces of chaos and evil.

46. Eaton, *Festal Drama,* 12.

47. Rahab and Yam ("the sea") are the mythical forces of chaos that Yahweh overcomes.

48. Eaton, *Festal Drama,* 13–7.

49. Jacobs, *Jewish Practice,* 109.

50. Eaton, *Festal Drama,* 17.

51. Ibid., 17–8.

52. See 2 Nephi 11:4; 25:29–30; Jacob 4:5; 7:7; Jarom 1:11; Mosiah 3:15; 13:27–28; 16:14–15; Alma 25:15–16; 30:3; 34:13; 3 Nephi 1:24–25; 9:17; 15:2–5; Ether 12:11.

Nephi's Use of Isaiah 2–14 in 2 Nephi 12–30

David Rolph Seely

Pride stands behind the many evils plainly exposed by Isaiah, and it also lies at the foundation of the devil's works, as explained and prophetically identified by Nephi.

It is no secret that Nephi loved the writings of the prophet Isaiah, nor is it surprising that the Isaiah passages in the Book of Mormon, particularly the long quotation found in 2 Nephi 12–24, provide great challenges to modern readers. Readers often ask why Nephi included particular passages from Isaiah in his writings and what message Nephi would have us learn from that passage. Nephi does much to help readers understand the words of Isaiah by answering these questions both directly and indirectly in his introductory statements and through his commentaries. For example, Nephi introduces his quotation of Isaiah 48 and 49 in 1 Nephi 20–21 by indicating that the prophet's words refer to the scattering and gathering of Israel: "Hear ye the words of the prophet, which were written unto all the house of Israel, and liken them unto yourselves" (1 Nephi 19:24). He then explains to his brothers Laman and Lemuel that these chapters refer to a temporal as well as a spiritual scattering of Israel, including the scattering and gathering of the Nephite and Lamanite seed (see 1 Nephi 22).

Nephi also gives us several important keys to reading and understanding the prophecies of Isaiah. For example, Nephi teaches that readers should read and interpret Isaiah's prophecies as "pertaining to things both temporal and spiritual" (1 Nephi 22:3); that readers should liken those prophecies to themselves and to "all men" (2 Nephi 11:8); and that readers will enhance their study and understanding of Isaiah by becoming familiar with the manner of prophesying among the Jews (see 2 Nephi 25:1), by being "filled with the spirit of prophecy" (2 Nephi 25:4), and by living "in the days that the prophecies of Isaiah shall be fulfilled" (2 Nephi 25:7).[1]

One other key to understanding Isaiah is to become familiar with the common themes he addresses. The poetry of Isaiah is like a musical fugue that intertwines several different themes. A reader unfamiliar with this style may feel lost with so many themes being treated at once, but one of the easiest and most effective ways to study Isaiah is to read for a specific theme and then follow that theme throughout the Isaiah passages and the accompanying commentary by the Book of Mormon prophets. John Welch has demonstrated how certain themes are found both in Nephite prophecy and throughout the Isaiah chapters quoted in the Book of Mormon. In particular he identifies the main themes of (1) Jesus Christ as the Messiah, (2) the scattering of Israel, (3) the day of the gentiles, and (4) the gathering and restoration of Israel, leading to the judgment of the world.[2] As we gain familiarity with each of the themes, we are better able to appreciate and understand the full score of Isaiah. This study will trace some of the prominent themes of Isaiah highlighted and emphasized by Nephi: the coming of the Messiah, the scattering and gathering of Israel, and pride.

The Coming of the Messiah in Isaiah's and Nephi's Writings

Nephi placed great emphasis on the coming of the Messiah, one of the central themes of Isaiah. He identifies this as one of the main reasons he included the long quotation of Isaiah 2–14 in his writings in 2 Nephi. Nephi first wove the messianic theme from Isaiah into his second book by including a sermon given by his brother Jacob (see 2 Nephi 6–10), who quoted extensively from Isaiah on the themes of the scattering and gathering of Israel and most prominently on the theme of the coming of the Redeemer, Jesus Christ. After recording Jacob's sermon, Nephi includes in his record "more of the words of Isaiah," because, he says, "my soul delighteth in his words. For I will liken his words unto my people, and I will send them forth unto all my children, for he verily saw my Redeemer, even as I have seen him" (2 Nephi 11:2). He then includes all of Isaiah 2–14 (in 2 Nephi 12–24), chapters that contain many explicit prophecies about the Messiah as well as several allusions to his coming. For example, in these chapters we find the verses "Behold, a virgin shall conceive, and shall bear a son, and shall call his name Immanuel" (2 Nephi 17:14, parallel to Isaiah 7:14) and "For unto us a child is born, unto us a son is given; and the government shall be upon his shoulder; and his name shall be called, Wonderful, Counselor, The Mighty God, The Everlasting Father, The Prince of Peace" (2 Nephi 19:6, parallel to Isaiah 9:6), and the prophecy of the stem of Jesse (see 2 Nephi 21, parallel to Isaiah 11). In his own prophecy, which follows the Isaiah chapters, Nephi explains the coming of the Messiah to the Jews (see 2 Nephi 25:12–13) and to the descendants of his people (see 2 Nephi 26:1–9), as well as Christ's manifestation to the gentiles (see 2 Nephi 26:12–13) and to all nations (see 2 Nephi 29:8–9).

The Succession of Nations in Nephi's Quotation of Isaiah

In addition to the theme of the Messiah, the themes of the scattering and gathering of Israel, destruction, and restoration are likewise intertwined and developed throughout these passages in 2 Nephi 12–30. Both Isaiah and Nephi are interested in the coming events that will affect the rise and fall and destinies of a series of national groups.

The Isaiah texts in 2 Nephi 12–24 deal with the succession of the Old World peoples and kingdoms of Judah, Ephraim, Syria, Assyria, and Babylon; likewise, Nephi's subsequent chapters, 2 Nephi 25–30, also deal with various groups of people, namely, the Jews, the Lehites, and the gentiles. Table 1 outlines the contents of 2 Nephi 12–30.

Table 1
**Isaiah's Prophecies in 2 Nephi 12–24,
Parallel to Isaiah 2–14**

2 Nephi / Isaiah[3]	People Addressed or Discussed
12/2	Judah and Jerusalem, destruction
13/3	Judah, Jerusalem, daughters of Zion
14/4	Zion's daughters
15/5	Judah as a vineyard, destruction
16/6	Isaiah's call, iniquity of Judah
17/7	Syria and Ephraim, destruction
18/8	Syria and Ephraim, destruction
19/9	Syria and Ephraim, destruction
20/10	Assyria, destruction
21/11	Israel, gathering
22/12	Israel, gathering
23/13	Babylon, type of the world, destruction
24/14	Babylon, type of the world, destruction

Nephi's Prophecies in 2 Nephi

2 Nephi	People Addressed or Discussed
25	**Jews, history**
26	Nephites/Lehites, history
26–29	Gentiles, history
30:1–2	Gentiles to enter the covenant
30:3–6	Lamanites to enter the covenant
30:7	Jews to believe in Christ
30:8–18	all nations to hear the Gospel

Table 1 shows that Isaiah 2–14 and 2 Nephi 12–24 pertain to a succession of ancient nations and peoples known from the world of Isaiah. A closer examination of these passages helps us better understand how these chapters fit together.

Chapters 12–16 of 2 Nephi present the iniquities of covenant Israel and Judah, including the vivid image of the mincing daughters of Zion (see chapters 13–14) and the allegory of the vineyard (see chapter 15). Because of its iniquities, Israel was destroyed and exiled by Assyria in 722 B.C., and Judah met the same fate in 587 B.C. Chapter 16 gives an account of the call of Isaiah to be a prophet.[4]

Chapters 17–19 discuss the apostasy of Ephraim and its collusion with Syria in an alliance that threatens Judah. In chapter 17, Isaiah warns Ahaz, king of Judah, not to join the Syro-Ephraimite alliance against Assyria, because the alliance would soon be destroyed. In fulfillment of this prophecy, Assyria destroyed the Syro-Ephraimite alliance in 732 B.C. Chapter 20 discusses Assyria, the nation that inflicted the divine punishment upon Syria and Ephraim in 732 B.C. but was itself destroyed in 612 B.C.

Chapters 21 and 22 juxtapose the theme of destruction in the preceding chapters with the glorious coming of the Messiah and his servants, who together will usher in the day of the Lord, delivering and gathering covenant Israel and thus leading to a reunification of Ephraim and Judah. Chapters 23 and 24 prophesy of the rise of Babylon, the nation that destroyed Assyria and inflicted the divinely ordained destruction of Judah and Jerusalem in 587 B.C. but was destroyed by the Medes in 539 B.C. Babylon represents the world, which must eventually be overcome by covenant Israel.[5]

In chapter 25, Nephi explains that Isaiah's words were difficult for his own people to understand. In contrast to the difficulty of understanding Isaiah's prophecies, Nephi says, "But behold, I proceed with mine own prophecy, according to my plainness; in the which I know that no man can err" (2 Nephi 25:7).

In 2 Nephi 25–30, then, Nephi prophesies "in plainness" (2 Nephi 25:4), looking into the future of three important groups of covenant Israel: the Jews (see 2 Nephi 25:9–30); the Lehites—that is, Nephites and Lamanites (see 2 Nephi 26:1–12); and the gentiles (see 2 Nephi 26:12–29:14). Nephi examines the relationship of the Messiah to each group, the problems each group has or will have with pride, the process by which Israel will be scattered for breaking the covenant, Israel's eventual gathering through the restoration of the gospel, and Israel's final acceptance of the Messiah. Nephi concludes his prophecy with a chiastic review of the status of each of these groups in relation to the Holy One of Israel, Jesus Christ. He prophesies that the last group, the gentiles, will repent, accept the Messiah, and enter into the covenant first (see 2 Nephi 30:1–2); then that the remnant of the Lehites, the Lamanites (see 2 Nephi 30:3–6), will do the same; and finally, the first group, the Jews, will embrace the Lord Jesus Christ (see 2 Nephi 30:7). The gospel will be taken to all nations (see 2 Nephi 30:8–18), leading to the millennium, which Nephi describes with citations from Isaiah 11.

Isaiah and Nephi Address the Theme of Pride

In a discussion about how to teach this particular sequence of Isaiah chapters in the Book of Mormon effectively to undergraduate students, one of my colleagues, Fred Woods, told me, "The key to these chapters is the theme of pride." Sure enough, as I began to read these passages looking for this theme, I discovered he was right. Pride is a central theme of the prophecies of Isaiah that Nephi quotes and also of Nephi's own prophecies. Recognizing this theme can help us better understand and appreciate these passages and to identify the metaphors used by Isaiah and Nephi to warn us against pride.

The sin of pride is identified by both Isaiah and Nephi as the common denominator in the fall, destruction, and scattering of all the nations and peoples discussed in Isaiah's prophecies. Table 2 names each of these groups and gives at least one passage representative of each group's acceptance or rejection of the Messiah and his gospel and containing Isaiah's condemnation of each group's pride.

Table 2

**The Theme of Pride in 2 Nephi 12–24
(Parallel to Isaiah 2–14)**

Speaking of the destruction of Judah and Jerusalem:

And it shall come to pass that the lofty looks of man shall be humbled, and the haughtiness of men shall be bowed down, and the Lord alone shall be exalted in that day. The day of the Lord shall be upon every one that is proud and lofty. (2 Nephi 12:11–12, parallel to Isaiah 2:11–12)

Moreover, the Lord saith: Because the daughters of Zion are haughty, and walk with stretched-forth necks and wanton eyes . . . the Lord will smite with a scab the crown of the head. (2 Nephi 13:16–17, parallel to Isaiah 3:16–17)

And the mean man shall be brought down, and the mighty man shall be humbled, and the eyes of the lofty shall be humbled. (2 Nephi 15:15, parallel to Isaiah 5:15)

[Isaiah's message will] make the heart of this people fat, and make their ears heavy, and shut their eyes . . . until the cities be wasted without inhabitant. (2 Nephi 16:10–11, parallel to Isaiah 6:10–11)

> **Speaking of the destruction of Syria and Ephraim:**
>
> And all the people shall know, even Ephraim and the inhabitants of Samaria, that say in the pride and stoutness of heart: The bricks are fallen down, but we will build with hewn stones; the sycamores are cut down, but we will change them into cedars. (2 Nephi 19:9–10)
>
> **Speaking of the destruction of Assyria:**
>
> [Assyria] saith: By the strength of my hand and by my wisdom I have done these things; . . . And my hand hath found as a nest the riches of the people. . . . Shall the ax boast itself against him that heweth therewith? Shall the saw magnify itself against him that shaketh it? (2 Nephi 20:13–15, parallel to Isaiah 10:13–15)
>
> Behold, the Lord, the Lord of Hosts shall lop the bough with terror; and the high ones of stature shall be hewn down; and the haughty shall be humbled. (2 Nephi 20:33, parallel to Isaiah 10:33)
>
> **Speaking of the destruction of Babylon:**
>
> And I will punish the world for evil, and the wicked for their iniquity; I will cause the arrogancy of the proud to cease, and will lay down the haughtiness of the terrible. (2 Nephi 23:11, parallel to Isaiah 13:11)
>
> [The King of Babylon, typified as Lucifer, has said in his heart:] I will ascend above the heights of the clouds; I will be like the Most High. Yet thou shalt be brought down to hell, to the sides of the pit. (2 Nephi 24:14–15, parallel to Isaiah 14:14–15)

Table 2 shows that the theme of pride is an important and recurring theme throughout the Isaiah passages that Nephi quotes. The theme of pride is also central to Nephi's own prophecy in 2 Nephi 25–30, which prophesies the futures of the Jews, the Lehites, and the gentiles. Nephi describes how the Messiah will present himself to each of these peoples and how in each case the main reason for their rejection of the Messiah and his gospel is pride. Ultimately, however, through the revelation of the Book of Mormon to the gentiles, each group will repent of its pride, be brought back to a knowledge of the Messiah, and enter into a covenant with the Lord. Table 3 outlines Nephi's progression through the groups' reactions to the Messiah and the gospel, giving representative passages of their attitudes and actions.

Table 3

Nephi's Prophecy: Pride in 2 Nephi 25–30

A The Jews' rejection of the Messiah, who will come first to them (see 2 Nephi 25:9–30):

"Behold, they will reject him, because of their iniquities, and the hardness of their hearts, and the stiffness of their necks" (2 Nephi 25:12).

B The Nephites' initial acceptance of the Messiah, who appeared to them after his death, and their subsequent rejection of him (see 2 Nephi 26:1–11):

After "the Son of righteousness shall appear unto them . . . For the reward of their pride and their foolishness they shall reap destruction; for because they yield unto the devil and choose works of darkness rather than light" (verses 9–10).

C The gentiles' reaction to the Messiah and to the restoration of the gospel in the latter days (see 2 Nephi 26:12–29:14):

"It must needs be that the Gentiles be convinced also that Jesus is the Christ, the Eternal God" (2 Nephi 26:12), but "the Gentiles are lifted up in the pride of their eyes, . . . and preach up unto themselves their own wisdom and their own learning, that they may get gain and grind upon the face of the poor" (2 Nephi 26:20).

"Because of pride, and because of false teachers, and false doctrine, their churches have become corrupted, and their churches are lifted up; because of pride they are puffed up" (2 Nephi 28:12).

"O the wise, and the learned, and the rich, that are puffed up in the pride of their hearts, and all those who preach false doctrines . . . revile against that which is good" (2 Nephi 28:15–16).

C' The gentiles' acceptance of the gospel (see 2 Nephi 28–30:3):

"As many of the Gentiles as will repent are the covenant people . . . for the Lord covenanteth with none save it be with them that repent and believe in his Son, who is the Holy One of Israel. . . . There shall be many [gentiles] who shall believe the words which are written; and they shall carry them forth unto the remnant of [the Jews]" (2 Nephi 30:2–3).

B' The Lamanites' acceptance of the gospel (see 2 Nephi 30:3–6):

"They shall be restored unto the knowledge of their fathers, and also to the knowledge of Jesus Christ, which was had among their fathers" (verse 5).

A' The Jews' acceptance of the gospel (see 2 Nephi 30:1–7):

"And it shall come to pass that the Jews which are scattered also shall begin to believe in Christ; and they shall begin to gather . . . [and] become a delightsome people" (verse 7).

The Isaiah passages in 2 Nephi 12–24 express pride using many different terms and images: "lofty looks," "haughtiness," "stretched forth necks and wanton eyes," "mighty man," "eyes of the lofty," "fat heart," "heavy ears," "shut . . . eyes," "pride and stoutness of heart," "strength of my hand," "high ones of stature," and "arrogancy of the proud." A close inspection of Nephi's prophecy (in 2 Nephi 26:12–29:14) shows that Nephi incorporated many of these Isaianic concepts and phrases. Consider the following five examples where Nephi apparently borrowed Isaiah's concepts (the italicized words and phrases indicate specific places where Nephi appears to have used Isaianic phraseology).

Example 1

Commentary by Nephi	Source from Isaiah
And the gentiles are lifted up in the pride of *their eyes*, and have stumbled, because of the greatness of their stumbling block, that they have built up many churches; nevertheless, they put down the power and miracles of God, and *preach up unto themselves their own wisdom and their own learning.* (2 Nephi 26:20)	Wo unto the *wise in their own eyes and prudent in their own sight!* (2 Nephi 15:21, parallel to Isaiah 5:21)
They may get gain and *grind upon the face of the poor.* (2 Nephi 26:20)	What mean ye? Ye beat my people to pieces, and *grind the faces of the poor.* (2 Nephi 13:15, parallel to Isaiah 3:15)

Nephi describes the gentiles in terms Isaiah used, in Isaiah's parable of the vineyard (found in Isaiah 5), to describe Israel. The irony of the gentiles' pattern is that they build up many churches but deny the power of God and preach their own learning as doctrine; the irony in Isaiah 5 is that Israel was "planted" and cared for by the Lord (Isaiah 5:2), and yet the

Israelites "regard not the work of the Lord, neither consider the operation of his hands" (Isaiah 5:12). Both Israel and theentiles glorified and relied on human instead of divine wisdom, and both took advantage of the poor to get gain.

Example 2

Commentary by Nephi	Source from Isaiah
And all the nations that fight against Zion, . . . yea, it shall be unto them, even as unto a hungry man which dreameth, and behold he eateth but he awaketh and his soul is empty; or like unto a thirsty man which dreameth, and behold he drinketh but he awaketh and behold he is faint, and his soul hath appetite. (2 Nephi 27:3)	And he shall snatch on the right hand and be hungry; and he shall not be satisfied; they shall eat every man the flesh of his own arm.[6] (2 Nephi 19:20, parallel to Isaiah 9:20)

Nephi used the vivid imagery of hunger and thirst that cannot be satisfied to describe those who seek to destroy Zion in the latter days. The imagery in Isaiah 9 refers to the quarreling between Ephraim, Manasseh, and Judah, who are unable to stand against Assyria. These three tribes of Israel were united only in one thing—to take advantage of the poor, widows, and orphans (see 2 Nephi 20:2, parallel to Isaiah 10:2), showing a greed that is manifest by the enemies of God in the latter days as well.

Example 3

Commentary by Nephi	Source from Isaiah
They *rob the poor* because of their fine sanctuaries; they *rob*	[They] turn away the needy from judgment, and to take away the

the poor because of their fine clothing; and they persecute the meek and the poor in heart, because in their pride they are puffed up. (2 Nephi 28:13)	right from *the poor* of my people, that widows may be their prey, and that they may *rob* the fatherless! (2 Nephi 20:2, parallel to Isaiah 10:2)

One of the first tenets of the eternal gospel is to care for the poor and the oppressed. Under the law of Moses, failing to care for the widows and orphans was a serious offense. The Lord said on Mount Sinai, "If thou afflict them in any wise, and they cry at all unto me, I will surely hear their cry; And my wrath shall wax hot, and I will kill you with the sword; and your wives shall be widows, and your children fatherless" (Exodus 22:23–24). The prophets in Israel all echoed the same theme. Not only did the covenant people of Israel neglect the poor, but they deliberately oppressed the poor and needy for their own gain. Worse, they did it in the name of religion. Ancient Israel was destroyed and scattered for breaking the covenant, and Nephi prophesies that the Nephites would eventually be destroyed for the same reason. The gentiles have the same problem, but they can still repent: "Nevertheless, I will be merciful unto them, saith the Lord God, if they will repent" (2 Nephi 28:32).

Example 4

Commentary by Nephi	**Source from Isaiah**
O the wise, and the learned, and the rich, that are puffed up in the pride of their hearts, and all those who preach false doctrines, . . . for they shall be thrust down to hell! (2 Nephi 28:15)	And it shall come to pass that the lofty looks of man shall be humbled, and the haughtiness of men shall be bowed down, and the Lord alone shall be exalted in that day. (2 Nephi 12:11, parallel to Isaiah 2:11)

The Book of Mormon and the book of Isaiah both teach the lesson that those who are proud will ultimately be humbled by being cast down. Isaiah and Nephi teach this lesson with the stories of Israel, Assyria, Babylon, and Persia. The Book of Mormon also illustrates it, with the stories of the fall of the Jaredites and the destruction of the Nephites. Both books warn all people, especially the latter-day covenant people, of the dangers of pride.

Example 5

Commentary by Nephi	**Source from Isaiah**
Cursed is he that putteth his trust in man, or *maketh flesh his arm,* or shall hearken unto the precepts of men, save their precepts shall be given by the power of the Holy Ghost. (2 Nephi 28:31)	Their land is also full of idols; they *worship the work of their own hands,* that which their own fingers have made. (2 Nephi 12:8, parallel to Isaiah 2:8)

One aspect of pride that Isaiah points out is the folly of putting trust in the things of men instead of in the things of God. In Isaiah, the lesson is dramatized in a parable about an idolatrous woodcutter who cuts down a tree with his own hands and makes an idol, which he then worships (see Isaiah 44:9–20). But the idol does not have the power to save. In 2 Nephi 28:4, Nephi prophesies the fate of those who "err because they are taught by the precepts of men." For the gentiles, just as for ancient Israel, to trust in the arm of flesh is a form of idolatry.

Isaiah looks into the future and sees the destruction of a series of nations and peoples, and in each case he cites pride as the cause of their rejection of the Lord and of their eventual scattering and destruction. In his own prophecy about the history of the Jews, Lehites, and gentiles, Nephi also identifies, often in the language of Isaiah, the main challenge that each of these groups faces as pride.

The Theme of Pride throughout the Writings of Nephi

Pride is a central theme in the writings of Nephi, and it is also one of the most important themes of the whole Book of Mormon. Nephi sees in vision the history and future of the world, including his own people's history, and he understands that the handling of pride is a determining factor in the welfare and future of all peoples. In Nephi's vision of the tree of life, the large and spacious building is identified as the "pride of the world" (1 Nephi 11:36), or the "pride of the children of men" (1 Nephi 12:18). The Messiah is opposed by the people "that were in [the] large and spacious building," which the angel identifies as "the world and the wisdom thereof," who are gathered up to fight against the Lamb (see 1 Nephi 11:35–36). For Nephi, the large and spacious building is the embodiment of the great and abominable church. The pride of the world is further defined in relation to the churches that will be founded in the day of the gentiles: "All churches which are built up to get gain, . . . to get power over the flesh, and those who are built up to become popular in the eyes of the world" (1 Nephi 22:23). Nephi affirms that the "church of the devil" has "dominion over all the earth, among all nations, kindreds, tongues, and people" (1 Nephi 14:10–11).

On a more personal level, Nephi identifies pride as one of the main reasons that his brothers Laman and Lemuel reject the teachings of their father and of Nephi. Nephi describes his brothers as stiff-necked (see 1 Nephi 2:11) and hard-hearted (see 1 Nephi 2:18; 7:8; 15:3). They refuse to listen to the words of Lehi and Nephi, rebel against the Lord, and ultimately seek to kill Nephi and his people.

To Nephi, Laman and Lemuel represent all Israel throughout history: just as Laman and Lemuel are hard of heart, so

are the ancient Israelites (see 1 Nephi 17:30, 42), the future
Lamanites (see 2 Nephi 5:21), the Jews (see 1 Nephi 19:7;
2 Nephi 25:12), and the Nephites, his own descendants, who
would in the end be destroyed "for the reward of their pride"
(2 Nephi 26:10).[7] Nephi, in his panoramic view of history,
also sees pride as a central issue for the gentiles: if they
"harden not their hearts against the Lamb of God, they shall
be numbered . . . among the house of Israel" (1 Nephi 14:2).
Nephi fervently teaches in his writings that just as the "proud
and lofty" of the past were destroyed, so will "every one
who is lifted up . . . be brought low" (2 Nephi 12:12, parallel
to Isaiah 2:12).

The sermon by Nephi's brother Jacob, in 2 Nephi 6–10,
also contains many references to pride. In that speech Jacob
warns of the imminent destruction of those who "when they
are learned . . . think they are wise, and they hearken not
unto the counsel of God, for they set it aside, supposing they
know of themselves" (2 Nephi 9:28) and of those worldly
rich, who, "because they are rich . . . despise the poor, and
they persecute the meek, and their hearts are upon their treasures; wherefore their treasure is their god" (2 Nephi 9:30).
Jacob defines true humility by juxtaposing it with learning
and wealth: "And the wise, and the learned, and they that
are rich, who are puffed up because of their learning, and
their wisdom, and their riches—yea, they are they whom he
[God] despiseth; and save they shall cast these things away,
and consider themselves fools before God, and come down
in the depths of humility, he will not open unto them"
(2 Nephi 9:42).

Nephi teaches that the solution to pride is humility. The
opposite of a prideful heart is a humble, softened heart, an
image occasionally expressed in the Book of Mormon.[8] When
Lehi receives his call to be a prophet, his family members
are faced with great challenges. Perhaps the greatest is their

decision whether to follow and obey Lehi. Because of the hardness of their hearts, Laman and Lemuel refuse to listen to their father, but Nephi turns to the Lord. He records, "Wherefore, I did cry unto the Lord; and behold he did visit me, and did soften my heart that I did believe all the words which had been spoken by my father; wherefore, I did not rebel against him like unto my brothers" (1 Nephi 2:16). One of the keys to overcoming pride is sincere and humble prayer—trusting in the Lord rather than ourselves. Through prayer we petition the Lord to extend his power and soften our hearts. Nephi learns this concept early in his life, and throughout his life he constantly turns to the Lord, while his brothers do not. Nephi alludes to his own struggles in the psalm of Nephi and concludes, "O Lord, I have trusted in thee, and I will trust in thee forever. I will not put my trust in the arm of flesh; for I know that cursed is he that putteth his trust in the arm of flesh" (2 Nephi 4:34). In the end, Nephi is able to endure trials and challenges, while his brothers become hardened and bitter, ultimately refusing to come to the tree of life.

The Lord is able to soften the hearts of the children of men in dramatic ways. After Laman and Lemuel tie Nephi up on the ship during their trip to the promised land, Nephi records, "And there was nothing save it were the power of God, which threatened them with destruction, could soften their hearts" (1 Nephi 18:20). King Lamoni describes the process by which the Lord softened the hearts of the Anti-Nephi-Lehies: "And behold, I thank my great God that he has given us a portion of his Spirit to soften our hearts" (Alma 24:8). And Jacob prophesies that in the latter days the Lord "will soften the hearts of the Gentiles, that they shall be like unto a father to [the Lamanites]; wherefore, the Gentiles shall be blessed and numbered among the house of Israel" (2 Nephi 10:18).

168 • *David Rolph Seely*

Conclusion

In 2 Nephi 11:2–7, Nephi explains that he desired to include the words of Isaiah in his record because his soul delighted in proving to his people the truth of the coming of Christ and of the covenant the Lord had made with their fathers. In verse 8, Nephi further announces that he would liken the words of Isaiah unto his own people. Throughout his own prophecy, which he delivers in "plainness" (2 Nephi 25:7), Nephi makes several specific allusions, often using Isaianic language, and many broad references to the Isaianic themes of the coming of the Messiah, the scattering and gathering of Israel, and destruction and restoration of covenant Israel and the nations around her. Crucial to the salvation of the covenant people and of all nations is the conquering of pride. Pride influences our relationships with ourselves, our fellow mortals, and our God. When we rely on the arm of flesh rather than on the Holy Ghost, when we ignore the poor and the oppressed, and when we worship idols—the works of our own hands—we separate ourselves from the Messiah. Isaiah and Nephi point to cases spanning thousands of years of history and prophecy in which pride plays a part in the downfall of the nations of Assyria and Babylon and the covenant peoples of Ephraim, Judah, and the Nephites and Lamanites.

Although pride is one of the greatest challenges we face in the latter days, the Book of Mormon's teachings can help us attain and maintain humility. As we read the warning against pride pronounced with eloquence by Isaiah and in plainness by Nephi, and as we study their other prophecies, may we remember the words Nephi wrote at the beginning of these prophecies and liken these words to ourselves (see 2 Nephi 11:8).

Notes

1. See Donald W. Parry, "Nephi's Keys to Understanding Isaiah (2 Nephi 25:1–8)," in this volume, which discusses these and other keys at length.

2. See John W. Welch, "Getting through Isaiah with the Help of the Nephite Prophetic View," in this volume.

3. The chapter numbers of the quotation of Isaiah 2–14 are 2 Nephi 12–24—numerically exactly ten more. An easy mnemonic device for identifying the Isaiah chapters in 2 Nephi 12–24 is simply to subtract ten from the 2 Nephi chapter numbers. To identify the 2 Nephi passage from the Isaiah 2–14 chapters, simply add ten.

4. See Stephen D. Ricks, "Heavenly Visions and Prophetic Calls in Isaiah, the Book of Mormon, and the Revelation of John," in this volume.

5. See also Sidney B. Sperry, "The Isaiah Quotation: 2 Nephi 12–24," *Journal of Book of Mormon Studies* 4/1 (1995): 192–208.

6. In the Old Testament, the closest parallel to the image of "trusting in the arm of flesh" is found in Jeremiah 17:5: "Cursed be the man that trusteth in man, and maketh flesh his arm, and whose heart departeth from the Lord." Since some of the writings of Jeremiah were on the brass plates (see 1 Nephi 5:1–13), Nephi may have borrowed this image from Jeremiah.

7. Nephi does not use the word *hard-hearted* in reference to the future Nephites, but it is a common phrase used by the other authors in the Book of Mormon to describe the Nephites in general. In particular, 4 Nephi 1:31 and 34 describe the beginning of the end for the Nephites, who "did harden their hearts" and attempted to kill the disciples of Jesus. Mormon used the image of the hard heart throughout his book to document the final destruction of the Nephites (see Mormon 1:17; 3:3, 12; 4:11).

8. For examples of the "hard heart" image, see 1 Nephi 3:28; 15:3; 16:2; for examples of images of a "softened heart" see 1 Nephi 2:16; 18:20.

Heavenly Visions and Prophetic Calls in Isaiah 6 (2 Nephi 16), the Book of Mormon, and the Revelation of John

Stephen D. Ricks

Isaiah's call, which involved a vision of God on his throne, a heavenly book, songs of praise, a commission, protests, and reassurances, compares instructively to the calls of Lehi and John.

From writing room table to the high throne of heaven, from the beginning of time to the end of the world, the visions of Isaiah, Lehi, and John the Revelator span the cosmos. Of all the prophets of ancient Israel or of the early church, none come as warmly recommended in the Book of Mormon as are Isaiah and John, the apostle of the Lamb. Nephi₃ records the risen Lord as saying, "Great are the words of Isaiah" (see 3 Nephi 23:1), and an angel affirmed to Nephi that the things that the apostle John should write "are just and true" (1 Nephi 14:23).

The writings of Isaiah and many parts of the Book of Mormon pronounce prophecies of judgment and hope on Israel. In the Bible, Isaiah's message is echoed in the Revelation of John, which provides hope for the people of the Lord but pronounces judgment on Babylon, or the world. This paper, illustrated with Christian religious art from the medieval and early Renaissance eras, considers common elements of these heavenly visions and prophetic calls as recorded in the writings of Isaiah, in the Book of Mormon, and in the book of Revelation.

Isaiah's call to be a prophet in Isaiah 6 and Lehi's call in 1 Nephi 1—experiences that are echoed by John in Revelation 1–5—contain basic elements of "call narratives": (1) a historical introduction that provides the setting of the vision; (2) the divine confrontation between the prophet and God or another holy being; (3) the prophet's reaction to the presence of God or to the holy being and the things he has heard; (4) the "throne-theophany," an experience in which the prophet sees the throne of God; (5) the receipt of a heavenly book; (6) the *qeḏuššāh*, a heavenly song in praise of God; (7) the receipt of the prophetic commission; (8) the prophet's objection or protest; and (9) the reassurance from God that the call is divine.[1] Isaiah's call contains elements that are also found in the calls of other Book of Mormon and biblical prophets. We will discuss these elements in relation to the account of Isaiah's call (as recorded not only in Isaiah 6, but also in 2 Nephi 16 in the Book of Mormon), other Book of Mormon prophets' calls (specifically that of Lehi), and the account of John's call in the book of Revelation.

Prophetic Call Narratives

1. Historical Introduction

The historical introduction provides the reader with information about the circumstances—such as the time, place, and setting—of the prophet's vision and call and may also contain biographical information about the prophet. The record of Isaiah's call in Isaiah 6 and 2 Nephi 16 indicates the specific time period and gives clues about the physical location: Isaiah's prophetic call takes place in the "year that king Uzziah died" (2 Nephi 16:1, parallel to Isaiah 6:1), and the experience may have occurred in the temple, possibly within the Holy of Holies. For instance, Isaiah indicates that he saw "the Lord sitting upon a throne, high and lifted up, and his train *filled the temple*" (2 Nephi 16:1, parallel to Isaiah 6:1). It has been suggested that the train of the robe represents the veil of the temple.[2] The account also explains that "the posts of the door moved at the voice of him that cried, and the house was filled with smoke" (2 Nephi 16:4, parallel to Isaiah 6:4). "The post of the door" and "the house" indicate that Isaiah was within a structure, and "the post of the door" seems to refer specifically to the doorway of the Holy of Holies.[3] The account also refers to what appears to be a religious sacrificial altar or, more likely, the incense altar within the temple:[4] "Then flew one of the seraphim unto me, having a live coal in his hand, *which he had taken with the tongs from off the altar*" (2 Nephi 16:6, parallel to Isaiah 6:6).

Lehi's call is set historically "in the commencement of the first year of the reign of Zedekiah, king of Judah," when "there came many prophets, prophesying unto the people that they must repent, or the great city Jerusalem must be destroyed" (1 Nephi 1:4). Nephi records that Lehi received his throne-theophany while "upon his bed" in "his own house at Jerusalem" (1 Nephi 1:7).

Though no specific date or setting is given in Revelation, John describes his own call to write letters to "the seven churches which are in Asia" (Revelation 1:11) as taking place when he was "in the Spirit on the Lord's day" (Revelation 1:10). The account also mentions his being "in the isle that is called Patmos" (Revelation 1:9).

2. Divine Confrontation

When a prophet is in the presence of a heavenly being, it is called "divine confrontation." The divine confrontation in Isaiah occurs during the throne-theophany itself. Isaiah records, "I saw also the Lord sitting upon a throne, high and lifted up, and his train filled the temple" (2 Nephi 16:1, parallel to Isaiah 6:1). He also describes seeing "seraphim" attending the Lord (see 2 Nephi 16:2, parallel to Isaiah 6:2). The divine confrontation usually involves the prophet's being presented to the council of heaven, and it often includes a reference to fire, which signifies the divine glory of God.[5] Isaiah's account implies that he saw the fire in his description of the smoke filling the house and possibly the "live coal" from the altar (2 Nephi 16:6, parallel to Isaiah 6:6). The smoke surrounds the heavenly messenger (often the Lord himself), making it possible for the mortal prophet's eye to endure the holy being's glory.[6]

Like the fire that preceded the children of Israel in the wilderness, a pillar of fire is also associated with Lehi's divine confrontation: "There came a pillar of fire and dwelt upon a rock before him; and he saw and heard much" (1 Nephi 1:6).[7] Shortly thereafter, Lehi experienced the throne-theophany: "And being thus overcome with the Spirit, he was carried away in a vision, even that he saw the heavens open, and he thought he saw God sitting upon his throne" (1 Nephi 1:8). Lehi also saw "One descending out of the midst of heaven, and he beheld that his luster was above that of the sun at noon-day. And he also saw twelve others following him, and their brightness did exceed that of the stars in the firmament" (1 Nephi 1:9–10).[8]

John experienced the divine confrontation when, being "in the Spirit," he heard behind him "a great voice, as of a trumpet, Saying, I am Alpha and Omega, the first and the last" (Revelation 1:10–11). Turning around to "see the voice," he saw "seven golden candlesticks; And in the midst of the seven candlesticks one like unto the Son of Man" (Revelation 1:12–13).

3. Reaction

In their visions, the prophets view God in his glory and learn of the nothingness of man and of the imminent destruction of the wicked. The effect of the divine confrontation and the knowledge conveyed in the visionary experience is both physical and emotional. In most accounts, besides being "astonished" and "overcome," the prophet is also physically weak or loses consciousness. Lehi, because of his vision of God's glory and of the imminent judgment on Jerusalem, "did quake and tremble exceedingly. . . . [A]nd he cast himself upon his bed, being overcome with the Spirit and the things which he had seen" (1 Nephi 1:6–7).

John reacted as did the prophet Ezekiel upon receiving his heavenly visitation: after seeing "one like unto the Son of Man," John "fell at his feet as dead." The Lord then "laid his right hand" upon John and commanded him to "Fear not" (Revelation 1:17; compare Daniel 10:7, 9).

Isaiah, overwhelmed by the majesty of the vision of God's glory and feeling his own nothingness, cried out, "Woe is me! for I am undone; because I am a man of unclean lips, and I dwell in the midst of a people of unclean lips; for mine eyes have seen the King, the Lord of Hosts" (2 Nephi 16:5, parallel to Isaiah 6:5). The angel reassured Isaiah by promising him forgiveness of his sins: "Then flew one of the seraphim unto me, having a live coal in his hand . . . ; And he laid it upon my mouth, and said: Lo, this has touched thy lips; and thine iniquity is taken away, and thy sin purged" (2 Nephi 16:6, parallel to Isaiah 6:6).[9] This act may have also served to prepare Isaiah for the calling he was about to receive.

4. Throne-Theophany

One of the most stressed parts of each prophet's call narrative is the receipt of the "throne-theophany," the experience in which the prophet sees the throne of God and sometimes even God himself sitting upon it, usually amidst the worshipping host of heaven. For example, the account of Lehi's throne-theophany records that God on his throne was "surrounded with numberless concourses of angels in the attitude of singing and praising their God" (1 Nephi 1:8).

The throne-theophany is such a powerful and significant experience and is so well described by prophets like

Ezekiel and John that many artists have attempted to capture the scene. As with most artwork, the accounts of throne-theophany are rich in symbolic elements. Throughout the remainder of this section, we will discuss examples of these artistic expressions, which help viewers imagine the power and glory of God manifested to his prophets.

Isaiah records, "I saw also the Lord sitting upon a throne, high and lifted up" (2 Nephi 16:1, parallel to Isaiah 6:1). Figure 1, an eleventh-century illustration of the vision of Isaiah, from the cathedral in Reichenau, Germany, depicts the Lord seated high on his throne, surrounded by a

Figure 1. Vision of Isaiah (11th century; Reichenau, Germany)

mandorla (an almond- or lozenge-shaped ornament). His feet are on the round orb of the sun, signifying his glory and transcendence. As recorded in 2 Nephi 16:2 (parallel to Isaiah 6:2), the Lord is also surrounded by angels with six wings—two covering the face, two covering the feet, and two with which to fly—who say to each other: "Holy, holy, holy, is the Lord of hosts: the whole earth is full of his glory" (2 Nephi 16:3, parallel to Isaiah 6:3). Note the angel in the lower left corner holding what appears to be a live coal.

Isaiah's description of the vision also influenced John's description of his vision of the heavenly temple: John records, "After this I looked, and, behold, a door was opened in heaven: and the first voice which I heard was as it were of a trumpet talking with me. . . . And immediately I was in the spirit: and, behold, a throne was set in heaven, and one sat on the throne" (Revelation 4:1–2).

Of the three accounts examined in this chapter, John's account of his throne-theophany contains the most detail about the symbolic elements he saw. A twelfth-century illustration from the Bible in the Bamberg Cathedral in Germany (see figure 2) depicts John's description of the exalted Lord sitting in glory upon a throne. Again, the Lord is surrounded by a *mandorla*. Around the throne are a man and three beasts—an eagle, a calf, and a lion—representing the four evangelists. Beneath the throne of heaven are twelve of the twenty-four elders, "clothed in white raiment [i.e., the garments of righteousness]; and they [have] on their heads crowns of gold" (Revelation 4:4). They also hold up horns that represent "seven lamps of fire burning before the throne, which are the seven Spirits of God" (Revelation 4:5). The Lord's feet rest upon a globe representing the glory of the cosmos, and beneath the globe is the "sea of glass like unto crystal" (Revelation 4:6). According to ancient style, this sea of glass is considered a person and has a face. The color scheme of this painting is striking: the Lord's throne and the *mandorla* are filled with blue; the green symbolizes the green lushness of the earth. The account in Revelation contains an element that is also found in the description of Ezekiel's vision—four creatures that were "full of eyes" (Revelation 4:6; compare Ezekiel 1:5, 18).

Accounts describing these visions of the throne of God, along with other scripture, have given us much understanding about the relationship between God's kingdom in

Figure 2. *Die Offenbarung des Johannes* (The Revelation of John) by Gertrud Schiller

heaven and his kingdom on earth. God's glory emanates over the earth from heaven, his temple. The basic Israelite conception of the world and God's dominion over the universe is given its finest expression in three places in the Old Testament: in the book's beginning, with the creation account in Genesis 1; near the middle of the book, in Psalm 24; and at its end, in Malachi 3.

Genesis 1 gives an account of the firmament separating the waters above the earth from the waters beneath the earth. Figure 3 shows the throne of heaven and the waters above located over the world and separated from the earth by a firmament. The waters below are also separated by a firmament. The firmament above is also equipped with "windows" (Hebrew *arubbāh*, plural *arubbôt*), which may also be rendered (as it is in the illustration in figure 3) "sluicegates" or "floodgates." In a world in which the waters of chaos are held at bay only by the firmament above the earth and the firmament beneath one's feet, it is no wonder that the great flood in Noah's day began when all "the fountains of the great deep [were] broken up, and the windows of heaven were opened" (Genesis 7:11).

From this passage in Genesis 1 and other passages in the Old Testament, we learn that the sequence of creation includes separating the waters from the dry land. The first firm places to emerge from the ocean are the mountains, after which comes the rest of the earth. The description in Genesis 1 is pertinent to our discussion of Isaiah's prophetic mission because, according to Jewish tradition, Jerusalem was the first dry land to have risen from the waters of chaos at the time of creation (see figure 3). We read in the Jewish *Midrash Tanḥuma*:

> Just as the navel is found at the center of a human being, so the Land of Israel is found at the center of the world. . . . Jerusalem is at the center of the Land of Israel,

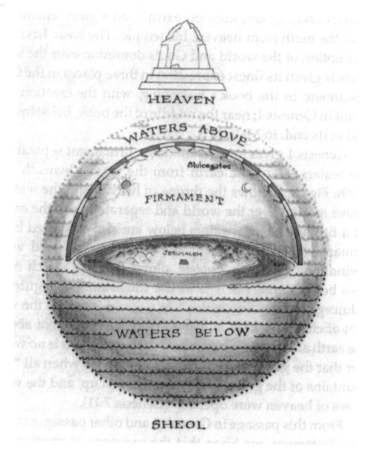

Figure 3. Throne of heaven and waters separated from earth by firmament

the Temple is at the center of Jerusalem, the Holy of Holies is at the center of the Temple, the Ark is at the center of the Holy of Holies and the Foundation Stone is in front of the Ark, which point is the foundation of the world.[10]

Thus it is not surprising to read in Psalm 24 (which may contain the world's first recorded temple recommend questionnaire)[11] the verse stating, "For he hath founded it [the temple in Jerusalem] upon the seas, and established it upon the floods" (Psalm 24:2).

As a final note on the earth's relationship to the heavens, we should consider the motif in the book of Isaiah of heaven as a house or tent over the earth. This is a common theme in ancient societies. The prophet Isaiah explains, "It is he that sitteth upon the circle of the earth, and the inhabitants thereof are as grasshoppers; that stretcheth out the heavens as a curtain, and spreadeth them out as a tent to dwell in" (Isaiah 40:22). And in Isaiah 44:24, he concludes, "Thus saith the Lord, thy redeemer, and he that formed thee from the womb, I am the Lord that maketh all things; that stretcheth forth the heavens alone; that spreadeth abroad the earth by myself." In figure 4, from the National Library in Paris, a cosmic tent is spread over the sacred tree of life. This connection may be reminiscent of the Arabs of the desert who constantly travel with a central tent post that represents the tree of life.[12] When the tent is pitched, this tree of life is set up first, then the tent is spread out from it, symbolizing the creation—or re-creation—of the universe.[13]

5. Presentation of a Heavenly Book

One common feature of many call narratives is the mention of a heavenly book or scroll from which the prophet is instructed to read. The book apparently contains judgments and teachings that the prophet should preach.[14] Although Isaiah's account in Isaiah 6 of his vision does not mention a heavenly book, we learn that he takes one later (see Isaiah 8:1; 30:8), and he is specifically instructed what to write and teach to the people. About Lehi's experience, Nephi records, "the first came and stood before my father, and gave unto him a book, and bade him that he should read. And . . . as he read, he was filled with the Spirit of the Lord. And he read, saying: Wo, wo, unto Jerusalem, for I have seen thine abominations! Yea, and many things did my father read

Figure 4. Cosmic tent spread over the sacred tree of life

concerning Jerusalem—that it should be destroyed, and the inhabitants thereof" (1 Nephi 1:11–13; compare Ezekiel 2:9–10). John also saw in vision "a book . . . sealed with seven seals" (Revelation 5:1) and was commanded to "Go and take the little book . . . and eat it up; and it shall make thy belly bitter, but it shall be in thy mouth sweet as honey" (Revelation 10:8–9).

6. The *Qeḏuššāh,* or Heavenly Song in Praise of God

The *qeḏuššāh,* or song in praise of God, is another element that is missing in the accounts of Isaiah's call narrative but is present in Lehi's and John's. Following the marvelous manifestations of God's greatness witnessed during the throne-theophany, Lehi is moved to praise the Lord's power and might. Nephi records, "And it came to pass that when my father had read and seen many great and marvelous things, he did exclaim many things unto the Lord; such as: Great and marvelous are thy works, O Lord God Almighty! Thy throne is high in the heavens, and thy power, and goodness, and mercy are over all the inhabitants of the earth; and, because thou art merciful, thou wilt not suffer those who come unto thee that they shall perish!" (1 Nephi 1:14). Isaiah does witness the seraphim praising the Lord, saying, "Holy, holy, holy,[15] is the Lord of hosts: the whole earth is full of his glory" (2 Nephi 16:3, parallel to Isaiah 6:2–3),[16] but there is no record of a *qeduššāh*. The passage in Revelation 4:8 repeats the same phrase glorifying God: "Holy, holy, holy, Lord God Almighty, which was, and is, and is to come,"[17] but several passages in John's account go on to describe the host of heaven praising, blessing, and honoring the Lord (see, for example, Revelation 4:9; 5:12–14; 11:17).

7. The Prophet Receives a Prophetic Commission

The height of the call narrative is the prophet's receipt of the command to speak forth boldly to the people. This command is his prophetic commission. It was a major responsibility of both Israel's prophets and Book of Mormon prophets, having themselves been warned, to warn the people of imminent destruction of the wicked. Much as Christ volunteered in the premortal council for his earthly mission, Isaiah volunteers for his call: "I heard the voice of the Lord, saying: Whom shall I send, and who will go for us? Then I said: Here am I; send me" (2 Nephi 16:8, parallel to Isaiah 6:8). Then comes the formal call: "And [God] said: Go and tell this people—Hear ye indeed, but they understood not; and see ye indeed, but they perceived not. Make the heart of this people fat, and make their ears heavy, and shut their eyes—lest they see with their eyes, and hear with their ears, and understand with their heart, and be converted and be healed" (2 Nephi 16:9–10, parallel to Isaiah 6:9–10).

John's prophetic commission appears in Revelation 1:19, where he is told, "Write the things which thou hast seen, and the things which are, and the things which shall be hereafter." Later, after John digests the book given him by an angel, he is commanded, "Thou must prophesy again before many peoples, and nations, and tongues, and kings" (Revelation 10:11).

Nephi's account of Lehi's vision obscures Lehi's formal call to prophesy, but Nephi records that his father did accept the call: "after the Lord had shown so many marvelous things unto my father, Lehi, yea, concerning the destruction of Jerusalem, behold he went forth among the people, and began to prophesy and to declare unto them concerning the things which he had both seen and heard . . . and also the things which he read in the book" (1 Nephi 1:18–19).

8. The Prophet Objects or Protests

Another common element in call narratives is for the prophet, once he has received the daunting commission to act as a representative of God's court, to address the Lord and the council, often in what seems to be an objection or protest or a request for reassurance. In response to the apparent difficulty of his call, Isaiah questions, "Lord, how long?" The Lord answers that Isaiah should serve as a prophet "until the cities be wasted without inhabitant, and the houses without man, and the land be utterly desolate; And the Lord have removed men far away, for there shall be a great forsaking in the midst of the land" (2 Nephi 16:11–12, parallel to Isaiah 6:11–12), thus confirming rather than dispelling the prophet's fears. No such objection occurs in Lehi's or John's account, although John's weeping before the council may be seen as such an outburst (see Revelation 5:4).

9. The Prophet Is Reassured

While the prophetic writings are tracts of judgment against a wayward Israel, they also express hope for the future. The Book of Mormon expresses a hope of reconstitution and return for a remnant of Israel. Isaiah maintains hope for a chastened though numerically diminished Israel to return to their Zion: "But yet [in the land] there shall be a tenth, and they shall return, . . . the holy seed shall be the substance thereof" (2 Nephi 16:13, parallel to Isaiah 6:13). The latter phrase is also rendered "the holy seed is its stock."[18] Gerhard Hasel states that

> on the basis of Job 14:7–9 it may be gathered that it was common knowledge that the root stock which was left in the ground at the felling of a tree was able to sprout again and thus bring forth new life. The felling of the tree certainly meant its destruction, but not the destruction of the life in the root stock. The root stock is thus the seat of new life.[19]

The idea of the holy seed sprouting leads to ideas found later in Isaiah that provide the structure for subsequent revelations about the new heaven and new earth: Isaiah records, "I will greatly rejoice in the Lord, my soul shall be joyful in my God; for he hath clothed me with the garments of salvation, he hath covered me with the robe of righteousness, as a bridegroom decketh himself with ornaments, and as a bride adorneth herself with her jewels" (Isaiah 61:10). This is certainly an image of hope and reassurance.

Once again, Nephi's writing makes no explicit reference to the Lord's reassurance to Lehi of the restoration of Israel, but we understand from later passages that convey Lehi's teachings to his children that this reassurance was in fact given (see 1 Nephi 1:16, 19). Lehi later received the Lord's blessing for the work he had performed: "For behold, it came to pass that the Lord spake unto my father, yea, even in a dream, and said unto him: Blessed art thou Lehi, because of the things which thou hast done; and because thou hast been faithful and declared unto this people the things which I commanded thee" (1 Nephi 2:1). Lehi's writing also says, "thou wilt not suffer those who come unto thee that they shall perish" (1 Nephi 1:14), a statement that shows that Lehi was reassured of the Lord.

John also apparently received a reassurance. Initially, when he "wept much, because no man was found worthy to open and to read the book, neither to look thereon" (Revelation 5:4), an angel approached him and told him to "Weep not: behold, [Christ] hath prevailed to open the book, and to loose the seven seals thereof" (Revelation 5:5). John was then assured that the time would come when the wicked would be destroyed and the Lord would reign over the righteous in the city of Jerusalem: "the fearful, and unbelieving, and the abominable . . . shall have their part in the lake which burneth with fire and brimstone" (Revelation 21:8), but "that great city, the holy Jerusalem," will descend "out of heaven from God" and shall shine with "the glory of God" (Revelation 21:10–11).

The Lord's Long-Term Perspective: Hope for Israel

Several chapters of Isaiah, including the final materials in Isaiah 55–66, describe a condition of restoration and redemption. So does the final part of the book of Revelation. A passage in the last chapter of Revelation is reminiscent of Lehi's dream of the tree of life as it is recorded in 1 Nephi 8:

> And he shewed me a pure river of water of life, clear
> as crystal, proceeding out of the throne of God and of the

> Lamb. In the midst of the street of it, and on either side of the river, was there the tree of life, which bare twelve manner of fruits, and yielded her fruit every month: and the leaves of the tree were for the healing of the nations. (Revelation 22:1–2)

This scene is illustrated in the Beatus commentary on the Apocalypse. In figure 5, the stream of water originates from the throne of God. On either side of the stream stands a tree of life. In Revelation we also read, "And to her [Zion] was granted that she should be arrayed in fine linen, clean and white: for the fine linen is the righteousness of saints" (Revelation 19:8). Just as the fine linen of the bride Zion stands as a metaphor for the righteous deeds of the saints, so are her ornaments symbols of the spiritual fidelity and holy conduct of those in the churches who "overcometh" the wickedness of the world (compare Revelation 2:7; see also Revelation 12:11). The overall message is one of healing, cleansing, and rebirth.

The task of Israel's prophets was to warn and to comfort. The formal calling of these prophets—Isaiah, Lehi, and John (a prophet and apostle of the New Israel)—came in "glorious" (2 Nephi 1:24) visions of God and his greatness in the heavens, of God's sovereignty and transcendence over the cosmos. In these callings, each prophet received instruction about what to preach: he must issue both the Lord's warnings and the hope of redemption and restoration.

Recording these calls serves a great purpose in the prophet's mission. The formal account of the call, though secondary to the call itself, establishes in the minds of the people the prophet's authority and his extraordinary standing with the Lord. As one commentator affirms, "the call narratives . . . [are] open proclamations of the prophet's claim to be Yahweh's agent at work in Israel."[20] The call

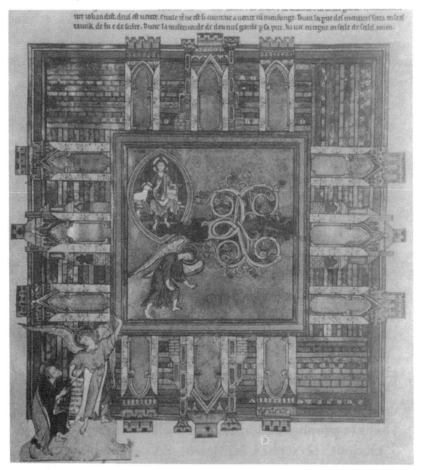

Figure 5. Stream of water originating from the throne of God

narrative not only portrays the "essence and function of the prophetic office," but it also gives insight into the nature of the call to be a prophet of God.[21] The prophet's glorious yet often unpleasant mission is to pronounce judgment on the wicked of the world and to preach hope to a chastened Israel.

Notes

The author wishes to express appreciation to Michael Lyon, John W. Welch, and Jessica Taylor for assisting in the preparation of this piece.

1. See Blake Thomas Ostler, "The Throne-Theophany and Prophetic Commission in 1 Nephi: A Form-Critical Analysis," *BYU Studies* 26/4 (1986): 67–95, esp. 69–70. See also John W. Welch, "The Calling of a Prophet," in *The Book of Mormon: First Nephi, The Doctrinal Foundation* (Provo: BYU Religious Studies Center, 1988), 35–54.

2. See Victor L. Ludlow, *Isaiah: Prophet, Seer, and Poet* (Salt Lake City: Deseret Book, 1982), 128.

3. See ibid., 129, 130.

4. See ibid., 131.

5. See Welch, "The Calling of a Prophet," 39–43.

6. George Reynolds and Janne M. Sjodahl, eds., *The Smaller Plates of Nephi*, vol. 1 of *Commentary on the Book of Mormon* (Salt Lake City: Deseret Book, 1955), 338. Compare Ezekiel 10:4.

7. See also the discussion of this aspect of Lehi's visionary experience in Welch, "The Calling of a Prophet," 39.

8. See also ibid., 42–3.

9. For additional examples of a man being forgiven of his sins before receiving a calling from the Lord, see Enos 1:5; Doctrine and Covenants 36:1; and Dean C. Jessee, ed., *The Papers of Joseph Smith* (Salt Lake City: Deseret Book, 1989), 1:6.

10. *Midrash Tanḥuma, Kedoshim* 10, cited in Arthur Hertzberg, *Judaism* (New York: Washington Square Press, 1963), 143.

11. See Donald W. Parry, "Temple Worship and a Possible Reference to a Prayer Circle in Psalm 24," *BYU Studies* 32/4 (1992): 57–62.

12. See Robert Eisler, *Weltenmantel und Himmelszelt* (Munich, Germany: Oskar Beck, 1910), 2:592.

13. See Hugh W. Nibley, *Temple and Cosmos* (Salt Lake City: Deseret Book and FARMS, 1992), 145.

14. The order of the giving of the heavenly book and the commission to preach is uncertain. Ezekiel's commission to preach directly followed his chariot vision but occurred just before the giving of the book: "And he said unto me, Son of man, go, get thee unto the house of Israel, and speak with my words unto them" (Ezekiel 3:4). See also Welch, "The Calling of a Prophet," 43–4.

15. On the *trisagion* (possibly *disagion*, a topic of debate), see Norman Walker, "Origin of the Thrice-Holy," *New Testament Studies* (1958–59): 132–3; Norman Walker, "Disagion Versus Trisagion," *New Testament Studies* 7 (1960–61): 170–1; B. M. Leiser, "The Trisagion," *New Testament Studies* 6 (1959–60): 261–3.

16. This compares with the *qeḏuššāh* in Ezekiel 3:12 and with the *Thanksgiving Hymns* of the Dead Sea Scrolls and the period of formative Judaism. See David Flusser, "Sanktus und Gloria," in *Abraham Unser Vater: Juden und Christen im Gespräch uber die Bibel: Festschrift für Otto Michel zum 60. Geburtstag*, ed. Otto Betz, Martin Hengel, and Peter Schmidt (Leiden: Brill, 1963), 129–52, especially pp. 131–8; J. Ellbogen, *Der jüdische Gottesdienst in seiner geschichtlichen Entwicklung* (Hildesheim, Germany: Olms, 1962), 61–7, 520–2, 586–7.

17. Gerhard Hasel renders the phrase "a holy seed is its stock" in *The Remnant: The History and Theology of the Remnant Idea from Genesis to Isaiah* (Berrien Springs, Mo.: Andrews University Press, 1974), 244. John D. W. Watts renders the phrase as "the seed of the holy (will be) its monument" in *Isaiah 1–33* (Waco, Texas: Word, 1985), 68.

18. Hasel, *The Remnant*, 244. Hasel uses *stock* and *stump* interchangeably; see Hasel, *The Remnant*, 238.

19. Ibid., 244–5. For other scriptural symbols regarding the seed, see Alma 32:28, 39; 33:23. For those regarding the regeneration of a tree stump, see Jacob 5.

20. Norman Habel, "The Form and Significance of the Call Narratives," *Zeitschrift für die Alttestamentliche Wissenschaft* 77 (December 1965): 317.

21. Ostler, "Throne-Theophany," 68.

Isaiah 29 and
the Book of Mormon

Robert A. Cloward

Nephi likened Isaiah 29 to his own circumstances, formulating an original prophecy that gave the old scripture new significance and saw fulfillment in the Book of Mormon.

Even among Latter-day Saints for whom most of Isaiah's writings remain obscure, phrases from chapter 29 are familiar. This is the chapter of "a marvellous work and a wonder"[1] (verse 14); "a book that is sealed," delivered to "one that is learned" (verse 11); and of a voice "out of the dust" (verse 4). It speaks of people who "draw near [to the Lord] with their mouth . . . but have removed their heart far from [him]" (verse 13); and of those who "seek deep to hide their counsel from the Lord"; or who "make a man an offender for a word" (verse 21). In the doctrinal and devotional writings of this dispensation, no chapter of Isaiah is more often cited.[2] The words of Isaiah 29 speak truths about the marvelous work of God, the coming forth of the Book of Mormon, and the foreknowledge by ancient prophets of the transcendent role of the Prophet Joseph Smith.

Before examining how and where this chapter appears in the Book of Mormon, it is vital to study it in its biblical context; then it will become clear how Book of Mormon writers applied Isaiah's words to truths they understood about themselves. This process, which Nephi and Jacob call "likening," was in part their justification for using Isaiah's words (see 1 Nephi 19:23–24; 22:8; 2 Nephi 6:5; 11:2, 8). Not only did they delight in "likening" scripture to themselves, they urged this process upon later readers as well. Their "likening" of Isaiah 29 provides a most interesting illustration of how this is done.

What Does Isaiah 29 Say?

After a series of burdens and woes on foreign nations in chapters 13–23, Isaiah speaks of the fate and future of Israel and Judah in chapters 24–35. Throughout these chapters, he prophesies the dire consequences of evil on the house of Israel in the short term and eventual blessings for the repentant in the long term.[3] Isaiah 29 includes both short-term woe and eventual rejoicing.

Isaiah 29:1–2

The chapter begins with a woe pronounced by the Lord upon "Ariel." References in verse 1 to the killing of sacrifices, and especially to "the city where David dwelt," make it clear that the Hebrew word "Ariel" refers to Jerusalem. Its fourfold repetition in verses 1–2 indicates that Jerusalem is the prophetic focus of Isaiah 29.

Various etymologies have been suggested for "Ariel."[4] The best clue to its meaning is its context in Ezekiel 43:15–16, where the King James Version (KJV) translates it "altar." A heavenly messenger is speaking of the hearth of Jerusalem's temple altar—the top portion where the actual burning of sacrifices took place. This explains the ominous climax of the woe in Isaiah 29:2: "It shall be unto me as Ariel." "It" refers to the city, and the meaning of the verse, punning on "Ariel," is "I [the Lord] will distress Ariel [Jerusalem], . . . and it [the city] shall be unto me as Ariel [an altar hearth or place of hot burning]."[5] The Lord thus announces that the holy city of Jerusalem, whose people have profaned their temple and polluted their sacrifices, will herself be burned as his own sacrifice.[6]

Isaiah 29:3–6

Following the pronouncement of the woe, the Lord reveals how his impending sacrifice will be made. Addressing

Jerusalem directly, he declares in verse 3, "I will camp against thee round about, and will lay siege against thee with a mount, and I will raise forts against thee." Siege was the dreaded horror of ancient warfare. It usually ended in slaughter and conflagration. Verses 5 and 7 refer to the multitude of nations that will accomplish Jerusalem's devastation, but the Lord himself takes responsibility for the siege. It is his retribution. He will send thunder, earthquake, great noise, storm, tempest, and finally, "the flame of devouring fire" (verse 6).

The result: Jerusalem and her people shall be "brought down" (verse 4). Isaiah uses this verb for figurative expressions of humiliation or abasement, like the felling of haughty trees (see Isaiah 10:33), the flattening of mountains (see Isaiah 40:4), or the humbling of men (see Isaiah 2:9; 5:15). In Isaiah 25:12, speaking to proud Moab, he says, "And the fortress of the high fort of thy walls shall he bring down, lay low, and bring to the ground, even to the dust." Similar language in Isaiah 26:5 describes the Lord's ability to humble "the lofty city." In Isaiah 29, the Lord announces that Jerusalem will suffer this fate. The city will be besieged, burned, and brought down to the ground.

Jerusalem's voice shall cease to be the voice of the living. Rather, it shall "speak out of the ground"; it "shall be low out of the dust" (verse 4). "Be low" translates the Hebrew verb meaning "to prostrate or bow oneself." Dust was the source of Adam's body (see Genesis 2:7; 3:19), and the dust often associated with abject humiliation in life is the same to which mankind bows in death.[7]

The image of a voice from the dead is first found in Genesis 4:10, where Abel's spilled blood cries from the ground to the Lord for vengeance. In Mosaic ritual, the blood of sacrifices was poured on the ground and covered with dust (see Leviticus 17:10–14; Deuteronomy 15:23; compare Ezekiel 24:7). When death was unwarranted, as in the case of Abel, the blood of the victim continued to speak for him, as if he were still alive.

The voice from Jerusalem's dust is said by the Lord to be "as of one that hath a familiar spirit" (verse 4). The string of English words "one that hath a familiar spirit" translates just one Hebrew word, which means "ghost."[8] Hence, Jerusalem will whisper out of the dust with a ghostly voice. Isaiah chastises those who advocate communicating with familiar spirits and heeding wizards who "peep" (the same Hebrew verb as "whisper"), saying, "should not a people seek unto their God? for the living to the dead?" (Isaiah 8:19; see also 2 Chronicles 33:6; Isaiah 19:3.)

Not just Jerusalem is to be brought to dust. Continuing the theme of destruction, the Lord applies the figure of "dust" and a parallel "chaff" in Isaiah 29:5 to Jerusalem's "strangers" and "terrible ones"—her enemies.[9] Their fate follows.

Isaiah 29:7–8

Though the destruction of Jerusalem will be a fierce and deadly reality, the Lord promises that in a turn of events, the multitude of nations that fight against Ariel or mount Zion will become "as a dream of a night vision" (verse 7). For Isaiah, "Zion" is another epithet for Jerusalem,[10] whose inhabitants verse 10 identifies as the dreamers. Their former terrible enemies will vanish as if they had been a dream. The very existence of these enemies is compared to dream-state food and drink, which neither fill the stomach nor quench the thirst (verse 8).

Isaiah 29:9–12

The Lord again addresses Jerusalem's people in verse 9. Jerusalem staggers and cries out as if drunk, but not from wine or strong drink.[11] Isaiah adds, "For the Lord hath poured out upon you the spirit of deep sleep" (verse 10). Indeed, the Lord has closed their eyes. This is the fourth of a series of poetic images of Jerusalem's downfall that began in verse 4. First the city was besieged and brought down to the dust, its voice like a ghost from the dead; then its inhabitants dreamed; then they staggered in a drunken-like stupor; and now they are in a "deep sleep." Not only has the Lord closed the eyes of the people, but he has also "covered" their prophets, their rulers, and their seers (verse 10).

Verse 11 follows directly from verse 10. In a fifth and culminating image, Isaiah states that Jerusalem's vision[12] is as obscured as the words of a sealed book. The Lord has made "the vision of all" so inaccessible that it is like words that cannot be read. English "learned" and "not learned" in the KJV (verses 11–12) translate a Hebrew idiom meaning literally "to know a book" or "to know writing," that is, "to be able to read." If the words are presented to one who can read, he will demur because the book is sealed; if to one who cannot read, he will say he cannot. The obscured vision or sealed book represents the eliminated words of Jerusalem's "covered" prophets, rulers, and seers.

Isaiah 29:13–16

In a sweeping statement of intent, and announcing the reason for his retribution upon Jerusalem, the Lord declares that "this people," the Jews, are hypocrites, and their worship is a fraud. His people have removed their hearts far from him (verse 13). Their wisdom and understanding will perish (verse 14). Hypocrites indeed, they have sought to hide their counsels from him. They have done their works in the dark (verse 15). The Lord labels their hypocrisy a "turning of things upside down."[13] It will be as worthless "as the potter's clay" (verse 16). In a biting pair of rhetorical questions in verse 16, he, the Potter, renounces their puerile declarations of independence. It is his turn to work. The works of mercy and righteousness that they did not do, he will now do, and in such a unique and powerful way that his will be "a marvellous work and a wonder" (verse 14).

Isaiah 29:17–24

In verse 17, a third rhetorical question heralds the Lord's marvelous work: "Is it not yet a very little while, and Lebanon shall be turned into a fruitful field, and the fruitful field shall be esteemed as a forest?" "Lebanon" is not literal here. The Lord is speaking about pride. He too will turn things upside down, as if Lebanon, renowned for tall cedar forests, were to become a fruit orchard, or a fruit orchard were to become a forest. With this metaphor of reversal, the Lord declares his intent to reshape and transform all of the misshapen foregoing scene.

In an impressive list, rippling open like a fan, the Lord describes his work:

1. "In that day shall the deaf hear the words of the book" (verse 18). In verses 11–12, the vision of all was like a sealed book, unread. Eventually, divine words will be heard by the deaf!

2. "The eyes of the blind shall see . . . out of darkness" (verse 18). Previous images of eyes closed in death, in dreaming, in sleep, and in drunken stupor are now replaced by seeing eyes, even the seeing eyes of the blind!

3. "The meek also shall increase their joy in the Lord."

4. "And the poor among men shall rejoice in the Holy One of Israel" (verse 19). Certainly the time of destruction

and distress will be forgotten in the day of the Lord's blessings.

5. "The terrible one is brought to nought" (verse 20). In verse 5, "terrible ones" referred to Jerusalem's enemies. Now they will be nothing.[14]

6. "And the scorner is consumed" (verse 20). Isaiah 28:14 spoke of the scornful rulers of Jerusalem; no longer will they rule.[15]

7. "All that watch for iniquity are cut off" (verse 20).[16]

8. "The house of Jacob . . . shall not now be ashamed,"

9. "Neither shall his face now wax pale" (verse 22). Israel will no longer be afraid.

10. "When [Jacob] seeth his children, the work of [the Lord's] hands, in the midst of him, they shall sanctify [the Lord's] name, and sanctify the Holy One of Jacob, and shall fear the God of Israel" (verse 23).

11. "They also that erred in spirit shall come to understanding" (verse 24). In verse 14, the understanding of the prudent was hid. Now, in his turning of things upside down, the One whose understanding they foolishly denied will mercifully grant understanding to them.

12. "And they that murmured shall learn doctrine" (verse 24).

Isaiah 29 is not a long chapter. Its message is clear: The Lord announces the destruction of Jerusalem and the death of her people as his response to pride and hypocritical worship. Then he foretells the miraculous era when he will revive and restore Jerusalem and the house of Jacob, calling this restoration "a marvellous work and a wonder."

Fulfillment of the Prophecies of Isaiah 29

Identifying the fulfillment of Isaiah 29 begins with the image of Jerusalem under siege. In 701 B.C., late in Isaiah's lifetime, Jerusalem was besieged by the Assyrian armies of Sennacherib (see Isaiah 36–37; compare 2 Kings 18:13–19:37), but this attack did not end in fiery destruction. The Lord acknowledged the pleadings and humble repentance of King Hezekiah by plaguing the Assyrians so that 185,000 of them died in one night (see Isaiah 37:36; 2 Kings 19:35).

About a century after Isaiah's death, the city was again besieged, this time by Babylonian armies in 597 B.C. Although they did not destroy the city, the Babylonians carried many of the leading Jews away into captivity and set King Zedekiah on Jerusalem's throne (see 2 Kings 24:10–17). Zedekiah "did that which was evil in the sight of the Lord" and also "rebelled against the king of Babylon" (2 Kings 24:19–20). Second Kings 25 reports the Babylonian response in words strikingly reminiscent of Isaiah's prophecy:

> And it came to pass in the ninth year of his reign, in the tenth month, in the tenth day of the month, that Nebuchadnezzar king of Babylon came, he, and all his host, *against Jerusalem,* and *pitched against it;* and *they built forts against it round about.* And *the city was besieged.* . . . And in the fifth month, on the seventh day of the month, which is the nineteenth year of king Nebuchadnezzar king of Babylon, came Nebuzar-adan, captain of the guard, a servant of the king of Babylon, unto Jerusalem: And *he burnt the house of the Lord, and the king's house, and all the houses of Jerusalem, and every great man's house burnt he with fire.* And all the army of the Chaldees, that were with the captain of the guard, *brake down the walls of Jerusalem round about.* (2 Kings 25:1–2a, 8–10; emphasis added)[17]

This time, no righteousness stood between Judah and her "terrible ones." Judah's inhabitants had ignored the warnings of Isaiah, Jeremiah, Lehi, Zephaniah, and "many prophets, prophesying unto the people that they must repent, or the great city Jerusalem must be destroyed" (1 Nephi 1:4). In 587 B.C. the fiery destruction became a fact. The Lord gave his people into the hand of the Babylonians, and Jerusalem became as an altar hearth unto him, or "as Ariel."[18]

Given the direct correlation of Isaiah's prophecy in 29:1–4, 6 with the 587 B.C. destruction of Jerusalem by Babylon, his prophecy in 29:5, 7–8 can be matched with the vanquishing of Babylon's power by the Medes and Persians (see Isaiah 13–14, 21, 41, 43–48). In 536 B.C., Cyrus the Great of Persia allowed the Jews to return to Jerusalem and re-build the temple (see Isaiah 44:28; 45:1; compare 2 Chronicles 36:22–23; Ezra 1, 3), but evidently this was not the restoration Isaiah prophesied in 29:14, 17–24. The books of Ezra, Nehemiah, Haggai, and Malachi indicate that, for the most part, Jerusalem's prophets, rulers, and seers were still "covered" during the sixth through the fourth centuries B.C., and "the vision of all" was still like the words of a sealed book.

Scripture reveals that the same sleep of apostasy prevailed in New Testament times. During his Galilean ministry, Jesus Christ declared to certain scribes and Pharisees from Jerusalem that Isaiah had prophesied *their* hypocrisy in Isaiah 29:13 (see Matthew 15:7–9; Mark 7:6–7). Similarly, Paul, speaking of God's people Israel in the first century A.D., used the phrase "the spirit of slumber" (compare "deep sleep" in Isaiah 29:10) to observe that Isaiah had prophesied *their* lack of vision, as compared to that of the gentiles (see Romans 11:8).[19] These passages imply that despite their return from Babylon, the Jews of the New Testament era were still in the state of blindness and stupor that Isaiah had foreseen.

During the last week of his life, the Savior prophesied a new destruction of Jerusalem (see Joseph Smith—Matthew 1:12–21). In A.D. 70, Roman armies besieged the city and burned it, eerily replaying the previous destruction by the Babylonians. In A.D. 135, Jerusalem was again ravaged by the Romans. This time, Jews were banished from the city's precincts on penalty of death.[20] In their turn, true to Isaiah's prophecy that "all the nations that fight against Ariel" would be "like small dust" and "as chaff that passeth away" (Isaiah 29:5, 8), the Romans eventually declined and became "as a dream of a night vision" (Isaiah 29:7).

Recognizing the fulfillment of the woe and destruction verses of Isaiah 29 is straightforward. What about the remainder of the chapter? Isaiah identifies Jerusalem and her people as the prophetic focus of chapter 29. A comparison of their latter-day condition with the twelve aspects of the Lord's "marvellous work and a wonder," listed above for Isaiah 29:17–24, reveals that most of these prophecies have not yet been fulfilled. The Lord promised a reversal of Jerusalem's physical and spiritual destruction, but today the hearts of Jerusalem's people are still far removed from him. Their fear toward him is still taught by the precept of men. He has not yet made them the work of his hands so that they "sanctify the Holy One of Jacob" and "fear the God of Israel," the Great Jehovah, Jesus Christ (Isaiah 29:23).

Isaiah lamented in Isaiah 29:11 that the vision of Jerusalem's people had become *as* the words of a sealed book. No specific book is mentioned. Isaiah's concern was the lost vision of his people, not books. His expression is symbolic—a simile, one of many similes and metaphors in Isaiah 29. Isaiah's symbolic sealed book is still sealed today. Jerusalem's vision has not yet been opened. Her people that erred in spirit have not yet come to understanding, and they that murmured have not yet learned doctrine (see verse 24).

It was Nephi who made Isaiah's symbolic book into a literal book. Nephi likened the symbolic book in Isaiah's simile to a literal, specific record the Lord had commanded him to write on gold plates. Nephi also foretold the latter-day role of his record in restoring vision, understanding, and doctrine to the house of Israel. To understand how this would occur, readers must turn to the Book of Mormon.

Isaiah 29 in the Book of Mormon

In 2 Nephi 12–24, Nephi copied from the brass plates onto his small plates, apparently verbatim, all of Isaiah 2–14. He introduced this section by saying, "And now I, Nephi, write more of the words of Isaiah, for my soul delighteth in his words" (2 Nephi 11:2) and, "I write some of the words of Isaiah, that whoso of my people shall see these words may lift up their hearts and rejoice for all men" (2 Nephi 11:8). Nephi also announced that he intended to liken these words to his people. Quoting and likening are not the same. He intended first to quote, then to liken.

After the lengthy quotation, the text indicates a clear break at 2 Nephi 25:1. There, Nephi begins his "own prophecy,"[21] so designated in 2 Nephi 25:7 and comprising six chapters, 2 Nephi 25–30. Nephi's "own prophecy" is easily definable in the text.[22] It has a distinct introduction in 2 Nephi 25:1–8 and a distinct end statement in 2 Nephi 30:18. The body of the prophecy contains two major sections. The first, in 2 Nephi 25:9–20, speaks of the Lord's dealings with the Jews, and the second, in 2 Nephi 25:21–30:18, broadens into his dealings with the Nephites, Lamanites, and gentiles, and the role of the Book of Mormon in the last days.

2 Nephi 25:1–8

In verse 1, Nephi reannounces his intent (compare 2 Nephi 11:8). He will now "speak somewhat concerning the words which [he has] written, which have been spoken by the mouth of Isaiah." Referring to his quotation of Isaiah 2–14, he says Isaiah's words are "hard for many of [his] people to understand" (verse 1). Nephi's "own prophecy" will be "according to [his] plainness; in the which [he knows] that no man can err" (verse 7).

In his "own prophecy," Nephi uses many words and themes from the quoted chapters. He also uses words and themes from other chapters of Isaiah, including words that sound like Isaiah 29 in 2 Nephi 25:17; 26:3, 6, 15–18; 27:1–7, 15, 17, 19, 25–35; 28:9, 14, 16, 20, 31; 29:1. He attributes none of these to Isaiah. In fact, he repeatedly claims the words as his own or attributes them to the Lord.[23]

Nephi announces his intention to "confine the words unto mine own people" (verses 7–8; compare with "my beloved brethren" in 2 Nephi 26:23), but his audience also includes those who suppose Isaiah to be of no worth (verse 8). Nephi's "own prophecy" they will understand, and it will be of worth to them.

2 Nephi 25:9–20

These twelve verses comprise the first section of Nephi's prophecy. This section is Nephi's commentary on Isaiah 29. In his introduction, he makes an important clarification about it: "I have made mention unto my children concerning the judgments of God, which hath come to pass among the Jews, unto my children, according to all that which Isaiah hath spoken, and I do not write them" (verse 6). In other words, he does not intend to quote Isaiah's prophecies about the Jews' destruction, as he earlier quoted Isaiah

2–14. He does give their meaning, however, in the form of commentary. These twelve verses are Nephi's recital of what Isaiah 29 means.

Nephi begins in verses 9–10 with the Jews' iniquity, their rejection of the prophets, and their destruction and captivity at the hand of the Babylonians. In verse 11, he prophesies the Jews' return to Jerusalem, but he makes clear that this is not their ultimate restoration. In verses 12–13, he notes that they will continue to have wars and rumors of wars, and when the Only Begotten of the Father comes among them, they will reject and crucify him. Then, according to verses 14–15, Jerusalem will be destroyed again, and the Jews will be scattered among all nations. Nephi adds a woe on those who fight against the people of the Messiah's church, and he observes that Babylon will be destroyed. So far, with a few added details, this section recognizably follows Isaiah 29.

In verse 16, Nephi begins a transition from destruction to the promises of restoration. He states that the scattering and scourging of the Jews will continue from generation to generation until they are "persuaded to believe in Christ, the Son of God, and the atonement." This corresponds to the promise in Isaiah 29:23. Nephi continues that when the Jews "worship the Father in [Christ's] name, with pure hearts and clean hands, and look not forward any more for another Messiah, then, at that time, the day will come that it must needs be expedient that they should believe these things" (verse 16). In verse 17, he summarizes: "Wherefore, he [the Lord] will proceed to do a marvelous work and a wonder among the children of men" (compare Isaiah 29:14). Nephi's "marvelous work and a wonder" has to do with "these things" in verse 16, but his explanation of this does not appear until the second section of his prophecy.

The second section (2 Nephi 25:21–30:18), particularly in chapters 26 and 27, contains the majority of the words that sound like those of Isaiah 29, but Nephi changes their meaning. The connection between Isaiah 29 and Jerusalem's destruction could not have been clearer in anyone's mind than in Nephi's,[24] but when Nephi wrote the words, "after the Lord God shall have camped against them round about, and shall have laid siege against them with a mount, and raised forts against them" (2 Nephi 26:15), "them" did not refer to the people of Jerusalem. The word "Ariel," a key to the meaning of Isaiah's chapter, is not found in the Book of Mormon. Nephi is not quoting from Isaiah 29 here. He is using words like those of Isaiah 29, but reinterpreting them and claiming them as his own. This is the process he calls "likening."[25]

To summarize, Isaiah 29 is not found in the Book of Mormon where readers usually look, that is, in 2 Nephi 27. The intent and meaning of Isaiah 29 are found in 2 Nephi 25:9–20. This first section of Nephi's "own prophecy" deals with Jerusalem and the Jews, just as Isaiah 29 does. Usually when looking for Isaiah in the Book of Mormon, readers look for Isaiah's actual words. Many words of Isaiah 29 do appear in the second section of Nephi's "own prophecy," but Nephi has given the words new meaning. He is no longer speaking of Jerusalem. He has likened the words of Isaiah 29 to his own people and to the gentiles.[26]

Nephi's Likening of the Words of Isaiah 29

Much longer than the first, the second section (2 Nephi 25:21–30:18) of Nephi's "own prophecy" covers several topics that converge on a single theme: the role of the Book of Mormon in bringing people to Christ. This theme was introduced in 2 Nephi 25:16–18, where Nephi states that the Lord will bring "his [the Lord's] words" to the Jews when they are ready for "these things." It is clear from 2 Nephi 25:21 that "these things" are Nephi's writings.

In verses 16–17, Nephi associates his writings with the marvelous work and wonder, but he also links them with a prophecy that "the Lord will set his hand again the second time to restore his people from their lost and fallen state" (verse 17). This wording is from Isaiah 11:11, but Nephi knows a significant difference. Second Nephi 25:17 says simply "his people," meaning the Jews. Isaiah 11:11 says "*the remnant of* his people" (emphasis added), among whom Nephi includes his own seed.[27] Nephi has begun to liken. The Book of Mormon, he prophesies, will play a role in restoring the Jews a second time from their lost and fallen state. But more broadly, he is about to reveal how it will restore his own people as well.

2 Nephi 25:21–26:11, with Words Likened from Isaiah 29:4, 6

Nephi begins the second section of his "own prophecy" by shifting away from the theme of Jerusalem and the Jews. He cites in verse 21 a promise made to the patriarch Joseph (his own ancestor) that Joseph's seed "should never perish as long as the earth should stand." He further prophesies that his own writings will be preserved and handed down among the Nephites from generation to generation. Nephi knows that his people will be stiffnecked, and he urges them not to deny the Christ, of whom his words testify (see 2 Nephi 25:28–29). Nevertheless, he prophesies that they will cast out the prophets and the saints and will stone and slay them, and "the cry of the blood of the saints shall ascend up to God from the ground against them" (2 Nephi 26:3). Consequently, the wicked among Nephi's people will be visited with all manner of destruction—with "thunderings, and lightnings, and earthquakes, and all manner of destructions, for the fire of the anger of the Lord shall be kindled against them, and they shall be as stubble" (2 Nephi 26:6). Although their Messiah will visit them and bring healing and peace to the righteous (see 2 Nephi 26:1–9), not many generations will pass after the Messiah's coming before Nephi's people will choose darkness and reap destruction (see 2 Nephi 26:10).

This sequence sounds familiar: rejection of the Lord, overwhelming wickedness and prophet-killing, blood crying from the ground, the Lord's retributive response, the Messiah's coming, the returning of wickedness, further destruction. Although the time frame for the destruction is different, the sequence applies to the Nephites just as it applied to the Jews in Isaiah 29; therefore, Nephi likens Isaiah's prophecy to his people.

2 Nephi 26:12–13

Nephi next introduces a new people into his likening—the gentiles. Intent on his overarching theme, he asserts in verse 12, "It must needs be that the Gentiles be convinced also that Jesus is the Christ, the Eternal God."

2 Nephi 26:14–15a, with Words Likened from Isaiah 29:3

Verse 14 signals a new time frame—the last days, when the Lord will bring forth Nephi's writings. In verse 15, Nephi foresees his people's clash with the gentiles. The context is very different from that of Isaiah 29:1–3. Nephi likens the destruction of Jerusalem to the destruction of his people. The fulfillment of Isaiah's prophecy began in 587 B.C., while Nephi's prophecy would not be fulfilled until after the gentiles have discovered the Western Hemisphere.[28]

Nephi's likening is a symbolic extension of the destruction of Jerusalem. Nephi had come from Jerusalem, and his people are the descendants of Jerusalem's people. Jerusalem's downfall can be likened to God's punishment of any Israelites anywhere. Nephi sees Jerusalem's destruction, and later restoration, as a type of the whole covenant of the Lord with Abraham, which, though abandoned for a time by the house of Israel, will be restored to them in the latter days (see also 1 Nephi 15:17–18).[29]

2 Nephi 26:15b–17, with Words Likened from Isaiah 29:4, 11

Isaiah spoke of the total destruction of Jerusalem, even to the dust of death, so that if her people speak at all, they whisper like ghosts. Nephi knows that the dead of his own people will actually speak from the ground—their writings will be preserved and revealed. He says of the "familiar spirit," or ghost, of the Nephites who wrote before their destruction, "The Lord God will give unto him power, that he may whisper concerning them, even as it were out of the ground" (verse 16). Nephi's likening makes real Isaiah's symbol of the speaking dead. He uses Isaiah's words, converts them to a literal application, and adds more according to his own prophetic understanding.

2 Nephi 26:18–19, with Words Likened from Isaiah 29:5

Isaiah spoke of the destruction of Jerusalem's "terrible ones," the Babylonians (and later the Romans). In verse 18, Nephi prophesies that the "terrible ones" of the destroyed of his own people will likewise be "as chaff that passeth away." Nephi likens in this case because he knows the wicked gentiles will be vulnerable to the curse cited by Lehi on those who are brought to the Americas but who reject the Lord and abound in iniquity (see 2 Nephi 1:5–7; compare Ether 2:7–12).

2 Nephi 26:20–33

Nephi elaborates on the pride of the gentiles in the last days. He contrasts their wickedness with the concept of "Zion." In Isaiah 29:8, "mount Zion" meant Jerusalem. Here, Nephi uses "Zion" symbolically for the principles of righteousness (verses 29–33).[30]

The description of the gentiles' rejection of Zion in verses 20–33 includes no long passages from Isaiah 29, but it does employ shared themes throughout. In verse 20, putting down the power of God bespeaks Isaiah 29:16, and preaching with their own wisdom recalls Isaiah 29:10–14. The secret combinations spoken of in verses 22–24 hark back to Isaiah 29:15. Casting people out of the synagogue, found in verse 26, reminds the reader of "turn[ing] aside the just" in Isaiah 29:21. The whole message of verses 24 through 33—free salvation based on the merciful love of God—is the essence of the redemption theme in Isaiah 29:22–24.

Nephi also weaves in themes from Isaiah 2–14, as he announced he would do in 2 Nephi 25:1. Verse 20 of 2 Nephi 26 alludes to Isaiah's contrast of a "sanctuary" versus "a stone of stumbling" from Isaiah 8:14, or for Nephi, churches of righteousness versus the gentile churches of pride.[31] Verse 20 also integrates the phrase "grind upon the face of the poor," adapted from Isaiah 3:15. Verse 23 speaks of darkness, where "the Lord God worketh not," reminiscent of Isaiah 9:2. From a passage of Isaiah not found in chapters 2–14, Nephi uses Isaiah's words but attributes them to the Lord in 2 Nephi 26:25 (compare Isaiah 55:1).

2 Nephi 27:1–5, with Words Likened from Isaiah 29:6–10

In Isaiah 29:6–10, the prophet included multiple images of the downfall of the Jews. Nephi takes a different turn in verse 1, declaring that in the last days—the days of the gentiles—"all the nations of the Gentiles and also the Jews, both those who shall come upon this land and those who shall be upon other lands, yea, even upon all the lands of the earth, behold, they will be drunken with iniquity and all manner of abominations" (compare Isaiah 29:9). He warns that they all will be visited with the same kinds of destruction Isaiah prophesied for the Jews.

Here, Nephi likens in a broad sense, knowing that wickedness always leads to destruction. He also knows, from the writings of Zenos, that the day will come when the whole earth will be engulfed in wickedness and apostasy, but the enemies of Zion will eventually be destroyed (see Jacob 5:30, 39, 65–66, 69, 73–75).

2 Nephi 27:6–35, with Words Likened from Isaiah 29:11–24

Very different from the wording of Isaiah 29:11, 2 Nephi 27:6 announces: "The Lord God shall bring forth unto you the words of a book." Isaiah's sealed book represented the obscurity of his people's vision, a negative image. In Nephi's prophecy, his partly sealed and partly unsealed book is always positive. From the first mention of it, Nephi's book is the future hope for his people. Isaiah's book is symbolic. Nephi's book is literal, real, tangible. Unlike those of Isaiah's, the words of Nephi's book, at least those of the unsealed part, are read; then the book itself is sealed up again until the day when the words of the sealed part will also be read, by the power of Christ, from the housetops (verse 11).

In chapter 27, Nephi adds a wealth of prophetic detail not found in Isaiah—about events that will occur thousands of years after his time. Nephi's book will not be shown to the world because "the Lord God hath said that the words of the faithful should speak as if it were from the dead" (verse 13), but it will be shown to three witnesses and then to a few others, as seemeth the Lord good (see verses 12–14). Part of the book will not be sealed (see verse 15), and the Lord God will deliver the words of this part first to a man who is not learned (see verses 9 and 15), rather than men delivering the words first to a learned man, as in Isaiah 29. Unlike Isaiah 29, the man who is not learned will deliver the words to a second man, a go-between, who will show them to a learned man (see verse 15). The learned man will demand that the book, not just its words, be brought to him "because of the glory of the world and to get gain" (verses 15–16). After the request of the learned man is denied, the Lord will command the man who is not learned to read the words (see verses 19–20), unlike Isaiah 29, where neither one reads the words.

Verses 25–35 are rich with words that sound like Isaiah 29:13–24, but "this people" in verses 25–26 refers to the gentiles, while in Isaiah 29:13–14 the same phrase referred to the Jews. Nephi prophesies that the Book of Mormon will come forth through the gentiles to accomplish the Lord's marvelous work. Nephi likens Isaiah's words to his own people in this section because he rejoices in the Lord's promise that his word will be preserved and brought forth through the gentiles to his descendants. Eventually, the same book will have a significant role in restoring the Jews to the knowledge of God and in restoring them a second time to the land of their inheritance.

Isaiah may also have known of what Nephi saw—the whispering of Nephite words out of the dust. Isaiah's vision of God's future dealings with the whole house of Israel was unparalleled. Isaiah may have been aware of the Lord's prophecy to Enoch: "And righteousness will I send down out of heaven; and truth will I send forth out of the earth, to bear testimony of mine Only Begotten" (Moses 7:62; compare D&C 128:19). He was probably aware of the prophecy of the patriarch Joseph, which Lehi quoted from the brass plates, which said that Joseph's seed would speak to their descendants out of the dust: "And they shall cry from the dust; yea, even repentance unto their brethren, even after many generations have gone by them" (2 Nephi 3:19–20; compare 2 Nephi 25:21). But Isaiah did not elaborate about the Nephites and their book. Nephi did.

Isaiah may have known the specifics about the three witnesses and other selected witnesses to the Book of Mormon, about the sealed and unsealed portions of that particular book, and about the three men—one who was not learned, one who was learned, and one go-between. It was Nephi, however, not Isaiah, who wrote about these things.

Once Nephi had likened the words of Isaiah 29 to the coming forth of the Book of Mormon, the Nephites accepted this likening as the standard interpretation of Isaiah's words for them, and they passed that interpretation down from generation to generation. At the end of his contribution to the Book of Mormon, Nephi wrote: "I speak unto you as the voice of one crying from the dust: Farewell until that great day shall come" (2 Nephi 33:13). In the final portions of the Book of Mormon, Moroni referred twice at length to Nephi's version of Isaiah 29:

> Search the prophecies of Isaiah. . . . [T]hose saints who have gone before me, who have possessed this land, shall cry, yea, even from the dust will they cry unto the Lord; and as the Lord liveth he will remember the covenant which he hath made with them . . . ; for out of the earth shall they come, . . . and it shall come even as if one should speak from the dead. And it shall come in a day when the blood of saints shall cry unto the Lord, . . . in a day when there shall be heard of fires, and tempests, and vapors of smoke in foreign lands; And there shall also be

heard of wars, rumors of wars, and earthquakes in divers places. (Mormon 8:23, 26–27, 29–30)

I exhort you to remember these things; . . . ye shall see me at the bar of God; and the Lord God will say unto you: Did I not declare my words unto you, which were written by this man, like as one crying from the dead, yea, even as one speaking out of the dust? (Moroni 10:27)

Moroni later introduced Nephi's likened version of Isaiah 29 to the latter-day dispensation when he appeared in 1823 to the Prophet Joseph Smith (see details below).

2 Nephi 28:1–2

Nephi bears testimony that the Spirit has guided his words thus far (see verse 1). He reminds his readers that the Book of Mormon will be of great worth unto the children of men and especially unto his seed, "a remnant of the house of Israel" (verse 2) in the days of their antagonists, the gentiles.

2 Nephi 28:3–32, with Words Likened from Isaiah 29:11, 13, 15, 21

Using fewer of Isaiah's words than he did in 2 Nephi 27, Nephi nevertheless continues to liken in chapter 28. Isaiah spoke of those among the Jews whose heart was far from the Lord (see Isaiah 29:13); of those who "seek deep to hide their counsel from the Lord, and their works are in the dark" (Isaiah 29:15); of those whose fear toward the Lord "is taught by the precept of men" (Isaiah 29:13); and of those who "turn aside the just for a thing of nought" (Isaiah 29:21). Each of these concepts finds place in Nephi's warnings to the gentile churches of the last days (see, respectively, 2 Nephi 28:9, 20; 28:9; 28:14, 31; and 28:16). These churches deny the Holy One of Israel (see verse 5) and, by teaching with their learning, deny also the Holy Ghost (see verse 4), but "the blood of the saints shall cry from the ground against them" (verse 10; compare Isaiah 29:4).[32]

The Lord's response to the cry from the ground is his judgment upon the wicked, a theme that recalls Isaiah 29:18–21. Nephi likens a phrase from Isaiah 29:18, "in that day shall the deaf hear the words of the book," to the role of the Book of Mormon in the final judgment of all peoples. Earlier, in 2 Nephi 25:3, he had announced that his "own prophecy" would speak of judgments to those who would receive his writings—2 Nephi 25:18 states that the Book of Mormon will judge the Jews; 2 Nephi 25:21–22 says the same of the Nephites and Lamanites; 2 Nephi 28:23 reveals that the gentiles will be judged according to their works, but 2 Nephi 29:11 clarifies that the works of all men are written in "the books," books that are "sealed" for the time of judgment. As in Isaiah's sealed-book image, ignored prophetic words are closed up by the Lord, to be opened someday as a testimony against the heedless.

As he did in 2 Nephi 26:20–33, in chapter 28 Nephi weaves together allusions to and phraseology from many chapters in Isaiah. Some are taken from Isaiah 2–14. He returns to the theme of pride in 2 Nephi 28:9, 12–15 (compare Isaiah 2:11–17) and the theme of the proud harming the poor in verse 13 (compare Isaiah 3:15). In verse 17, Nephi uses the Book of Mormon version of Isaiah 2:9 (see 2 Nephi 12:9) to portray the theme of the people's unwillingness to repent. The fall of the "abominable" in verses 18–23 is likened from Isaiah 14:19 (see the context in Isaiah 14:4–23), including the concept of being brought "down to hell" in verse 21, from Isaiah 14:15. The eight "wo" statements of verses 16–32, with the lengthening out of the Lord's arm in verse 32, are patterned after the five woes of Isaiah 5:8–23, with the Lord's hand stretched forth in Isaiah 5:25.

From elsewhere in Isaiah, Nephi takes "eat and drink; for to morrow we shall die" from Isaiah 22:13 (compare 2 Nephi 28:7–8); "I am the Lord's" from Isaiah 44:5 (compare 2 Nephi 28:3); and "precept upon precept; line upon line" from Isaiah 28:10, 13 (compare 2 Nephi 28:30). Nephi's "own prophecy" displays his total mastery of Isaiah's concepts and doctrines. No one with cursory knowledge could have written this. Because he knows them intimately, Nephi can integrate Isaiah's complex teachings into his likening in such a way that they become "plain."

2 Nephi 29:1, with Words Likened from Isaiah 29:14

Before continuing with the gentiles, Nephi repeats what he earlier said in 2 Nephi 25:17. He juxtaposes in a single verse the themes of a marvelous work and a wonder, from Isaiah 29:14, and the Lord's setting his hand the second time, from Isaiah 11:11.[33] There is intentional structure here. In effect, 2 Nephi 25:17 and 29:1 could be called "thematic link verses" between the messages of Isaiah chapter 29 and Isaiah chapter 11. Nephi's "own prophecy" begins with Isaiah 29 themes in 2 Nephi 25:9–20 and ends with Isaiah 11 themes in 2 Nephi 30:9, 11–15. The two thematic link verses are in between.

Themes from Isaiah 11 abound in the second section of Nephi's "own prophecy." The remnant of the house of Israel (see Isaiah 11:11, 16) has already been mentioned, but Isaiah's root of Jesse in the last days (see Isaiah 11:10), commonly identified as Joseph Smith,[34] is also foreseen by Nephi in 2 Nephi 27:9, 12, 15, 19 as the man who is not learned, to whom the Lord will deliver the Book of Mormon in the last days. In 2 Nephi 27:20–35, Nephi even quotes a long instruction that the Lord will later give to Joseph

Smith. Moreover, Nephi's whole emphasis on the gentiles in 2 Nephi 26–30, which is not found in Isaiah 29, draws on Isaiah 11:10, as does his prophecy of the restoration of the gospel, which Isaiah calls "an ensign" to which the gentiles seek (compare Isaiah 10:12, where "nations" is translated from the same Hebrew word as "gentiles" in Isaiah 11:10).[35] Isaiah 11:11 locates part of the remnant on "the islands of the sea," to which Nephi refers in 2 Nephi 29:7 and with which the Nephites identified themselves (see 2 Nephi 10:20–21). Isaiah 11:12 speaks of the assembling of the outcasts of Israel and the gathering of the dispersed of Judah from the four corners of the earth.[36] Isaiah 11:13 prophesies the reconciliation of Ephraim and Judah.[37] Isaiah 11:3–5 speaks of the day of judgment. Isaiah 11:6–9 foretells the millennium, when "the earth shall be full of the knowledge of the Lord, as the waters cover the sea." All of these themes appear in the second section of Nephi's "own prophecy." Even as he uses words from Isaiah 29, Nephi is developing themes from Isaiah 11. Of the many Isaiah chapters incorporated into Nephi's likening, none is more pervasive than Isaiah 11. The second section of Nephi's "own prophecy" could be called Nephi's explanation of the fulfillment of Isaiah 11.

2 Nephi 29:2–14, with Words Likened from Isaiah 29:5, 7, 22–23

Nephi speaks specifically of the wicked gentiles' rejection of his words: "A Bible! A Bible! We have got a Bible, and there cannot be any more Bible" (verse 3). Then he recapitulates that the house of Israel will be gathered to the lands of their possessions and that the Lord's word will also be gathered in one. The Lord will show those who fight against his word and his people that "[He is] God, and that [He] covenanted with Abraham that [He] would remember his seed forever" (verse 14). In 2 Nephi 29, themes from Isaiah 29:5, 7, and 22–23 have again been broadened in concept and application.

2 Nephi 30:1–18, with Words Likened from Isaiah 29:13

Nephi concludes the second section of his prophecy with the reassurance that "as many of the Gentiles as will repent are the covenant people of the Lord; and as many of the Jews as will not repent shall be cast off" (verse 2). The Lord's judgment criterion is the grand theme of the whole second section—those who "repent and believe in his Son, who is the Holy One of Israel" will be part of his covenant (verse 2). Nephi prophesies that many gentiles will believe the words of his book and will carry them to his seed, restoring them to the knowledge of Christ and his gospel and convincing them that they are "descendants of the Jews," so that they will rejoice and become a delightsome people (verses 3–6). The Jews, too, will be gathered, and those among them who believe in Christ will also become delightsome (see verse 7).

In verse 8, the climax of Nephi's "own prophecy," again recalling Isaiah 11:11, Nephi prophesies, "And it shall come to pass that the Lord God shall commence his work among all nations, kindreds, tongues, and people, to bring about the restoration of his people upon the earth." Thereafter, in verses 9–15, Nephi adds many words like those of Isaiah 11:4–9, culminating his linkage of Isaiah chapters 29 and 11. As Isaiah did in Isaiah 11:4, Nephi speaks of righteous judgment upon the poor and the meek in 2 Nephi 30:9. Isaiah 29:19 also singled out the poor and the meek in the judgment. Nephi declares that the Lord "shall smite the earth with the rod of his mouth; and with the breath of his lips shall he slay the wicked" (verse 9). This language echoes

Isaiah 29:20, where "the terrible one is brought to nought, and the scorner is consumed." As Isaiah did in Isaiah 11:6–9, Nephi announces the glorious millennial day, when "Satan shall have power over the hearts of the children of men no more, for a long time" (2 Nephi 30:18). This is the promised return of the errant hearts that were far removed from the Lord (compare Isaiah 29:13).

Thus, Isaiah's "marvellous work and a wonder" becomes fully Nephi's. Isaiah prophesied that the Lord would turn aright all that the wicked Jews of Isaiah's day had turned upside down. In his "own prophecy," Nephi reveals how, in the last days, the Lord will bring the gentiles, then the descendants of the Nephites and Lamanites, and finally the Jews to their Messiah and Redeemer, all through the instrumentality of the Book of Mormon. What a marvelous prophecy it is!

Fulfillment of Nephi's Likening of Isaiah 29 in 2 Nephi 25–30

The words of Isaiah 29 figure in the events of the restoration from Joseph Smith's earliest visionary experience. He asked the Father and the Son in the spring of 1820 which church he should join. The reply—

> I was answered that I must join none of them, for they were all wrong; and the Personage who addressed me said that all their creeds were an abomination in his sight; that those professors were all corrupt; that: "they draw near to me with their lips, but their hearts are far from me, they teach for doctrines the commandments of men, having a form of godliness, but they deny the power thereof." (JS–H 1:19)

The churches of Joseph Smith's inquiry were the gentile churches of America, whose pride and lack of the Spirit are detailed in 2 Nephi 26:20–27:5, who deny the power of God, as 2 Nephi 28:5 says, and whose hearts, lips, and doctrines are described by Nephi in 2 Nephi 27:25. They were not the Jews, whose hearts, lips, and doctrines are described in Isaiah 29:13 and in the aforementioned New Testament citations. Therefore, the Savior, in speaking to the Prophet Joseph, was not quoting Isaiah in the traditional sense. He was using a likening similar to Nephi's. In fact, the Savior's words were the very instruction Nephi had prophesied that the Lord would give to the man who was not learned (see 2 Nephi 27:24–25).

Words like those of Isaiah 29 also figure in Joseph Smith's second visionary experience. When Moroni appeared to him repeatedly on the night of 21–22 September 1823, Moroni cited many scriptures about coming events. The account of this vision in Joseph Smith—History 1:27–47 says that after Moroni announced the purpose of his visit and the location and significance of the gold plates, "he commenced quoting the prophecies of the Old Testament" (JS–H 1:36). The account then specifies Malachi 3–4, Isaiah 11, Acts 3:22–23, and Joel 2:28–32. Moroni said Isaiah 11 "was about to be fulfilled" (JS–H 1:40), and "the fulness of the Gentiles was soon to come in" (JS–H 1:41).

Joseph Smith said Moroni "quoted many other passages of scripture, and offered many explanations which cannot be mentioned here" (JS–H 1:41). The "many other passages" included citations with words like those in Isaiah 29, as evidenced by another account of Moroni's visit,[38] which appears in the fourth of Oliver Cowdery's series of eight letters to William W. Phelps, published in the *Messenger and Advocate* beginning in October 1834.[39] Oliver Cowdery says Moroni declared that he had come "that the scriptures might be fulfilled."[40] To which scriptures did he refer? Moroni first cited 1 Corinthians 1:27–29, concerning the foolish things of the world confounding the mighty, but then he continued:

> Therefore, says the Lord, I will proceed to do a marvelous work among this people, even a marvelous work and a wonder; the wisdom of their wise shall perish, and the understanding of their prudent shall be hid; for according to his covenant which he made with his ancient saints, his people, the house of Israel must come to a knowledge of the gospel, and own that Messiah whom their fathers rejected, and with them the fulness of the gentiles be gathered in to rejoice in one fold under one Shepherd.[41]

The Isaiah 29:14 words are forthright, and the promise to the house of Israel agrees with Nephi's understanding of Isaiah 29 in the first section of his "own prophecy" (see especially 2 Nephi 25:17–18). But Moroni's concern for the gentiles is a focus of the second section of Nephi's "own prophecy" and of Isaiah 11:10, 12, not of Isaiah 29.

Oliver Cowdery says Moroni went on to announce that the prophecies could not occur until "certain preparatory things are accomplished," among them the choosing of Joseph Smith by the Lord "as an instrument in his hand to bring to light that which shall perform his act, his strange act, and bring to pass a marvelous work and a wonder."[42] The angel again used words like Isaiah 29 but themes from Isaiah 11.

Moroni continued:

> Wherever the sound shall go it shall cause the ears of men to tingle, and wherever it shall be proclaimed, the pure in heart shall rejoice, while those who draw near to God with their mouths, and honor him with their lips, while their hearts are far from him, will seek its overthrow, and the destruction of those by whose hands it is carried.[43]

This Isaiah 29:13 allusion would have recalled to Joseph Smith's mind the prophesied instruction he received in the First Vision.

After giving "a general account of the promises made to the fathers" and "a history of the aborig[i]nes of this country," saying they were literal descendants of Abraham, Moroni told Joseph Smith he would have the privilege, if obedient, to translate the history of these people by means of the Urim and Thummim.

> "Yet," said he [Moroni], "the scripture must be fulfilled before it [the history] is translated, which says that the words of a book, which were sealed, were presented to the learned; for thus has God determined to leave men without excuse, and show to the meek that his arm is <not> short[e]ned that it cannot save."
>
> A part of the book was sealed, and was not to be opened yet. The sealed part, said he, contains the same revelation which was given to John upon the isle of Patmos, and when the people of the Lord are prepared, and found worthy, then it will be unfolded unto them.[44]

The question arises whether "the scripture" to which Moroni refers is from Isaiah 29 or 2 Nephi 27. Oliver Cowdery's account is subject to the weaknesses of non-eyewitness sources, but it should be examined at face value. Note that he says Moroni gave "a history of the aborig[i]nes of this country," introducing the Book of Mormon. However, Moroni also said that sealed words were presented to the learned. Neither Isaiah nor Nephi said that.[45] Like Moroni, both sources mention the meek (see Isaiah 29:19 and 2 Nephi 27:30), but only the Book of Mormon differentiates sealed and unsealed *parts* of a book (see 2 Nephi 27:7–11, 14–22). The Book of Mormon, not the book of Isaiah, speaks specifically about the coming forth of the words of John, establishing that after the contents of the unsealed part go forth, the sealed part will be read from the housetops (see 2 Nephi 27:11; Ether 4:16–17). Thus, if only the Bible were available, as was the case when Joseph Smith heard Moroni's words, the conclusion would be that "the scripture" to be fulfilled was from Isaiah 29. This was, in fact, the Prophet Joseph's conclusion. But since the Book of Mormon is now translated, the details of Moroni's statements show that the source of "the scripture" was much more likely 2 Nephi 27.

Oliver Cowdery next says Moroni gave specific instructions, indicating that even the bringing forth of the unsealed portion of the book was to be done with an eye single to the glory of God. Centuries earlier, as a mortal, Moroni had prophesied this detail (see Mormon 8:15).

In his eighth letter, Oliver Cowdery comments on Moroni's meeting with Joseph Smith at the Hill Cumorah on 22 September 1823. When Joseph attempted to get the plates for their monetary value, Oliver Cowdery notes that the Prophet was shown a vision of the power of Satan. Moroni had also foreseen this (see Mormon 8:14). The angel sternly warned Joseph Smith, using words from Isaiah 29:11–14 but with a Book of Mormon interpretation:

> These things are sacred, and must be kept so, for the promise of the Lord concerning them must be fulfilled. No man can obtain them if his heart is impure, because they contain that which is sacred; and besides, should they be entrusted in unholy hands the knowledge could not come to the world, because they cannot be interpreted by the learning of this generation; consequently, they would be considered of no worth, only as precious metal. Therefore, remember, that they are to be translated by the gift and power of God. By them will the Lord work a great and a marvelous work: the wisdom of the wise shall become as nought, and the understanding of the

prudent shall be hid, and because the power of God shall be displayed those who profess to know the truth but walk in deceit, shall tremble with anger; but with signs and with wonders, with gifts and with healings, with the manifestations of the power of God, and with the Holy Ghost, shall the hearts of the faithful be comforted.[46]

And further:

Your name shall be known among the nations, for the work which the Lord will perform by your hands shall cause the righteous to rejoice and the wicked to rage: with the one it shall be had in honor, and with the other in reproach; yet, with these it shall be a terror because of the great and marvelous work which shall follow the coming forth of this fulness of the gospel.[47]

Like the Savior in the First Vision, Moroni was not quoting Isaiah in the traditional sense. He too was using a likening similar to Nephi's.

Moroni attached Nephi's "marvelous work and a wonder" to the call of Joseph Smith and the coming forth of the Book of Mormon.[48] It was to have an even wider application. In February 1829, the Lord prefaced a revelation to Joseph Smith for his father, who was visiting him in Harmony, Pennsylvania: "Now behold, a marvelous work is about to come forth among the children of men" (D&C 4:1). Although he certainly had reference to the Book of Mormon, which appeared a year later, in 1830, the content of the revelation suggests that the Lord was using the phrase "a marvelous work" for the whole of his work in the latter-day restoration.[49]

The framework for a comprehensive fulfillment of 2 Nephi 25–30 is the latter days, yet the fulfillment of these prophecies is often attributed to Isaiah 29. Earlier, it was noted that there was no published Book of Mormon at the time of Joseph Smith's early visions, and there exists no record that the Savior or Moroni attributed their words in these visions to Isaiah or to Nephi.[50] Naturally, Joseph Smith compared what he learned in the visions to the Bible[51] and attributed the Isaiah-like words to Isaiah. This has been the common attribution in the Church ever since.

Nephi's likening in 2 Nephi 27:9–10 and 15–20 is the source of the prophecy of the Martin Harris interview with Professor Charles Anthon of Columbia College. It is interesting to consider when and how the fulfillment of this prophecy was first attributed to Isaiah 29:11–12. When Moroni said "the scripture must be fulfilled before it [the history] is translated," he was probably speaking of "the scripture" in 2 Nephi 27. Relevant details about the learned man and the go-between and about the book and the words, often assumed biblical, are only found in Nephi's "own prophecy." A review of historical events and sources can shed further light on why the Isaiah attribution was made.[52]

From the moment Joseph Smith removed the gold plates from the Hill Cumorah in the early morning hours of 22 September 1827, he was hounded by persecutors in his Manchester, New York, environs. It was clear that the translation of the record could not progress unless he moved away from the meddling. With a gift of fifty dollars from Martin Harris, Joseph left for Harmony, Pennsylvania, the home of his wife's parents, where he had met Emma while boarding there in October 1825 during his employment with Josiah Stowell.[53] Despite some difficulties,[54] Joseph Smith began the process of translation in Harmony. Emma and her brother Reuben served as scribes,[55] and Joseph translated a few pages during the months of December 1827 through February 1828.[56]

In February 1828, Martin Harris arrived in Harmony. In *History of the Church*, the account of Harris's trip from Harmony to New York is brief, and based for the most part on his report upon his return. After recounting Professor Anthon's assessment, which included an affidavit that "they [the Book of Mormon characters] were true characters, and that the translation of such of them as had been translated was also correct,"[57] Martin Harris said Professor Anthon asked how and where he had obtained them. When Harris told him, the following exchange ensued:

> He then said to me, "Let me see that certificate." I accordingly took it out of my pocket and gave it to him, when he took it and tore it to pieces, saying, that there was no such thing now as ministering of angels, and that if I would bring the plates to him, he would translate them. I informed him that part of the plates were sealed, and that I was forbidden to bring them. He replied, "I cannot read a sealed book."[58]

Additional details can be found in the Prophet's 1832 history, from the first six pages of his "Letterbook 1":

> [O]n the 22d day of Sept of this same year I obtained the plates and ~~the~~ in December following we mooved to Susquehana by the assistence of a man by the name of Martin Haris who became convinced of the visions and gave me fifty Dollars to bear my expences and because of his faith and this righteous deed the Lord appeared unto him in a vision and shewed unto him his marvilous work which he was about to do and <he> imediately came to Su[s]quehanna and said the Lord had shown him that he must go to new York City with some of the c[h]aracters so we proceeded to coppy some of them and he took his Journy to the Eastern Cittys and to the Learned <saying> read this I pray thee and the learned said I cannot but if he would bring the plates they would read it but the Lord had fo<r>bid it and he returned to me and gave them to <me to> translate and I said ~~I said~~ [I] cannot for I am not learned but the Lord had prepared

~~spectticke~~ spectacles for to read the Book therefore I commenced translating the characters and thus the Prop[h]icy of Is<ia>ah was fulfilled which is writen in the 29 chapter concerning the book[.][59]

This account states that Martin Harris was told by the Lord in vision to take characters from the plates to the East.[60] Although the Prophet's description of Martin Harris's vision uses the phrase "his marvilous work which he was about to do," it is not stated that Martin knew when he journeyed to the East in February 1828 that the result would be a fulfillment of scripture. It may be assumed that Joseph Smith either knew or suspected that the journey had relevance to what Moroni had told him. If Joseph Smith had not by this time told Martin Harris the details of his advance tutoring by Moroni, Harris's vision would constitute an interesting orchestration of events by the Lord to accomplish the fulfillment of Nephi's prophecy.

In later recollections, Martin Harris stated that he did *not* know that he was fulfilling scriptural prophecy. There are at least two reports of this. One is from William Pilkington, who was thirteen years old when he boarded with the Martin Harris Jr. family in Cache County, Utah, for a year and a half beginning in October 1874. Martin Harris Sr., the Book of Mormon witness, was living with his son Martin at the time and died at Clarkston the year after William Pilkington's arrival. Pilkington later wrote in a sworn affidavit:

> He told me it was he who took some of the copied characters, along with the interpretation "which Joseph Smith had made through the gift and power of God" to Professor Charles Anthon . . . and thus the prophecy of Isaiah was fulfilled, which will be found in the 29th chapter and 11 verse, but I did not know that I was fulfilling it at the time.[61]

Anthony Metcalf, who also interviewed Martin Harris in Utah, made a similar statement, with interesting additions. He wrote:

> Harris told me about his trip to New York and what Prof. Anthon told him. He (Anthon) said the characters were translated correctly. After Harris had told the professor how the plates had been found, the professor said that it was his opinion that he (Harris) was being duped by sharpers, and advised Harris to take care of himself. I asked him if he knew what the prophet Isaiah had said about that event. He said, "No," but that Joseph Smith had shown that chapter to him after his return.[62]

Whether or not the outcome of Martin Harris's journey was uncertain to Joseph Smith at its outset, it was apparently clear to the Prophet after Martin returned. The entry in Joseph Smith's 1832 history, cited above, implies that for the Prophet, a remarkable connection with Isaiah became obvious in Professor Anthon's words. Within a few years, the Isaiah connection was being spread as a proselytizing testimonial for the new scripture, and the Harris/Anthon interview became a matter of importance in recitals of the facts of the restoration.[63]

It is not surprising that Isaiah rather than Nephi continues to be cited even though 2 Nephi 27 is the source of the prophecy of the interview. It has been important for many Church members to find evidences for the Book of Mormon's truthfulness in the Bible. Furthermore, after Martin Harris returned from the East, convinced of the authenticity of Joseph Smith's work, and Joseph showed "that chapter [Isaiah 29]" to him,[64] more than a year passed before the Book of Mormon translation revealed Nephi's prophecy.[65] Joseph Smith must have been fascinated to encounter the details of the Harris/Anthon interview in written form on the ancient plates.

JST Isaiah 29 and Nephi's "Own Prophecy"

After the Book of Mormon was published and the Church organized, Joseph Smith commenced the new translation of the Bible now called the Joseph Smith Translation (JST). The date he began this work is not certain, but it could have been as early as the summer of 1830.[66] The manuscripts of the JST provide eloquent witness of the importance of Nephi's likening and of its relationship to Isaiah's original vision.

The Prophet did not translate the Bible in the order of the chapters as they appear in the King James Version. Although he started with Genesis, he shifted to the New Testament before returning to finish the Old Testament. His work on Isaiah was part of the final section of the translation, which consisted of Genesis 24 through Malachi, and the changes were recorded in Sidney Rigdon's handwriting on the manuscript now referred to as Old Testament Manuscript 3 (OT 3).[67] Although it covered most of the Old Testament, this section was completed in just five months, from 2 February to 2 July 1833.[68] It was "rather hurriedly done and did not receive as thorough a review as did the New Testament."[69] For the most part, the notation system developed to speed up the New Testament translation was used—words or phrases were written, accompanied by chapter and verse numbers to indicate where they were to be inserted into the biblical text.[70] Relatively few verses were written out in their entirety.

A notable exception is Isaiah 29. OT 3 includes nearly five pages of changes for this chapter. In the 1828 KJV that Joseph Smith used for the translation,[71] every verse in chapter 29 except verses 1 and 7 is marked for correction.[72] Isaiah 29 is twice as long in the JST as in the KJV.

Why did the Prophet single out Isaiah 29 for such comprehensive revision? Two intriguing discoveries about the source of the changes provide the answer. First, Joseph Smith used the Book of Mormon for his translation of Isaiah 29.[73] Second, the switch from the normal source, the 1828 KJV, to the Book of Mormon does not occur at the beginning of the chapter, but after verse 7. From verse 8 to the end of Isaiah 29, Joseph Smith replaced Isaiah's prophecy with Nephi's.[74]

Before discussing the implications of these discoveries, the evidence for them must be examined, based on descriptions of the original sources—Joseph Smith's KJV (1828); the first edition of the Book of Mormon (1830); and the OT 3 manuscript's Isaiah section (1833).[75]

JST Isaiah 29:1–7

The following observations tie the first seven verses of JST Isaiah 29 to the KJV:

1. Changes for the early verses are based on KJV wording, and internal error corrections in OT 3 move its text in the direction of the KJV. This is evident in the verses written out in their entirety (verses 2–4) and the verses only partially written out (verses 1, 5, 6). For example, the opening words of verse 1 are written, "Wo to Ariel, to Ar"; then they are lined through, suggesting that the KJV text of that verse was considered even though the verse was left unchanged. The KJV pun in verse 2, "it shall be unto me as Ariel" (Jerusalem shall be like an altar hearth), is changed into an introduction for verse 3: "thus hath the Lord said unto me, it shall be unto Ariel, [here, a verse number "3"] That I the Lord will camp against her round about." Verse 3 in the manuscript begins with "That I"; then it has a "w," overwritten as "t" to continue "the Lord will camp against"; then a dark ink

smudge (a form of erasure), overwritten as "her" to continue "her round about." The two overwrites correct the JST in the direction of the KJV verse "And I will camp against thee"—the "w" corresponds to KJV "will," changed to "the," and the smudge erasure corresponds to KJV "thee" (illegible in the smudge), changed to "her."

2. KJV verse numbers accompany the Prophet's changes for verses 1–6, showing that he and Sidney Rigdon were correlating JST verse content to the KJV. (Since no change is indicated for verse 7, no number is written for that verse.)

3. Changes for the early verses in OT 3 do not correspond to the 1830 Book of Mormon. For example, both OT 3 and the KJV read "as *of* one that hath a familiar spirit" for Isaiah 29:4 (emphasis added), whereas 2 Nephi 26:16 reads "as one that hath a familiar spirit." The JST "of" was probably dictated from the KJV.

4. Topically, the early verses coincide with the KJV, while Nephi's prophecy is different. For example, the city Ariel is the focus of verses 2–4 in the JST, just as in the KJV. The JST does not mention the focus of 2 Nephi 26:14— Nephi's seed and the seed of his brethren. Also absent in the JST are the elaborations in 2 Nephi 26:15–18—the prophecy that "the words of the righteous shall be written, and the prayers of the faithful shall be heard, and all those who have dwindled in unbelief shall not be forgotten"; the prophecy that the Lord will give power to the familiar spirit of the destroyed Nephites and Lamanites to whisper concerning their seed; and the warning about the sins and iniquities of the days of the gentiles (see 2 Nephi 26:19–27:1).

5. Verses 5 and 6 in OT 3 use the word and phrase insertion notation mentioned above. For verse 5, only the word "her" is written, and for verse 6, only the phrase "for they shall." Joseph Smith's Bible indicates insertion points for these words in the KJV text with an inked circle around

"thy" in verse 5 and a line through "Thou shalt" in verse 6.[76] The absence of verse 7 in OT 3 implies that this verse was to remain unchanged from the KJV. Thus, the JST maintains the KJV concept of the fate of "the multitude of all the nations that fight against Ariel [the city]," not the Book of Mormon concept of the fate of "all the nations that fight against Zion [the principles of righteousness]."

JST Isaiah 29:8–32

The following observations tie JST Isaiah 29:8–32 to the Book of Mormon:

1. Beginning with verse 8, the entire text for the remainder of Isaiah 29 is written out in OT 3. The content corresponds to 2 Nephi 27:3b–35 in the 1830 Book of Mormon. For example, JST Isaiah 29:8 is equivalent to 2 Nephi 27:3b in all but two words—both of them "who" replacing "which." This verse differs radically from KJV Isaiah 29:8. Verses 9 and 10 are exactly the same in OT 3 and 2 Nephi 27:4–5, and together they are quite different from the KJV. Where KJV Isaiah 29:11–12 would be expected, OT 3 includes all the content of 2 Nephi 27:6–24, not found in the KJV (see JST Isaiah 29:11–25). This is the clearest evidence for the source switch. Included in the JST are all of the unique Book of Mormon details about the man who is learned and the man who is not learned, the part that is sealed and the part that is not sealed, and the three witnesses plus a few others who will view the book. All the remainder of JST Isaiah 29, corresponding to KJV Isaiah 29:13–24, continues to parallel the content of the Book of Mormon, not the KJV (see JST Isaiah 29:26–32).

2. KJV verse numbers do not continue to the end of chapter 29 in OT 3. After the number for verse 8, the remainder of the text is interrupted only by "9 verse" written before

the content for verse 9, "10" written before the content for verse 10, and a long dash after each of these two verses. A number 11 is placed near the beginning of the content for that verse, but the number looks like an afterthought—small, between the levels of two horizontal text lines, and uncharacteristically to the left in the margin. Three subsequent pages of replacement content are not labeled with verse numbers.

3. Idiosyncrasies in the 1830 edition of the Book of Mormon also appear in OT 3. For example, in 2 Nephi 27:9, the grammatical error "they which" in "he shall deliver the words of the book, which are the words of they which have slumbered in the dust; and he shall deliver these words unto another" also appears in OT 3. "They" has been lined through and corrected between lines to "those".[77] In 2 Nephi 27:11, the grammatical error "hath" in "all things shall be revealed unto the children of men which ever hath been among the children of men" also appears in OT 3. The "th" in "hath" has been lined through and corrected interlineally to "ve".[78]

4. Several internal error corrections in OT 3 move its text in the direction of the 1830 Book of Mormon. For example, at JST Isaiah 29:24, "the" is written above the line with a caret between "read" and "words" to correct "when thou hast read words which I have commanded thee" in the direction of 2 Nephi 27:21. For the same verse, "Touch not things" is corrected in the direction of the Book of Mormon's "Touch not the things" by the smudge erasure of "things," the placement of "the" beneath the smudge, then the rewriting of "things." At JST Isaiah 29:29, "thus" is lined through to correct "thus saith the Lord of hosts" in the direction of 2 Nephi 27:28 "saith the Lord of Hosts."

5. Sidney Rigdon's handwriting, though usually very legible, is in these verses noticeably neater and more consistent

in letter formation, word spacing, and slant. This could result from straight copying of an existing text.

There is no question that Joseph Smith—and the Lord—took the JST very seriously.[79] Those living in the latter days are blessed to have it. In pondering the Prophet's changes, JST readers are left to draw their own conclusions on why each was made, since he left no systematic commentary to explain them. With that in mind, the significance of Joseph Smith's treatment of Isaiah 29 should be assessed.

First, the Prophet confirmed that KJV Isaiah 29 and 2 Nephi 26–27 are different and independent texts. He consciously used part of each. If he had understood the Book of Mormon to preserve a more complete and correct text of Isaiah 29 from the brass plates, he would likely have substituted for chapter 29 *all* of the Book of Mormon version.[80]

Second, Joseph Smith confirmed the focus that has been discussed here for Isaiah's original prophecy. He retained all the references to Jerusalem in the first seven verses. If he had understood Isaiah to prophesy that the Nephites and Lamanites would be brought down and would "speak out of the ground" and "whisper out of the dust," he would likely have copied 2 Nephi 26:15–16 into the JST. Not only did he not do that, but, by changing eight instances of first person "thee," "thy," and "thou" in verses 3–5 to "her" and "she," he *strengthened* the identification of Jerusalem as the one brought down.

Third, the JST confirms that Isaiah prophesied the destruction of all nations that fight against Ariel. Joseph Smith left that concept in verses 5 and 7. Had he understood Isaiah to prophesy that "all the nations of the Gentiles and also the Jews, both those who shall come upon this land [the Western Hemisphere] and those who shall be upon other lands, yea, even upon all the lands of the earth" would be "drunken with iniquity and all manner of abominations," he could readily have copied 2 Nephi 27:1 into the JST. He could have changed the city "Ariel" to the abstract concept of Zion in verse 7 as Nephi did. Not only did he not do that, he *strengthened* the reference to Jerusalem's strangers and terrible ones (her enemies) by changing "thou" to "they" in verse 6 to make that verse refer to the enemies, as do verses 5 and 7, rather than to Jerusalem, as in the KJV.

Fourth, Joseph Smith chose to give the inspired translation of two-thirds of Isaiah 29 an application more apropos to the latter days.[81] By copying Nephi's words into the JST from verse 8 to the end, Joseph Smith likened Isaiah 29 to his own dispensation.[82]

Seeing the Scriptures As One

So we come full circle. Isaiah foresaw both the fate and the future restoration of Jerusalem and her people. Nephi, who was also of Israel, likened Isaiah's words to his people in a new prophecy, showing how Nephite writings would advance the Lord's work in the latter days. Book of Mormon prophets perpetuated Nephi's likening among their people until the time of Moroni. Then, the Savior and the resurrected Moroni taught the significance of Nephi's likening for this dispensation to the Prophet Joseph Smith. Joseph Smith, in turn, replaced Isaiah's words in his inspired translation of the Bible with his new understanding of how they had been likened to him and to the Lord's latter-day work.

In this process, Isaiah's sealed book was reinterpreted as Nephi's gold plates and as Joseph Smith's Book of Mormon. Isaiah's dust of death was reinterpreted as Nephi's source of renewed life and as Joseph Smith's Cumorah. Isaiah's "learned" and "not learned," both denied access to spiritual vision, became Nephi's future translator, Joseph the seer, and his foil, Professor Charles Anthon. This is the process of likening. Prophets do it readily. Students of the scriptures are urged to liken as well. When readers in any era are moved upon by the Holy Ghost, there is no impropriety in their giving old scripture new meaning for their lives. As readers do this, the Lord can reveal new truths to them and enlarge their understanding.

By 1833, Joseph Smith, Nephi, and Isaiah all rejoiced that the Book of Mormon was beginning to cause the eyes of the spiritually blind to "see out of obscurity and out of darkness" (2 Nephi 27:29). Eventually, as the Lord said, "They also that erred in spirit shall come to understanding, and they that murmured shall learn doctrine" (2 Nephi 27:35). Latter-day readers have begun to see and will yet know the fulness of the Lord's marvelous work and a wonder—the ultimate fulfillment of both Isaiah's and Nephi's prophecies.

Notes

1.　All direct quotes in this study preserve variant or erroneous spellings from original sources, e.g., "marvellous."

2.　Monte S. Nyman makes this observation in his *"Great Are the Words of Isaiah"* (Salt Lake City: Bookcraft, 1980), 101, apparently based on data in his Appendix B, 259–81. The same observation is supported in the published sermons and writings of Joseph Smith by data found in the appendix of Grant Underwood, "Joseph Smith's Use of the Old Testament," in *The Old Testament and the Latter-day Saints,* Sperry Symposium 1986 (Orem, Utah: Randall, 1986), 399–411.

3.　Isaiah 24 opens the series of chapters with the foreboding announcement that the Lord will empty the earth and make it waste. He will turn it upside down and scatter abroad its inhabitants. Chapters 28–33 contain a series of six woe pronouncements: 28:1; 29:1, 15; 30:1; 31:1; and 33:1. Shorter messages of hope are interspersed, and the culmination of the section is a promise of millennial rejoicing in chapter 35.

4. Suggested translations for "Ariel" include "lion (or lioness) of God," "altar of God," or even "Arishalem" (an early equivalent of Jerusalem?), with the name of the deity Shalem replaced by El. It could also derive from a corrupt spelling of "harel," meaning "mountain of El." Any thorough Bible dictionary or critical commentary on Isaiah will detail the meanderings for this term. See for example Edward J. Young, *The Book of Isaiah: The English Text, with Introduction, Exposition, and Notes* (Grand Rapids, Mich.: Eerdmans, 1965–72), 2:304–5; R. B. Y. Scott, "The Book of Isaiah," in *The Interpreter's Bible,* ed. George Arthur Buttrick (New York: Abingdon Press, 1951–57), 5:323; W. Harold Mare, "Ariel," in *The Anchor Bible Dictionary,* ed. David Noel Freedman (New York: Doubleday, 1992), 1:377–8.

5. Some suggest that the Hebrew text be read with "it" feminine, clarifying the antecedent relationship, although the wordplay does not require this. See *Biblia Hebraica Stuttgartensia* (Stuttgart: Deutsche Bibelstiftung, 1977), footnote *sub loc.*

6. Isaiah speaks of the Lord's contempt for Jerusalem's polluted and hypocritical sacrifices in Isaiah 1:11–15; 43:22–24; 65:3; and 66:3–4. The image of the Lord making the city into his own symbolic sacrifice is repeated in Isaiah 34:5–8.

7. The book of Job, in which the man Job is brought down low, nigh unto death, illustrates biblical usage of the poetic figures of ground and dust. Job and his friends associate dust with death in Job 7:21; 10:9; 17:16; 20:11; 21:26; 34:15; 40:13, and dust or the ground with mourning and oppression in Job 1:20; 2:12–13; 7:5; 16:13, 15; 30:19; 42:6. Isaiah applies these figures to Jerusalem in Isaiah 2:10; 3:26; 5:24; 34:9; and 51:23. The theme of the dead or oppressed rising or speaking from the dust is repeated in Isaiah 26:19; 51:17, compare verse 23; 52:1–15.

8. The same Hebrew word can also refer to a wizard or witch acting as a medium through whom a ghost is consulted. The implication is always necromancy or seeking instruction from the dead. Consulting familiar spirits was strongly condemned by the Lord. The penalty was, at best, banishment, and, at worst, death by stoning (see Leviticus 19:31; 20:6, 27;

Deuteronomy 18:11). When the deranged King Saul received no response from the Lord and longed for help from the departed Samuel, he sought a medium with a familiar spirit, contrary to his own edict of death for wizards and witches in Israel (see 1 Samuel 28:3–25; 1 Chronicles 10:13). The witch of Endor agreed to the séance and claimed to bring up Samuel's ghost. Interestingly, the Joseph Smith Translation of the Bible (JST) links contact with the dead to words "ascending out of the earth." In the JST, the witch's inquiry to Saul was, "*The word of* whom shall I bring up unto thee?" and Saul's reply was "Bring me up *the word of* Samuel." Subsequently, "when the woman saw *the words of* Samuel, she cried with a loud voice; and the woman spake unto Saul, saying, Why hast thou deceived me? for thou art Saul. And the king said unto her, Be not afraid; for what sawest thou? And the woman said unto Saul, I saw *the words of Samuel ascending out of the earth.* And she said, I saw Samuel also" (JST 1 Samuel 28:11–13, emphasis added).

9. Isaiah, Jeremiah, and Ezekiel all use the plural epithet "terrible [ones]," with occasional parallel "strangers," to refer to the enemies of Jerusalem and its environs, usually the Babylonians (Isaiah 13:11; 25:3, 5; 49:24–25; Jeremiah 15:21; Ezekiel 28:7; 30:11; 31:12; 32:12).

10. In the days of Enoch, the Lord called his people "Zion" because of their righteousness (Moses 7:18; compare D&C 97:21). Judah's historians called Jerusalem "Zion" (2 Samuel 5:6–7; 1 Kings 8:1; 1 Chronicles 11:4–5; 2 Chronicles 5:2). Isaiah and later prophets used "Zion," "mount Zion," "the daughter of Zion," and like terms, for Jerusalem (e.g., Isaiah 1:27; 10:32; 30:19; 31:4–5; 33:20), probably because it had been idealized as the city of God (see, for example, Psalm 87).

11. By contrast, in Isaiah's woe on Ephraim (the Northern Kingdom of Israel) in Isaiah 28 (see especially verse 7), the Lord decries drunkenness that *does* result from strong drink. The Isaiah 29 image of the wineless drunkenness of Jerusalem before the Lord helps the city is repeated in Isaiah 51:21 (compare 2 Nephi 8:21).

12. The dual force of the English word *vision,* meaning "sight" as well as "revelation," renders well the corresponding Hebrew word, based on a poetic root "to see." A related form gives us "seer," as in Isaiah 29:10.

13. Isaiah 5:20 also speaks of the wrongful turning of things upside down, in that case "calling evil good, and good evil."

14. The singular "terrible one" in Isaiah 29:20 (and its parallel singular, "scorner") could refer to Satan, the ultimate enemy of Jerusalem and the antithesis of the Lord of Hosts.

15. See the previous note. Perhaps "the scorner," as Satan, could be considered the symbolic ruler of Jerusalem during its time of destruction.

16. The Hebrew means "to be alert or wakeful" for iniquity. Isaiah's three examples in Isaiah 29:21 are (1) making a man an offender for a word, (2) entrapping judges, and (3) condemning good people for trivial cause.

17. The Lord similarly described the 587 B.C. siege of Jerusalem to Ezekiel (see Ezekiel 4:1–2).

18. For a succinct review of the Assyrian and Babylonian sieges of Jerusalem, see John Bright, *A History of Israel,* 3rd ed. (Philadelphia: Westminster, 1981), 285–8, 327, 329–30; or Siegfried Herrmann, *A History of Israel in Old Testament Times,* rev. ed. (Philadelphia: Fortress, 1981), 257–9, 278–80, 282–5.

19. Romans 11:8 is actually a conflate quote of Deuteronomy 29:3–4 with the added phrase from Isaiah. Paul also cited Isaiah 29:16 in Romans 9:20–21 and Isaiah 29:14 in 1 Corinthians 1:19. For an exhaustive list of New Testament Isaiah citations, see Gleason L. Archer and Gregory C. Chirichigno, *Old Testament Quotations in the New Testament* (Chicago: Moody Press, 1983), 92–135.

20. On the Roman quash of the First and Second Jewish Revolts, see Flavius Josephus, *De Bello Judaico,* Books 4–6 (English translation *Josephus, The Jewish War,* ed. Gaalya Cornfeld [Grand Rapids, Mich.: Zondervan, 1982], 263–452), and Eusebius Pamphili, *Historia Ecclesiastica,* Book 4 (English translation *The History of the Church from Christ to Constantine,* trans. G. A. Williamson [New York: Dorset, 1984], 157–8), respectively. For a

synopsis, see A. R. C. Leaney, *The Jewish and Christian World, 200 BC to AD 200,* Cambridge Commentaries on Writings of the Jewish and Christian World, 200 BC to AD 200, vol. 7 (Cambridge: Cambridge University Press, 1984), 115–25.

21. The prophecy could also be called Nephi's "plain prophecy," but he uses "plain" again in 2 Nephi 31:2–3 to characterize his explanation of the doctrine of Christ in that chapter.

22. The first edition of the Book of Mormon (1830), with topical chapters, generally longer than in the current editions, divides Nephi's "own prophecy" into just two: Chapter XI, equivalent to 2 Nephi 25–27, and Chapter XII, equivalent to 2 Nephi 28–30.

23. Nephi claims Isaiah-like words as his own in 2 Nephi 25:1–4, 7–8, 13, 20, 28; 26:14; 28:1, 6; 30:1, 3. He attributes Isaiah-like words to the Lord in ways that Isaiah does not in 2 Nephi 26:18; 27:28; 29:1.

24. Nephi, his father Lehi, and his brother Jacob each received a divine witness of Jerusalem's destruction (see 1 Nephi 19:20; 2 Nephi 1:4; 6:8).

25. Other prophets have often likened scriptural words to new contexts for their own purposes. President Spencer W. Kimball used the criteria the Lord gave Moses in Leviticus 26:2–4 for meriting rain in the land of Canaan to urge Sabbath observance and other commandment-keeping during the 1977 drought in the Western United States. Citing the scripture, President Kimball said, "This applies to you and me" (*Conference Report* [April 1977]: 5–6). Elder Bruce R. McConkie called the words of earlier scriptural writers "my own words" in his eloquent final testimony of the Savior (*Conference Report* [April 1985]: 9). In an extended allegory, Joseph Smith likened the Savior's parables in Matthew 13 to the expanding kingdom of God in the latter days (see "To the Elders of the Church of the Latter Day Saints," *Latter Day Saints' Messenger and Advocate* 2/3 [December 1835]: 225–30; reprinted in Joseph Smith, *History of the Church of Jesus Christ of Latter-day Saints,* ed. B. H. Roberts [Salt Lake City: The Church of Jesus Christ of Latter-day Saints, 1932–51], 2:264–72).

26. It is sometimes claimed that words that are *not* like Isaiah 29 in 2 Nephi 26:15–27:35 come from the brass plates text of Isaiah or restore plain and precious things taken from Isaiah's writings (see 1 Nephi 13:20–41). These approaches are misdirected for these chapters. Nephi is not quoting here. Both the new words and the Isaiah-like words are Nephi's. They are part of his "own prophecy." Similarly misdirected are claims that Nephi is paraphrasing Isaiah 29 in 2 Nephi 26:15–27:35. He is doing exactly the opposite. "Paraphrase" gives new words for the same meaning. "Likening" gives new meaning for the same words.

27. The term "remnant" pervades biblical and Book of Mormon scripture. Passages showing the Nephite understanding include 1 Nephi 13:34; 2 Nephi 28:2 (compare 2 Nephi 25:4–5); and 2 Nephi 30:3–4. Isaianic usage is illustrated in Isaiah 1:9; 10:20–23; 11:16; and 46:3.

28. Comparison with 2 Nephi 26:9–11 shows that this destruction is not the slaughter of the Nephite civilization in the fourth century A.D. (see Mormon 6). The gentiles didn't begin to arrive in the Western Hemisphere until more than a thousand years later. Their devastation of so many of Lehi's descendants is the focus of 2 Nephi 26:15–19 (see also 1 Nephi 13:34; 15:17; 2 Nephi 1:10–11).

29. On Nephite awareness of the scattering and the restoration, see John W. Welch, "Getting through Isaiah with the Help of the Nephite Prophetic View," in this volume.

30. See note 10. For a concise statement on the symbolic usage of "Zion," see A. D. Sorensen, "Zion," in *The Encyclopedia of Mormonism*, ed. Daniel H. Ludlow (New York: Macmillan, 1992), 4:1624–6.

31. David Rolph Seely identifies pride as the main theme of Isaiah 2–14 in "Nephi's Usage of Isaiah 2–14 in 2 Nephi 12–30," in this volume.

32. Second Nephi 28:10, like 2 Nephi 26:3, uses the concept of a voice from the ground to portray the vindication of the wrongfully slain, showing that Nephi recognized the Genesis 4:10 implications of Isaiah 29:4. Moroni uses the same concept in Ether 8:24.

33. The "second time" phrase on the gathering, from Isaiah 11:11, appears to be very important to Nephi. He refers to it in 2 Nephi 6:14; 21:11; 25:17; and 29:1. His brother Jacob also refers to it in Jacob 6:2. Doctrine and Covenants 137:6 gives the prophecy a latter-day fulfillment, according to the understanding of Joseph Smith.

34. Such identifications are discussed in interpretive commentaries on Isaiah 11, including Duane S. Crowther, *Prophets and Prophecies of the Old Testament* (Salt Lake City, Deseret Book, 1966), 354–6; Victor L. Ludlow, *Isaiah: Prophet, Seer, and Poet* (Salt Lake City: Deseret Book, 1982), 167–78; Bruce R. McConkie, *The Millennial Messiah: The Second Coming of the Son of Man* (Salt Lake City: Deseret Book, 1982), 339–40; Monte S. Nyman, *An Ensign to All People: The Sacred Message and Mission of the Book of Mormon* (Salt Lake City: Deseret Book, 1987), 18–20; Nyman, *"Great Are the Words,"* 61–4, 71–7; Sidney B. Sperry, *The Voice of Israel's Prophets* (Salt Lake City: Deseret Book, 1952), 33–8.

35. See previous note; also see Ellis T. Rasmussen, *A Latter-day Saint Commentary on the Old Testament* (Salt Lake City: Deseret Book, 1993), 512; and Joseph Fielding Smith, *The Way to Perfection* (Salt Lake City: Deseret Press, 1975), 134–48.

36. The assembling of the outcasts of Israel includes the recovery of the latter-day Nephites and Lamanites to belief in Christ by means of the Book of Mormon.

37. The conversion of the Jews by the Book of Mormon is part of the fulfillment of this prophecy, since "Ephraim" can represent Joseph's descendants, the book's writers. In Doctrine and Covenants 27:5, the Lord refers to the Book of Mormon as "the stick of Ephraim."

38. Collections of various accounts of the visits of Moroni and other heavenly messengers to Joseph Smith are found in Milton V. Backman Jr., *Eyewitness Accounts of the Restoration* (Orem, Utah: Grandin, 1983), 33–56; Paul R. Cheesman, *The Keystone of Mormonism: Little Known Truths about the Book of Mormon* (Salt Lake City: Deseret Book, 1973), 1–31; H. Donl Peterson, "Moroni: Joseph Smith's Teacher," in *Regional Studies in Latter-day*

Saint Church History: New York, ed. Larry C. Porter, Milton V. Backman Jr., and Susan Easton Black (Provo, Utah: Department of Church History and Doctrine, Brigham Young University, 1992), 49–70.

39. In the preface to the first letter of this series, Oliver Cowdery says his letters are intended to give "a full history of the rise of church of the Latter Day Saints, and the most interesting parts of its progress, to the present time [September 7, 1834]" (*Messenger and Advocate,* 1/1 [October 1834]: 13). He adds, "That our narrative may be correct, and particularly the introduction, it is proper to inform our patrons [the readers of the *Messenger and Advocate*], that our brother J. SMITH jr. has offered to assist us. Indeed, there are many items connected with the fore part of this subject that render his labor indispensible." Oliver Cowdery's eight letters were copied into Joseph Smith's "large journal" and republished in the *Times and Seasons,* November 1840–May 1841, and elsewhere, most recently in Dean C. Jessee, *Papers of Joseph Smith* (Salt Lake City: Deseret Book, 1989), 1:26–96. Subsequent citations from the letters herein follow Jessee's edition.

40. Jessee, *Papers of Joseph Smith,* 1:52.

41. Ibid., 1:52–3.

42. Ibid., 1:53.

43. Ibid.

44. Ibid., 1:53–4. The theme of a sealed book is found in Revelation 5 (compare D&C 77:6–7) as well as in Isaiah 29.

45. Isaiah said, speaking of the words of a symbolic book, that they are delivered to "one that is learned" (Isaiah 29:11), but neither learned nor unlearned can read them. Nephi said, speaking of the words of a literal book, and using a phrase more like Moroni's, that they are presented to "the learned" (2 Nephi 27:15), but he goes on to say (in 2 Nephi 27:19–20) that the Lord *tells* "him that is not learned" to read them (Moroni says "translate" them).

46. Jessee, *Papers of Joseph Smith,* 1:88.

47. Ibid., 1:90.

48. The Three Witnesses would later testify that "this *work*"—the Book of Mormon—was "*marvelous* in our eyes" ("The

Testimony of Three Witnesses," Book of Mormon front matter, emphasis added).

49. Illustrating the wider application, the Lord again spoke of the "marvelous work" in April 1829 after Oliver Cowdery had begun to serve as Joseph Smith's scribe (see D&C 6:1); to various associates of the Prophet in May and June 1829 in connection with their part in the work (see D&C 11:1; 12:1; 14:1); and to David Whitmer and Oliver Cowdery in conjunction with their call in June 1829 to search out the first Twelve of the latter-day dispensation (see D&C 18:44).

50. Nephi may have personally visited Joseph Smith before the Book of Mormon was translated, but his words to the Prophet are not known. A probable scribal error substituted Nephi's name for Moroni's in some early publications, including the 1851 edition of the Pearl of Great Price (see Cheesman, *The Keystone of Mormonism*, 27–31), but other statements that Nephi appeared to the Prophet are found in George Q. Cannon, *Journal of Discourses* (Liverpool: Latter-day Saints' Book Depot, 1885–86), 3:47; John Taylor, *Journal of Discourses,* 17:374; 21:161–4; and Orson Pratt to John Christensen, 11 March 1876, Orson Pratt Letter Book, Church Archives, Historical Department, The Church of Jesus Christ of Latter-day Saints, Salt Lake City, Utah (hereafter, LDS Church Archives), cited in H. Donl Peterson, *Moroni: Ancient Prophet, Modern Messenger* (Bountiful, Utah: Horizon, 1983), 131. On an alleged statement in Thomas Bullock's journal, see Cheesman, *The Keystone,* 6.

51. Joseph Smith observed that for Moroni's citation from Malachi 3–4, the angel quoted it "with a little variation from the way it reads in our Bibles" (JS–H 1:36) and for the verses of Acts 3:22–23, "precisely as they stand in our New Testament" (JS–H 1:40).

52. Commentary and sources on the Harris/Anthon interview are found in Backman, *Eyewitness Accounts of the Restoration,* 57–68, 79–83; Richard Bushman, *Joseph Smith and the Beginnings of Mormonism* (Urbana: University of Illinois Press, 1984), 84–90; Ariel L. Crowley, "The Anthon Transcript: An Evidence for the

Truth of the Prophet's Account of the Origin of the Book of Mormon," *Improvement Era* 45 (1942): 14–5, 58–60, 76–80, 124–5, 150–1, 182–3; Donna Hill, *Joseph Smith: The First Mormon* (Garden City, New York: Doubleday, 1977), 74–9; Stanley B. Kimball, "The Anthon Transcript: People, Primary Sources, and Problems," *Brigham Young University Studies* 10 (spring 1970): 325–52; Francis W. Kirkham, *A New Witness for Christ in America: The Book of Mormon; Evidence of Divine Power in the "Coming Forth" of the Book of Mormon*, vol. 1, special 4th ed. (Salt Lake City: Utah Printing, 1967), 1:155–71, 414–22; "Martin Harris' Visit with Charles Anthon: Collected Documents on the Anthon Transcript and 'Shorthand Egyptian,'" (Provo, Utah: FARMS, 1990); Larry C. Porter, "A Study of the Origins of the Church of Jesus Christ of Latter-day Saints in the States of New York and Pennsylvania, 1816–1831" (Ph.D. diss., Brigham Young University, 1971), 138–44; B. H. Roberts, *A Comprehensive History of the Church of Jesus Christ of Latter-day Saints* (Salt Lake City: Deseret News Press, 1930), 1:99–109.

53. See Smith, *History of the Church*, 1:17–9.

54. Joseph Smith and his wife Emma were not allowed to live in her parents' home when Joseph refused to show his father-in-law the plates. See Bushman, *Joseph Smith and the Beginnings of Mormonism*, 85–6.

55. See Hill, *Joseph Smith: The First Mormon*, 73.

56. See Smith, *History of the Church*, 1:19.

57. Ibid., 20.

58. Ibid.

59. Jessee, *Papers of Joseph Smith*, 1:9. This account is all the more significant since the 1832 history is Joseph Smith's only journal that contains his own handwriting. Much of the material quoted here is in the Prophet's handwriting in the original. For background information on the 1832 history, see Jessee, *Papers of Joseph Smith*, 1:1, 3; and *The Personal Writings of Joseph Smith*, ed. Dean C. Jessee (Salt Lake City: Deseret Book, 1984), 3–4. The latter includes photofacsimiles of the original holograph on pages 9–14.

60. The Prophet's mother recalled that Martin Harris had told Joseph Smith he would come to Harmony as soon as Joseph

had had sufficient time to copy and translate some of the characters. She also said Joseph Smith and Martin Harris had agreed
that Harris was to take the characters and translation to the East
and stop in at all the professed linguists along the way to give
them an opportunity to display their talents in translating them.
See Lucy Mack Smith, *History of Joseph Smith by His Mother*, ed.
Preston Nibley (Salt Lake City: Bookcraft, 1954), 119. This could
refer, however, to an agreement made in Harmony, or she could
have confused the timing of the agreement.

61. William Pilkington Affidavit, 3 April 1934, Archives,
Brigham Young University, Provo, Utah, 2. On Pilkington's ac-
quaintance with Martin Harris generally, see William Pilkington,
"A Biography of William Pilkington Jr.. written By Himself," LDS
Church Archives.

62. A. Metcalf, *Ten Years before the Mast* (Malad, Idaho: by the
author, 1888), 71, cited in Bushman, *Joseph Smith and the Beginnings of Mormonism*, 219 n. 31.

63. See the discussion in Bushman, *Joseph Smith and the Beginnings of Mormonism*, 89, and 219 n. 33. Later inquiries to Professor
Anthon by both the curious and the anti-Mormon resulted in attempts to distance himself from what he considered an embar-
rassing association with Mormonism. He denied giving Martin
Harris a certificate in an 1834 letter to E. D. Howe, reprinted in
Eber D. Howe, *Mormonism Unvailed* (Painesville, Ohio: by the author, 1834), 269–72, but contradicted himself in an 1841 letter to
Rev. Thomas W. Coit, reprinted in John A. Clark, *Gleanings by the
Way* (Philadelphia: W. J. & J. K. Simon, 1842), 233–8, saying that
he did write a certificate to the effect that the marks on the paper
[shown him by the farmer] appeared to be an imitation of various
alphabetical characters that had no meaning at all connected with
them. His 1841 letter says no one had ever requested a written
statement from him about the meeting, further contradicting the
Howe letter. The two letters are reprinted in Roberts, *A Comprehensive History of the Church*, 1:102–7, with observations on the
contradictions.

64. We assume here that Joseph Smith showed Martin Harris
the Isaiah 29 passage as soon as Harris returned to Harmony

from New York, although no historical source clearly states this.

65. The translation initiated shortly after Martin Harris's return, for which he acted as scribe, produced the 116 foolscap pages that were subsequently lost (see D&C 3, 10). Several months passed before the Urim and Thummim and the plates were returned to the Prophet by Moroni. Mother Smith says Joseph Smith got the Urim and Thummim back on 22 September 1828 (see Lucy Mack Smith, *History of Joseph Smith by His Mother*, 134), and the translation that included 2 Nephi was not made until after Oliver Cowdery became the Prophet's scribe on 7 April 1829 (see Smith, *History of the Church*, 1:32–3).

66. On the historical chronology of Joseph Smith's translation of the Bible, see Robert J. Matthews, *"A Plainer Translation": Joseph Smith's Translation of the Bible, A History and Commentary* (Provo, Utah: Brigham Young University Press, 1975), 21–39.

67. Ibid., 78–80.

68. Ibid., 79, 96.

69. Ibid., 86.

70. Ibid., 59–60, 75, 79–81. Matthews discusses the insertion notation and explains the need for access to both Joseph Smith's Bible and the corresponding JST manuscript for understanding its interpretation.

71. Ibid., 56–60.

72. This and all subsequent statements on the contents of the JST manuscripts and Joseph Smith's 1828 KJV Bible are based on an examination of the microfilm copy at the LDS Church Archives, catalogued as "Inspired Version of the Bible manuscript, ca. 1830–1833." The original Bible and manuscripts are in the possession of Library—Archives, Reorganized Church of Jesus Christ of Latter Day Saints, Independence, Missouri.

73. Royal Skousen, personal communication, 29 October, 1994. In his "Textual Variants in the Isaiah Quotations in the Book of Mormon," in this volume, Skousen lists this as one of the findings of his ongoing Book of Mormon Critical Text Project. See also an earlier perspective in Richard P. Howard, *Restoration Scriptures: A Study of Their Textual Development,* 2nd ed. (Independence, Missouri: Herald House, 1995), 94–102.

74. It is not clear whether Joseph Smith dictated this material or had Sidney Rigdon copy it directly out of the Book of Mormon. Textual evidence does not support one theory to the exclusion of the other. In fact, some combination may have occurred. The two men could have been looking at the Book of Mormon while Joseph Smith read aloud and Sidney Rigdon wrote, or the words could have been dictated by Joseph Smith from the Book of Mormon and then visually compared by Sidney Rigdon with the written text.

75. Neither the 1830 edition of the Book of Mormon nor the Isaiah 29 section of OT 3 is fully versified. To facilitate the discussion, portions of them will be cited using chapter and verse numbers from current published editions.

76. The italicized words *"shall be"* in KJV Isaiah 29:5 are also lined through in Joseph Smith's Bible, but no replacement is indicated in OT 3.

77. "Those who" appears in recent editions of both the Book of Mormon and the JST.

78. "Have" appears in recent editions of the Book of Mormon.

79. In the introduction to the revelation now known as Doctrine and Covenants 71, received 1 December 1831, Joseph Smith referred to the Bible translation as "this branch of my, <calling>" ("calling" was inserted in the manuscript of the revelation) (Joseph Smith, "History of the Church, A–1," manuscript [1839], 174, in Jessee, *Papers of Joseph Smith*, 1:369; compare Smith, *History of the Church*, 1:238). The Lord's concern with the translation is seen in its important role in the unfolding revelations of the Doctrine and Covenants. See Robert L. Millet, "From Translations to Revelations: Joseph Smith's Translation of the Bible and the Doctrine and Covenants," in Porter, Backman, and Black, eds., *Regional Studies in Latter-day Saint Church History: New York*, 215–34; and Larry E. Dahl, "The Joseph Smith Translation and the Doctrine and Covenants," in *Plain and Precious Truths Restored: The Doctrinal and Historical Significance of the Joseph Smith Translation*, ed. Robert L. Millet and Robert J. Matthews (Salt Lake City: Bookcraft, 1995), 104–33.

80. It is interesting to consider why Joseph Smith did not copy the full text of Isaiah 2–14 from the Book of Mormon into the JST. The changes in OT 3 for Isaiah 2–14 generally use the word and phrase insertion notation. Joseph Smith obviously saw Nephi's detailed prophecies in 2 Nephi 27 in a different light than the less extensive dissimilarities between 2 Nephi 12–24 and KJV Isaiah 2–14.

81. Speaking of the Prophet's translation of the New Testament, but just as applicable to Isaiah 29, the Lord taught Joseph Smith that one purpose of the JST was to prepare us for things to come (see D&C 42:56–58, 60–61).

82. The replacement of Isaiah 29:8–24 with 2 Nephi 27:3b–35 in the JST could fit the third of the four categories Robert J. Matthews proposes for types of changes in the JST. He describes the third category as follows: "Portions [of the JST] may consist of inspired commentary by the Prophet Joseph Smith, enlarged, elaborated, and even adapted to a latter-day situation. This may be similar to what Nephi meant by 'likening' the scriptures to himself and his people in their particular circumstance" (Matthews, *"A Plainer Translation,"* 253). In the case of JST Isaiah 29, the replacement process itself, in addition to the chapter content, was commentary.

"How Beautiful upon the Mountains" The Imagery of Isaiah 52:7–10 and Its Occurrences in the Book of Mormon

Dana M. Pike

Many writers quote Isaiah's rejoicing at the messenger who will bring the beleaguered city victorious news, a prophecy that rewards close analysis and primarily refers to Christ.

Nestled in the middle of Isaiah 52 is a passage that contains intriguing imagery and brims with joyous hope:

> How beautiful upon the mountains
> are the feet of him that bringeth good tidings,
> that publisheth peace;
> that bringeth good tidings of good,
> that publisheth salvation;
> that saith unto Zion,
> Thy God reigneth! (Isaiah 52:7)[1]

This beautiful passage has been frequently quoted or paraphrased, often along with the three verses following it, by later prophets in other passages of Latter-day Saint scripture. What is it about this passage that has had, and still has, so much appeal? A study of what the prophet Isaiah intended by these words and an exploration of how other prophets—especially those whose teachings are contained in the Book of Mormon—have understood and employed them will allow us to appreciate the impact of this prophecy in the lives of past saints, as well as its significance for our time.

The Context

In order to understand the imagery and significance of Isaiah 52:7–10, it is important to appreciate how this passage fits into the larger text of which it is a part. As with many ancient prophetic texts, Isaiah 52, with the exception of verses 3–6, is written in poetic form, although this is not apparent in the King James Version. Most modern English translations preserve the poetic versification of this and other similar material. Because of its poetic nature, this text is filled with wonderfully vivd imagery but is at the same time ambiguous in many respects.

For example, in Isaiah 52:1–2, Zion—that is, Jerusalem—is urged to "awake, awake; put on thy strength . . . , shake thyself from the dust, . . . loose thyself from the bands of thy neck."[2] Latter-day Saints often consider Jerusalem and Zion to be names applied to distinctly different locations, Jerusalem in Israel and "Zion (the New Jerusalem) . . . upon the American continent" (Article of Faith 10). This is true, but in addition to referring to "the pure in heart" (D&C 97:21) wherever they may be, the term *Zion* has been applied in the scriptures to specific places where the pure in heart have gathered, such as Enoch's city (see Moses 7:18) and the so-called Old Jerusalem, especially the area originally captured by David from the Jebusites and the area that later became the temple mount (see 2 Samuel 5:6–7; 1 Kings 8:1; Isaiah 2:1–3; and so on).[3] For the present purpose, it is sufficient to know that the name Zion has been applied to Old and New Jerusalem, just as both of these cities are called Jerusalem.

Many, if not most, of Isaiah's contemporaries would have viewed his use of the names Zion and Jerusalem in Isaiah 52:1–2 as a function of the interchangeability of a poetic pair of terms both of which referred to Jerusalem in Judah. These names are often used in the Bible in just such a way.[4] Such use is illustrated here in Isaiah 52 verses 1 and 2:

> put on thy strength, O Zion;
> put on thy beautiful garments, O Jerusalem . . .
> arise, and sit down, O Jerusalem:

loose thyself from the bands of thy neck, O captive
daughter of Zion.

Such statements as these actually refer to Jerusalem and
those Israelites living there at any given time. But these passages can function typologically in the scriptures, so that,
conceptually, they apply by extension to other Israelites in
different times and places.

Pronouncements by Joseph Smith recorded in Doctrine
and Covenants 113:7–10 make it clear that these prophetic
promptings at the beginning of Isaiah 52 apply to such
events as the latter-day gathering and redemption of Israel:

> Questions by Elias Higbee: What is meant by the
> command in Isaiah, 52d chapter, 1st verse, which saith:
> Put on thy strength, O Zion—and what people had Isaiah
> reference to?
>
> He had reference to those whom God should call in
> the last days, who should hold the power of priesthood
> to bring again Zion, and the redemption of Israel; and to
> put on her strength is to put on the authority of the priest-
> hood, which she, Zion, has a right to by lineage; also to
> return to that power which she had lost.
>
> What are we to understand by Zion loosing herself
> from the bands of her neck; 2d verse?
>
> We are to understand that the scattered remnants are
> exhorted to return to the Lord from whence they have
> fallen; which if they do, the promise of the Lord is that he
> will speak to them, or give them revelation. See the 6th,
> 7th, and 8th verses. The bands of her neck are the curses
> of God upon her, or the remnants of Israel in their scat-
> tered condition among the Gentiles.

The word *Jerusalem* is not used in these verses in Doctrine
and Covenants 113, but it is clear from Joseph's answers concerning this passage that he had a much broader vision of Zion
in mind than just the city of Jerusalem in Judah.

On a different occasion, Joseph quoted Isaiah 52:8, "thy watchmen shall lift up the voice; with the voice together shall they sing: for they shall see eye to eye, when the Lord shall bring again Zion," when he spoke of the Lord designating the spot in Jackson County, Missouri, where the city of Zion would someday be built.[5] This should not be understood as an indication that Isaiah 52:7–10 exclusively applies to or is to be fulfilled only by events in Missouri; it is rather an example of the prophetic application of an earlier prophetic statement to one particular circumstance.[6]

Whether one understands the primary sense of the terms *Zion* and *Jerusalem* in Isaiah 52:1–2 as restricted to Old Jerusalem—the likely view with which most of Isaiah's audience would have understood his teachings—or whether one prefers the broader application of some latter-day prophets, it is clear that Joseph's declaration concerning these verses indicates that the primary focus of the prophecy in Isaiah 52 is the last days. The latter-day content of Isaiah 52 is also indicated in the first verse by the promise that "henceforth there shall no more come into thee [that is, Jerusalem] the uncircumcised and the unclean," a condition that has yet to be fulfilled. Compare the similar language in Joel 3:17 in which it is stated that after the (second) coming of the Lord, "shall Jerusalem be holy, and there shall no strangers pass through her any more."[7]

In Isaiah 52:3–6 the Lord also speaks of a future time. He reminds the Israelites that even though "ye have sold yourselves for nought" (verse 3), and though some have been, and others would yet be, exiled (verse 5), "in that [future] day" he would fulfill all his promises to them—"my people shall know my name" (verse 6). The Jews who were exiled to and returned from Babylonia (about 597–535 B.C.) probably applied this and similar passages to their circumstances. However, the historical context of the Jews returning from exile to a land dominated by foreigners (Judah was then a province of the Persian empire; Jerusalem was hardly redeemed) and our understanding of the latter-day focus of verses 1–2 indicates that verses 3–6 have not yet been fulfilled. The primary occurrence of this redemption and renewed knowledge is the latter days, when Israel as a people will be a faithful, covenant partner with Jehovah.

Similarly, Isaiah 52:7–10 beautifully conveys the (yet-future) exultation in Jerusalem created by the "good tidings" that "God reigneth" (Isaiah 52:7) and that he is about to "comfort his people" and "redeem Jerusalem" (Isaiah 52:9). This news causes the city's "watchmen" to "sing" for joy (Isaiah 52:8). According to verse 9, however, Jerusalem is still in ruins. The messenger announces the *beginning*, not the completion, of the process of redemption and comfort that commences because "the Lord hath made bare his holy arm . . . and all the ends of the earth shall see the salvation of our God" (Isaiah 52:10). Compare the similar message in Isaiah 40:1–2: "Comfort ye, comfort ye my people, saith your God. Speak ye comfortably to Jerusalem, and cry unto her, that her warfare is accomplished, that her iniquity is pardoned."

Isaiah 52 continues with an exhortation to Israelites: "go ye out" (verse 11) from your places of dispersement and "gather" (as verse 15 in the JST reads for "sprinkle" in KJV). They are instructed to be clean (see verse 11) and promised that "the Lord will go before you" (verse 12). Once again, the latter days seems to be the time of the primary fulfillment of these instructions (compare 2 Corinthians 6:17 and D&C 133:5–15, especially verses 14–15).

Verses 13–15 tell of the Lord's "servant" who will "deal prudently," who will be "exalted and extolled" (verse 13), although "his visage was so marred more than any man" (verse 14), and whose works will cause kings to "shut their mouths" (verse 15) because they had not previously heard of nor understood the things accomplished by the servant. But who is this servant? An identity is not clearly specified in the text. Proposed identifications include, first, the nation of Israel, referred to as Jehovah's servant in Isaiah 49:1–3; second, the mortal Lord, especially suggested by those who prefer to connect these last verses of Isaiah 52 with the prophecy of the mortal Messiah that follows in chapter 53 (see verse 11, "my righteous servant"); third, the resurrected Lord, who, though "marred more than any man" in the sense of the atoning load he bore (compare Isaiah 53:2–5), will be powerful and exalted at his second coming (an interpretation in keeping with the latter-day focus of this chapter, specifically verse 10); and, fourth, Joseph Smith, an identification especially based on Jesus' use of this passage in 3 Nephi 20:43–45 and 21:7–10 (discussed below).[8] The first option is the least likely in this context; the latter two are the most likely and may both apply (some people see multiple fulfillments in many of Isaiah's prophecies).[9]

The Particulars

The imagery embodied in the poetry of Isaiah 52:7–10 is that of watchmen on a city wall who witness the approach and arrival of a messenger who travels on foot. Walled cities were commonplace in ancient Israel and throughout the ancient Near East, and watchmen, or lookouts, were regularly posted above city gates. The job security and probably the life of a watchman depended on his ability to remain alert to anyone or anything approaching his city, especially things appearing suspicious in nature.[10]

Lacking the technological advances available in our era, people of the ancient Near East regularly entrusted messengers with communications. We learn a great deal about messengers in the ancient Near East from a variety of documents that span more than two millennia before the Christian era. For instance, messages were given to messengers for delivery sometimes in oral but often in written form.[11] Two very important qualities of a good messenger were speed and accuracy in delivering a message. Accurate delivery was especially a concern when the message was in oral form only.[12]

The Hebrew word that is most often used to designate a messenger is *mal'āk*, from *L'K*. While *mal'āk* is usually translated as "messenger," the translation is "ultimately context-sensitive: 'envoy,' 'messenger,' 'representative,' 'ambassador,' 'agent' all may comfortably apply depending on the situation."[13]

Messengers and watchmen are mentioned in a number of passages in the Bible. The text that best illuminates the present discussion is 2 Samuel 18:19–28. Ahimaaz, a son of Zadok the priest, requests of Joab the general that he be allowed to deliver news from the battlefield to King David in Jerusalem. The subsequent actions of the watchman in Jerusalem who observes the approach of Ahimaaz, and David's anticipation of what he thinks will be good news, are clearly recounted:

> Let me [Ahimaaz] now run, and bear the king tidings, how that the Lord hath avenged him of his enemies. . . . And he [Joab] said unto him, Run. . . . And the watchman went up to the roof over the gate unto the wall [of Jerusalem], and lifted up his eyes, and looked, and behold a man running alone. And the watchman cried, and told the king. . . . And the watchman said, Me thinketh the running . . . is like the running of Ahimaaz the son of Zadok. And the king said, He is a good man, and cometh with good tidings. (2 Samuel 18:19, 23–25, 27)[14]

Such real-life activities clearly provided the imagery of a messenger and watchmen that are incorporated into Isaiah's prophecy, especially verses 7–8 of chapter 52.

The role of a watchman on a city wall was used in Israelite literature to represent a significant aspect of a prophet's duty. In Ezekiel 33:1–9 the Lord clearly draws an analogy between the critical function of an actual urban watchman and that of a "spiritual" watchman, reminding Ezekiel, "I have set thee a watchman unto the house of Israel; therefore thou shalt hear the word at my mouth, and warn them from me" (verse 7).[15] In this passage, the Lord functions as the messenger. Ezekiel is the watchman who receives the message from the messenger and conveys it to the leadership or to the inhabitants of the city.

Israelite prophets also functioned as spiritual messengers to the inhabitants of ancient Israel, delivering Jehovah's message to the people.[16] This role is illustrated by the description of the prophet Haggai as "the Lord's messenger [*mal'āk*]" who delivered "the Lord's message unto the people" (Haggai 1:13). Note also the chronicler's observation, made while indicating that the sinfulness of those living in Jerusalem and Judah had led to their destruction by the Babylonians, that

> the Lord God of their fathers sent to them by his messengers [*mal'ākāyw*] . . . ; because he had compassion on his people, and on his dwelling place: But they mocked the messengers [*mal'ăkê*] of God, and despised his words, and misused his prophets, until . . . there was no remedy. (2 Chronicles 36:15–16)

The Hebrew word commonly used to designate a human messenger, *mal'āk*, is the same word that is translated "angel" when used in referring to a heavenly messenger. Angels are "messengers" commissioned by the Lord to deliver a message from the divine realm to the human one.[17] An interesting coincidence of these uses of *mal'āk*, in reference to both human and divine beings, is found in the narration of Jacob's departure from Laban's house to return to the land of Canaan: "And Jacob went on his way, and the angels of God [*mal'ăkê 'ělōhîm*] met him. . . . And Jacob sent messengers [*mal'ākîm*] before him to Esau his brother" (Genesis 32:1, 3).

The Hebrew word used in Isaiah 52:7, however, is not the common noun *mal'āk*, "messenger," but the masculine singular active participle *mĕbaśśēr*, "one who brings news, a herald," derived from *BŚR*, "to bring news."[18] The term itself is neutral, not revealing the nature of the news. Sometimes it was tragic, as illustrated in 1 Samuel 4:17: "And the messenger [*mĕbaśśēr*] answered and said, Israel is fled before the Philistines, and there hath been also a great slaughter among the people" (see verses 12–18 for the context). In Isaiah 52:7 the news is good. The text clearly states that the *mĕbaśśēr* brings "good tidings."[19] Actually, the term *mĕbaśśēr* occurs two times in Isaiah 52:7:

> How beautiful upon the mountains
> are the feet of <u>him that bringeth good tidings</u>
>   [*mĕbaśśēr*],
> that publisheth peace [*mašmîaʿ šālôm*];
> <u>that bringeth good tidings</u> [*mĕbaśśēr*] of good,
> that publisheth salvation [*mašmîaʿ yĕšûʿâ*];
> that saith unto Zion,
> Thy God reigneth!

An alternative, more literal rendition of this verse follows:

> What beauty on (or over) the mountains:
> the feet of a herald
> announcing peace,
> declaring (heralding) good,

announcing salvation,
saying to Zion
"your God reigns."

What is fascinating about Isaiah's use of imagery here is that not only does he mention a messenger or herald, but he also focuses on the messenger's feet with the notation that they are "beautiful." Feet are not generally considered among the more attractive body parts; they are functional, yes, but not beautiful. What did Isaiah intend by this description?

Interestingly, the word rendered "beautiful" in verse 7 is the Hebrew term *nā^ɔwû* (from the rarely attested verbal root *N^ɔH*), the word from which Joseph Smith coined the city name "Nauvoo."[20] This particular form is used only here and in Song of Solomon 1:10, where it is rendered "comely" in the KJV.

Since walking on dirt roads with sandal-shod feet was the major form of transportation for most people in ancient Israel, feet were not only quite visible but required daily washing and attention. The cleansing and care of a guest's feet was long considered a basic act of hospitality.[21] However, despite the importance of foot care in ancient Israel, when Isaiah described the messenger's feet on the mountains as "beautiful," he was probably not suggesting that the arriving herald had remarkably clean and well-manicured feet![22]

It is not the condition of the feet but their observable activity, their *progress*, that is being emphasized by the description "beautiful." It might be suggested that Isaiah employed metonymy here, using "feet" to represent the whole messenger. Whether viewed this way or not, the emphasis in this passage is on the feet of the messenger because the focus of the passage is on the delivery of the message as well as on the arrival of the messenger. The hope-inspiring approach of the herald elicits the reaction on Mount Zion that the messenger's feet are beautiful, and the delivery of the anticipated message produces the expression of exultation in Jerusalem (see Isaiah 52:8–10). Some modern translations of Isaiah 52:7 have tried to convey this sense. Consider this rendition: "How welcome on the mountain are the footsteps of the herald announcing happiness" (NJPS). Here Isaiah depicts the arrival of a messenger recognized by watchmen who joyfully anticipate his message. It appears that they already know the message and the messenger; it is the actual delivery of the message, the *fulfillment*, that is so exciting.

Verses 9–10 relate the exhortation to "sing together, ye waste places of Jerusalem" because the Lord has "comforted his people" and "redeemed Jerusalem" by baring "his holy arm in the eyes of all the nations." This suggests some type of deliverance that those in Jerusalem could not attain on their own.

Three Interpretive Questions

Readers should ask three questions regarding Isaiah's use of real-life imagery in Isaiah 52:7–10 when considering the fulfillment of the prophecy therein. Given that the fulfillment of the prophecy in Isaiah 52:7–10 involves some future event or events through which a message of hope and comfort will be delivered to and welcomed by a people in need of assistance, readers must ask three questions regarding Isaiah's use of real-life imagery in this passage. First, in Isaiah 52:7–10, the messenger with glad tidings for Zion is depicted as arriving alone. As mentioned above, the grammatical form is masculine singular, and the messenger is not named. Is the herald in this passage a specific individual in the latter days, or should he be viewed as a type,

representing many people? The answer is not clear in the
passage itself. Second, Jerusalem alone is depicted as the
destination of the herald, and Isaiah's imagery draws on
Jerusalem's location on a ridge amidst hills ("mountains").
But should Jerusalem also be understood as a type, depict-
ing any city or group of people receiving glad tidings?
Third, although the message itself is described in glowing
terms and is prophesied as being well received, what is the
actual content of the message? Is the message of a political
or military nature integral to an actual event that is yet to
be, or might this message be spiritual, meant to convey deliverance from a different kind of bondage and destruction?
Again, this is not clearly stated by Isaiah.

As noted above, we will specifically address these
points focusing first on the prophetic use of this Isaianic
passage in the Book of Mormon, and then we will briefly
examine how this passage has been utilized by prophets in
scriptures other than the Book of Mormon.

Isaiah 52:7–10 in the Book of Mormon

Given the favor Nephi and other Book of Mormon
prophets accorded Isaiah's prophecies, it would be very
surprising if Isaiah 52:7–10, a passage of such poetic promise, was not mentioned in that volume of scripture. Actually, much of Isaiah 52, including verses 7–10, is given considerable attention in the Book of Mormon.[23]

Nephi's Teachings of Isaiah

About 125 years after Isaiah, the Lord taught Nephi that

I will manifest myself unto thy seed, that they shall
write many things which I shall minister unto them . . .
behold, these things [the Book of Mormon record] shall
be hid up, to come forth unto the Gentiles, by the gift and

power of the Lamb. . . . And blessed are they who shall
seek to bring forth my Zion *at that day*, for they shall have
the gift and power of the Holy Ghost; . . . and whoso shall
publish peace, yea, tidings of great joy, how beautiful
upon the mountains shall they be. (1 Nephi 13:35, 37,
emphasis added)

The context of this passage in 1 Nephi 13 indicates that the
Lord is referring to the latter-day restoration of the gospel.
The imagery and phrasing of this passage clearly draw on
Isaiah 52:7, and the perspective is wholly positive: those
who participate in this activity will be greatly blessed.
However, this passage is quite general, exhibiting neither
development nor detail. Since "my Zion" may refer to
Jerusalem, the American Zion, or to the Lord's kingdom in
general, it is not clear which, if any one of these in particular, is intended, although the latter is the most likely. Addi-
tionally, *beautiful* does not modify *feet* in this passage, but
has general reference to those who proclaim the peace of the
gospel, and in contrast to Isaiah 52:7, it is explicitly stated
that *many* ("they") will bring glad tidings, not just one -
messenger.

Abinadi's Teachings of Isaiah

The most extensive development and application of
Isaiah 52:7–10 in the Book of Mormon is found in the teachings of the heroic prophet Abinadi, who lived about 150 B.C.
Abinadi is brought before King Noah and his court and is
questioned by Noah's priests, one of whom asks: "What
meaneth the words which are written, and which have been
taught by our fathers, saying: 'How beautiful upon the
mountains are the feet of him that bringeth good tidings;
that publisheth peace?'" (Mosiah 12:20–21 [verses 21–24
quote Isaiah 52:7–10]). With this question we anticipate a prophetic commentary on the passage just quoted; however,

Abinadi, seizing the moment, begins to castigate his audience: "Are you priests . . . and yet desire to know of me what these things mean?" (Mosiah 12:25). He then proceeds to review basic gospel teachings such as the ten commandments and the coming atonement of the Messiah. Partway through his sermon, Abinadi even reminds them that he has not forgotten their question (see Mosiah 13:3). After teaching that salvation did not come through the law of Moses alone, but that the law was a type to point Israelite minds and hearts toward the one truly efficacious sacrifice (see Mosiah 13), Abinadi quotes Isaiah's poignant and powerful prophecy of the Messiah's mortal ministry and atoning sacrifice as recorded in Isaiah 53 (see Mosiah 14).

Finally, in Mosiah 15, Abinadi provides the requested commentary, but in two portions: one in a context of praise and gratitude in which he draws on Isaiah 52:7, and one in a context of condemnation in which he utilizes Isaiah 52:8–10. Mosiah 15 begins with Abinadi's declaration of the nature and identity of the Son of God and the significance of his sacrifice (see verses 1–9). He then continues in verse 10, employing quotations from Isaiah in his remarks: "And now I say unto you, who shall declare his [Jesus'] generation [see Isaiah 53:8]?[24] Behold, I say unto you, that when his soul has been made an offering for sin he shall see his seed [see Isaiah 53:10]. And now what say ye? And who shall be his seed?" The Savior's "seed" are those people in all ages who are spiritually reborn through the power of his atoning sacrifice.[25] Thus, Abinadi exclaims that those who obey the Lord and follow the prophets (see verses 11–12), as well as the prophets themselves (see verse 13), are the "seed" of the Lord and thus "heirs of the kingdom of God" (verse 12).

It is at this point in his exposition of the redemptive power of Jesus' sacrifice that Abinadi employs Isaiah 52:7. Mosiah 15:14 begins with Abinadi's declaration that "these are they who have published peace." While the term *they* might refer exclusively to the prophets mentioned in the verse 13, it seems more likely to me that *they* refers to the saints and prophets to which Abinadi has just made reference in verses 11–13, since he describes both groups as the spiritual "seed" of Christ. Abinadi uses phrases from Isaiah 52:7 as he continues:

> And these are they who have published peace, who have brought good tidings of good, who have published salvation; and said unto Zion: Thy God reigneth!
> And O how beautiful upon the mountains were their feet!
> And again, how beautiful upon the mountains are the feet of those that are still publishing peace!
> And again, how beautiful upon the mountains are the feet of those that shall hereafter publish peace, yea, from this time henceforth and forever!
> And behold, I say unto you, this is not all. For O how beautiful upon the mountains are the feet of him that bringeth good tidings, that is the founder of peace, yea even the Lord, who has redeemed his people. (Mosiah 15:14–18)

Abinadi is here declaring, based on the interpretation just given above, that everyone, everywhere, whoever has or will receive and proclaim the true gospel of Jesus Christ, including and especially the Lord himself, was, is, or will be a messenger with "beautiful feet." Jesus as the "founder of peace" provides the opportunity for spiritual rebirth, and all who truly embrace this good tiding not only enjoy his peace but proclaim the same. The "good tidings" are identified in this passage as the message of redemption, and the phrase *beautiful feet* is employed to indicate that those who receive this message will consider it welcome and wonderful. While Abinadi clearly refers to *many* people's feet as "beautiful," my reading of this episode suggests that Abinadi, and probably also the priests, viewed the prophesied Messiah as *the* messenger with glad tidings. These tidings were from and about the Redeemer. Remember that Abinadi has just taught that Jesus was the God who would "come down among the children of men, and redeem his people" (Mosiah 15:1) and that Christ alone had the power to save. It is in this context that Abinadi employs Isaiah 52:7 (see Mosiah 15:14–18), thus indicating that Jesus was the primary fulfillment of the prophecy in Isaiah 52:7 of the messenger with glad tidings. His "seed," by extension, assist in declaring the same message.

It is instructive at this point to inquire why Abinadi was asked to explain the meaning of Isaiah 52:7–10 by a priest of Noah. It seems clear from the tenor of the preserved account that the priests were trying to frame, and thus eliminate, this prophet who was troubling them. A likely possibility is that they asked Abinadi to interpret Isaiah 52:7–10 because this passage indicates that a messenger of the Lord would come with *good* tidings, and Abinadi's tidings to Noah and his priests were anything but good. Assuming this, the priests could then charge Abinadi with false prophecy, for which they, with their twisting of the scripture, would punish him.[26]

Abinadi continues his discourse to Noah and his priests by explaining that Jesus had power over death through his redeeming sacrifice (see Mosiah 15:19–20) and that all those who qualify for redemption will be part of the "first resurrection" (verses 22–25). Having laid this doctrinal groundwork, Abinadi here shifts in his remarks from testifying of the Redeemer and the redeemed to condemning his audience: "But behold, and fear, and tremble before God, for ye ought to tremble; for the Lord redeemeth none such that rebel against him and die in their sins; yea, even all those . . . that have known the commandments of God, and would not keep them; these are they that have no part in the first resurrection" (verse 26; see also verse 27). Abinadi then teaches that despite the feeble apostate efforts and misguided views of Noah's priests, "the time shall come that the salvation of the Lord shall be declared to every nation, kindred, tongue, and people" (verse 28). He continues,

> Yea, Lord, thy watchmen shall lift up their voice; with the voice together shall they sing; for they shall see eye to eye, when the Lord shall bring again Zion. Break forth into joy, sing together, ye waste places of Jerusalem; for the Lord hath comforted his people, he hath redeemed Jerusalem. The Lord hath made bare his holy arm in the eyes of all the nations; and all the ends of the earth shall see the salvation of our God. (Mosiah 15:29–31, parallel to Isaiah 52:8–10)

Abinadi instructs the priests, using Isaiah 52:8–10, that the time will come when the wicked who fight against Zion, the Lord's people, will be destroyed as the Lord demonstrates his power to "all the ends of the earth" (this theme continues into much of Mosiah 16). Thus, Jesus' suffering at his first coming allows him to exercise justice, to save or destroy, at his second coming, which is the context in which Abinadi places Isaiah 52:8–10. At *that* day, the watchmen of the Lord will rejoice as he arrives to destroy the wicked, redeem the faithful, and establish his millennial kingdom. This all seems intended as a requisite last witness and warning from Abinadi to the priests as he applies a prophecy concerning the last days to the priests and the destruction they will bring on themselves. While there are several facets to the Lord's work of redemption, it is interesting to see how Abinadi connected Isaiah 52:7 with one facet and 52:8–10 with another.

Isaiah's Teachings in the Book of Mosiah

Portions of Isaiah 52:7 also occur in Mosiah 27:37, although the context is much more restricted than that of Mosiah 15. Mosiah 27 contains the account of an angel visiting Alma the Younger and the four sons of King Mosiah as they were persecuting the church, and their subsequent conversion and efforts to reverse the effects of their spiritually destructive activities. In speaking of Mosiah's sons, the record states that "they traveled throughout all the land . . . zealously striving to repair all the injuries which they had done to the church . . . and thus they were instruments in the hands of God in bringing many to the knowledge of the truth, yea, to the knowledge of their Redeemer. And how blessed are they! For they did publish peace; they did publish good tidings of good; and they did declare unto the people that the Lord reigneth" (Mosiah 27:35–37).

It is not presently possible to determine whether the portion of Isaiah 52:7 that is in verse 37 was originally employed in this context by Mormon, as an editorial comment, or whether he found it an account by Alma the Elder or Alma the Younger. While this abbreviated form of the passage does not contain the imagery of the first part of Isaiah 52:7 (the mountains, the beautiful feet, and so forth), the passage is specifically employed in reference to the four sons of Mosiah as messengers (plural) and their own teaching of the good tidings of the gospel as part of their repentance.

Jesus' Teachings of Isaiah in 3 Nephi 16

The resurrected Lord employed the contents of Isaiah 52 twice in his teachings to the Nephites during his post-resurrection visit to the Americas, as recorded in 3 Nephi. In the first of these, 3 Nephi 16:18–20, Jesus uses Isaiah's description of rejoicing "watchmen" (Isaiah 52:8–10) in the context of teaching the Nephites of future events that would take place in the Americas. Jesus teaches them that his sacrifice fulfilled the law of Moses (3 Nephi 15:1–10) and reminds them that as a branch of the house of Israel they represented some of his "other sheep" (3 Nephi 15:11–16:3). He further explains that the latter-day gentiles would be intermediaries in bringing these teachings about him to Lehite descendants as part of the latter-day gathering of Israel, since they would be in a scattered condition "because of their unbelief" (3 Nephi 16:4–7). Jesus also sounds a warning to citizens of the latter-day gentile nations that if they "shall reject the fulness of my gospel, behold, saith the Father, I will bring the fulness of my gospel from among them. And *then* will I remember my covenant which I have made unto my people, O house of Israel, and I will bring my gospel unto them . . . but if the Gentiles will repent and return unto me, saith the Father, behold they shall be numbered among my people, O house of Israel" (3 Nephi 16:10–11, 13; see also 3 Nephi 16:8–13). The emphasis is clearly on the last days when the process of gathering Israel is well underway.

It is in this context of latter-day Israelites and gentile nations that Jesus proclaims:

> Verily, verily, I say unto you, thus hath the Father commanded me—that I should give unto *this people this land* for their inheritance. *And then* the words of the prophet Isaiah shall be fulfilled, which say: Thy watchmen shall lift up the voice; with the voice together shall they sing, for they shall see eye to eye when the Lord shall bring again Zion. Break forth into joy, sing together, ye waste places of Jerusalem; for the Lord hath comforted his people, he hath redeemed Jerusalem. The Lord hath

made bare his holy arm in the eye of all the nations; and
all the ends of the earth shall see the salvation of God.
(3 Nephi 16:16–20)

It seems quite clear that the expression *this land* is used
in reference to the Americas.[27] However, the phrase *this
people* may refer either specifically to Lehite descendants,
since he is speaking to Lehites, or it may refer more broadly
to other Israelites (especially non-Lehite descendants of
Joseph) in addition to Lehites, given Jesus' repeated use of
the title "house of Israel" in the previous verses of this chapter.[28] Either way, these Israelites will be inheriting the
Americas as their allotment of promised land during the
Lord's millennial reign.

The question thus arises: What is the relationship between the phrases "that I should give unto this people this
land for their inheritance" and "and *then* the words of the
prophet Isaiah shall be fulfilled"? This may be intended to
indicate that the inheritance of the Americas ("this land")
by some Israelites is *a* fulfillment of the words of Isaiah contained in Isaiah 52:8–10. Thus, faithful Israelites in the
Americas would be the "watchmen" who rejoice when the
Lord's saving power is manifest in this hemisphere as well
as in the land of Israel, as he "bring[s] again Zion."[29] This
interpretation requires that the reference to Jerusalem in the
quotation of Isaiah 52:9 (parallel to 3 Nephi 16:19) be understood as figuratively applying to a branch of Israelites and
not to the city itself (unless he intends it to be understood as
the *New* Jerusalem to be built in the Americas in the last
days, as prophesied elsewhere in the scriptures [see, for example, Ether 13 and Article of Faith 10]). Alternatively, the
clauses "that I should give unto this people this land for
their inheritance" and "and *then* the words of the prophet
Isaiah shall be fulfilled" may indicate that the gathering in
the Americas would take place, perhaps as a sign, before the

prophecy in Isaiah 52:8–10 is fulfilled *elsewhere*, without it having specific reference to the activity in the Americas. In that case the name Jerusalem would indicate the actual city. Given the audience being addressed and other statements regarding the gathering in the Americas (such as 3 Nephi 20, cited below), it seems more likely to me that Jesus was here applying Isaiah's words to an American context. This is not to say that such use represents the primary sense of the original prophecy, but it does represent an appropriate application.

Jesus' Teachings of Isaiah in 3 Nephi 20

Jesus' second use of Isaiah 52 is found in 3 Nephi 20:29–46. Following a second administration of the sacrament to the Nephites (see verses 1–10), Jesus reminds his audience that "the words of Isaiah should be fulfilled" when latter-day Israel had been gathered both physically and spiritually (see verses 11–13). He also reiterates that "the Father hath commanded me that I should give unto you [and their latter-day Lehite descendants] this land [the Americas], for your inheritance" (verse 14) and that "this people will I establish in this land, unto the fulfilling of the covenant which I made with your father Jacob; and it shall be a New Jerusalem" (verse 22). After further comments about the Lehites being part of Israel and heirs to the covenant blessings (see verses 25–27) and about the latter-day gentiles being accountable since they will have the "fulness of [his] gospel" (verses 27–28), Jesus seems to shift his perspective away from the Americas when he states: "And I will remember the covenant which I have made with my people; and I have covenanted with them that I would gather them together in mine own due time, that I would give unto them again the land of their fathers for their inheritance, which is the land of Jerusalem, which is the promised land unto them forever, saith the Father" (3 Nephi 20:29).

The emphasis is still on the latter-day gathering, but as Jesus specifically speaks of the "land of Jerusalem," the context is no longer the Americas. Jesus' statement in verse 29 serves as an important contextualizing preface to what follows, including his use of passages from Isaiah 52. He continues, "the time cometh, when the fulness of my gospel shall be preached unto them; and they shall believe in me, that I am Jesus Christ, the Son of God" (3 Nephi 20:30–31). "*Then* shall their watchmen lift up their voice, and with the voice together shall they sing; for they shall see eye to eye" (3 Nephi 20:32, parallel to Isaiah 52:8). This clearly indicates that accepting the gospel causes the rejoicing and the unity of perspective among the watchmen. Presumably, the modification of "thy watchmen" in Isaiah's text to "their watchmen" in this passage in 3 Nephi 20 is audience dependent. Jesus is here speaking to American Israelites about future watchmen among non-American Israelites (rather than applying Isaiah's prophecy to Israelites in the Americas, as he did in 3 Nephi 16, as noted above). This suggests that the original or primary sense of Isaiah's prophecy related to the broader house of Israel, who would gather to the land of Israel.

Following these statements concerning the spiritual component of the gathering of Israel, Jesus continues,

> *then* will the Father gather them together again, and give unto them Jerusalem for the land of their inheritance. *Then* shall they break forth into joy—Sing together ye waste places of Jerusalem; for the Father [not "the Lord" as in Isaiah 52:9] hath comforted his people, he hath redeemed Jerusalem. The Father [not "the Lord" as in Isaiah 52:10] hath made bare his holy arm in the eyes of

all the nations; and all the ends of the earth shall see the salvation of the Father [not "our God" as in Isaiah 52:10]; and the Father and I are one. *And then* shall be brought to pass that which is written: Awake, awake again, and put on thy strength, O Zion . . . [verses 36–38, parallel to Isaiah 52:1–3]. Verily, verily, I say unto you, that my people shall know my name; yea, *in that day* they shall know that I am he that doth speak. *And then* shall they say: How beautiful upon the mountains are the feet of him that bringeth good tidings unto them, that publisheth peace. (3 Nephi 20:33–40)

Jesus then quotes Isaiah 52:11–15 (in 3 Nephi 20:41–45), and observes, "all these things shall surely come . . . *then* shall this covenant . . . be fulfilled; and *then* shall Jerusalem be inhabited again with my people, and it shall be the land of their inheritance" (3 Nephi 20:46).

Although Isaiah 52:7 is rendered with no appreciable differences in 3 Nephi 20:40, Jesus respectfully attributes some of the activities prophesied in Isaiah 52:9–10 to his Father's power (see verses 33, 35). He also includes a few introductory phrases (such as, "and then shall they say," just before "how beautiful upon the mountains") and rearranges the order of the passages from Isaiah 52 that he includes in his remarks.[30] Zion here represents Old Jerusalem, and Jesus' arrangement of this material suggests that Isaiah's prophecy will not be fulfilled until he comes again. Jesus' references to himself in verse 39 ("my people shall know my name" and "I am he that doth speak" [this latter phrase is also found in Isaiah 52:6]) followed by his quotation of Isaiah 52:7 suggests to me that *he* is the primary messenger who will announce deliverance to Israelites who have gathered to Jerusalem at the last day. They will know *his* name and will say how beautiful are *his* feet!

Quotations of Isaiah without Commentary

There are a few other passages in the Book of Mormon in which portions of Isaiah 52 are quoted but with little or no discussion in the text. For example, Nephi records that Jacob quotes Isaiah 52:1–2 after relating Isaiah 51 to his Nephite audience (see 2 Nephi 8:24, 25). Although there is no explicit commentary on this passage, Jacob employs Isaiah 51, which contains prophecy about the redemption of Zion, in support of his comments concerning the gathering of Israel. Also, in his closing exhortation to readers of the Book of Mormon to "come unto Christ" (Moroni 10:30–32), Moroni creatively paraphrases from Isaiah 52:1–2 (verse 31: "awake, and arise from the dust, O Jerusalem; yea, and put on thy beautiful garments, O daughter of Zion") and alludes to Isaiah 52:11 (verse 30: "touch not the evil gift, nor the unclean thing"). He also employs phrases from Isaiah 54:2–4 in Moroni 10:31. The context of Moroni's remarks indicates that he understands that the passages of Isaiah 52 that he quotes have to do with the Lord's covenant people in the last days.[31]

Let's summarize the use of Isaiah 52:7–10 in the Book of Mormon. Isaiah 52:8–10 is consistently employed in Mosiah 15:29–31 and in 3 Nephi 16:18–20 and 20:32, 34–35 in the context of the last days when the Lord will redeem his people by delivering them from the nations of the world. However, Isaiah 52:7 is employed with greater variety. In 3 Nephi 20:40, Jesus relates it to his coming in the last days to declare deliverance for his people. Likewise, in Mosiah 15:18, Abinadi envisions the Lord as the primary messenger who will bring glad tidings because he is the Redeemer, although he also broadly applies this verse to the Lord's prophets and people in every age (see Mosiah 15:14–17). Phrases from Isaiah 52:7 also appear in 1 Nephi 13:37, where the application is to the many who will assist in the latter-day restoration, and in Mosiah 27:37, where they are applied to the sons of Mosiah and their own gospel teaching.

Isaiah 52:7–10: Other Textual Witnesses

Having thus reviewed the occurrences of Isaiah 52:7–10 in the Book of Mormon and how it was employed in that volume of scripture, it is instructive to survey the use of this passage in other canonical and noncanonical contexts before making some concluding observations.

Similarities in the Old Testament

Two passages in the Old Testament, Isaiah 40:9 and Nahum 1:15, contain expressions similar to those in Isaiah 52:7–10. The composer Georg Handel, in his oratorio "The Messiah," follows the lead of the apostle Matthew (see Matthew 3:1–3) in applying the first portion of Isaiah 40 to the mission of John the Baptist (a voice in the wilderness crying "prepare ye the way of the Lord" [Isaiah 40:3]). However, the *primary* focus of this passage seems to me to be the last days and the *second* coming of the Lord, when "every valley shall be exalted" (verse 4) and the "glory of the Lord shall be revealed" (verse 5).[32] In this last-day context, the following invitation is found:

> O Zion, that bringest good tidings, get thee up into the high mountain; O Jerusalem, that bringest good tidings, lift up thy voice with strength; lift it up, be not afraid; say unto the cities of Judah, Behold your God! Behold, the Lord GOD will come with a strong hand, and his arm shall rule for him. (Isaiah 40:9–10)

The names Zion and Jerusalem, used here as synonyms, represent the inhabitants of this city who, having received glad tidings (see Isaiah 52:7), are now to be messengers of similar tidings to the rest of the cities of Judah. The phrase "his arm shall rule for him" (verse 10) recalls Isaiah 52:10, which says, "the Lord hath made bare his holy arm."

The book of Nahum contains a "burden" or prophecy of doom against Nineveh (see Nahum 1:1), which functioned as the capital city of the Assyrian empire from 705–612 B.C. Judah and her neighbors were vassals of the Assyrian empire for much of the seventh century, but Nahum here announces the downfall of Assyria as he prophesies the destruction of Nineveh. Thus, the book was probably composed during the latter half of the seventh century. Nahum 1 serves as a preface to the rest of the book, announcing that while "the Lord is slow to anger" he is also "great in power" (Nahum 1:3). His might will be unleashed to deliver Judah: "Thus saith the Lord . . . I break his yoke from off thee, and will burst thy bonds in sunder. . . . Behold upon the mountains the feet of him that bringeth good tidings, that publisheth peace! O Judah, keep thy solemn feasts, perform thy vows: for the wicked shall no more pass through thee; he is utterly cut off" (Nahum 1:12–15).[33] While the adjective *beautiful* is not employed in reference to "feet" in this passage, as in Isaiah 52:7, the messenger is represented as singular, and we would expect that the tidings of deliverance and peace were certainly welcome.

If this prophecy in Nahum 1 merely foretells the deliverance of Judah from the yoke of Assyria, then the "good tidings" were received when Assyrian domination ended, historically fulfilled when the Babylonians and Medes terminated Assyrian sovereignty in the Near East in 612 B.C. However, there are indications that this "burden" against Nineveh typologically represents the destruction of the wicked at the second coming of Christ. These clues include the description in verse 5, "the mountains quake at him, and the hills melt, and the earth is burned at his presence, yea, the world, and all that dwell therein," which is reminiscent of other prophecies of Jesus' second coming (see, for example, Psalms 97:3, 5; Malachi 4:1; 3 Nephi 26:3; and D&C 133:41, 44), as well as the statement at the end of verse 15 that "the wicked shall no more pass through thee [Judah]." This latter phrase is similar to expressions in Isaiah 52:1 and Joel 3:17 that in the final day the "unclean" and "strangers" will no longer control nor occupy Jerusalem, a condition that was not achieved with the removal of the Assyrian yoke from Judah. The fact that the Babylonians, Persians, Greeks, Romans and others followed the Assyrians in a centuries-long line of conquerors suggests that the real fulfillment of this prophecy has yet to be realized.

Thus, while Nahum the prophet may himself represent a fulfillment of the prophecy of the messenger who announces "good tidings" (Nahum 1:15) concerning the demise of historic Nineveh, it seems to me that this prophecy is meant as a type of the final deliverance of Jerusalem. In such a reading, the Lord is the messenger of good tidings, and he will declare peace for the last time. This is interesting in light of the use Abinadi makes of Isaiah 52:7, in which he indicates that while prophets function as messengers of salvation, the ultimate messenger is the Lord, who has the power to deliver physically and spiritually. This understanding of Nahum's prophecy thus correlates with Jesus' teachings in 3 Nephi 20, where Jesus indicates that he is the primary messenger of salvation at the last day.

Isaiah Quotations from the Septuagint

The Septuagint (hereafter designated LXX) is the name given to the Greek translation of the books of the Hebrew Bible produced by Jews living in Alexandria, Egypt, in the third and second centuries B.C. It was common for Christians in the first century A.D. to use the LXX when studying books in our "Old Testament." The rendition of Isaiah 52 in the LXX is somewhat different from that preserved in the Masoretic Text, which is the standard, "received" text of the Hebrew Bible on which most English translations are based. We will not go into detail; it is sufficient to observe that in the version of Isaiah 52 represented in the LXX, first, the Lord is clearly depicted as the one speaking, and second, he identifies himself as the one who is "*like* beauty on the mountains" and "*like* the feet of one who proclaims peace" (emphasis added). In the LXX then, the language of Isaiah 52:7 metaphorically represents Jehovah *as if he were a messenger* proclaiming the deliverance of his people.[34] There is no ambiguity concerning the identity of this messenger! While I consider this passage in the LXX an interpretive rendition of Isaiah's original prophecy, not the original version itself, I have no quarrel with the messianic sense of the interpretation.

The LXX makes explicit what is implicit in the Masoretic Text in representing the Lord speaking the contents of Isaiah 52:7. This contrasts with Jesus' use of this material in 3 Nephi 20:40 (discussed above), in which "they," the Israelites, are represented as speaking the contents of Isaiah 52:7. The clear depiction of Jehovah as the messenger in the LXX (although in a metaphorical sense) is reminiscent of Abinadi's interpretation of Isaiah 52:7 in Mosiah 15:18.

Insights from the Dead Sea Scrolls

Discovered among the Dead Sea Scrolls are the remains of twenty-one copies of the book of Isaiah. Only a few of these, however, preserve any portion of Isaiah 52:7–10; the so-called Great Isaiah Scroll, *1QIsaiah*[a], preserves the whole passage, while *1QIsaiah*[b] and *4QIsaiah*[b,c,d] preserve only por-

tions of it. Despite minor differences in spelling and wording, none of these manuscripts preserves text that differs in
any significant way from the text of Isaiah 52:7–10 that is
preserved in the Masoretic Text, which became the standard
version of the Hebrew Bible.

However, there is another document among the Dead
Sea Scrolls that is of greater interest for this study. A first-
century-B.C. text, partially preserved on thirteen fragments
and known as *11QMelchizedek (11Q13)*, appears to have
been composed by the Qumran community. It relates some
of the future activities of a heavenly figure designated
Melchizedek who "is portrayed as presiding over the final
Judgment and condemnation of his demonic counterpart,
Belial/Satan, the Prince of Darkness."[35] The portion of the
text relevant for this study is as follows:

> *13* But, Melchizedek will carry out the vengeance of
> God's judges [on this day, and they shall be freed from
> the hands] of Belial and from the hands of all the sp[irits
> of his lot.] *14* To his aid (shall come) all «the gods of [jus-
> tice»; he] is the one [who will prevail on this day over] all
> the sons of God, and he will pre[side over] this [assem-
> bly.] *15* This is the day of [peace about which God] spoke
> [of old through the words of Isa]iah the prophet, who
> said: *Isa 52:7* «How beautiful *16* upon the mountains are
> the feet of the messenger who announces peace, of the
> mess[enger of good who announces salvation,] saying to
> Zion: 'your God [reigns.'»] *17* Its interpretation: The
> mountains are the pro[phets …] *18* And the messenger is
> [the ano]inted of the spirit about whom Dan[iel] spoke
> [. . . and the messenger of] *19* good who announces
> salv[ation is the one about whom it is written that] he will
> send him *Isa 61:2–3* «to comfo[rt the afflicted, to watch
> over the afflicted ones of Zion».] *20* «To comfo[rt the af-
> flicted», its interpretation:] to instruct them in all the ages
> of the worl[d. . .] *21* in truth. [. . .] *22* [. . .] it has been

turned away from Belial and it [. . .] 23 [. . .] in the judgments of God, as is written about him: *Isa 52:7* «Saying to
Zion: 'your God rules'». [«Zi]on» is 24 [the congregation of
all the sons of justice, those] who establish the covenant,
those who avoid walking [on the pa]th of the people.
«Your God» is 25 [. . . Melchizedek, who will fr]ee [them]
from the hand of Belial. *(11QMelchizedek [11Q13],* col. 2)[36]

While this is not the place to evaluate the manner of interpretation at Qumran, nor for a detailed evaluation of this
passage, it is noteworthy that, first, the fulfillment of the
prophecy of a messenger announcing peace in Isaiah 52:7–10
is envisioned as occurring at the last day, when Belial, or
Satan, and his followers will be vanquished, and second,
that the messenger is described as one who "is [the
ano]inted of the spirit about whom Dan[iel] spoke [, . . . and
the messenger of] good who announces salv[ation is the
one about whom it is written that] he will send him *Isa
61:2–3* «to comfo[rt the afflicted, to watch over the afflicted
ones of Zion»]." The Hebrew word rendered "anointed" is
meššiaḥ, "messiah." Daniel 9:25 contains a difficult prophecy about *a* "messiah and prince" who the people at
Qumran identified as the messenger who would bring glad
tidings and comfort to the afflicted of Israel. The contents of
11QMelchizedek suggests that an *angelic* Melchizedek would
deliver true Israel and would judge the world by destroying
the sons of darkness with the power of God. The sense of
deliverance in this passage is similar to that in Jesus' use of
Isaiah 52:7–10 in 3 Nephi 20:33–40 and Abinadi's use of
Isaiah 52:8–10 in Mosiah 15:26–31.

Latter-day Saints should recall that "Melchizedek" is a
name-title meaning "King of Righteousness" that is used as
an alternate designation of the Holy Priesthood of the Son
of God (see D&C 107:1–4), because Melchizedek the person
was such a faithful follower and powerful "type" of Christ.

Thus, the name itself is an appropriate title for Jesus. I consider this passage in *11QMelchizedek* to be a corrupted tradition of an earlier, authentic teaching that the Lord, the true "King of Righteousness," would be the messenger of deliverance and peace in Isaiah 52:7.[37]

Significantly, the two noncanonical texts of significance for this study, the LXX rendition of Isaiah 52 and *11QMelchizedek*, both preserve interpretations of key elements of Isaiah 52:7–10 that are similar to those found in the Book of Mormon: *11QMelchizedek* envisions a last-day fulfillment (and in its own way preserves an interpretation of the messenger as a heavenly being with power over the world and Satan), and the LXX specifically associates the image of the messenger with the Lord himself. Of course, these texts do not prove that a last-day, messianic interpretation of Isaiah's prophecy should be preferred over others, but they do support the view that we have already seen in the Book of Mormon.

Letter of Paul

The apostle Paul's letter to the Romans in the New Testament preserves an interesting form and use of Isaiah 52:7. It is likely that Paul has paraphrased this passage since the text of Romans 10:15 does not exactly match either the traditional Hebrew text or the LXX of Isaiah 52:7. Paul taught that "whosoever shall call upon the name of the Lord shall be saved" (verse 13).

> How then shall they call on him in whom they have not believed? and how shall they believe in him of whom they have not heard? and how shall they hear without a preacher? And how shall they preach, except they be sent? as it is written, How beautiful are the feet of them that preach the gospel of peace, and bring glad tidings of good things! (Romans 10:14–15)

Paul employs some of Isaiah's imagery, but not all. For example, he mentions neither mountains nor Jerusalem. By excluding the phrase *thy God reigneth* at the end of Isaiah 52:7 and 52:8–10 and the message of judgment contained therein, Paul is able to apply Isaiah's prophecy to his own circumstances. Paul refers to the beautiful feet of "them," not a singular herald as in Isaiah's text. These messengers preach the "gospel" of peace, which, in the context of Paul's remarks, clearly refers to the message of salvation through Christ. Furthermore, the destination of these messengers is not restricted to Jerusalem, for in the process of "likening" Isaiah's passage to the first century A.D., Paul depicts Christian missionaries of his day delivering the gospel message to the Mediterranean world. This is conceptually analogous to Nephi's use of Isaiah 52:7 in the context of the latter-day spread of the gospel (see 1 Nephi 13:37), to Abinadi's use of Isaiah 52:7 in reference to prophets and saints who publish peace and salvation in all ages (see Mosiah 15:14–17), and to the use of Isaiah 52:7 in relation to the missionary efforts of the sons of Mosiah (see Mosiah 27:37).

Modern Witnesses

In more recent times, Joseph Smith, in a doctrinal letter to the church dated 6 September 1842, declared:

> Now what do we hear in the gospel which we have received? A voice of gladness! A voice of mercy from heaven; and a voice of truth out of the earth; glad tidings for the dead; a voice of gladness for the living and the dead; glad tidings of great joy. How beautiful upon the mountains are the feet of those that bring glad tidings of good things, and that say unto Zion: Behold thy God reigneth! As the dews of Carmel, so shall the knowledge of God descend upon them! (D&C 128:19)

The important imagery of feet, mountains, and Zion are all included in the prophet Joseph's paraphrase of Isaiah 52:7. However, significant differences include the phrase "the feet of those," indicating more than one messenger, and the context in which this passage is employed. Joseph is speaking about baptism for the dead. In the following two verses he mentions a number of divine messengers who had restored authority, keys, and knowledge that made possible vicarious ordinances for the dead, as well as such ordinances for the living ("a voice of gladness for the living and the dead"). It thus seems likely that the phrase "those that bring glad tidings" was used in reference to such messengers. The concluding phrase in verse 19, "so shall the knowledge of God descend upon them," likely refers to the living and the dead. According to this interpretation, the term *Zion* refers to the church and the phrase "thy God reigneth" refers to the Lord's power and desire to reveal the teachings and authority necessary for the salvation of his children so that those who are faithful may reign with him. There is no passage in the Book of Mormon that exactly parallels the use made of Isaiah 52:7 here.

Elsewhere, in Doctrine and Covenants 19:29, 31:3, and 79:1, the Lord commissioned and encouraged Joseph Smith, Thomas B. Marsh, and Jared Carter, respectively, to declare "glad tidings" as part of their missionary efforts. The Lord instructed Jared Carter to go forth "proclaiming glad tidings of great joy, *even the everlasting gospel*" (D&C 79:1, emphasis added). Although most of the imagery of Isaiah 52:7 is absent from these passages, the content of the "glad tidings" is specifically explained in this context as the gospel. Nephi employed the phrase "tidings of great joy" from Isaiah 52:7 in reference to the preaching of latter-day missionaries (see 1 Nephi 13:35–37). In like manner, but without specific reference to the last days, we have seen how Paul (see Romans 10:14–15) and Abinadi (see Mosiah 15:14–17) utilized Isaiah 52:7 in reference to those who have preached the gospel at various times. Thus, passages from the Book of Mormon, Bible, and the Doctrine and Covenants illustrate how prophets in different dispensations have drawn upon the words of Isaiah 52:7 to express the preaching of "glad tidings" or "good news," the gospel, by faithful missionaries.

In addition to these passages from the Doctrine and Covenants, Latter-day Saint General Authorities have employed Isaiah 52:7–10 in their teachings, typically in the context of missionary work. Consider this modern example:

> As we live righteous and unselfish lives, the Spirit of the Lord enters our souls and then radiates from us. We become beautiful, even as a holy temple is beautiful. And as missionaries we can help others to become beautiful. "How beautiful upon the mountains are the feet of him that bringeth good tidings."[38]

Summary and Conclusion

The preceding review demonstrates that the Book of Mormon is a valuable resource for understanding Isaiah 52:7–10. It assists us in appreciating what I consider to be the primary sense of this passage, as well as the broader or secondary sense in which this passage is often employed.

If the "messenger" and "Jerusalem" referred to by Isaiah in 52:7 were meant as figures or types representing any number of people and places, then the passages cited above represent various prophetic uses of what Isaiah intended as a general theme: faithful messengers, prophets, and missionary saints in all ages would be welcomed by at least some watchmen and watchwomen who would rejoice when the glad tidings of the gospel were preached to them. This is the way in which several prophets who lived after Isaiah (such as Nephi, Paul, Joseph Smith, and even the Lord) employed Isaiah 52:7–10 in their teachings. This perspective represents one major interpretive possibility.

If, on the other hand, Isaiah ultimately had a single latter-day herald in mind who would bring glad tidings specifically to *Old* Jerusalem, then we can see how some of the teachings of Abinadi (in Mosiah 15) and Jesus (in 3 Nephi 20) that Isaiah 52:7–10 is or will be fulfilled by the Messiah are of considerable significance in understanding the original intent of Isaiah's words. This fulfillment—that of a single latter-day, messianic herald—represents a second major interpretive possibility.

A conceptual middle ground that many Latter-day Saints are inclined to occupy results from combining the specific and the more general perspectives just presented by accepting the multiple fulfillment of Isaiah's prophecy. Thus, Jesus, as *the* messenger of salvation who can deliver both temporally and spiritually, represents the primary fulfillment of Isaiah's prophecy. However, Jesus' mission as deliverer serves as a type of all his followers who, in an expanded application of Isaiah's passage, carry the gospel message of peace and hope to the world in all dispensations. According to this view, prophets in the passages cited above broadened the focus of Isaiah's original prophecy. This took place either as an appropriate process of likening the scriptures to their own or previous circumstances (as in the case of Paul, Alma or Mormon in relation to the sons of Mosiah, Abinadi, and Joseph Smith) or to circumstances that they understood would prevail in the future (as in the case of Nephi, Abinadi, and Jesus).

Wherever *you* are on this interpretive spectrum, I conclude with what *I* consider to be the primary fulfillment of this prophecy in the mortal phase of this earth's history: Jesus' second coming to Jerusalem, in power and glory, to people who will recognize him and be grateful for his message. Prophesying through Joseph Smith as he had earlier through Zechariah (chapters 13, 14), the Lord declared, concerning his own second coming:

> Then shall the arm of the Lord fall upon the nations. And then shall the Lord set his foot upon this mount [of Olives], and it shall cleave in twain, and the earth shall tremble, and reel to and fro, and the heavens also shall shake. And the Lord shall utter his voice, and all the ends of the earth shall hear it. . . . Then shall they know that I am the Lord; I am he who was lifted up. I am Jesus that was crucified. I am the Son of God. And then shall they weep because of their iniquities; then shall they lament because they persecuted their king. (D&C 45:47–53)

Jesus, the "messenger of salvation" (D&C 93:8), the "messenger of the covenant" (Malachi 3:1), will "bare his holy arm" and bring "good tidings" of deliverance and peace to a war-ravaged Jerusalem that is in ruins by comforting and redeeming a portion of his people both physically *and* spiritually. How beautiful will be his feet, or in other words, how welcome will be his appearance and message, as he descends upon the Mount of Olives. Then and only then will Jerusalem know, as Isaiah prophesied (see Isaiah 40:1–2), that "her warfare is accomplished" and "that her iniquity is pardoned." Then shall the watchmen of that portion of the Lord's people shout for joy, and his "people shall [finally] know his [true] name" (Isaiah 52:6)—Jesus the Messiah. While I consider this the primary focus of Isaiah's prophecy, in a very real way this interpretation of Isaiah 52:7 is merely a type of what Jesus can and does do in delivering us from the yoke of mortality as we continue in our eternal progress. The extension of such power and compassion to us represents "glad tidings" indeed.

Addendum

Several months after this paper was delivered at the FARMS symposium on Isaiah and the Book of Mormon, Elder Jeffrey R. Holland made the following comments in the October 1996 semi-annual General Conference of the Church of Jesus Christ of Latter-day Saints:

> A general conference of this Church is a remarkable occasion indeed—it is an institutional declaration that the heavens are open, that divine guidance is as real today as it was for the ancient house of Israel, that God our Heavenly Father loves us and speaks His will through a living prophet.
>
> The great Isaiah foresaw such moments and foretold this very setting in which we find ourselves:
>
> "And it shall come to pass in the last days, that the mountain of the Lord's house shall be established in the top of the mountains, and shall be exalted above the hills; and all nations shall flow unto it.
>
> "And many people shall go and say, Come ye, and let us go up to the mountain of the Lord, to the house of the God of Jacob; and he will teach us of his ways, and we will walk in his paths: for out of Zion shall go forth the law, and the word of the Lord from Jerusalem." [Isaiah 2:2–3]
>
> Of such comforting latter-day direction, including its divine source, Isaiah would go on to say: "How beautiful upon the mountains are the feet of him that bringeth good tidings, that publisheth peace." [Isaiah 52:7]
>
> Peace and good tidings; good tidings and peace. These are among the ultimate blessings that the gospel of Jesus Christ brings a troubled world and the troubled people who live in it, solutions to personal struggles and

human sinfulness, a source of strength for days of weariness and hours of genuine despair. This entire general conference and The Church of Jesus Christ of Latter-day Saints which convenes it declare that it is the Only Begotten Son of God Himself who gives us this help and this hope. . . . As the Book of Mormon prophet Abinadi made clear in a slight variation of Isaiah's exclamation:

"O how beautiful upon the mountains are the feet of him that bringeth good tidings, that *is the founder of peace,* yea, even the Lord, who has redeemed his people; yea, him who has granted salvation unto his people." [Mosiah 15:18]

Ultimately it is Christ who is beautiful upon the mountain. And it is His merciful promise of "peace in this world," His good tidings of "eternal life in the world to come" [see D&C 59:23] that make us fall at His feet and call His name blessed and give thanks for the restoration of His true and living Church. (*Ensign* [November 1996]: 82; second italics added)

Notes

The author expresses his appreciation to John W. Welch and Larry E. Dahl who helped so much in refining his ideas as they are presented here.

1. All Bible quotations are from the King James Version (hereafter KJV) unless otherwise indicated.

2. This language is part of a literary pattern that begins in the preceding chapter; see Isaiah 51:9, 17. Also, compare Lehi's adaptation and use of this language and imagery as he addresses his rebellious sons in 2 Nephi 1:13, 14, 21, 23.

3. Joseph Smith, of course, also taught that "the whole of America is Zion itself from north to south" (Joseph Fielding Smith, comp., *Teachings of the Prophet Joseph Smith* [Salt Lake City: Deseret Book, 1970], 362 [hereafter *TPJS*]).

4. See, for example, 2 Kings 19:21, 29–32; Psalms 102:21; 147:12; Isaiah 2:3; 4:3; 31:9; and so on.

5. *TPJS*, 79–80.

6. I take a different position than Monte S. Nyman in his *"Great Are the Words of Isaiah"* (Salt Lake City: Bookcraft, 1980), 199, when he states that "Joseph Smith designated Jackson County, Missouri, as the Zion spoken of in verse 8." Applying a prophecy of Isaiah to a particular situation is not the same as saying that the prophecy is exclusively fulfilled by that situation. The prophetic use and application of earlier prophecies is a concept that is demonstrated by this paper.

7. Note also that Isaiah 52:10 is quoted in Doctrine and Covenants 133:3, and portions of Isaiah 52:8–9 are paraphrased in a millennial song recorded in Doctrine and Covenants 84:98–9, again suggesting the time when this prophecy will actually be fulfilled.

8. For a review of these interpretive options, see Victor L. Ludlow's *Isaiah: Prophet, Seer, and Poet* (Salt Lake City: Deseret Book, 1982), 438–41. Ludlow favors identifying the servant in this passage as Joseph Smith. See also, Nyman, *Words of Isaiah*, 204–6. See also the brief discussion of Isaiah 52 by David R. Seely, "The Lord Will Bring Salvation," in *1 Kings to Malachi*, vol. 4 of *Studies in Scripture*, ed. Kent P. Jackson (Salt Lake City: Deseret Book, 1993), 148–51.

9. Consider, for example, such well-known prophecies as those recorded in Isaiah 2:1–5; 7:14; and 40:1–5.

10. There are no indications of which I am aware that women functioned in such positions in the ancient Near East, thus I use masculine pronouns throughout this discussion. For examples of passages mentioning watchmen but not messengers, see 2 Samuel 13:34 and 2 Kings 9:17–20. See also the LDS Topical Guide, s.v. "Watchman, Watchmen." For biblical citations mentioning messengers, both secular and religious (i.e., prophetic), see the LDS Topical Guide, s.v. "Message, Messenger."

11. For a convenient review of the available evidence, see Samuel A. Meier, *The Messenger in the Ancient Semitic World*, Harvard Semitic Monographs no. 45 (Atlanta: Scholars Press, 1988). Biblical texts relating to the form of the message are dealt with on pages 37–42 and 191.

12. Meier, *Messenger*, 13–30, 163–79. Note the *written* comment of Amenophis III, king of Egypt, to King Kadašman-Enlil of Babylonia that "your messengers don't speak truly to you. . . . Don't listen to

your messengers whose mouths are false.... I swear ... they told lies" (el-Amarna letter 1:81–88, as quoted in Meier, *Messenger,* 169).

13. Ibid., 2 n. 6.

14. See ibid., 168–9, 188–9, for a convenient discussion of this passage.

15. See also Isaiah 62:6; Jeremiah 6:17; and Ezekiel 3:17.

16. Israelite prophets seem to have also been messengers, in some way, to surrounding nations, judging from prophecies to and about foreign nations preserved in the Old Testament. Some examples are found in Isaiah 13–17; Jeremiah 46–51; Amos 1–2; Jonah 3; Nahum; and Zephaniah 2.

17. For examples of heavenly messengers, see Judges 2:1–4; 1 Kings 19:5–7; and the LDS Topical Guide, s.v. "Messenger."

18. Note, however, how the New International Version renders it as plural, without any notation: "the feet of those who bring good news."

19. Note that in Isaiah 41:27, *mĕbaśśēr* is rendered in the KJV as "one that bringeth good tidings." This translation is presumably based on the translators' understanding of the context. In comparison, *mĕbaśśēr* is rendered simply as "herald" in the same verse in *Tanakh, A New Translation of the Holy Scriptures* (Philadelphia: Jewish Publication Society, 1988), hereafter cited as NJPS.

20. *TPJS,* 182.

21. See Genesis 18:4; Luke 7:44; and John 12:3.

22. I note here the suggestion of Larry Dahl (private communication) that perhaps the feet are described as beautiful because they *are* clean. Larry rightly observes that some of the scriptural passages that mention feet refer to the washing or cleansing of feet, symbolizing forgiveness of sins and acceptance by the Lord that can only come through the true gospel (see, for example, Exodus 30:17–21; D&C 88:74–75). Thus, in his view, the gospel is the message and the feet of the messenger(s) are clean because he/they represent the Lord. Those who accept the message share in the hope of becoming clean through Christ.

23. In addition to the work of LDS authors (Ludlow and Nyman) mentioned above, see John A. Tvedtnes, Study Aid to "The Isaiah Variants in the Book of Mormon," (Provo, Utah:

FARMS, 1981), 89–91, for notes on the occurrence of Isaiah 52 in the Book of Mormon; see also Monte S. Nyman, "Abinadi's Commentary on Isaiah," in *Mosiah: Salvation Only Through Christ.* ed. Monte S. Nyman and Charles D. Tate Jr. (Provo, Utah: BYU Religious Studies Center and Bookcraft, 1991), 176–9.

24. Isaiah 53:8 is the only passage in the Hebrew Bible in which the expression *dôrô*, rendered "his generation" in the KJV, occurs (although see Genesis 6:9: *dôrōtāyw*, literally "his generations," in reference to Noah). It may mean "his lifetime," since the Hebrew term *dôr* refers to the period of a life, a generation. It often occurs in the expression *dôr wĕdôr*, "generation to generation," indicating a long time, even forever. Thus, to "declare his generation" seems to mean to announce what he accomplished during his life, or the value of his lifetime. Others have explained this phrase with more specific reference to the Lord's genealogy and origin as the son of God through Mary. See, for example, Bruce R. McConkie, *The Promised Messiah* (Salt Lake City: Bookcraft, 1978), 471–3.

25. In Mosiah 5:7, Benjamin refers to the "children of Christ, his sons, and his daughters," whom "he hath spiritually begotten."

26. This view is developed by John W. Welch, "Judicial Process in the Trial of Abinadi" (Provo, Utah: FARMS, 1981). See also Paul Y. Hoskisson, "A Singular Explanation of the Atonement: Abinadi Speaks of Those Beautiful Feet upon the Mountain" (October 1996; presently unpublished). I appreciate both of these colleagues sharing their work with me.

Although it is ancillary to the present discussion, it is also interesting to ask why this is the only question from the priests to Abinadi that is preserved for us. We are told that the priests of Noah "began to question him, that they might cross him, . . . but he answered them boldly, and withstood all their questions" (Mosiah 12:19), and this took place *before* they asked Abinadi the question regarding Isaiah 52:7–10. While it is not possible to discern the extent to which the *present* form of the account of Abinadi reflects Alma's initial efforts to record this incident (Alma was "concealed for many days [and] did write all the words which Abinadi had spoken" [Mosiah 16:4]) in relation to

Mormon's later editorial work on and use of Alma's record, it seems to me that the singular reason for the decision to include this episode in our Book of Mormon is Abinadi's powerful teaching of the Savior, which the Nephite prophet delivered and then sealed his testimony with his life. All other questions and considerations regarding this pericope on Abinadi must be considered with this perspective in mind.

27. Interestingly, the original pronoun "thy" in the phrase "thy watchmen" is retained. This may suggest that he is speaking about watchmen in the Americas. Contrast the situation in 3 Nephi 30:32, discussed below.

28. A third possibility is that Jesus is speaking specifically of the gentiles, as opposed to the house of Israel, although this does not seem likely to me given that he has said that if the gentiles repent and convert they "shall be numbered among my people" (3 Nephi 16:13), and if they do not repent they will be "trodden under the foot of my people" (3 Nephi 16:15).

29. This interpretation is given, for example, in Nyman, *Words of Isaiah*, 199.

30. Third Nephi 20:32, 34–35, parallel to Isaiah 52:8–10; 3 Nephi 20:36–38, parallel to Isaiah 52:1–3; 3 Nephi 20:39–40, parallel to Isaiah 52:6–7; 3 Nephi 20:41–54, parallel to Isaiah 52:11–15. Isaiah 52:4–5 is not included in 3 Nephi 20.

31. Angela M. Crowell, "The Hebrew Literary Structure of the Book of Mormon," *Restoration Studies V* (Independence, Mo.: Herald House, 1993): 166, has classified Moroni's use of Isaiah in this passage as "narrative midrash." I thank John W. Welch for this reference.

32. See, for example, Doctrine and Covenants 33:10. This is not meant to suggest that the passage should not be applied to John the Baptist, as in Matthew 3, but only that such usage appears to be a secondary application of Isaiah 40.

33. There are a number of challenges to interpreting this chapter, such as the identity of the "wicked counselor" (verse 11) and the nature of the poetic description of the Lord's power and its effects (see verses 3–6, 8), that cannot be dealt with in this paper.

34. I thank my colleague Michael Rhodes for discussing this passage with me.

35. Geza Vermes, *The Dead Sea Scrolls in English,* 4th ed. (New York: Penguin, 1995), 360.

36. This translation is from F. García Martínez, *The Dead Sea Scrolls Translated,* trans. W. G. E. Watson. (New York: Brill, 1994), 140. Note that the text within brackets has been restored; it is not on the fragments that have survived. The italicized numerals indicate the line numbers in this column of text. See also Vermes, *The Dead Sea Scrolls in English,* 361, and the comments of James VanderKam, *The Dead Sea Scrolls Today* (Grand Rapids, Mich.: Eerdmans, 1994), 52–4. A critical study of *11QMelchizedek* is available in Paul J. Kobelski, *Melchizedek and Melchiresaʿ* (Washington, DC: Catholic Biblical Association of America, 1981), 4–23.

37. While it is not likely in my opinion, it may be that the Qumran view of Melchizedek is a variant of the teaching that Michael will not only assist but actively lead out in the last great battle against Satan at the *end* of the millennium, as recorded in Doctrine and Covenants 88:100–15 (see also Revelation 20:7–10, although Michael is not specifically mentioned there). Note that Vermes, *The Dead Sea Scrolls in English,* 360, considers Melchizedek in *11QMelchizedek* as "identical with the archangel Michael."

38. Elder Keith W. Wilcox, "Look for the Beautiful," *Ensign* (May 1985): 28. It is interesting to note how Orson Pratt, in *Journal of Discourses* 13:355–6, evoked the sense of going out from Zion with glad tidings in a manner similar to that found in Isaiah 40:9–10, quoted above: "We came here [to the mountains of Utah] to fulfil these ancient prophecies. God has lifted up this Church. . . . Beautiful indeed are the feet of those who are sent forth from the mountains of Zion to publish glad tidings of great joy among the various nations and kingdoms of the earth." Again, the "beautiful feet" are those of multiple missionaries preaching the gospel.

Isaiah 53, Mosiah 14,
and the Book of Mormon

John W. Welch

*While Abinadi and others in antiquity interpreted Isaiah's
suffering servant messianically, the Hebrew text left enough
unstated that Noah's wicked priests could adopt another reading.*

Isaiah 53 is unsurpassed in the Book of Mormon, if not
in all of scripture, for its detailed prophetic images of the
suffering and death of the supernally meek servant of God.
Quoted in its entirety by Abinadi in Mosiah 14, near the
middle of his response to the priests of Noah, this beautiful
poem formed not only the crux of Abinadi's theological testimony and legal defense, but also comprised one of the
mainstays of prophetic knowledge in the Book of Mormon
about the coming atonement of the Savior.

In this poem, Isaiah speaks in short, powerful phrases.
His compact expressions project strong bursts of imagery;
he does not dwell long on each painful scene in the travail
of the Redeemer. Each of these flashes evokes sober reflec-
tion. Isaiah has seen the suffering of the servant, but it is
almost as if he cannot stand to look.

In this study, I will explore several issues: (1) How does
Isaiah 53 connect with Isaiah 52? Why did Abinadi quote
Isaiah 53 in answering the question raised against him by
the priests from Isaiah 52? (2) How did Abinadi use and
understand Isaiah 53? To what extent is his discourse in
Mosiah 15-16 grounded in the words and phrases of Isaiah
53? (3) How much was Isaiah 53 understood and used by
Book of Mormon prophets before Abinadi? (4) In light of
the fact that Isaiah 53 seems to have been clearly understood by many Nephites, what linguistic features in the text
of Isaiah 53 may have contributed to the priests' thorough

misunderstanding of this text? Finally, because Isaiah 53 offers the most extensive description in the Old Testament of the suffering servant of God, I will survey in an addendum the comments made by LDS scholars on this exquisite text. Readers of the Book of Mormon should have little difficulty getting through this section of Isaiah if they follow Abinadi as their guide.

Narrative Setting in the Trial of Abinadi

Abinadi recited and interpreted Isaiah 53 because his accusers, the priests of Noah, had challenged him to explain the meaning of Isaiah 52:7–10. What was the thrust of their challenge? It appears that the priests intended, by their direct examination of Abinadi, to catch him in conflict with that scripture and thereby convict him of false prophecy—a capital offense under the law of Moses (see Deuteronomy 18:20).[1] In essence, they were apparently asking Abinadi why he bore tidings of doom and destruction when Isaiah had declared that the beautiful and true prophet brings good tidings and publishes peace: "How beautiful upon the mountains are the feet of him that bringeth *good* tidings" (Mosiah 12:20–22, emphasis added). Isaiah gave cause for great joy: "They shall see eye to eye when the Lord shall bring again Zion; break forth into joy" (Mosiah 12:22–24), and yet Abinadi had brought nothing but bad tidings of destruction.

Abinadi's rebuttal was an extensive and brilliant explanation of the true essence of redemption and how it brings good tidings to those who accept Christ (see Mosiah 12:29–37 and chs. 13–16). His words comprise an elaborate midrash or explanation of the text quoted to him by the priests from Isaiah 52, especially in light of Isaiah 53. Abinadi's fundamental position was based on solid ground, for Isaiah had also clearly stated that "they that rule over them make them to howl" (Isaiah 52:5), and accordingly, Abinadi predicted that the people of Noah "shall howl all the day long" due to the wickedness of their leaders (Mosiah 12:4).

Readers might wonder if Abinadi's speech was responsive to the specific question posed to him by the priests. On examination it becomes clear that his answer was constructed around specific words and phrases in Isaiah 52, interpreted in connection with Isaiah 53. His discourse sheds great light on the meaning of these two closely related texts.

Connections between Isaiah 52 and Isaiah 53

Abinadi quoted Isaiah 53:1–12 in Mosiah 14. That chapter stands as the central passage in his legal defense and prophetic message. Although some scholars have wondered whether the song of the suffering servant should begin at Isaiah 53:1 or 52:13, the fact that Abinadi began quoting at Isaiah 53:1 implies that he and the ancient Nephites understood that a poetical unit began at Isaiah 53:1, as it does today in the traditional chapter divisions in the Bible, not at Isaiah 52:13, as has been suggested by such scholars as Dion and Clines.[2] Indeed, other biblicists, including Orlinsky and Whybray, have argued in favor of commencing the unit at 53:1, the traditional starting point.[3]

Even though Abinadi's quotation begins at Isaiah 53:1, his discourse still supports the general idea that Isaiah 53 is closely linked to and should be understood in connection with Isaiah 52. In explaining the meaning of Isaiah 52, Abinadi readily turned to Isaiah 53, weaving together phrases from both chapters in his summation in Mosiah 15–16 of the mission of the Messiah. Beginning where the priests had left off when they asked him the meaning of Isaiah

52:7–10 (see Mosiah 12:21–24), Abinadi first paraphrased and interpreted the remaining verses in Isaiah 52, and they work together marvelously in Abinadi's hand. Although Abinadi did not expressly quote Isaiah 52:11–15 (the five verses between the text quoted by the priests and the beginning of Isaiah 53), four of the ideas in those verses were integral and sequential parts of Abinadi's argument:

1. Immediately after Isaiah 52:7–10, quoted by the priests, comes a stern admonition concerning the worthiness of those who officiate in the house of the Lord: "Touch no unclean thing, . . . Be ye clean that bear the vessels of the Lord" (Isaiah 52:11). Consistent with this sequence in Isaiah 52, Abinadi commenced his answer by challenging the worthiness of the priests of Noah (see Mosiah 12:26–31). One might wonder why Abinadi did not *quote* Isaiah 52:11 at this point. Perhaps Abinadi sensed that it would do no good to tell the priests of Noah in so many words, "be ye clean," for it was too late to prevent the impurity of the priests; they had continued to violate several of the ten commandments in spite of Abinadi's warning two years earlier (see Mosiah 11:20–25; 12:36–37). In light of God's judgment concerning them, Abinadi probably knew that they would not respond favorably to righteous counsel.

2. The text in Isaiah 52 continues, "My servant shall deal prudently, he shall be exalted and extoled, and be very high" (Isaiah 52:13). Abinadi may well have seen in these words a prediction of Christ's final exalted station (compare Mosiah 16:9). These words may also have reassured Abinadi that he himself, as one of the Lord's servants, would be blessed in many ways by God: "I finish my message, and then it matters not whither I go, if it so be that I am saved" (Mosiah 13:9).

3. Isaiah 52 next declares that people would be astonished by the prophet's message: "As many were astonied at thee" (Isaiah 52:14). Abinadi expected and remarked the same: "Yea, and my words fill you with wonder and amazement" (Mosiah 13:8).

4. Finally, the amazing and shocking sight seen by Isaiah was this: "His visage was so marred more than any man, and his form more than the sons of men" (Isaiah 52:14). Again, compatible with the sequence in Isaiah 52, Abinadi next declared that Christ would live among "the children of men [in] the form of man, [to] be oppressed and afflicted" (Mosiah 13:34–35), immediately before he began quoting Isaiah 53.

The evidence thus sustains the observation that Abinadi was very familiar with the Isaiah text between Isaiah 52:10 and 53:1, for he used its elements in bridging the question of the priests with the answer of the Lord.

Abinadi's Use of Isaiah 53:1–12

After Abinadi called the priests to repentance, declared that salvation would not come by observance of the law of Moses alone, withstood the priests by radiating the power of God, and rehearsed to them the ten commandments, the prophet turned his attention to the coming of the Messiah to explain the true source of salvation and redemption. Approaching Abinadi's use of Isaiah 53 from a forensic standpoint, one might wonder why he decided to quote this particular chapter as his main defense against the accusations of the priests of Noah.

It appears that the priests intended, by their direct examination, to catch Abinadi in conflict with Isaiah 52 on five potential points: (1) Why did he bear tidings of doom and destruction when Isaiah had declared that the beautiful and true prophet brings *good* tidings (see Mosiah 12:20–22)? (2) How could he condemn them when Isaiah said that the redemption of the land was a cause for great joy, and they had *redeemed* the land of Nephi (see Mosiah 12:23–24)? (3) How could he accuse the people of not keeping the law of Moses when Isaiah had said that the uncircumcised and unclean would *not* come in (see Isaiah 52:1)? (4) How did Abinadi dare to prophesy that the people "shall be brought into bondage" (Mosiah 12:2), when Isaiah had spoken of Jerusalem *loosing* herself "from the bands of thy neck" (Isaiah 52:2)? And (5), How could Abinadi value Noah's life as a garment in a furnace when the true prophet had invited Zion to "put on thy beautiful garments" (Isaiah 52:1)? Potential arguments such as these made Isaiah 52 a potent choice as the point of departure in the priests's examination of Abinadi.

Abinadi's response was effective and inspired. By quoting Isaiah 53, Abinadi put himself in a position to answer each of these five potential arguments of the priests: (1) Through Isaiah 53, Abinadi could explain the good tidings of the gospel; the suffering and death of the Lord's servant was a cause of eternally good news, and thus it pleased even God to bruise his servant. (2) In Isaiah 53, one finds several clear statements about the correct meaning of redemption: Only when a person "makes [Christ's] soul an offering for sin" will the Lord "prolong his days" and bring prosperity to his hand (verse 10). True redemption comes when the Father "shall see of the travail of [the Savior's] soul" and "shall be satisfied" (verse 11). By bearing "the sin of many," the Savior shall make "intercession [redemption] for the transgressors" (verse 12). Moreover, because Isaiah

53 prophesied that the people would not esteem Christ (verse 3) and would "esteem him stricken, smitten of God" (verse 4), it was evident (3) that they had not properly understood or kept the law, and, therefore, (4) the law would not protect them from bondage or, even more so, (5) from death and destruction. The priests had taken Isaiah 52:7–10 out of context in accusing Abinadi; he averted their attack by putting that passage of scripture back into its surrounding context.

In addition, several of Isaiah's phrases would have taken on trenchant local meanings that would have set the priests of Noah back in their bold affront against Abinadi. For example, Isaiah had asked, "Who hath believed our report?" (Isaiah 53:1). This plaintive question must have taken on a new ring of truth when Abinadi quoted these words, directing his quote squarely at the unbelieving priests, and Abinadi probably took some solace knowing that disbelief was the typical response of many people to the messages of the prophets. In the same way, the question "and to whom is the arm of the Lord revealed?" (Isaiah 53:1) invites the retort, "Not to Noah and his priests."

But most importantly, Isaiah 53 not only provided Abinadi with a defense against his accusers, but it allowed him to take the higher ground of an affirmative defense. Abinadi used Isaiah 53 to declare the plan of salvation and testify of the resurrection and day of judgment whereby the wicked priests would be punished by God. Isaiah 53 teaches clearly enough the basic messages that were consistently promoted by Book of Mormon prophets.

Isaiah 53 understands many details involved in the life and death of the coming Messiah: "For he [the Messiah] shall grow up before him [the Father] as a tender plant, and as a root [the root of Jesse] out of a dry ground [in the land of Israel]" (verse 2). Isaiah knew that Christ's people would reject their Savior because he would not come as an exalted, glorious being; thus, Isaiah taught that Christ "hath no form nor comeliness" (verse 2); "when we shall see him, there is no beauty that we should desire him" (verse 2); and "he is despised and rejected of men, . . . he was despised, and we esteemed him not" (verse 3). In lieu of recognizing Christ's worth, Isaiah taught, "we [his friends] hid as it were our faces from him" (verse 3), and "we did esteem him stricken, smitten of God, and afflicted" (verse 4). But the people will be in error: "All we like sheep have gone astray; we have turned every one to his own way" (verse 6).

Isaiah 53 poignantly affirms that Jesus will suffer pain and grief, according to the will of God: He will be "a man of sorrows, and acquainted with grief" (verse 3); "surely he hath borne our griefs, and carried our sorrows" (verse 4); "he was wounded for our transgressions, he was bruised for our iniquities" (verse 5); "he was oppressed, and he was afflicted" (verse 7); "he was taken from prison and from judgment" (verse 8); and "Yet it pleased the Lord to bruise him; he hath put him to grief." (verse 10).

Not only will Christ suffer, but he will die: "And he made his grave with the wicked, and with the rich in his death" (verse 9); "He hath poured out his soul unto death" (verse 12); and "For he was cut off out of the land of the living" (verse 8).

Despite the fact that people would erroneously number him "with the transgressors" (verse 12), Christ would be innocent: "He had done no violence, neither was any deceit in his mouth" (verse 9). Yet he would go voluntarily: "He opened not his mouth: he is brought as a lamb to the slaughter, and as a sheep before her shearers is dumb, so he openeth not his mouth" (verse 7).

The astounding purpose in all of this is that Christ's suffering will benefit all humanity: "The chastisement of our peace was upon him; and with his stripes we are healed" (verse 5). This is the peace that the messenger would publish. The expiation of sin would not come through the sacrifices called for by the law of Moses (as the priests of Noah taught), but instead our iniquities are taken up *by him*: "the Lord hath laid on him the iniquity of us all" (verse 6); "for the transgression of my people was he stricken" (verse 8); "for he shall bear their iniquities" (verse 11), "and he bare the sin of many, and made intercession [with the Father] for the transgressors" (verse 12). This messianic offering will satisfy the demands of justice and will bring about a reconciliation and atonement between God and mankind: "He [the Father] shall see of the travail of [the Savior's] soul, and shall be satisfied" (verse 11). But each person will need to accept his offering, which will become efficacious "when thou shalt make his soul an offering for sin" (verse 10).

In this way, the Lord shall have spiritual offspring: "he shall see his seed" (verse 10), and he will be able to reward and prosper his people: At the day of judgment, "by his knowledge shall my righteous servant justify many" (verse 11), and this shall pave the way for eternal rewards: "He shall prolong his days, and the pleasure of the Lord shall prosper in his hand" (verse 10). These blessings, the spoils of the war against evil, will be turned over to the Servant for division among his followers: "Therefore will I divide him a portion with the great, and he shall divide the spoil with the strong" (verse 12).

The Grounding in Isaiah 53 of Abinadi's Theological Explanations in Mosiah 15–16

To the casual reader, the relationship between Isaiah 53 (parallel to Mosiah 14) and the remainder of Abinadi's discourse to the priests (see Mosiah 15–16) may seem slight; but on closer inspection, it becomes clear that Abinadi's theology and prophetic understanding of God's salvation are deeply grounded in the words and phrases of Isaiah 53.

One of Abinadi's main messages was that God himself would come down among his people (see Mosiah 15:1). This idea is imbedded in the text of Isaiah 53. For example, Isaiah 53:1–2 says that "the arm of the Lord" will be revealed when "he [that is the Lord] shall grow up before him as a tender plant." Abinadi attributes to God all of the humiliation, pain, and death of the suffering servant here on earth among his people.

A closely related point is Abinadi's insistence that this Lord, "the Son of God," will subject his flesh "to the will of the Father" (Mosiah 15:2). Nevertheless, Abinadi hastens to add that the Son of God is "one God," called the Father (not of the spirits, but "of heaven and earth") and also called the Son ("because of the flesh").[4] Abinadi's words were carefully selected—perhaps to avoid further controversy with the priests and possibly another legal accusation, this time on the grounds that he had violated the commandment that is often read as requiring monotheism, "thou shalt have no other God before me" (Mosiah 13:35)—and he appears to teach the priests all that their understanding allowed. But beyond those limitations, it remains clear that Abinadi understood that at least two distinct beings are involved in the godhead, and he could have found some support for this in Isaiah 53, if he understood Isaiah to be speaking of two divine beings: *"He* [the Son] shall grow up before *him* [the Father]" (verse 2); *"the Lord* [God the Father] laid *on him* [the Son] the iniquities of us all" (verse 6); "it pleased *the Lord* to bruise *him"* (verse 10); *"he* hath put *him* to grief" (verse 10); *"he* shall see the travail of *his* soul, and shall be satisfied" (verse 11); *"I* will divide *him* a portion" (verse 12).

Used by Abinadi' as part of his testimony that God himself shall redeem his people, Isaiah's prophecy affirmed that the Son would "suffer temptation," but "yield not"; would allow himself "to be mocked and scourged" (compare Isaiah's words: esteemed him not, grief, wounded, oppressed, afflicted), and to be "cast out and disowned by his people" (compare Isaiah: despised and rejected), yet "he opened not his mouth" (Mosiah 15:5–6). He would become "subject even unto to death" (compare Isaiah: he hath poured out his soul unto death), and the will of the Son would be "swallowed up in the will of the Father" (Mosiah 15:7; compare Isaiah: it pleased the Lord to bruise him). Thus he would gain "the victory over death" (compare Isaiah: and divide the spoils, i.e. the spoils of victory), which would give the Son "power to make intercession for the children of men" (Mosiah 15:8; in Isaiah's words: and made intercession for the transgressors), having "satisfied the demands of justice" (Mosiah 15:9; compare Isaiah: he shall see of the travail of his soul, and shall be satisfied).

Next, Abinadi turned to answer another pressing issue raised by the priests: Who are the true messengers of the Lord, and was Abinadi one of them? As Isaiah had asked, "Who shall declare his generation?" (Isaiah 53:8). Abinadi proceeded to explain that "when his soul has been made an offering for sin" (Isaiah 53:10) then shall Jesus "see his seed" (Mosiah 15:10); and all prophets who declare this message, and all people who believe their words are his seed, "for whom he has died, to redeem them from their transgressions" (Mosiah 15:12; compare Isaiah: he shall bear their iniquities). Thus, those prophets are the ones "who have published peace, who have brought good tidings of good, who have published salvation; and said unto Zion: Thy God reigneth!" (Mosiah 15:14). Accordingly, if and when the priests of Noah will repent and recognize that Christ's sacrifice is the proper offering for sin, then Christ will see his seed and how beautiful upon the mountains will be their message of peace (see Mosiah 15:15–18). In this way, Abinadi answered effectively the question, "Who is entitled to speak as a prophet?" and thereby countered the charge that he had committed the crime of false prophecy.

Abinadi went on to explain that "the Son reigneth" (compare Isaiah 52:7) because the Son will overcome death (see Mosiah 15:20–25), and that indeed "the ends of the earth shall see the salvation of our God" (Isaiah 52:10) at the day of judgment before every nation (see Mosiah 15:26–28); and for that reason the "watchmen" (Isaiah 52:8) shall sing for joy (see Mosiah 15:29–31).

Abinadi concluded his speech by explaining the rewards that will be given in the resurrection (see Mosiah 16:1–12), and, with this theme, he turns to the final concepts found in Isaiah 53. The wicked, such as the priests of Noah, will weep (see Mosiah 16:2–7), for there will be a victory over death (compare Isaiah: he shall divide the spoil), and only in Christ will there be "a life which is endless" (compare Isaiah: he shall prolong his days) and the Lord's judgment will stand and the righteous of God will prevail (see Mosiah 16:8–12; compare Isaiah: the pleasure of the Lord shall prosper in his hand).

Thus, each segment in Isaiah 53 contributes to the main points of Abinadi's speech. Indeed, Mosiah 18:2 confirms and summarizes these as the main precepts taught by

Abinadi. As Alma began to teach the words of Abinadi, Alma crystallized from this discourse the same concepts we have seen here: Alma taught "concerning that which was to come, and also concerning the resurrection of the dead, and the redemption of the people, which was to be brought to pass through the power, and sufferings, and death of Christ, and his resurrection and ascension into heaven" (Mosiah 18:2).

Was Isaiah 53 Known and Used by Earlier Nephite Prophets?

The teachings of Abinadi, of course, were not new in Nephite history. Abinadi's death occurred about 150 B.C. Four hundred years earlier, Nephi and Jacob had taught, in the same city as Abinadi, similar points about the coming of Christ, the suffering and death of the Messiah, and the resurrection of the dead. Interestingly, the set of doctrines taught by Abinadi closely tracks these key elements in the messianic portions of the Nephite prophetic worldview articulated in 1 Nephi 11, 1 Nephi 19, 2 Nephi 9, 2 Nephi 25, and in other early Nephite and brass plates texts.[5] The similarity between Abinadi's set of doctrines and the writings of Nephi and Jacob raises the following additional questions: To what extent was Nephi's messianic expectation, like Abinadi's, grounded in Isaiah 53? Did Nephi and Jacob use Isaiah 53 in formulating their teachings about the coming of the Messiah? Several concepts and phrases in Nephite writings, together with the fact that Nephi and Jacob made extended use of Isaiah 48–51, make it likely that Abinadi was not the first Nephite to use Isaiah 53 as an extensive source of knowledge about the coming of Christ.

Isaiah 53 begins by describing Christ's condescension and life upon the earth (see Isaiah 53:2). Nephi similarly saw and declared that "the Son of Man [would go] forth among the children of men" (1 Nephi 11:24).[6] Nephi also concurred with Isaiah's vision of Christ being "exalted" (Isaiah 52:13) as he taught that Christ would be "lifted up" (1 Nephi 11:33; 19:10) both in death and in his ascension.

As Isaiah prophesied that Christ would be "taken from prison and from judgment" (Isaiah 53:8) and we would hide "as it were our faces from him" (Isaiah 53:3), Nephi taught that Christ would be "taken by the people . . . and judged of the world" (1 Nephi 11:32) and would be put "into the hands of wicked men" (1 Nephi 19:10), and that people would "turn aside their hearts against the Holy One" (1 Nephi 19:15).

Regarding Christ's rejection and suffering (see Isaiah 53:3, 8, 14), Nephi prophesied that the "Holy One of Israel" would be "despised" (1 Nephi 19:14; 2 Nephi 15:24) and "rejected" (2 Nephi 25:18). Isaiah wrote that Christ will be "acquainted with grief" and "a man of sorrows" (Isaiah 53:3); Nephi said the same, explaining that "they scourge him, and he suffereth it; and they smite him, and he suffereth it. Yea, they spit upon him, and he suffereth it" (1 Nephi 19:9). Isaiah said that Christ would suffer "more than any man" (Isaiah 52:14), and this detail was also expressed by Jacob: "he suffereth the pains of all men, yea, the pains of every living creature, both men, women, and children, who belong to the family of Adam" (2 Nephi 9:2).

Isaiah wrote that Christ suffered for our sake—he was "wounded for our transgressions, he was bruised for our iniquities" (Isaiah 53:5). Again, Nephi and Jacob each declared that Christ would be "lifted up upon the cross and slain for the sins of the world" (1 Nephi 11:33; see also Jacob

1:8). Similarly, Isaiah wrote that Christ should die—that he would be "cut off out of the land of the living" (Isaiah 53:8), and this is recorded in the Book of Mormon as well (1 Nephi 11:33; Jacob 1:8).

The beautiful benefits of Christ's suffering and death were also described in Isaiah, and similar points are found in the teachings of the early Book of Mormon prophets. Isaiah says that Christ would be led like "a lamb to the slaughter" (Isaiah 53:7); Nephi refers to Christ as a lamb nearly sixty times in 1 Nephi chapters 11–14, gratefully aware that Christ "suffereth it, because of his loving kindness and his long-suffering towards the children of men" (1 Nephi 19:9; compare Isaiah 53:5, "with his stripes we are healed"). Because of Christ's sacrifice, those who partake of his gift will receive the blessings (compare Isaiah 53:12, "he shall divide the spoil with the strong"); Nephi and Jacob promised that those who believe in the Son (see 1 Nephi 11:6), "seek to bring forth . . . Zion" (1 Nephi 13:37), and "labor diligently in his vineyard" (Jacob 6:3) will be "a blessed people upon the promised land forever" (1 Nephi 14:2) and that God will "bestow [blessings] upon [their] children" (2 Nephi 9:3).

And this is not all. After Christ's death, Isaiah prophesied, Christ would be resurrected (see Isaiah 53:12). Likewise Nephi declared that Christ "shall rise from the dead, with healing in his wings" (2 Nephi 25:13), punishing the wicked and effecting the "resurrection of the dead" (2 Nephi 26:3; see also 2 Nephi 2:8).

The words, phrases, concepts, and expressions are similar enough in all these cases that one may readily conclude that Book of Mormon prophets prior to Abinadi knew and used Isaiah 53 and understood the relevance of this song of the suffering servant to their own revelations concerning the coming Messiah.

Parenthetically, it is interesting to note that the Book of Mormon prophets were not the only Jews or members of the house of Israel before the time of Jesus Christ who understood Isaiah 53 messianically and who expected the Messiah to suffer at the hands of his people. One recently published Dead Sea Scroll, 4Q541, fragment 9, column I, reads: "They will utter many words against him, and an abundance of lies; they will fabricate fables against him, and utter every kind of disparagement against him. His generation will change the evil, and [. . .] established in deceit and in violence."[7] The translator, Florentino García Martínez, sees in this text an important confirmation that the messianic interpretation of Isaiah 53 was "not an innovation of purely Christian origin," but rather was already "the result of previous developments."[8] Some scholars have even proposed that this ancient Jewish text from Qumran may have "contained the idea of the violent death of this 'Messiah-priest,'"[9] but unfortunately the text appears too fragmentary to allow solid conclusions in this regard.

For a summary, verse by verse, of the extensive Latter-day Saint messianic interpretation of Isaiah 53, see the bibliographic addendum in this volume, pages 495–502.

Why Did the Priests of Noah Not Understand the Messianic Content of Isaiah 52–53?

Because Abinadi's interpretation and use of Isaiah 53 was complete, cogent, and bound up with Nephite tradition, one naturally wonders why the priests of Noah did not understand or accept what he said to them. Likewise, if Isaiah 53 had been understood all along as a messianic text, how could the priests of Noah and others, like Sherem, who rejected the Nephite prophetic view, not agree with this basic interpretation? There is no reason to believe that the priests of Noah were unfamiliar with Isaiah 53 before

Abinadi quoted it to them, for they knew and introduced Isaiah 52 into the discussion. People of their persuasion must have somehow understood Isaiah 53 differently.

While hindsight is 20/20, making it much easier for Christian readers to perceive the relevance of Isaiah 53 on the mission and passion of Jesus Christ, several ambiguities in the Hebrew in Isaiah 53 have, indeed, given rise over the years to other interpretations. It seems quite likely that these ambiguities would have been an even greater source of uncertainty about the meaning of Isaiah 53 in the minds of people like the priests of Noah, who lived before the time of Christ. Clines concisely and conveniently summarizes the main points of debate among modern Isaiah scholars concerning the veiled meanings of Isaiah 53.[10] Several problems exist, arising mainly from the fact that Isaiah used so many pronouns or other grammatical constructions with unspecified antecedents:

1. In Hebrew, the identity of the servant is ambiguous. Who is *he?* The servant is never actually named or identified, except by the things that he suffered. In fact, it is difficult to determine the antecedent of many of the pronouns in Isaiah 53. To whom do these pronouns refer: "we" (verse 6), "our" (verses 3–6), "I" (verse 12), or "thou" (verse 10)?

2. The song is unclear about when the servant had lived in the past or would yet live in the future. It is fair to ask, should Isaiah 53 be read in reference to the past, the present, or the future? Because the Hebrew verbs are in the perfect mode, some people have argued that Isaiah 53 speaks only of a person who lived in Isaiah's own day, whom he knew, who was despised, rejected, and wrongly put to death, perhaps an innocent prophet who went silently to his death, executed because of some testimony he bore. Others read Isaiah 53 as a "prophetic

retrospective," looking back in vision at the future death of the Messiah as if it had already occurred. According to this view, Isaiah 53 is written in the "prophetic past." Accordingly, it is debatable whether this text was written in the historical past or the prophetic past. Apparently, this was in fact a major issue for the priests of Noah, for Abinadi had to explain to them that he, like Isaiah, spoke "of things to come *as though they have already come*" (Mosiah 16:6, emphasis added), a marvelous description of the Hebraic prophetic perfect.[11] This grammatical comment by Abinadi is an important acknowledgment from antiquity that people were aware of this manner of speaking, which is known today by grammarians as the prophetic past.

3. Other questions include, What did he suffer or will he suffer? and What led the "we" to change their minds about the servant? At first people despised him, but later they agreed that he had borne their griefs. The text is not specific about the answers to such questions, and thus it is open to a variety of interpretations.

Behind all of these questions, however, stands the ultimate interpretive issue: whether or not the servant is a divine future being. This is the crucial point of departure in determining how one reads Isaiah 53, and it is possible to read this text several ways. Because of the open texture of Isaiah 53 in this regard, Abinadi was textually vulnerable on this very point, and thus it is logical that the priests attacked him precisely on this position, that a divine being, "that God himself should come down" (Mosiah 17:8). However, Abinadi's words and his blood stand as a testimony of this crucial declaration, for which Abinadi too went like a lamb to the slaughter. He also was innocent—another servant of the Lord who suffered death and was cut off from the land of the living.

The Book of Mormon says nothing about Abinadi's children or posterity, but his legacy or prophetic seed lived on in Alma and his converts. Abinadi was more than a witness in word alone; his life and death show that he also knew that meaning of Isaiah 53 from the inner workings of personal suffering and testing to the extreme.

Notes

1. For a detailed discussion of the legal aspects of the trial of Abinadi, see John W. Welch, "Judicial Process in the Trial of Abinadi," (Provo: FARMS Preliminary Report, 1981); and "The Trial of Abinadi," in John W. Welch, *Law in the Book of Mormon: The Nephite Court Cases* (Provo: BYU Law School, 1996); see also Lew W. Cramer, "Abinadi," in *Encyclopedia of Mormonism*, Daniel H. Ludlow ed. (New York: Macmillan, 1992), 1:5–6, and Paul Y. Hoskisson, "How Beautiful Were the Feet of Abinadi," unpublished manuscript (1997). I am grateful to Paul Hoskisson for reviewing this chapter and discussing his paper with me.

2. Paul-Eugéne Dion, "Les chants du Serviteur de Yahweh et quelques passages apparentés d'Is 40–55. Un essai sur leurs limites précises et sur leurs origines respectives," *Biblica* 51 (1970); 17–38, cited in David J. A. Clines, *I, He, We and They: A Literary Approach to Isaiah 53* (Sheffield, England: University of Sheffield, 1983), 11.

3. Harry M. Orlinsky, "The So-Called 'Servant of the Lord' and 'Suffering Servant' in Second Isaiah," in *Studies on the Second Part of the Book of Isaiah* (Netherlands: Brill, 1967), 17–23; R. N. Whybray, *Thanksgiving for a Liberated Prophet: An Interpretation of Isaiah Chapter 53* (Sheffield, England: University of Sheffield, 1985), 110–3; R. N. Whybray, *Isaiah 40–66* (London: Oliphants, 1975), 169.

4. See the discussion of Jeffrey R. Holland in this volume; see also Robert L. Millet, "Jesus Christ, Fatherhood and Sonship of," in *Encyclopedia of Mormonism*, Ludlow ed., 2:739–40.

5. On the Nephite prophetic outlook, see my essay on that subject earlier in this volume.

6. Benjamin, a few years after Abinadi, likewise taught that Christ would "dwell in a tabernacle of clay" (Mosiah 3:5), and it was widely known among the Nephites that he would "take upon him flesh and blood, and go forth upon the face of the earth" (Mosiah 7:27).

7. Florentino García Martínez, "Messianic Hopes in the Qumran Writings," in Donald W. Parry and Dana M. Pike, *LDS Perspectives on the Dead Sea Scrolls* (Provo: FARMS, 1997), 136-7.

8. Ibid., 137.

9. Ibid., 138, referring to E. Puech, cited in ibid., 167 n. 5.

10. Clines, *I, He, We and They*, 25–33.

11. See Gesening, section 106: "perfectum propheticum."

The Lord's Covenant of Kindness
Isaiah 54 and 3 Nephi 22

Cynthia L. Hallen

*Linguistic analysis of key words shows how a barren woman
is symbolically associated with Zion, the earth, and the Lord's
servants in God's beautiful, astonishing, merciful love.*

In 3 Nephi 22, the Saints who gathered at the temple to
hear the message of the resurrected Jesus had recently survived terrible tempests and upheavals in their lives. The
more wicked part of the people had been destroyed, and the
more righteous part of the people mourned the loss of their
loved ones. As part of his sermon to the Nephites, Jesus
shared a message of comfort from the prophecies of Isaiah.
Isaiah 54 is one of the richest passages of scripture ever spoken by the Lord, so it is not surprising that Jesus would re-
cite this passage in its entirety for the faithful at the temple
in Bountiful.[1]

Chapter 22 of 3 Nephi is a blessing of comfort from the
Lord to his covenant people. In many ways it reads like a
love letter from a husband to his wife, a *billet-doux*[2] with covenant blessings and promises encoded into every verse. The
verses of the text also resemble an *epithalamium*,[3] a wedding
song or poem that celebrates the joy of a bride and her groom.
The language sings with poetic figures, scriptural allusions,
and multilayered metaphors. All of these language features
emphasize the kindness that the Lord feels for his people,
making the Lord's love seem impossible to fully express.
One can only attempt to "mention the lovingkindnesses of
the Lord . . . according to all that the Lord hath bestowed on
us, and the great goodness toward the house of Israel, which
he hath bestowed on them" (Isaiah 63:7).

In English, the word *kindness* is a key to understanding the Lord's relation to his covenant people.[4] The earliest etymological meaning of *kindness* is the reconstructed Indo-European root *gen-*, meaning "to give birth, beget; with derivatives referring to . . . procreation and to familial and tribal groups."[5] Several other terms come from the same semantic root as *kindness* and have underlying meanings related to gospel themes in Isaiah and the Book of Mormon: *gentile, gentle, generation, gene, genealogy, genesis, progenitor, pregnant, natal, nation, nativity, kin, kindred, king,* and *kinder.*[6] Kindness is the key to the covenant that turns the hearts of the children to their parents and the hearts of the parents to each other in the plan of salvation. Loving-kindness is the chief characteristic of the covenant that binds the heart of the Lord to his people and the hearts of his people to the Lord: "Yea, I have loved thee with an everlasting love: therefore with lovingkindness have I drawn thee" (Jeremiah 31:3; see also John 12:32; 3 Nephi 27:14–15; D&C 88:63).

In the scriptures, the Lord often uses a metaphor of marriage to describe his covenant of kindness: "I will betroth thee unto me in righteousness, and in judgment, and in lovingkindness, and in mercies" (Hosea 2:19). The Hebrew word for *kindness* is *hesed,* which has connotations of mercy, courtship, favors, loyalty, cherishing, marital duty, and constant attention (see 3 Nephi 22:8, 10, parallel to Isaiah 54:8, 10).[7] In 3 Nephi 22, the Lord discusses his everlasting covenant of kindness by comparing latter-day Zion to a barren woman. Throughout the chapter and in related scriptures, the barren woman is symbolically associated with the destiny of (1) Zion and the church, (2) the earth and all creation, and (3) the Lord's servants and the Latter-day Saints. Each verse of 3 Nephi 22 weaves various combinations of these elements together into a beautiful song of loving-kindness.

This chapter identifies thirteen motifs in Isaiah 54 (paralleled in 3 Nephi 22) and explores their literary and theological nuances by examining the linguistic and scriptural backgrounds of key words or phrases in this beautiful text.

Sing!

In Jewish culture, childbirth is associated with singing, rejoicing, and reciting psalms. A woman sings when she first discovers that she will have a baby, as Mary does after Gabriel's annunciation that she would bear the Christ child: "My soul doth magnify the Lord, And my spirit hath rejoiced in God my Saviour" (Luke 1:46–47). A woman also sings when her baby is safely delivered, as Hannah does after the birth of Samuel: "My heart rejoiceth in the Lord, mine horn is exalted in the Lord: my mouth is enlarged over mine enemies; because I rejoice in my salvation" (1 Samuel 2:1). Even today, an orthodox Jewish mother will use the words of a psalm to give thanks for the birth of her firstborn child: "Sing aloud unto God our strength: make a joyful noise unto the God of Jacob" (Psalm 81:1).[8] Singing is a token of the covenant that promises that barren women will have posterity, that the Lord will have children in Zion, and that the Lord's people will have children in their homes. The singing of angels heralded the birth of Jesus, who will redeem the whole earth with a covenant of peace and goodwill (see Luke 2:13–14).

In 3 Nephi 22:1, Jesus assures the Nephites that his covenant promises will be fulfilled in the latter days. He then quotes a sacred annunciation from Isaiah:

> Sing, O barren, thou that didst not bear;
> break forth into singing, and cry aloud, thou that didst
> not travail with child;

> for more are the children of the desolate
> than the children of the married wife, saith the Lord.

In these three phrases—(1) *sing*, (2) *break forth into singing,* and (3) *cry aloud*—the Lord encourages the barren woman literally to rejoice in song and figuratively to give birth to children.

The command to sing is a command for all Saints to rejoice in spite of difficult circumstances. We are to sing for joy in spite of present sorrows because the Lord will comfort us in our affliction (see 1 Nephi 21:13). We are to sing together because the Lord will redeem the waste places and the devastated peoples of the earth (see Isaiah 52:9; Mosiah 12:23; 15:30; 3 Nephi 16:19; 20:32–34). We "break forth into singing" because the Lord has done great things for us just as he once did great things for the Nephites and for Mary, the mother of Jesus (see 3 Nephi 4:31; Luke 1:49). We worship the Lord by singing in our hearts, in our homes, and in our church meetings because, as Elder Dallin H. Oaks has said, "music has a unique capacity to communicate our feelings of love for the Lord."[9] When we sing, we remember the covenant of the Lord's loving-kindness.

Cry aloud means "shout," especially to make a joyful noise as in singing (see Psalm 55:17; Isaiah 24:14). The Lord tells the barren woman to cry aloud with joyful singing because she will soon cry aloud with paradoxical pain as she breaks forth into the joys of childbirth. The crying aloud of the woman for joy in marriage and childbirth foreshadows the glad shouts of the mountains, valleys, seas, dry lands, rivers, brooks, rills, woods, trees, rocks, sun, moon, stars, and all creation at the second coming of the Son of God, who gives new birth to all creatures and creations through the pain of his atoning sacrifice (see D&C 128:23; see also Isaiah 14:7; 42:11; 55:12; D&C 128:22).

O Barren

The message in 3 Nephi 22 is addressed to a barren woman with whom the Lord has made a covenant of kindness. With marriage as a metaphor for the covenant, we would expect the Lord to address the woman as a bride or as a married wife with children. However, in keeping with the plan of salvation, the faith and the faithfulness of the woman must be tried; she experiences a temporary separation from her husband and promised children. The woman lives alone as if she has been widowed or as if she has never been married. She has never been able to bear the children that she was promised in the covenant. The woman feels abandoned and fearful because she does not have a companion; she feels sad and desolate because she has no children to care for; she feels ashamed and vulnerable because in her culture singleness is a stigma and barrenness is a curse. Other women in her society have the blessings of family life, while she is "afflicted, tossed with tempest, and not comforted!" (3 Nephi 22:11, parallel to Isaiah 54:11).

The Lord acknowledges the woman's affliction in four parallel phrases: (1) *O barren*, (2) *thou that didst not bear*, (3) *thou that didst not travail with child*, and (4) *the desolate* (see 3 Nephi 22:1, parallel to Isaiah 54:1). By addressing the woman as "barren," the Lord evokes the stories of various female progenitors in the house of Israel whose blessings of posterity came after the trial of their faith: Sarah, Rebekah, Rachel, Hannah, the mother of Sampson, and Elisabeth.

At first Sarah was barren (see Genesis 11:30), but the Lord's covenant with Abraham included blessings for his wife:

> I will bless her, and she shall be a mother of nations; kings of people shall be of her. Then Abraham fell upon his face, and laughed, and said in his heart, Shall a child

be born unto him that is an hundred years old? and shall
Sarah, that is ninety years old, bear? . . . And God said,
Sarah thy wife shall bear a son indeed; and thou shalt call
his name Isaac: and I will establish my covenant with him
for an everlasting covenant, and with his seed after him.
(Genesis 17:16–19)

Abraham and Sarah's response to the Lord's promise is
to laugh, but their humor is prompted by joy, not just incre-
dulity (see Genesis 18:9–15). The Hebrew word *tzachak* means
"to laugh" and "to rejoice" (see Genesis 21:6 note a; 17:17,
note a).[10] When Isaac is born, Sarah rejoices: "God hath made
me to laugh, so that all that hear will laugh with me" (Genesis 21:6). In the Lord's covenant, the joy of Abraham and
Sarah is extended to their posterity and to all of the Lord's
children in Zion:[11]

> Look unto Abraham your father,
> and unto Sarah that bare you:
> for I called him alone,
> and blessed him, and increased him.
> For the Lord shall comfort Zion:
> he will comfort all her waste places;
> and he will make her wilderness like Eden,
> and her desert like the garden of the Lord;
> joy and gladness shall be found therein,
> thanksgiving, and the voice of melody.
>
> (Isaiah 51:2–3, parallel to 2 Nephi 8:2–3)

The Lord will comfort Zion, in spite of barrenness, old
age, and death, and the earth will become a millennial garden, full of music.

In addressing Zion as "thou that didst not bear" (3 Nephi
22:1, parallel to Isaiah 54:1), the Lord evokes the story of
Sampson's mother, the wife of Manoah: "And the angel of
the Lord appeared unto the woman, and said unto her, Behold now, thou art barren, and bearest not: but thou shalt

conceive, and bear a son" (Judges 13:3). Not only does the angel's message announce the birth of Sampson, but it also foreshadows Gabriel's annunciation to Mary of the birth of Jesus: "thou shalt conceive in thy womb, and bring forth a son, and shalt call his name Jesus" (Luke 1:31).[12]

Some women might welcome the idea of being exempt from the labor of childbirth, but the emotional agony of the woman who does not travail with child may be more severe than physical pain. Despite her husband's kindness, the childless Hannah grieves intensely: "Then said Elkanah her husband to her, Hannah, why weepest thou? and why eatest thou not? and why is thy heart grieved? am not I better to thee than ten sons? . . . And she was in bitterness of soul, and prayed unto the Lord, and wept sore[, saying] . . . I am a woman of a sorrowful spirit" (1 Samuel 1:8, 10, 15).

The woman who gives birth may also experience sorrow, but she usually experiences great joy in family life: "A woman when she is in travail hath sorrow, because her hour is come: but as soon as she is delivered of the child, she remembereth no more the anguish, for joy that a man is born into the world" (John 16:21). Women who bear children may carry heavy burdens of pain in raising a child, but the barren woman may carry an even heavier burden of emptiness. The childless woman may feel ashamed, saying to herself, "I travail not, nor bring forth children, neither do I nourish up young men, nor bring up virgins" (Isaiah 23:4). The childless woman's anguish is intensified by her desolation. Yet the barren woman will not always be desolate; she will someday have more children than any married wife can give birth to in one mortal lifetime (see 3 Nephi 22:1, parallel to Isaiah 54:1).[13] The offspring of the barren woman will be infinite in number because she symbolizes the earth, individuals, and groups of people that will eventually receive the full blessings of the Lord's covenant.

The barren wife is a scriptural type for faithful people who must wait for promised blessings, not a symbol of the covenant-breakers personified in Jeremiah's backsliding harlot or Hosea's unfaithful wife. When explaining the marriage metaphor, many scholars interpret all references to the woman as references to people who break their covenants.[14] They read the Lord's kind words as an offer of forgiveness to a wayward but eventually repentant people.[15] We should not equate the faithful barren wife with the adulterous wife. Although "all we like sheep have gone astray" (Isaiah 53:6), the language of 3 Nephi 22 suggests that the Lord is addressing a woman who has tried to remain faithful to her covenants, not a woman who has been rejected because of infidelity.

The Lord explicitly equates the barren woman with "the servants of the Lord" (3 Nephi 22:17, parallel to Isaiah 54:17). Each individual man or woman who enters into a covenant relationship is a servant of the Lord. Couples who make sacred marriage covenants in the temple act as servants of the Lord when they pray to bring children into their homes. Every prophet, apostle, seventy, or missionary who bears the glad tidings of the gospel is a servant in the Lord's vineyard. Just as a barren woman would willingly experience labor pains in order to give physical life to children, so are the servants of the Lord willing to labor as missionaries so that all of God's children might be born again in the name of Jesus Christ.[16] The enemies of the Lord try to prevent the work from going forward, and the efforts of the servants may seem futile, but the Lord's servants will see the fruits of their labors if they endure to the end in the latter-day harvest of souls (see Jacob 5).

The chapter heading of 3 Nephi 22 identifies the barren woman as Zion: "In the last days, Zion and her stakes shall be established." Zion the woman symbolizes a city or community of people in a covenant relationship with God. In the last days, all of the righteous inhabitants of the earth will become citizens of Zion. Zion will fulfill her destiny as a city of holiness, a New Jerusalem for the Jews, a habitation for the gentiles, a haven for the scattered tribes of Israel, a church for the followers of Christ, a millennial home for faithful children of God, and a kingdom for the King of Kings. The formal name of Zion as an institution is the Church of Jesus Christ of Latter-day Saints. Christ (the Bridegroom) works with the church (the bride) to teach the gospel of peace and to publish the plan of salvation. Members of the church become the children of Christ, then help others to enter into spiritual kinship with the Lord through faith, repentance, baptism, and the gift of the Holy Ghost.

Enlarge Thy Tent

In five lexically parallel phrases, the Lord instructs the barren woman to make room in her home for children: (1) *enlarge the place of thy tent*, (2) *let them stretch forth the curtains of thy habitations*, (3) *spare not*, (4) *lengthen thy cords*, and (5) *strengthen thy stakes* (see 3 Nephi 22:2, parallel to Isaiah 54:2). *Enlarge the place of thy tent* literally means "make the place where you set up your tent larger" and figuratively means "make room in your life for promised blessings" (see Genesis 9:27). *Let them stretch forth the curtains of thine habitations* means "let the birth of children cause you to enlarge your home." The childbearing images of enlarging, stretching, and cords make the woman's home a metaphor for her own body. The Lord asks married women to enlarge their bodies in order to provide bodies as tabernacles or temples for his spirit children. The desolate woman must have a great deal of faith to enlarge her tent to prepare for the blessing of children.

The tent is reminiscent of the tabernacle in the wilderness, which provided a place of worship for the children of Israel (see Numbers 3:25–26).[17] The tent is also a metaphor for the Lord's covenant with the descendants of Noah's sons Shem, Japheth, and Ham: "God shall enlarge Japheth, and he shall dwell in the tents of Shem; and Canaan shall be his servant" (Genesis 9:27; see also Acts 10:9–48). Just as the Lord promised Japheth that his people would someday become members of the household of Shem, so the Lord promises that Ham and all other nations will have the opportunity to dwell in the tent of gospel covenants in the latter days (see 3 Nephi 22:3, 5, parallel to Isaiah 54:3, 5; see also D&C: Official Declaration—2).

The image of stretching forth curtains describes not only childbirth but also how the Lord created the earth as a dwelling place for his children: "Bless the Lord . . . who stretchest out the heavens like a curtain . . . who laid the foundations of the earth" (Psalm 104:1–2, 5; see also Zechariah 12:1). The same image occurs often in Isaiah: "Have ye not understood from the foundations of the earth? It is he . . . that stretcheth out the heavens as a curtain, and spreadeth them out as a tent to dwell in" (Isaiah 40:21–22). Images of singing, birth, creation, protection, and temple-building combine in another Isaiah passage:

> Sing, O ye heavens; for the Lord hath done it:
> shout, ye lower parts of the earth:
> break forth into singing, ye mountains,
> O forest, and every tree therein:
> for the Lord hath redeemed Jacob,
> and glorified himself in Israel.
> Thus saith the Lord, thy redeemer,
> and he that formed thee from the womb,
> I am the Lord that maketh all things;
> that stretcheth forth the heavens alone;
> that spreadeth abroad the earth by myself;

That frustrateth the tokens of the liars; . . .
That confirmeth the word of his servant . . . ;
that saith to Jerusalem, Thou shalt be inhabited;
and to the cities of Judah, Ye shall be built, . . .
even saying to Jerusalem, Thou shalt be built;
and to the temple, Thy foundation shall be laid.

(Isaiah 44:23–26, 28)

Variations on these themes carry over into the beautiful music of kindness in Isaiah 54 and 3 Nephi 22.[18]

Enoch also testifies of the Lord's kindness toward his creations. The Lord stretches out curtains and creates countless worlds for his children because his mercy is infinite: "And were it possible that man could number the particles of the earth, yea, millions of earths like this, it would not be a beginning to the number of thy creations; and thy curtains are stretched out still; and yet thou art there, and thy bosom is there; and also thou art just; thou art merciful and kind forever" (Moses 7:30).

Not only does the Lord allow us to observe his creations, he also invites us to participate in creation. Childbirth is the Lord's way of teaching his children about love; bearing children and building homes teaches the Lord's covenant people about the creation of worlds. Church members can teach each other to renew the covenant of kindness on a weekly basis and to perform good works on a daily basis. Saints can magnify their callings and enlarge the influence of Christlike service in a world hungry for loving-kindness.

Childbirth teaches the Lord's people how to establish his church family on earth. To Zion, *let them stretch forth the curtains* means "let missionary work cause you to enlarge the church." When the Lord needs more room for gathering his children, he provides mission fields: "When there is found no more room for them . . . I have other places which I will appoint unto them, and they shall be called stakes, for the curtains or the strength of Zion" (D&C 101:21). The missionaries of the church help the Lord make room for his children: "Go ye forth unto the land of Zion, that the borders of my people may be enlarged, and that her stakes may be strengthened, and that Zion may go forth unto the regions round about" (D&C 133:9).

To the woman enlarging her tent, *spare not* means "do not hold back the curtains." In missionary work, *spare not* means "do not refrain from speaking the truth": "Cry aloud, spare not, lift up thy voice like a trumpet" (Isaiah 58:1). The Lord tells his servants to "open your mouths and spare not, and you shall be laden with sheaves upon your backs" (D&C 33:9; see also D&C 43:20). *Spare not* also figuratively means "cry aloud," echoing the meaning of *sing, break forth,* and *cry aloud* in 3 Nephi 22:1. The call to spare not is a sacred call. In the affirmative sense, *spare not* means "do whatever is necessary to accomplish something for good." To Zion it means "do not neglect to feed the poor," and to the church it means "use the best materials to build the Lord's kingdom." To the Latter-day Saint it means "do not be stingy with your time and money in serving others." To the married woman, it means "do not refrain from having children; do not hold back your love." To the barren woman, it means "love in spite of loneliness"; it means "do not forget to prepare for future children" (see Proverbs 21:26). The Lord asks us to do whatever is necessary to prepare a place for children, just as Heavenly Father was willing to give his Only Begotten Son, Jesus Christ, in order to prepare a place for us in his kingdom: "He that spared not his own Son, but delivered him up for us all" (Romans 8:32).

If we live the law of consecration, the Lord will help us progress and endure: "Look upon Zion . . . thine eyes shall see . . . a tabernacle that shall not be taken down; not one of the stakes thereof shall ever be removed, neither shall any of the cords thereof be broken" (Isaiah 33:20). But if we break our covenants, the Lord will not be able to protect us: "My tabernacle is spoiled, and all my cords are broken: my children are gone forth of me, and they are not: there is none to stretch forth my tent any more, and to set up my curtains" (Jeremiah 10:20). Family members lengthen their cords through prayer, scripture study, and family reunions. Church members strengthen their stakes through home teaching, visiting teaching, temple worship, and regular attendance at meetings and conferences. Zion arises from the dust and puts on sacred garments of righteousness, which are like the curtains of a sanctuary: "Put on thy beautiful garments . . . strengthen thy stakes and enlarge thy borders forever, that thou mayest no more be confounded, that the covenants of the Eternal Father . . . may be fulfilled" (Moroni 10:31; see also D&C 82:14).

Break Forth

After instructing Zion to sing for joy and enlarge her tent, the Lord makes three parallel promises: (1) *thou shalt break forth on the right hand and on the left*, (2) *thy seed shall inherit the Gentiles*, and (3) *thy seed shall make the desolate cities to be inhabited* (see 3 Nephi 22:3, parallel to Isaiah 54:3). The command to break forth is a pun: in the first verse it has connotations of singing; in this verse it has connotations of childbirth, light, and growth. *Break forth on the right hand and on the left* means literally to "enlarge, stretch forth, or spread out in all directions": "Then shall thy light break forth as the morning" (Isaiah 58:8).[19] *Break forth* also means "give birth": "The sorrows of a travailing woman shall come upon him . . . for he should not stay long in the place of the breaking forth of children" (Hosea 13:13; see also Genesis 38:29).

On the right hand and on the left means "in all directions" or "on all sides": "I saw the Lord sitting upon his throne, and all the host of heaven standing on his right hand and on his left" (2 Chronicles 18:18). If she is faithful to her covenants, the barren woman will give light and peace to all around her. If they are faithful, church members will radiate the light of Christ. They will reach out to others instead of withdrawing in fear and self-pity. To the surprise of many, the earth will go into labor and bring forth the children of Zion in one day (see Isaiah 66:7–8). Zion will receive so many children that she will not know where they came from: "Who hath begotten me these, seeing I have lost my children, and am desolate, a captive, and removing to and fro?" (Isaiah 49:21, parallel to 1 Nephi 21:21).

Thy seed shall inherit the Gentiles means that the children of the covenant will take the light of the gospel to all nations: "And when the times of the Gentiles is come in, a light shall break forth among them that sit in darkness, and it shall be the fulness of my gospel" (D&C 45:28). Those who come into the church from out of the world will strengthen the children of Zion: "I will lift up mine hand to the Gentiles . . . and they shall bring thy sons in their arms, and thy daughters shall be carried upon their shoulders. And kings shall be thy nursing fathers, and their queens thy nursing mothers" (Isaiah 49:22–23, parallel to 1 Nephi 21:22–23). The children of the faithful will inherit the earth (see Psalm 25:12–13).

The image of the desolate woman in 3 Nephi 22:1 now shifts to the desolate cities and lands of Zion that have been ravaged because of Israel's apostasy in earlier dispensations. The faithful children of latter-day Zion will "make the desolate cities to be inhabited" (3 Nephi 22:3, parallel to Isaiah 54:3). The restored gospel will bring many people back into the covenant family of God: "Thy desolate places, and the land of thy destruction, shall even now be too narrow by reason of the inhabitants" (Isaiah 49:19, parallel to 1 Nephi

21:19). Israel will no longer be ashamed and confounded by iniquity, but will instead prepare the earth for the millennium: "This land that was desolate is become like the garden of Eden; and the waste and desolate and ruined cities are become fenced, and are inhabited" (Ezekiel 36:35). Zion will no longer be forsaken and the land will no longer be desolate; instead Zion will be the Lord's delight, and the land will be called "married wife" (Isaiah 62:4).

Fear Not

The Lord counsels Zion not to be afraid and not to let enemies silence her singing: "fear not ... neither be thou confounded" (3 Nephi 22:4, parallel to Isaiah 54:4). *Confounded* can mean "disturbed," "humiliated," "terrified," "confused," "destroyed," or "silenced by foes." Women need not fear the pain and risks of childbirth; righteous servants need not fear being mistreated or misunderstood. The single woman need not fear that her blessings will never come; the childless woman need not fear being ostracized; the woman alone should not be afraid of those who mock her efforts to rejoice in spite of rejection or loneliness. The church need not fear the power of the adversary. Zion should not be afraid of opposition: "fear ye not the reproach of men, neither be ye afraid of their revilings" (2 Nephi 8:7, parallel to Isaiah 51:7). The Saints should not heed the worldly scorn of those who reside in the "great and spacious building" (1 Nephi 11:36). The servants of the Lord need not fear, even when they are surrounded by hostile armies: "Fear not: for they that be with us are more than they that be with them" (2 Kings 6:16). The earth need not fear destruction by flood because the Lord will keep the covenant that he made with Noah and the prophets: "I have sworn that the waters of Noah should no more go over the earth" (3 Nephi 22:9). We need not fear that death is final or that Christlike love is in vain: "fear not

them which kill the body, but are not able to kill the soul"
(Matthew 10:28).

To ease her fears, the Lord comforts Zion in four parallel
phrases: (1) *thou shalt not be ashamed,* (2) *thou shalt not be put
to shame,* (3) *thou shalt forget the shame of thy youth,* and
(4) *[thou] shalt not remember the reproach of thy widowhood
any more* (see 3 Nephi 22:4, parallel to Isaiah 54:4). *Thou shalt
not be ashamed* means that ultimately the barren woman need
not feel ashamed because of her vulnerability. The Lord's
servants may have to endure shame and spitting for a time
as Jesus did, but he will succor them in their afflictions:
"therefore shall I not be confounded: therefore have I set my
face like a flint, and I know that I shall not be ashamed"
(Isaiah 50:7).

Thou shalt not be put to shame means that the wicked will
never be able to shame those who have "tender and chaste
and delicate" feelings (Jacob 2:7). Instead, the people who
choose wickedness instead of kindness will lose their children: "thou shalt no more be called tender and delicate . . .
[thou] sayest in thine heart . . . I shall not sit as a widow,
neither shall I know the loss of children: But these two things
shall come to thee in a moment in one day, the loss of children, and widowhood" (Isaiah 47:1, 8–9).

People who choose goodness will temporarily experience "the shame of [their] youth," that is, the vulnerability
of being childlike, but such meekness helps them to become
Christlike. Christ faced Gethsemane and the crucifixion just
as each of us must face our own *Sabachthani* of afflictions:
"Thou hast known my reproach, and my shame, and my
dishonor: mine adversaries are all before thee. Reproach hath
broken my heart; and I am full of heaviness: and I looked
for some to take pity, but there was none; and for comfort-
ers, but I found none. They gave me also gall for my meat;
and in my thirst they gave me vinegar to drink" (Psalm

69:19–21). Because Christ endured the agonies of death upon the cross, he suffered an "open shame" from his persecutors (Hebrews 6:6). Likewise, the barren woman appears to be cursed. She may have to bear the reproach of her peers instead of bearing promised children. The widowed or divorced person may also experience discomfort or disgrace. The church may suffer ridicule or condemnation from those who do not recognize its divine origins. Prophets may suffer martyrdom in spite of their holy calling. The earth suffers in the shadow of Satan's wrath in spite of her glorious destiny. Notwithstanding these sorrows, Zion will forget the temporary disgrace of not having a husband, and the Lord will remember Zion eternally: "I will remember my covenant with thee in the days of thy youth, and I will establish unto thee an everlasting covenant" (Ezekiel 16:60). Zion "shall not be ashamed nor confounded world without end" (Isaiah 45:17).

Thy Maker Is Thine Husband

The Lord identifies himself as the messenger of the covenant with Zion (see 3 Nephi 22:1, 8, 10, 17, parallel to Isaiah 54:1, 8, 10, 17). He refers to himself by several different names and roles: (1) *Maker,* (2) *Husband,* (3) *Lord of Hosts,* (4) *Redeemer,* (5) *Holy One of Israel,* and (6) *God of the whole earth* (see 3 Nephi 22:5, parallel to Isaiah 54:5). "Thy Maker is thine husband" means that the Creator of the world is the one who acts as our main companion and nurturer: "as the bridegroom rejoiceth over the bride, so shall thy God rejoice over thee" (Isaiah 62:5). Our Maker is the one who cultivates us and helps us grow in the plan of salvation.[20] When Zion begins to fear "the fury of the oppressor," the Lord reminds her of the covenant: "forgettest the Lord thy maker, that hath stretched forth the heavens, and laid the foundations of the earth?" (2 Nephi 8:13, parallel to Isaiah 51:13).

The etymology of the English word *husband* is a compound of *house* and *prepare;* thus a *husband* is "one who prepares or builds a house."[21] Our Maker is our husband because he prepares the earth as a house for all creatures; he prepares our bodies as houses or temples for our spirits; he prepares temples as places of worship in Zion, and he promises to prepare mansions for us in heaven (see John 14:2). He transforms the dwelling place of the barren woman from a tent into a temple as she makes room for future children: "I will lay thy stones with fair colors, and lay thy foundations with sapphires. And I will make thy windows of agates, and thy gates of carbuncles, and all thy borders of pleasant stones. And all thy children shall be taught of the Lord" (3 Nephi 22:11–13, parallel to Isaiah 54:11–13).

The husband's name is Jehovah,[22] or the Lord of Hosts: "I have made the earth, and created man upon it: I, even my hands, have stretched out the heavens, and all their host have I commanded" (Isaiah 45:12).[23] The Lord is not ashamed to be called the "God of the whole earth" (3 Nephi 22:5, parallel to Isaiah 54:5). In former days, he was a husband to the house of Israel, even when the people broke their covenants (see Jeremiah 31:32). In Book of Mormon times, he invited the more righteous part of the Nephite people to touch the wounds in his hands and feet and side: "that ye may know that I am . . . the God of the whole earth, and have been slain for the sins of the world" (3 Nephi 11:14). Surely he will care for Zion, who has been faithful in the latter days. Zion's Redeemer is the "Holy One of Israel," who hallows and heals everyone who has lived on the earth: "For I will restore health unto thee, and I will heal thee of thy wounds, saith the Lord; because they called thee an Outcast, saying, This is Zion, whom no man seeketh after" (Jeremiah 30:17).

Called to Grief

In two parallel phrases, the Lord tells Zion that she has temporarily been called as "a woman forsaken and grieved in spirit" and as "a wife of youth, when thou wast refused" (3 Nephi 22:6, parallel to Isaiah 54:6). Christ understands Zion as a woman "forsaken and grieved" because he was a man "despised and rejected of men; a man of sorrows, and acquainted with grief" (Isaiah 53:3). For a moment, it may seem as if the Lord has abandoned Zion, just as for a moment it seemed that God the Father abandoned Jesus, who cried out from the cross, "My God, my God, why hast thou forsaken me?" (Psalm 22:1; see also Matthew 27:46). As part of our earthly probation, we must endure periods of separation from God, but the Lord will never forsake his covenant people: "But Zion said, The Lord hath forsaken me, and my Lord hath forgotten me. Can a woman forget her sucking child, that she should not have compassion on the son of her womb? yea, they may forget, yet will I not forget thee. Behold, I have graven thee upon the palms of my hands; thy walls are continually before me" (Isaiah 49:14–16, parallel to 1 Nephi 21:14–16).

"A wife of youth" implies childlike submission to the will of the Father. The Lord's calling and that of the woman are similar: the barren woman will give birth to her children after suffering desolation; Jesus spiritually gives birth to his children after suffering rejection. Christ can console the woman who was refused as a wife in her youth, because he was refused as a Savior in his mortal life: "The stone which the builders refused is become the head stone of the corner" (Psalm 118:22). Zion may be alone now, but the Lord's law of love will compensate for her losses: "Whereas thou hast been forsaken and hated, so that no man went through thee, I will make thee an eternal excellency, a joy of many generations" (Isaiah 60:15). If we can endure the pain, the Lord will bless us with peace: "thine adversity and thine afflictions shall be but a small moment; And then, if thou endure it well, God shall exalt thee on high; thou shalt triumph over all thy foes" (D&C 121:7–8).

For a Small Moment

The Lord explains Zion's calling as a forsaken woman in two verses that are connected by parallelism, antithesis, and word repetition:

> For a **small moment** have I **forsaken** thee,
> but with **great mercies** will I **gather** thee.
> In a **little wrath** I hid my face from thee for a **moment**,
> but with **everlasting kindness** will I have **mercy** on thee,
> saith the Lord thy Redeemer.
>
> (3 Nephi 22:7–8, parallel to Isaiah 54:7–8)

The phrase *for a small moment have I forsaken thee* makes it seem that the Lord has been angry with Zion. The barren woman may feel that she is forsaken because the Lord has left her childless. Noah's family may have felt that the Lord abandoned them when the storms beat upon the ark for forty days. Christ may have felt that the Father had forsaken him when he writhed in agony on the cross. Yet because of the ark of the covenant, the fear and anguish are not in vain: "For our light affliction, which is but for a moment, worketh for us a far more exceeding and eternal weight of glory" (2 Corinthians 4:17). The Lord will gather the barren woman with great mercies, and Zion will gather children into her land: "Lift up thine eyes round about, and behold: all these gather themselves together, and come to thee. As I live, saith the Lord, thou shalt surely clothe thee with them all, as with an ornament, and bind them on thee, as a bride doeth" (Isaiah 49:18, parallel to 1 Nephi 21:18).

The phrase *I hid my face from thee for a moment* implies a temporary withdrawal of the Lord's presence (see 3 Nephi 22:8). The Lord will never completely abandon his people, even if his presence seems to be withdrawn for a little while: "he hath not despised nor abhorred the affliction of the afflicted; neither hath he hid his face from him; but when he cried unto him, he heard" (Psalm 22:24). In Jewish culture, a husband is not permitted to see his wife going through the travail of childbirth, but he does not abandon her. He sits in the corner of the room with his back turned so that she will not feel embarrassed or immodest in her hour of agony. She recites psalms as she goes through contractions. When the woman can no longer sing because of the pain, her husband takes over, reciting the psalms for her.[24] Though we cannot see the Lord, when we weep, he weeps with us; when we sing, he rejoices with us. He understands our pain because he "hid not [his] face from shame and spitting" (Isaiah 50:6, parallel to 2 Nephi 7:6), even though sometimes "we [hide] as it were our faces from him" (Isaiah 53:3, parallel to Mosiah 14:3).

The Waters of Noah

From the Lord's perspective, the small moment of forsaking and wrath that Zion experiences is like the flood that Noah experienced:

> For this, **the waters of Noah** unto me,
> for as **I have sworn** that **the waters of Noah** should
> no more go over the earth,
> so **have I sworn** that I would not be **wroth** with thee.

> (3 Nephi 22:9, parallel to Isaiah 54:9)

The people of Zion are the children of Noah, who must remember the shining promises of salvation even as storms threaten to dash their arks into oblivion. Noah and his family experienced forty days of storms in the ark, but the Lord preserved Noah and his posterity in a covenant of kindness (see Genesis 7:6–7). The flood destroyed every living substance on the earth, but the barren earth was then ready to become a garden, having been born again and cleansed of mankind's wickedness in a baptismal covenant (see Moses 7:47–64). After the flood, the house of Israel was scattered by wickedness, but the Lord will bring them home again so that "after they [are] restored they should no more be confounded, neither should they be scattered again" (1 Nephi 15:20). The earth still labors under the curses of sin and death, but the Lord sent Noah, the angel Gabriel, to Mary to announce the birth of the Savior Jesus Christ who conquered sin and death (see Luke 1:26–38).[25]

The barren woman experiences distress, but the Lord comforts Zion by comparing her to Noah, whose Hebrew name means "rest" or "comfort." The Lord reminds Zion of his promises to Noah, who was spared destruction like the Nephites because of his faithfulness. After the floods of sin, affliction, sorrow, and barrenness abate, the Lord will gather or embrace Zion with great mercies: "For his merciful kindness is great toward us" (Psalm 117:2). Those who cry out in pain will someday celebrate the Lord's everlasting kindness: "And now the year of my redeemed is come; and they shall mention the loving kindness of their Lord, and all that he has bestowed upon them according to his goodness, and according to his loving kindness, forever" (D&C 133:52).

The rhetorical figures in 3 Nephi 22:10 show that the Lord's loving-kindness is related to his covenant of peace:

> For the **mountains** shall **depart** and the **hills** be **removed**,
> but my **kindness** shall **not depart** from thee,
> neither shall the **covenant of my peace** be **removed**,
> **saith the Lord** that hath **mercy** on thee.
>
> (3 Nephi 22:10, parallel to Isaiah 54:10)

Mountains and *hills* have parallel meanings. "The mountains shall depart, and the hills be removed" suggests the disappearance of the mountains and hills in the flood waters of Noah: "the waters prevailed exceedingly upon the earth; and all the high hills, that were under the whole heaven, were covered. Fifteen cubits upward did the waters prevail; and the mountains were covered" (Genesis 7:19–20).

"The mountains shall depart" also reminds us that kindness is greater than the power to move mountains: "though I have all faith, so that I could remove mountains, and have not charity, I am nothing" (1 Corinthians 13:2). No matter what happens in our lives, the Lord's covenant of kindness will comfort us: "Therefore will not we fear, though the earth be removed, and though the mountains be carried into the midst of the sea; Though the waters thereof roar and be troubled, though the mountains shake with the swelling thereof" (Psalm 46:2–3). The Lord protects all those who put their trust in him: "They that trust in the Lord shall be as mount Zion, which cannot be removed, but abideth for ever. As the mountains are round about Jerusalem, so the Lord is round about his people henceforth even for ever" (Psalm 125:1–2).

"My kindness" is parallel to the "covenant of my peace," implying that the main characteristic of the Lord's covenant is kindness, a charity that is characterized by peace. The covenant of kindness will not depart: "Charity never faileth: but whether there be prophecies, they shall fail; whether there be tongues, they shall cease; whether there be knowledge, it shall vanish away" (1 Corinthians 13:8). The rainbow that the Lord presented after the flood is a token of the covenant of kindness:

> This is the token of the covenant which I make between me and you and every living creature that is with

you, for perpetual generations: I do set my bow in the cloud, and it shall be for a token of a covenant between me and the earth. . . . And the bow shall be in the cloud; and I will look upon it, that I may remember the everlasting covenant between God and every living creature of all flesh that is upon the earth. (Genesis 9:12–13, 16)

The Noachian covenant includes a renewal of creation and generation, a restoration of the command to give birth to children: "And God blessed Noah and his sons, and said unto them, Be fruitful, and multiply, and replenish the earth" (Genesis 9:1). This is the same command that the Lord gives to the barren woman in 3 Nephi 22.

The "covenant of peace" will remove the natural enmity between creatures: "And I will make with them a covenant of peace, and will cause the evil beasts to cease out of the land: and they shall dwell safely in the wilderness, and sleep in the woods" (Ezekiel 34:25). Warfare will cease, and the Lord will redeem Israel: "I will make a covenant of peace with them; it shall be an everlasting covenant with them: and I will place them, and multiply them, and will set my sanctuary in the midst of them for evermore" (Ezekiel 37:26).

Pleasant Stones

The Lord empathizes with the woman who suffers affliction, trouble, and grief: "Sing, O heavens; and be joyful, O earth; and break forth into singing, O mountains: for the Lord hath comforted his people, and will have mercy upon his afflicted" (Isaiah 49:13, parallel to 1 Nephi 21:13). He promises to comfort Zion by revealing her beauty and her worth through temple covenants and ordinances. He promises that her children will learn the gospel and receive the covenant of peace. The image of the tempest resolves into the image of a temple:

O thou afflicted, tossed with tempest, and not
comforted!
Behold, I will lay thy stones with fair colors,
and lay thy foundations with sapphires.
And I will make thy windows of agates,
and thy gates of carbuncles,
and all thy borders of pleasant stones.
And all thy children shall be taught of the Lord;
and great shall be the peace of thy children.

(3 Nephi 22:11–13, parallel to Isaiah 54:11–13)

The tempest image is an echo of the previous references
to the waters of Noah and to other scriptural storms (see
3 Nephi 22:9, parallel to Isaiah 54:9). The Lord will lead Zion
to a promised land as he led the Jaredites: "God caused that
there should be a furious wind blow upon the face of the
waters, towards the promised land; and thus they were
tossed upon the waves of the sea before the wind" (Ether
6:5). The disciples of Jesus were frightened by a tempest on
the Sea of Galilee, but he calmed the waters and built their
faith: "there arose a great tempest in the sea, insomuch that
the ship was covered with the waves: but he was asleep. . . .
Then he arose, and rebuked the winds and the sea; and there
was a great calm" (Matthew 8:24, 26). The more wicked part
of the Nephites were killed by tempests and other disasters,
but the Lord appeared to the righteous Nephite remnant at
the temple in Bountiful and established his covenant of peace
(see 3 Nephi 8:17; 9:13).

The Lord comforts Zion with images of temple-building.
I will lay thy stones with fair colors means "I will use beautifully colored stones to make a foundation for you" (3 Nephi
22:11). Whenever the Lord commands his people to build a
temple, the best possible materials are procured: "I have
prepared with all my might for the house of my God . . .
onyx stones, and stones to be set, glistering stones, and of

divers colours, and all manner of precious stones, and marble stones in abundance" (1 Chronicles 29:2). Choosing the stones is an important part of laying the foundation of the temple: "they brought great stones, costly stones, and hewed stones, to lay the foundation of the house" (1 Kings 5:17). The cornerstone of the temple is a symbol of the redeeming sacrifice of Jesus Christ: "thus saith the Lord God, Behold, I lay in Zion for a foundation a stone, a tried stone, a precious corner stone, a sure foundation: he that believeth shall not make haste" (Isaiah 28:16). Zion will no longer be comfortless because the Lord is the foundation of her life: "Behold, I lay in Sion a chief corner stone, elect, precious: and he that believeth on him shall not be confounded" (1 Peter 2:6).

The Lord's servants sing and make beautiful music when the foundations of the temple are laid: "And when the builders laid the foundation of the temple of the Lord, they set the priests in their apparel with trumpets . . . to praise the Lord" (Ezra 3:10). Laying foundations also refers to the creation of the earth and its inhabitants: "Where wast thou when I laid the foundations of the earth? . . . When the morning stars sang together, and all the sons of God shouted for joy?" (Job 38:4, 7).

When the Lord promises to lay the foundations of Zion with sapphires (see 3 Nephi 22:11), he suggests that she will one day enter his presence:[26] "And they saw the God of Israel: and there was under his feet as it were a paved work of a sapphire stone, and as it were the body of heaven in his clearness" (Exodus 24:10). Sapphires, beautiful blue gemstones, are often associated with heaven and the presence of the Lord:

> And above the firmament that was over their heads was the likeness of a throne, as the appearance of a sapphire stone: and upon the likeness of the throne was the likeness as the appearance of a man above upon it. . . . As

> the appearance of the bow that is in the cloud in the day
> of rain, so was the appearance of the brightness round
> about. This was the appearance of the likeness of the glory
> of the Lord. (Ezekiel 1:26, 28)

The light and colors of the temple stones shine like rainbows, reminding Zion of the Lord's covenant with the children of Noah. Similar stones will shine in the celestial city of the New Jerusalem: "And the foundations of the wall of the city were garnished with all manner of precious stones" (Revelation 21:19).

Zion's temple will have windows made of beautiful multicolored agates (see 3 Nephi 22:12; see also 1 Kings 6:4). Agates are one of the precious gems found on the breastplate of the high priest, along with sardius, topaz, carbuncle, emerald, sapphire, diamond, ligure, amethyst, beryl, onyx, and jasper (see Exodus 28:15–20): "And the stones shall be with the names of the children of Israel" (Exodus 28:21). The gate of Zion's temple will be made of carbuncles, the valuable red garnets mentioned in a lamentation for the once-great king of Tyrus:[27] "Thou hast been in Eden the garden of God; every precious stone was thy covering, the sardius, topaz, and the diamond, the beryl, the onyx, and the jasper, the sapphire, the emerald, and the carbuncle, and gold" (Ezekiel 28:13). If Zion is faithful to her covenants, all her possibilities, perspectives, and perimeters will be as lovely as "borders of pleasant stones" (3 Nephi 22:12, parallel to Isaiah 54:12).

The most beautiful temple blessing for Zion will be in her posterity: "thy children shall be taught of the Lord" (3 Nephi 22:13, parallel to Isaiah 54:13). Her yet unborn children will live in peace, and the Lord will teach all her children (see Psalm 132:12). The Lord will teach his commandments to the children of Zion so that they may "enter into his rest" (Alma 13:6), and those commandments will lead Zion's children into the covenant of peace: "Great peace have they which love thy law: and nothing shall offend them" (Psalm 119:165). The children of the barren woman will thus become the children of the Lord: "Blessed are the peacemakers: for they shall be called the children of God" (Matthew 5:9).

Established in Righteousness

The Lord tells the afflicted woman that he will verify her righteousness. She will not be afraid, so oppression will not touch her. She will not panic, so terror will not affect her. Some people will conspire to harm Zion, but the Lord will not support them; in their conspiracy against her they will destroy themselves:

> In righteousness shalt thou be established;
> thou shalt be far from oppression for thou shalt not fear,
> and from terror for it shall not come near thee.
> Behold, they shall surely gather together against thee,
>   not by me;
> whosoever shall gather together against thee shall fall
>   for thy sake.
>
> (3 Nephi 22:14–15, parallel to Isaiah 54:14–15)

Zion and her children will be established, or qualified, to enter into the presence of the Lord because of their righteousness: "As for me, I will behold thy face in righteousness: I shall be satisfied, when I awake, with thy likeness" (Psalm 17:15). The Lord, who has called Zion as a woman of grief, has also called Zion as a woman of righteousness: "I the Lord have called thee in righteousness, and will hold thine hand, and will keep thee, and give thee for a covenant of the people" (Isaiah 42:6). The servants of the Lord will be able to build the city of Zion, or the New Jerusalem (see Isaiah 45:13), and they will be blessed with children who will carry on the Lord's work: "The children of thy servants shall continue, and their seed shall be established" (Psalm 102:28).

Zion will be "far from oppression" (3 Nephi 22:14). She will be calm in the face of affliction: "For the oppression of the poor . . . now will I arise, saith the Lord; I will set him in safety from him that puffeth at him" (Psalm 12:5). Zion will not be afraid of her enemies: "Ye shall not fear them: for the Lord your God he shall fight for you" (Deuteronomy 3:22). Zion will trust in the Lord in spite of the plans of her opponents: "Though an host should encamp against me, my heart shall not fear: though war should rise against me, in this will I be confident" (Psalm 27:3).[28] Zion will not be terrified when her enemies seek to destroy her, even if she is called to suffer temporarily: "if ye suffer for righteousness' sake, happy are ye: and be not afraid of their terror, neither be troubled" (1 Peter 3:14). Not even the threat of death can harm Zion because she has faith in the atonement of Christ: "they never did look upon death with any degree of terror, for their hope and views of Christ and the resurrection" (Alma 27:28).

Wicked people will certainly conspire to humiliate Zion: "They have gaped upon me with their mouth; they have smitten me upon the cheek reproachfully; they have gathered themselves together against me" (Job 16:10). Some will plot to destroy Zion because they resent her goodness: "They gather themselves together against the soul of the righteous, and condemn the innocent blood" (Psalm 94:21). In spite of their craftiness, however, the plans of the wicked will backfire because Zion has kept her covenants.

The nations of the world may collaborate furiously against Zion, but they will not escape the hand of the Lord: "Now also many nations are gathered against thee, that say, Let her be defiled, and let our eye look upon Zion. But they know not the thoughts of the Lord, neither understand they his counsel: for he shall gather them as the sheaves into the floor" (Micah 4:11–12). Zion's enemies cannot succeed because their power does not come from the Lord: "They have set up kings, but not by me: they have made princes, and I knew it not" (Hosea 8:4). Every person or group that fights against Zion will fail miserably: "And every nation which shall war against thee, O house of Israel, shall be turned one against another, and they shall fall into the pit which they digged to ensnare the people of the Lord. And all that fight against Zion shall be destroyed" (1 Nephi 22:14). Because Zion has endured persecution for the Lord's sake, he will protect her. The Lord is no stranger to tyranny; he patiently suffered injustice for us all: "Because for thy sake I have borne reproach; shame hath covered my face" (Psalm 69:7).

The Servants of the Lord

The Lord has created the people who make weapons to destroy his servants, but he will not allow the weapons of oppressors to be successful against Zion. Zion will be able to refute the arguments of all the people who speak evil against her. The Lord gives such protection to all people who serve him, and he is the source of their righteousness:

> Behold, I have created the smith
> that bloweth the coals in the fire,
> and that bringeth forth an instrument for his work;
> and I have created the waster to destroy.
> No weapon that is formed against thee shall prosper;
> and every tongue that shall [revile / rise against] thee
>   in judgment thou shalt condemn.
> This is the heritage of the servants of the Lord,
> and their righteousness is of me, saith the Lord.
>
> (3 Nephi 22:16–17, parallel to Isaiah 54:16–17)

The adversary may call upon skilled laborers to create weapons for the destruction of Zion, but the skill of those workers is in the hands of the Lord who created them. No matter how shrewd they are, those who work against Zion will not be able to destroy the Lord's work:

> All his fellows shall be ashamed: and the workmen, they are of men: let them be gathered together, let them stand up; yet they shall fear, and they shall be ashamed together. The smith with the tongs both worketh in the coals, and fashioneth it with hammers, and worketh it with the strength of his arms: yea, he is hungry, and his strength faileth: he drinketh no water, and is faint. (Isaiah 44:11–12)

Satan may assign bloodthirsty agents to ravage the work of the Lord: "Their feet run to evil, and they make haste to shed innocent blood . . . wasting and destruction are in their paths" (Isaiah 59:7). But no power of darkness can overcome the power of the Lord's covenant of peace: "Violence shall no more be heard in thy land, wasting nor destruction within thy borders; but thou shalt call thy walls Salvation, and thy gates Praise" (Isaiah 60:18).

No weapon that is formed against Zion can prosper. No murder, no slander, no torture can stop the Lord from endowing his people in holy places, as evidenced by the dedicatory prayer at the temple in Kirtland, Ohio:

> We ask thee, Holy Father, to establish the people that shall worship, and honorably hold a name and standing in this thy house, to all generations and for eternity; That no weapon formed against them shall prosper; that he who diggeth a pit for them shall fall into the same himself; That no combination of wickedness shall have power to rise up and prevail over thy people upon whom thy name shall be put in this house. . . . And if they shall smite this people thou wilt smite them; thou wilt fight for

thy people as thou didst in the day of battle, that they may be delivered from the hands of all their enemies. We ask thee, Holy Father, to confound, and astonish, and to bring to shame and confusion, all those who have spread lying reports abroad, over the world, against thy servant or servants, if they will not repent. (Doctrine and Covenants 109:24–26, 28–29)

The enemies of Zion will revile or rise against the servants of the Lord (see Alma 30:31). Instead of suffering permanent damage, however, Zion will be blessed because she will feel the Lord's kind words of affirmation: "And blessed are ye when men shall revile you and persecute, and shall say all manner of evil against you falsely, for my sake" (3 Nephi 12:11).

The sentence *this is the heritage of the servants of the Lord* (see 3 Nephi 22:17, parallel to Isaiah 54:17) refers to all of the promises that the Lord has made to the barren woman: (1) that she will have children, (2) that she will be a gathering place for the gentiles and all other nations, (3) that she will not be ashamed or desolate, (4) that the Lord will encircle her with everlasting kindness, (5) that her children will be taught in the temple, and (6) that her enemies will not be able to destroy her. The heritage of the Lord is an inheritance or an endowment. For her inheritance, Zion will receive the earth as a promised land: "And I will bring you in unto the land, concerning the which I did swear to give it to Abraham, to Isaac, and to Jacob; and I will give it you for an heritage: I am the Lord" (Exodus 6:8). Zion will help the earth become the celestial kingdom: "In an acceptable time have I heard thee, and in a day of salvation have I helped thee: and I will preserve thee, and give thee for a covenant of the people, to establish the earth, to cause to inherit the desolate heritages" (Isaiah 49:8, parallel to 1 Nephi 21:8).

Like the barren woman, the servants of the Lord will sing praises: "Praise, O ye servants of the Lord, praise the name of the Lord" (Psalm 113:1). Zion will be blessed because she has taken upon her the name of the Lord: "For thou, O God, hast heard my vows: thou hast given me the heritage of those that fear thy name" (Psalm 61:5). All who come to Zion will receive the Lord's covenant of kindness: "there shall they fall down and be crowned with glory, even in Zion, by the hands of the servants of the Lord, even the children of Ephraim" (D&C 133:32). Their righteousness will be established because of their faith: "that which is through the faith of Christ, the righteousness which is of God by faith" (Philippians 3:9). The servants of the Lord will receive all the blessings of Abraham, Isaac, and Jacob: "Then shalt thou delight thyself in the Lord; and I will cause thee to ride upon the high places of the earth, and feed thee with the heritage of Jacob thy father" (Isaiah 58:14).

Children Are the Heritage of the Lord

Zion will receive children and eternal increase as an inheritance from the Father: "Lo, children are an heritage of the Lord: and the fruit of the womb is his reward" (Psalm 127:3). Because the Lord loves his spirit children with perfect kindness, children are the greatest blessing he can bestow upon his servants on earth. In Zion or the church, children are signs of sacred covenants and ordinances of salvation. For the earth, children are signs of genesis, renewal, and preparation for celestial glory. For church members, children are the tangible representations of the power of godliness.

The Lord uses the promise of children to represent important events and blessings in the plan of salvation: "Behold, I and the children whom the Lord hath given me are for signs and for wonders" (2 Nephi 18:18, parallel to Isaiah

8:18). The promise of children is the greatest blessing a barren woman can hope for, even if she must wait in faith. For the promise of this blessing, Christ was willing to be called as a man rejected, like a barren woman who is willing to suffer in order to be eventually blessed with children. Christ wanted us to be his children spiritually. We are to be like him, also desiring to give birth and work hard to raise children in a covenant of infinitely tender loving-kindness. The only barrenness we need ever fear is a lack of kindness; the only desolation we need ever dread is the loss of charity. We are to sing.

Notes

1. For fairly standard LDS interpretations of Isaiah 54, see Sidney B. Sperry, *The Old Testament Prophets* (Salt Lake City: Deseret Sunday School Union, 1965); *Book of Mormon Compendium* (Salt Lake City: Bookcraft, 1968); and Victor L. Ludlow, *Isaiah: Prophet, Seer, and Poet* (Salt Lake City: Deseret Book, 1982).

2. From French *billet doux*, "sweet letter."

3. From Greek *thalamos*, "bridal chamber." For more information on the covenant significance of bridal chamber imagery, see John A. Tvedtnes, "Olive Oil: Symbol of the Holy Ghost," in *The Allegory of the Olive Tree*, ed. Stephen D. Ricks and John W. Welch (Salt Lake City: Deseret Book and FARMS, 1994), 439–41, 447.

4. Making an analysis based on the etymology of English words translated from Isaiah's Hebrew text or from the Book of Mormon's unidentified source language may seem questionable to some. However, because the Lord has chosen English as the main language of translation for the Book of Mormon, attention to the English words is relevant. Furthermore, comparative historical linguists have been working to reconstruct genetic connections between the Indo-European family of languages to which English belongs and the Afroasiatic family to which Hebrew and Egyptian belong. See Allan R. Bomhard, *Toward Proto-Nostratic: A*

New Approach to the Comparison of Proto-Indo-European and Proto-Afroasiatic (Philadelphia: John Benjamins, 1984).

5. From the appendix of *The American Heritage Dictionary of the English Language*, 3rd ed., s.v. "gen-."

6. *Kinder* is the German word for *children*, as in the English word borrowed from the German word *kindergarten* (a garden for children).

7. Special thanks to Robert J. Norman, former director of the Tucson Institute of Religion, for the Hebrew lexis.

8. Lynn Clark Callister, "Cultural Meanings of Childbirth," *Journal of Obstetric, Gynecologic and Neonatal Nurses* 24 (May 1995): 327.

9. Dallin H. Oaks, "Worship through Music," *Ensign* (November 1994): 10.

10. The Lord tells Abraham to name the child Isaac, which means "he laugheth" or "he rejoiceth."

11. Sarah's son Isaac married Rebekah, who was barren until she conceived Esau and Jacob (see Genesis 25:21–24). Jacob's wife Rachel was barren, but the Lord finally remembered her and took away the reproach (see Genesis 29:31; 30:22–23).

12. Although Mary is described as a virgin rather than as a barren woman, the unique circumstances of Christ's conception make her as vulnerable as the woman alone until Joseph agrees not to put her away from him privately.

13. *Married wife* in 3 Nephi 22:1 has several possible interpretations: (1) any woman who has a husband and children, in contrast to the desolate woman who has neither husband nor children; (2) the Lord's former-day covenant peoples in contrast to the Lord's latter-day covenant peoples; (3) anyone who appears to be blessed, while some covenant people appear to be cursed, being denied blessings in spite of their faithfulness.

14. David Rolph Seely, "The Allegory of the Olive Tree and the Use of Related Figurative Language in the Ancient Near East and the Old Testament," in *The Allegory of the Olive Tree*, 298–9.

15. Richard K. Hart, "The Marriage Metaphor," *Ensign* (January 1995): 27.

16. The act of travailing to give birth to a child is compared to the struggle for spiritual birth in Galatians 4:19 and to the rebirth of the earth in Doctrine and Covenants 84:101.

17. The Lord's cloud and pillar of fire showed the Israelites where to pitch their tents and where to place the tabernacle in the wilderness (see Numbers 9:17; Deuteronomy 1:33).

18. Images of creation and singing combine in Isaiah 42:5–12: the Lord is he that "created the heavens, and stretched them out; he that spread forth the earth, and that which cometh out of it"; the Lord commands the earth and its inhabitants to "sing unto the Lord a new song" (see also Isaiah 51:3, 11).

19. *Break forth* can also mean "appear": "And let the priests also, which come near to the Lord, sanctify themselves, lest the Lord break forth upon them" (Exodus 19:22).

20. The Lord's husbandry extends not only to Israel and Zion but to other kings and nations such as Cyrus of Elam, who allowed the Jews to rebuild the temple: "I have even called thee by thy name: I have surnamed thee, though thou hast not known me" (Isaiah 45:4).

21. The *–band* morpheme in the English word *husband* comes from Old Norse *būa* (to live, prepare) and *būask* (to make oneself ready). See the Indo-European root *bheu–* (to be, exist, grow) in the appendix of the *American Heritage Dictionary*, 3rd edition.

22. The Hebrew word *Yahweh* is translated as *Lord* in the King James Version of the Bible. See *The NIV Interlinear Hebrew-English Old Testament*, ed. John R. Kohlenberger III (Grand Rapids, Mich.: Zondervan, 1985), 110.

23. See also Isaiah 47:4; 48:2; 51:15; Jeremiah 31:35; 50:34.

24. Lynn Callister, conversation, 24 June 1995.

25. Thanks to Linda Smith for pointing out this connection.

26. Just as the Nephites are blessed in 3 Nephi 11 to be in the presence of Jesus after their trial of faith.

27. For more about the king of Tyrus, see John A. Tvedtnes, "Lucifer, Son of the Morning," unpublished paper (1995).

28. See also "The Lord is my helper, and I will not fear what man shall do unto me" (Hebrews 13:6); "And the righteous need not fear, for they are those who shall not be confounded" (1 Nephi 22:22); "Wherefore, be of good cheer, and do not fear, for I the Lord am with you, and will stand by you" (D&C 68:6).

PART THREE

Isaiah and the Restoration

Joseph Smith and
the Words of Isaiah

Ann N. Madsen

*The prophet of the restoration was extensively instructed by Moroni,
Jesus Christ himself, and in other ways, concerning the significance
of Isaiah's prophecies, which Joseph frequently cited.*

How much did young Joseph Smith know of Isaiah, the man and the prophet? Probably not very much at first. Perhaps the question should be reversed: How much did Isaiah know of young Joseph, the prophet of the restoration? Surely Isaiah prophesied of him. Isaiah's writing is permeated with restoration imagery. Could he have known that many of his own prophecies would be used to expand the boy prophet's vision?

Instruction of the Young Prophet

What Joseph Smith as an impressionable young man saw and heard and delivered to the world profoundly links Isaiah to each of our lives. It all began in 1820 when Joseph Smith saw a pillar of light exactly over his head and was visited three years later by the angel Moroni, being called to bring to pass a great and marvelous work. Centuries ago, Isaiah described his own call in ways that also involved heavenly manifestations: he "saw also the Lord sitting upon a throne, high and lifted up, and his train filled the temple" (Isaiah 6:1). Isaiah became God's messenger in an earlier day, and he continues to speak to the people of this dispensation through Joseph Smith.

In his first vision, after regaining composure enough to speak, Joseph asked God the Father and Jesus Christ which church he should join. He was answered that he must join none of them. He was told by Christ, who paraphrased the words of Isaiah, "They draw near to me with their lips, but their hearts are far from me, they teach for doctrines the commandments of men" (JS–H 1:19; compare Isaiah 29:13). So at age fourteen, in the spring of 1820, in the grove we have come to call sacred, Joseph heard Isaiah's words spoken by Jesus Christ—or rather, Christ's words as revealed to Isaiah 2,500 years earlier.

On 21 September 1823 Joseph was first visited by the angel Moroni and was again instructed from the words of Isaiah. The method apparently used by Moroni in teaching the fledgling prophet is interesting. He quoted scriptures and stated when they were to be fulfilled and "offered many explanations" (Joseph Smith—History 1:40–41). In answer to the boy's plea that September evening to know of his "state and standing" before the Lord (see Joseph Smith—History 1:29), Moroni gave Joseph an impressive array of prophecies that sounded like a patriarchal blessing to the young boy. Moroni explained to him that God had a work for him to do that included translating a book written on golden plates. The book, he was told, gave an account of the former inhabitants of the Americas and contained the fulness of the everlasting gospel as delivered by the Savior himself to these ancient Americans. The messenger also quoted several prophecies from the Bible, beginning with Malachi 3 and then moving on to Malachi 4, with a little variation (see Joseph Smith—History 1:36). Malachi 3 announces the coming of a messenger to prepare the way before the coming of the Lord and describes the apostate conditions in the world that will need to be corrected. Malachi 4 speaks of the hearts of fathers and children turning to one another before the "great and dreadful day of the Lord" (Joseph Smith—History 1:38).

Then Moroni quoted all of Isaiah 11, saying the prophecies therein were about to be fulfilled. By way of background, although not quoted by Moroni, the last few verses of Isaiah 10 speak of a scattering and apostasy, using the metaphor of trees being cut down and branches being lopped off, leaving only stumps. In Jerusalem it is common for such stumps to sprout and grow (one whole garden of such fruitful stumps is called Gethsemane). Emerging out of these images of destruction, Isaiah 11 begins:

> And there shall come forth a rod out of the stem of Jesse, and a Branch shall grow out of his roots: And the spirit of the Lord shall rest upon him, the spirit of wisdom and understanding, the spirit of counsel and might, the spirit of knowledge and of the fear of the Lord; ... [and] with righteousness shall he judge the poor, and reprove with equity for the meek of the earth: and he shall smite the earth with the rod of his mouth, and with the breath of his lips shall he slay the wicked. And righteousness shall be the girdle of his loins, and faithfulness the girdle of his reins. (Isaiah 11:1–2, 4–5)

In 1838 the revelation now found in Doctrine and Covenants 113:1–2 revealed that these verses refer to Christ. The next few verses in Isaiah 11 speak of the latter days and the peace and enlightenment of the millennium:

> The wolf also shall dwell with the lamb, and the leopard shall lie down with the kid; and the calf and the young lion and the fatling together; and a little child shall lead them.... They shall not hurt nor destroy in all my holy mountain: for the earth shall be full of the knowledge of the Lord, as the waters cover the sea. (Isaiah 11:6, 9)

The Prophet Joseph was to play the key role in the restoration, which would prepare the world for the millennium:

> And in that day there shall be a root of Jesse, which shall stand for an ensign of the people; to it shall the Gentiles seek: and his rest shall be glorious. And it shall come to pass in that day, that the Lord shall set his hand again the second time to recover the remnant of his people, . . . And he shall set up an ensign for the nations, and shall assemble the outcasts of Israel, and gather together the dispersed of Judah from the four corners of the earth. The envy also of Ephraim shall depart, and the adversaries of Judah shall be cut off: Ephraim shall not envy Judah, and Judah shall not vex Ephraim. (Isaiah 11:10–13)

Doctrine and Covenants 113 applies these passages to "a servant in the hands of Christ, . . . on whom there is laid much power" (verse 4). This servant is often identified as Joseph Smith.[1]

After quoting Isaiah 11, Moroni quoted Acts 3:22–23 to Joseph:

> For Moses truly said unto the fathers, A prophet shall the Lord your God raise up unto you of your brethren, like unto me; him shall ye hear in all things whatsoever he shall say unto you. And it shall come to pass, that every soul, which will not hear that prophet, shall be destroyed from among the people.

Moroni explained that "that prophet" was Christ, the perfect model for the young Joseph.

Among other scriptures, the angel also quoted Joel 2:28–32, which speaks of the Lord's Spirit being poured out on all flesh and of young men seeing visions. In addition, he "offered many explanations," on which Joseph said he could not elaborate in his writings.

Later the Prophet and Oliver Cowdery, in whom Joseph confided the vision, cited thirty-one scriptural references

Moroni used to tutor Joseph.[2] On this list are nine Isaiah references in addition to Isaiah 11. They include Isaiah 1:7, 23–24, 25–26; 2:1–4; 4:5–6; 29:11, 13, 14; and 43:6. These passages cover the topics of the apostasy, the gathering, the restoration, the Book of Mormon, and a latter-day temple in the tops of the mountains. That was quite a curriculum for the seventeen year old!

The Words of Isaiah in the Book of Mormon

It is interesting to note how very often Joseph encountered Isaiah in the formative years of his ministry. Although Joseph received the plates of the Book of Mormon in 1827, the translation of what we now have did not begin until 7 April 1829, when Oliver Cowdery first served as his scribe. As he translated the Book of Mormon, Joseph soon learned the importance and value of Isaiah, just as Nephi had more than two thousand years earlier. Nephi reports:

> And now I, Nephi, write more of the words of Isaiah, for my soul delighteth in his words. For I will liken his words unto my people, and I will send them forth unto all my children, for he verily saw my Redeemer, even as I have seen him. . . . And now I write some of the words of Isaiah, that whoso of my people shall see these words may lift up their hearts and rejoice for all men. Now these are the words, and ye may liken them unto you and unto all men. (2 Nephi 11:2, 8)

What does Nephi choose to copy into his record from the words of Isaiah contained in the plates of brass? He copies the passage that speaks of the mountain of the Lord's house—a temple (2 Nephi 12). Further in the record, Nephi prophesies using words from Isaiah 29 (paralleled in 2 Nephi 27), which prophesies of events in the last days. Since the work of translation was arduous, time-consuming, and demanding, Joseph probably had little opportunity to ponder Isaiah's words while translating the Book of Mormon, but he was at least exposed to these new insights about his times as he saw his own mission in Nephi's words.

In translating the speech of Abinadi, delivered about four hundred years later in the record, Joseph again came upon words of Isaiah. Abinadi refers to Isaiah 53, beginning, "Yea, even doth not Isaiah say: Who hath believed our report, and to whom is the arm of the Lord revealed?" (Mosiah 14:1). Mosiah 15 then contains Abinadi's enlightening commentary on the lengthy passages of Isaiah he has just quoted, which describe the atonement of Jesus Christ in inspired detail.

Did Joseph wonder why he was encountering so much Isaiah? Why are so many of Isaiah's teachings found in the Book of Mormon? Let us explore some possible answers to that question.

1. Isaiah's teachings are so important that Jesus Christ himself quoted all of Isaiah 54 to the righteous Nephites then commanded them to search the words of Isaiah (see 3 Nephi 22; 23:1–5). Moroni also emphasizes their importance to God's children: "Search the prophecies of Isaiah, behold, I cannot write them" (Mormon 8:23).

2. The Book of Mormon's purpose is to testify that Jesus is the Christ (see title page of the Book of Mormon). Isaiah's writings are messianic. Nephi and Jacob saw Christ in a vision, as did Isaiah (see Isaiah 6; 2 Nephi 11:2–3; Joseph Smith—History 1:17–20). Those prophets surely felt an extraordinary familiarity with Jesus, which Joseph must have shared because of his experience in his first vision.

3. Many of Isaiah's prophecies describe the last dispensation. Readers and hearers in his time ignored his message;

hence his words are more completely relevant for those who would live in the time period he describes. That message is spotlighted for us in the Book of Mormon.

Joseph Teaches the Words of Isaiah

After the publication of the Book of Mormon and the organization of the church in 1830, Joseph often used the words of Isaiah to instruct his growing flock, just as he had been tutored by Isaiah's words. As modern scriptures were revealed through him and the canon of scripture expanded, the influence of Isaiah's words is evident. The Doctrine and Covenants is a major repository of Isaianic language. Many of its sections either interpret verses in Isaiah or use phrases that are also found in Isaiah. Two researchers, Ellis T. Rasmussen and Lois Jean Smutz, have identified parallels between the Bible and the Doctrine and Covenants.[3] Although they use different methodologies, they both find that in its wording the Doctrine and Covenants more often resembles the New Testament than the Old Testament. "However," says Smutz, "paralleled passages referring to the latter days are particularly abundant in Isaiah, Joel, Zephaniah and Malachi, raising the ratio of frequency of parallels in these books considerably."[4] Their studies show that the Old Testament passages most often paralleled or alluded to in the Doctrine and Covenants come from Isaiah, particularly in sections 1, 45, 49, 66, 88, 101, 109, 117, 124, and 133.

The Prophet Joseph Smith also used the words of Isaiah while producing the Joseph Smith Translation of the Bible. Joseph did the bulk of his work translating the Old Testament in the Gilbert-Whitney store in Kirtland between 2 February and 2 July 1833.[5] In Doctrine and Covenants 90:13 we learn that on 8 March 1833 Joseph was in the midst of translating the prophets. So, as early as 1833 Joseph was deeply involved with the words of Isaiah, making corrections and additions that, in some cases, can make a difference as one studies those words.[6] For instance, opposite meanings are given to clarify the sense of the passage in Isaiah 65:1:

> King James Version: "I am sought of them that asked *not* for me; I am found of them that sought me *not*."
>
> Joseph Smith Translation: "I am found of them who seek after me, I give unto all them that ask of me; I am not found of them that sought me not, or that inquireth not after me."

The Lord used Isaianic language in the revelations he gave to Joseph Smith. Similarly, Joseph Smith used the words of the ancient prophet in his discourses and correspondence. A scouring of the standard sources of Joseph's writings[7] produces many references to Isaiah as early as 1828 and continuing until his martyrdom in 1844. In a survey of Joseph's references to the Old Testament in the books *Teachings of the Prophet Joseph Smith, The Words of Joseph Smith,* and *The Personal Writings of Joseph Smith,* Grant Underwood found that "over 200, or nearly half the total number of references are drawn from just three books."[8] Ninety-nine of them—the greatest number—are from Isaiah. The next most oft-cited books, Psalms and Genesis, contribute fifty-eight and fifty-seven phrases, respectively. Underwood also noted that in these compilations, most scriptures occur only once. Those that occur more often include Isaiah 29:21, which refers to persecution, cited six times; Isaiah 51:3 or 58:12, which refers to the gathering to and restoration of Zion, one or the other being cited six times; and Isaiah 2:2–3, which refers to latter-day temples, cited four times.[9]

As the Prophet cited Isaiah's teachings, three themes occurred repeatedly: First, a "voice from the dust," a book brought forth to the world—the Book of Mormon; second, a gathering to Zion, a restoration; and third, the mountain of the Lord—latter-day temples.

The Book of Mormon, a Voice from the Dust

Joseph saw the coming forth of the Book of Mormon as fulfilling the prophecy in Isaiah 29:11–12, which says, "And the vision of all is become unto you as the words of a book that is sealed, which men deliver to one that is learned, saying, Read this, I pray thee: and he saith, I cannot; for it is sealed: And the book is delivered to him that is not learned, saying, Read this, I pray thee: and he saith, I am not learned." The Prophet's recognition of this fulfillment is evidenced in a passage he wrote in his personal history. During the early months of the Book of Mormon translation, Martin Harris came to Joseph and told him that

> the Lord had shown him [Martin] that he must go to New York City with some of the characters so we proceeded to copy some of them and he took his Journey to the Eastern Cities and to the Learned saying, "read this, I pray thee," and the learned said "I cannot" but if he would bring the plates they would read it, but the Lord had forbidden it and he returned to me and gave them to me to translate and I said "[I] cannot for I am not learned," but the Lord had prepared spectacles for to read the Book therefore I commenced translating the characters and thus the Prophecy of Isaiah was fulfilled which is written in the 29th chapter concerning the book.[10]

Clearly, Joseph saw the coming forth of the Book of Mormon as fulfillment of Isaiah 29:11–12.[11]

Establishing Zion

In June 1831 Joseph arrived in Jackson County, Missouri, where the gathering to Zion was just beginning. He wrote,

> [The Lord] designed to commence the work of the gathering, and the upbuilding of an "holy city," which should be called Zion—Zion, because it is a place of righteousness, and all who build thereon are to worship the true and living God, and all believe in one doctrine, even the doctrine of our Lord and Savior, Jesus Christ. [Then, quoting Isaiah 52:8 directly, he said:] "Thy watchmen shall lift up the voice; with the voice together shall they sing: for they shall see eye to eye, when the Lord shall bring again Zion." [12]

All will believe in one doctrine and be united in righteousness. This interpretation of watchmen or prophets proclaiming together and "seeing eye to eye" as referring to Zion is striking. Only a few times in the world's history have so many prophets lived on earth at the same time. The latter days are unique in this regard. The councils of the First Presidency and Quorum of the Twelve, sustained as prophets, seers, and revelators, as well as the Seventy, take action only by unanimous vote (see D&C 107:27).

The idea of Zion was compelling to early converts. Gathering to Zion was an ideal that inspired early pioneers in Europe and Great Britain. Joseph Smith said that the "Land of Zion . . . consists of all North and South America but that any place where the Saints gather is Zion, which every righteous man will build up for a place of safety for his children."[13] Members of the church today take comfort in this idea, that wherever the Saints gather is Zion. It is not so much where we live but how we live that matters to the Lord. Zion is the living of righteous principles contained in the restored gospel, the unity of seeing eye to eye, just as Isaiah envisioned (see Isaiah 52:8).

The Mountain of the Lord

As late as 8 April 1844, only a few weeks before his martyrdom, Joseph proclaimed triumphantly:

> I have now a great proclamation for the Elders to teach the Church hereafter, which is in relation to Zion. The whole of North and South America is Zion. The mountain of the Lord's House is in the center of North and South America. When the House is done, [the] Baptismal font erected and finished, and the worthy are washed, anointed, endowed, and ordained kings and priests, . . . then the Elders are to go through all America and build up Churches until all Zion is built up. But [they are] not to commence to do this *until the Temple is built up here and the Elders endowed*. Then go forth and accomplish the work and build up stakes in all North and South America.[14]

Here we see the close connection of Zion, conversion, and temple ordinances. The elders are not to go until they are endowed. They will lead their converts to the temple, and the cycle will repeat. The centerpiece of the establishment of Zion is to be a temple, the image of which is spoken of with clarity in this proclamation:

> And it shall come to pass in the last days, that the mountain of the Lord's house shall be established in the top of the mountains, and shall be exalted above the hills; and all nations shall flow unto it. And many people shall go and say, Come ye, and let us go up to the mountain of the Lord, to the house of the God of Jacob; and he will teach us of his ways, and we will walk in his paths: for out of Zion shall go forth the law, and the word of the Lord from Jerusalem. (Isaiah 2:2–3)

Joseph and Isaiah shared many visions, some of which would be fulfilled by Joseph himself. Isaiah foretold "a marvelous work and a wonder" taking place that would include the gathering of scattered Israel to Zion, a process that would be facilitated by the flooding of the earth with the Book of Mormon, which Joseph translated. The wondrous work would also include building a latter-day temple to which all nations would flow to be taught and to be sealed together as an eternal family.

We have an unbroken line of prophets from Joseph Smith to our own day who teach of the significance of temple work. As recently as October 1994, President Howard W. Hunter said,

> All of our efforts in proclaiming the gospel, perfecting the Saints, and redeeming the dead lead to the holy temple. This is because the temple ordinances are absolutely crucial; we cannot return to God's presence without them. I encourage everyone to worthily attend the temple or to work toward the day when you can enter that holy house to receive your ordinances and covenants.
>
> May you let the meaning and beauty and peace of the temple come into your everyday life more directly in order that the millennial day may come, that promised time when [as Isaiah promised] "they shall beat their swords into plowshares, and their spears into pruninghooks: nation shall not lift up sword against nation, neither shall they learn war any more. . . [but shall] walk in the light of the Lord" (Isaiah 2:4–5).[15]

Thus a common bond unites the great prophets Isaiah, Joseph Smith, and our latter-day leaders. That bond is the temple, with Jesus Christ and his atonement standing at its center. The prophets all invite us to come to Christ. They teach us of him in many ways, but especially through their own lives of devotion and faith. They offer us the hope of returning to his presence through righteous living and essential temple ordinances.

Conclusion

How much did Joseph Smith know of Isaiah? It is hard to evaluate the extent of his knowledge before the first vision when he was fourteen years old, but from then on we can trace this great prophet's words in a curriculum beginning with his receiving Isaianic quotations as instructions from Jesus Christ himself, progressing as he encounters those words throughout the Book of Mormon, and later culminating in his incorporation of them into his own sermons and writings. The themes in the book of Isaiah that become themes in Joseph's ministry are the coming forth of the Book of Mormon, "a voice from the dust"; establishing Zion, a place of righteous unity; and temple building, "the mountain of the Lord." Jesus Christ is the centerpiece of Isaianic writing, often directly, and many times indirectly as the Holy One of Israel. He is mentioned and alluded to again and again.

Joseph Smith was inspired, motivated, and empowered profoundly by his connection to Isaiah's teachings. In the past ten years, my immersion in the words of Isaiah has led me to know that clarity, power, and inspiration await anyone willing to search his words.

Notes

1. In his book *Isaiah: Prophet, Seer, and Poet* (Salt Lake City: Deseret Book, 1982), 170–4, Victor L. Ludlow discusses the ways in which Joseph Smith could possibly be identified as "the root of Jesse," but he leaves open the possibility of other interpretations. Ludlow points out that Doctrine and Covenants 113:1–2 identifies "the stem of Jesse" as Christ (see p. 168), but Doctrine and

Covenants 113:3–4 does not explicitly identify "the rod of Jesse" or "the root of Jesse."

2.   Kent P. Jackson, *From Apostasy to Restoration* (Salt Lake City: Deseret Book, 1996), 104.

3.   Ellis T. Rasmussen, "Textual Parallels to the Doctrine and Covenants and Book of Commandments as Found in the Bible," (master's thesis, Brigham Young University, 1951); Lois Jean Smutz, "Textual Parallels to the Doctrine and Covenants (Sections 65 to 133) as Found in the Bible" (master's thesis, Brigham Young University, 1971).

4.   Smutz, 255.

5.   Robert J. Matthews, *"A Plainer Translation": Joseph Smith's Translation of the Bible: A History and Commentary* (Provo, Utah: Brigham Young University Press, 1975), 92.

6.   See Royal Skousen, "Textual Variants in the Isaiah Quotations in the Book of Mormon," in this volume for a discussion of Joseph's use of the Book of Mormon in his inspired translation of Isaiah.

7.   Sources include Joseph Smith, *History of the Church of Jesus Christ of Latter-day Saints,* 7 vols. (Salt Lake City: Deseret Book, 1978); Joseph Fielding Smith, ed., *Teachings of the Prophet Joseph Smith* (Salt Lake City: Deseret Book, 1976); N. B. Lundwall, ed., *Lectures on Faith* (Salt Lake City: Bookcraft, n.d.); Dean C. Jessee, ed., *The Personal Writings of Joseph Smith* (Salt Lake City: Deseret Book, 1984); Dean C. Jessee, ed., *Papers of Joseph Smith,* 2 vols. (Salt Lake City: Deseret Book, 1989); and Andrew F. Ehat and Lyndon W. Cook, eds., *The Words of Joseph Smith* (Orem, Utah: Grandin Book, 1991).

8.   Grant Underwood, "Joseph Smith's Use of the Old Testament," in *The Old Testament and the Latter-day Saints: Sperry Symposium 1986* (Salt Lake City: Randall Books, 1986), 382.

9.   Ibid, 383.

10.   "History [1832]," *The Papers of Joseph Smith,* 1:9; spelling and punctuation standardized for modern audience.

11.   Note that these verses come immediately before those quoted to Joseph by Jesus in Joseph's first vision about the minis-

ters drawing near to him with their lips while their hearts are far from him (see Isaiah 29:13 and Joseph Smith—History 1:19).

12. *Teachings of the Prophet Joseph Smith,* 80.

13. *The Words of Joseph Smith,* 415. The date for this utterance is uncertain, but it may have been 1843. See also TPJS Conference 8 April 1844 cited below. He made similar references to Zion being North and South America at both conferences.

14. *The Words of Joseph Smith,* 363–4; spelling and punctuation standardized for modern audience; italics added.

15. Howard W. Hunter, "Follow the Son of God," *Ensign* (November 1994): 88.

Textual Variants in the Isaiah Quotations in the Book of Mormon

Royal Skousen

Comparing the 1829 Book of Mormon manuscripts with the King James Version generates eight findings about the Prophet's translation of the Isaiah passages.

In analyzing the textual variants for the Isaiah quotations in the Book of Mormon, we first have to decide which passages are actual quotes, in distinction to paraphrases or phrasal allusions. The first step in this process is to determine the degree to which a Book of Mormon passage can be lined up with a proposed corresponding Isaiah passage. Ultimately, I have decided to consider only those passages that can be lined up at the sentence level, thus eliminating phrasal allusions or situations involving the mixture of phrases within the same sentence.

In the resulting list of selected passages, I have distinguished three types of similarity. If a passage shows a high degree of correspondence, I have marked it with a *q* to indicate that it is a quote. In two cases the quote is only secondarily from Isaiah. In one of these cases, the quote is actually the same as the quotation of Isaiah from the synoptic Gospels (Matthew, Mark, and Luke); in the other case the quote is from Malachi. I have marked these two secondary quotes of Isaiah with a 2. The remaining examples are clearly paraphrastic; these I have left unmarked.

q	Isaiah 2:1–14:32	2 Nephi 12:1–24:32
	Isaiah 5:26	2 Nephi 29:2
	Isaiah 5:26	2 Nephi 29:3
q	Isaiah 11:4	2 Nephi 30:9
q	Isaiah 11:5–9	2 Nephi 30:11–15

	Isaiah 11:11	2 Nephi 25:17
	Isaiah 11:11	2 Nephi 29:1
	Isaiah 28:10	2 Nephi 28:30
	Isaiah 28:13	2 Nephi 28:30
	Isaiah 29:3–4	2 Nephi 26:15–16
	Isaiah 29:4	2 Nephi 27:6–9
q	Isaiah 29:5	2 Nephi 26:18
	Isaiah 29:6	2 Nephi 6:15
q	Isaiah 29:6–10	2 Nephi 27:2–5
	Isaiah 29:11	2 Nephi 26:17
	Isaiah 29:11–12	2 Nephi 27:15–19
	Isaiah 29:13	2 Nephi 28:9
	Isaiah 29:13	2 Nephi 28:14
q	Isaiah 29:13–24	2 Nephi 27:25–35
	Isaiah 29:14	1 Nephi 14:7
	Isaiah 29:14	1 Nephi 22:8
	Isaiah 29:14	2 Nephi 25:17
	Isaiah 29:14	2 Nephi 29:1
	Isaiah 29:15	2 Nephi 28:9
	Isaiah 29:21	2 Nephi 28:16
	Isaiah 40:3	1 Nephi 10:7
2	Isaiah 40:3	1 Nephi 10:8
	Matthew 3:3	
	Mark 1:3	
	Luke 3:4	
	Isaiah 44:27	Helaman 12:16
	Isaiah 45:18	1 Nephi 17:36
2	Isaiah 47:14	1 Nephi 22:15
	Malachi 4:1	
q	Isaiah 48:1–49:26	1 Nephi 20:1–21:26
	Isaiah 49:22	2 Nephi 29:2
	Isaiah 49:22–23	1 Nephi 22:6
	Isaiah 49:22–23	1 Nephi 22:8
q	Isaiah 49:22–23	2 Nephi 6:6–7
q	Isaiah 49:24–52:2	2 Nephi 6:16–8:25
	Isaiah 51:10	Helaman 12:16

	Isaiah 52:1–2	Moroni 10:31
q	Isaiah 52:1–3	3 Nephi 20:36–38
q	Isaiah 52:6–7	3 Nephi 20:39–40
	Isaiah 52:7	1 Nephi 13:37
	Isaiah 52:7	Mosiah 15:14
	Isaiah 52:7	Mosiah 15:15–18
q	Isaiah 52:7–10	Mosiah 12:21–24
q	Isaiah 52:8	3 Nephi 20:32
q	Isaiah 52:8–10	Mosiah 15:29–31
q	Isaiah 52:8–10	3 Nephi 16:18–20
q	Isaiah 52:9–10	3 Nephi 20:34–35
	Isaiah 52:10	1 Nephi 22:10
	Isaiah 52:10	1 Nephi 22:11
q	Isaiah 52:11–15	3 Nephi 20:41–45
	Isaiah 52:12	3 Nephi 21:29
q	Isaiah 52:15	3 Nephi 21:8
q	Isaiah 53:1–12	Mosiah 14:1–12
q	Isaiah 53:7	Mosiah 15:6
	Isaiah 53:10	Mosiah 15:10
q	Isaiah 54:1–17	3 Nephi 22:1–17
	Isaiah 54:2	Moroni 10:31
q	Isaiah 55:1	2 Nephi 9:50
	Isaiah 55:1	2 Nephi 26:25
	Isaiah 55:2	2 Nephi 9:51

The next step is to prepare a computerized collation to compare the various textual sources. This step involves the following Book of Mormon and Bible texts:

1. the original manuscript of the Book of Mormon (the manuscript the scribes wrote down as Joseph Smith dictated the text)

2. the printer's manuscript of the Book of Mormon (the copy that the scribes produced to take to the printer of the 1830 edition)

3. the first three editions of the Book of Mormon (editions that Joseph Smith had some control over):

    (a) 1830, Palmyra
    (b) 1837, Kirtland
    (c) 1840, Cincinnati

4. the current LDS edition of the Book of Mormon (dating from 1981, with minor revisions)

5. the King James Version of the Bible (namely, the current Cambridge text)

6. the Joseph Smith Translation of the Bible[1]

No more than 30 percent of the original manuscript of the Book of Mormon is extant; only part of the Isaiah quotations are found in what remains:

1 Nephi 20–21 / / Isaiah 48–49
>   virtually extant
>   LDS Church Historical Department

2 Nephi 6–8 / / Isaiah 49–52
>   large fragments
>   Wilford Wood Foundation

2 Nephi 23–24 / / Isaiah 13–14
>   large fragments
>   Wilford Wood Foundation

3 Nephi 20 / / Isaiah 52
>   one minor fragment
>   LDS Church Historical Department

The printer's manuscript, which is owned by the Reorganized Church of Jesus Christ of Latter Day Saints, is fully extant except for three lines near the beginning of 1 Nephi.

In the King James Version there are words set in italics and others set in all caps. The italics represent words that do not occur in the original biblical languages, but which the

King James translators added to make the text read sensibly in English. Words set in all caps represent the translation of the sacred Hebrew name for God (*JHWH*).

In the remainder of this paper, I will briefly describe the basic findings from comparing these Isaiah passages.

First Finding: *The base text for the Isaiah quotations in the Book of Mormon is indeed the King James Version of the Bible.*

The King James Version of the Bible is not an independent translation from the original biblical languages, but instead is a revision based on early English Bibles published in the 1500s.[2] An example of this dependence on earlier translations is found when we briefly compare the King James Version with the Geneva Bible. The Geneva Bible was translated by Protestant exiles in Geneva, Switzerland, and was first published in 1560. It was the popular English Bible prior to the 1611 King James Version and served as the Bible of the Puritans and Shakespeare.[3] The similarity between the Geneva Bible and the King James Bible is striking, as in the following comparison for Isaiah 53. (Here word differences are printed in bold; italics are preserved from the original.)

Isaiah 53: Geneva Bible versus King James Version

GNV who **will believe** our report and to whom is the arm
KJV who **hath believed** our report and to whom is the arm

GNV of the Lord revealed **but** he shall grow up before him
KJV of the LORD revealed **for** he shall grow up before him

GNV as a **branch** and as a root out of a dry ground he
KJV as a **tender plant** and as a root out of a dry ground he

GNV hath **neither** form nor **beauty** when we shall
KJV hath **no** form nor **comeliness and** when we shall

GNV see him there **shall be** no **form** that we should desire
KJV see him *there is* no **beauty** that we should desire

GNV	him he is despised and rejected of men **he is** a man **full**
KJV	him he is despised and rejected of men a man
GNV	of sorrows and **hath experience of infirmities** we
KJV	of sorrows and **acquainted with grief** **and** we
GNV	hid as it were our faces from him he was despised and
KJV	hid as it were *our* faces from him he was despised and
GNV	we esteemed him not surely he hath borne our
KJV	we esteemed him not surely he hath borne our
GNV	**infirmities** and carried our sorrows yet we did **judge**
KJV	**griefs** and carried our sorrows yet we did **esteem**
GNV	him **as plagued and** smitten of God and **humbled** but
KJV	him **stricken** smitten of God and **afflicted** but
GNV	he was wounded for our transgressions he was **broken**
KJV	*he was* wounded for our transgressions *he was* **bruised**
GNV	for our iniquities the chastisement of our peace *was* upon
KJV	for our iniquities the chastisement of our peace *was* upon
GNV	him and with his stripes we are healed all we like sheep
KJV	him and with his stripes we are healed all we like sheep
GNV	have gone astray we have turned every one to his own
KJV	have gone astray we have turned every one to his own
GNV	way and the Lord hath laid **upon** him the iniquity
KJV	way and the LORD hath laid **on** him the iniquity
GNV	of us all he was oppressed and he was afflicted yet
KJV	of us all he was oppressed and he was afflicted yet
GNV	**did he not open** his mouth he is brought as a **sheep** to
KJV	**he opened not** his mouth he is brought as a **lamb** to
GNV	the slaughter and as a sheep before her **shearer** is dumb
KJV	the slaughter and as a sheep before her **shearers** is dumb
GNV	so he openeth not his mouth he was taken **out** from
KJV	so he openeth not his mouth he was taken from
GNV	prison and from judgment and who shall declare his
KJV	prison and from judgment and who shall declare his

GNV	**age** for he was cut out of the land of the living
KJV	**generation** for he was cut **off** out of the land of the living
GNV	for the transgression of my people was he **plagued** and
KJV	for the transgression of my people was he **stricken** and
GNV	he made his grave with the wicked and with the rich in
KJV	he made his grave with the wicked and with the rich in
GNV	his death **though** he had done no **wickedness** neither
KJV	his death **because** he had done no **violence** neither
GNV	*was* any deceit in his mouth yet the Lord
KJV	*was any* deceit in his mouth yet **it pleased** the LORD
GNV	**would break** him **and** **make** him **subject** to
KJV	**to** **bruise** him **he hath put** *him* to
GNV	**infirmities** when **he** **shall** make his soul an offering
KJV	**grief** when **thou shalt** make his soul an offering
GNV	for sin he shall see *his* seed **and** shall prolong *his* days
KJV	for sin he shall see *his* seed **he** shall prolong *his* days
GNV	and the **will** of the Lord shall prosper in his hand
KJV	and the **pleasure** of the LORD shall prosper in his hand
GNV	he shall see of the travail of his soul *and* shall be satisfied
KJV	he shall see of the travail of his soul *and* shall be satisfied
GNV	by his knowledge shall my righteous servant justify many
KJV	by his knowledge shall my righteous servant justify many
GNV	for he shall bear their iniquities therefore will I **give**
KJV	for he shall bear their iniquities therefore will I **divide**
GNV	him a portion with the great and he shall divide the spoil
KJV	him *a portion* with the great and he shall divide the spoil
GNV	with the strong because he hath poured out his soul unto
KJV	with the strong because he hath poured out his soul unto
GNV	death and he was **counted** with the transgressors and
KJV	death and he was **numbered** with the transgressors and
GNV	he bare the sin of many and **prayed** for the
KJV	he bare the sin of many and **made intercession** for the

GNV	**trespassers**
KJV	**transgressors**

For Isaiah 53, 88 percent of the King James text is identical with the Geneva Bible.

In fact, the Geneva Bible itself is a revision, not a translation from scratch. All the early translations of the English Bible are ultimately based on the biblical translation made by William Tyndale in the 1530s.[4] Jon Nielson's recent master's thesis shows that in the portions of the Bible that Tyndale translated before he was martyred, about 82 percent of the King James text is identical, word-for-word, with Tyndale's translation.[5]

So an important question is whether the biblical quotations in the Book of Mormon actually come from the King James Bible. Andrew Stewart, a student in my 1991 course on textual criticism of the Book of Mormon, identified unique readings in the various early English Bibles (including the King James Version); he then compared those readings with the Book of Mormon text. Not surprisingly, in every case except one Stewart found that the Book of Mormon agreed with the unique readings in the King James Version.[6]

But the one exception is very interesting. In 2 Nephi 12:16, the text reads "upon all the ships of the sea and upon all the ships of Tarshish."

2 Nephi 12:16 / / Isaiah 2:16

> *upon all the ships of the sea*
> Septuagint (Greek)
> Coverdale 1535
>
> *and upon all the ships of Tarshish*
> Masoretic text (Hebrew)
> all early English Bibles except for Coverdale

The first phrase is found in the Septuagint (or Greek) version of Isaiah, the second in the Masoretic (or traditional Hebrew) text. While looking for unique readings, Stewart discovered that the first phrase (but not the second) occurs in Coverdale's 1535 Bible as "upon all shippes of the sea," while all the other early English Bibles have only the other phrase, "upon all the ships of Tarshish."[7] Quite possibly Coverdale's translation is based on the Greek version of Isaiah.

Second Finding: *The original manuscript for the biblical quotes shows that the text was dictated by Joseph Smith; no physical copy was given to Oliver Cowdery to copy from.*

Some scholars have assumed that Joseph Smith used a King James Bible to dictate the biblical passages in the Book of Mormon.[8] The reason for this claim is that the biblical quotations are based on the King James text. Yet witnesses who observed Joseph Smith dictating the Book of Mormon claimed that Joseph Smith used no books at all.[9] In any event, we can definitely establish that Joseph Smith did in fact dictate the biblical quotations to his scribe; he did not hand over an emended Bible for the scribe to visually copy the text from. This conclusion can be seen when we examine Oliver Cowdery's spellings in the Isaiah portions of the original manuscript. Here we find the normal spelling variants that Oliver used when writing down other portions of the Book of Mormon. For example, in 1 Nephi 20–21 (quoting Isaiah 48–49), we find the following typical spelling errors:

the Lord of *hoasts*
I have *declaired*
least thou shouldst say
& my *moulton* image
even *hiden* things

> hath *spaned* the heavens
> cut off nor *destroid*
> he *lead* them
> in an *exceptable* time
> for a *covanent*
> shall not *hungar*
> thou shalt surely *cloath* thee
> & *removeing* to & fro

We also find that Oliver Cowdery sometimes misinterpreted what Joseph Smith dictated, as in 1 Nephi 21:11, which has *away* in the original manuscript (as well as in the printer's manuscript) instead of the correct *a way:*

1 Nephi 21:11 / / Isaiah 49:11

> and I will make all my mountains *away*
> (instead of *a way*)

Oliver Cowdery also interpreted unfamiliar words in terms of more familiar words; for example, in 2 Nephi 24:23, he wrote *the bosom of destruction* (in both the original and printer's manuscripts) since the word *besom,* meaning 'broom,' was totally unknown to him:

2 Nephi 24:23 / / Isaiah 14:23

> and I will sweep it with the *bosom* of destruction
> (instead of *besom*)

Third Finding: *The original Book of Mormon chapter divisions of the Isaiah quotations follow a larger thematic grouping, not the interruptive chapter system found in the King James Bible.*

Although the base text for the Isaiah quotations in the Book of Mormon is the King James Version, the original Book of Mormon chapter divisions ignore the chapter system found in the King James Bible. The division into the

66 relatively short chapters in Isaiah dates from late medieval times.[10] The original Book of Mormon chapters are based on narrative unity and group the King James chapters into more coherent units. And in one case, the grouping does not overlap with the beginning and ending of the King James chapters:

Original *Book of Mormon*	*King James* *Version*	*Current* *Book of Mormon*
1 Nephi VI	Isaiah 48–49	1 Nephi 20–21
2 Nephi V	Isaiah 49:24–52:2	2 Nephi 6–8
2 Nephi VIII	Isaiah 2–5	2 Nephi 12–15
2 Nephi IX	Isaiah 6–12	2 Nephi 16–22
2 Nephi X	Isaiah 13–14	2 Nephi 23–24

Of course, the current LDS chapter system in the Book of Mormon does agree with the King James chapter system, but this has only been true since 1879, when Orson Pratt divided up the original Book of Mormon chapters to facilitate the versification of the text.

Fourth Finding: *The original Book of Mormon text is closer to the King James Version.*

In working with the original manuscript, I have discovered a number of cases where the original reading is different from our current reading and in each case the original reading agrees with the King James reading—or is at least much closer to the King James reading. As an example, consider a large fragment of the original manuscript from 2 Nephi 7.[11] When Oliver Cowdery produced the printer's manuscript by copying from this portion of the original manuscript, he made at least six changes, five of which appear to be accidental and are probably due to tiring:

2 Nephi 7:2, 4, 5 / / Isaiah 50:2, 4, 5

Original Manuscript	*Printer's Manuscript*
2 wherefore when I *came* there was no man	wherefore when I *come* there was no man
I make *the* rivers a wilderness	I make *their* rivers a wilderness
they *dieth* because of thirst	they *die* because of thirst
4 he *wakeneth* morning by morning	he *waketh* morning by morning
he *wakeneth* mine ear	he *waketh* mine ear
5 the Lord God hath *opened* mine ear	the Lord God hath *appointed* mine ear

In each of these six cases, the original reading agrees with or is closer to the King James reading.

Another example of an original King James reading is in 2 Nephi 24:

2 Nephi 24:25 / / Isaiah 14:25

Original Manuscript	*Printer's Manuscript*
25 I will *break* the Assyrian in my land	I will *bring* the Assyrian in my land

Here the Wilford Wood fragment has *brea* at the end of a line, with the *a* only partially visible. The original *k* was presumably written at the beginning of the next line, but this part of the page is no longer extant. In any event, Oliver Cowdery, in his copying, misread the line-final *brea* as the beginning of the word *bring*, which seems to fit semantically and makes an interesting reading—but nonetheless wrong. Oliver Cowdery typically made copying errors at the end of lines by accidentally changing or omitting a word.

For most of the Book of Mormon—in fact, for most of the Isaiah quotations in the Book of Mormon—the original manuscript is no longer extant. The preceding examples (in which the original manuscript restores a King James reading) should warn us that single-word differences may simply be due to copying errors, especially when the words are visually similar. Other examples of possible scribal errors include the following:

2 Nephi 20:13 / / Isaiah 10:13

> BoM   and I have **moved**   the **borders** of the people
> KJV   and I have **removed** the **bounds** of the people

2 Nephi 23:15 / / Isaiah 13:15

> BoM   every one that is **proud** shall be thrust through
> KJV   every one that is **found** shall be thrust through

2 Nephi 24:19 / / Isaiah 14:19

> BoM   and   the **remnant** of those that are slain
> KJV   *and as* the **raiment** of those that are slain

Fifth Finding: *The majority of differences between the Book of Mormon text and the Isaiah text are **not** associated with italicized words in the King James Version.*

Stan Larson, along with others, has claimed that Joseph Smith used a copy of the King James Bible to produce the biblical quotations in the Book of Mormon.[12] Larson has also argued that Joseph Smith knew what the italics in the King James Version meant; namely, that the italicized words had been added by the translators of the King James Bible and could therefore be altered.[13] Yet it is doubtful whether Joseph Smith would have even known what the italics meant, especially since no explanation for their use is ever given in the King James Bible. This use of italics originated with the Geneva Bible, which did explain its purpose.[14]

William Calhoun and Margaret Robbins, two students in my 1991 class on textual criticism of the Book of Mormon, studied this issue regarding italics and concluded that there was little evidence in support of Larson's hypothesis.[15] More recently, I have made an actual count for all the Isaiah quotations in the Book of Mormon. In my analysis I used only the direct quotes and ignored the paraphrastic passages since their differences are even less predictable by reference to the italicized words in the King James Bible. The results are as follows:

total number of differences	516
total number of italicized words	392
overlap: differences + italicized words	150
differences linked to italicized words	150/516 = 29%
italicized words linked to differences	150/392 = 38%

For direct quotes there was a total of 516 differences between the Book of Mormon text and the King James text. Of those differences, only 29 percent could be linked to italicized words in the King James Bible. In other words, 71 percent of the differences are unrelated to italics and must be explained in terms of other factors. Moreover, the majority (62 percent) of italicized words are unchanged in the Book of Mormon. If the italicized words have an effect, they do not explain very much.

Sixth Finding: *Corrections in the original manuscript give very little evidence for the hypothesis that Joseph Smith altered the text while he supposedly read it off from a King James Bible.*

Stan Larson has argued that we can find evidence for this hypothesis by identifying examples where Joseph Smith first dictated the King James text and then made changes away from that text.[16] Supposedly, the original manuscript should thus show the scribe first writing the King James textual version, then correcting it to agree with Joseph Smith's revised text. The major problem with this proposal is that there are very few cases that can even be considered examples of editing while dictating. In the Isaiah quotations, there are only three examples in the extant portions of the original manuscript where the scribe first wrote something like the King James text and then altered it away from that text.

In 1 Nephi 20:11, Oliver Cowdery first wrote "for how should I suffer my name to be polluted," which is somewhat close to the King James text "for how should *my name* be polluted." Then, in heavier ink, Oliver Cowdery crossed out the words "how should I" and wrote above the crossout, again in heavier ink, "I will not," which agrees with the beginning of the following clause ("and I will not give my glory unto another"). The heavier ink flow suggests that the change is not immediate; moreover, it removes a difficult reading. In the original and printer's manuscripts, virtually all corrections in heavier ink that remove difficult readings reflect conscious editing later on the part of the scribe rather than immediate editing by Joseph Smith. In the following comparison, we give both the reading of the original Book of Mormon text (BM*) and the reading of the current text (BMc), as well as the King James Version (KJV) and the Joseph Smith Translation (JST):

1 Nephi 20:11 // Isaiah 48:11

BM*	for **how should I suffer**	my name	**to**	be polluted
BMc	for **I will not**	**suffer**	my name	**to**	be polluted
KJV	for **how should**		*my name*	be polluted
JST	for **how should**		my name	be polluted

BM*	and I will not give my glory unto another
BMc	and I will not give my glory unto another
KJV	and I will not give my glory unto another
JST	and I will not give my glory unto another

A clear example demonstrating that Oliver Cowdery did indeed make conscious changes in the Book of Mormon text is found in 2 Nephi 7. Here the printer's manuscript shows Oliver Cowdery using heavier ink to cross out *dieth* and then writing *die* above the crossout, again in heavier ink. A difficult reading is removed (since the *–eth* ending is not supposed to occur with plural subjects). And we know this change represents conscious editing on Oliver Cowdery's part since the original manuscript has only *dieth* and Oliver originally wrote *dieth* when producing the printer's manuscript; only later did he replace *dieth* with *die.*

2 Nephi 7:2 // Isaiah 50:2

BM*	because **the waters are dried up**
BMc	because **the waters are dried up**
KJV	because *there is* **no water**
JST	because **the waters are dried up**

BM*	and **they dieth** **because of** thirst
BMc	and **they die** **because of** thirst
KJV	and **dieth for** thirst
JST	and **they die** **because of** thirst

The other two examples of possible editing away from the King James text seem quite weak and can be readily explained in other ways:

1 Nephi 21:21 // Isaiah 49:21

BM*	behold I was left alone these where **had** they been
BMc	behold I was left alone these where **have** they been
KJV	behold I was left alone these where *had* they been
JST	behold I was left alone these where **had** they been

1 Nephi 21:24 / / Isaiah 49:24

BM*		shall the prey be taken from the mighty
BMc	**for**	shall the prey be taken from the mighty
KJV		shall the prey be taken from the mighty
JST		shall the prey be taken from the mighty

In each case, the scribe in the original manuscript (Oliver Cowdery) first wrote the text of the King James Version, then corrected the text to read slightly differently. In these two examples the corrections in the original manuscript appear to be made with the same ink level as the surrounding text. The past tense form *had* in the first example may represent the King James text, but it may just as easily be due to tense agreement with the past-tense form *was* in the preceding clause ("behold I was left alone"). In the second example, agreement with a null or zero reading does not seem particularly persuasive when the only word involved is such a frequent function word as the conjunction *for*.

In any case, what is surprising is that there are so few potential examples of Joseph Smith's changing his mind, not only in the Isaiah passages but throughout the extant portions of the original manuscript.

Seventh Finding: *The few Isaiah passages that have been quoted more than once in the Book of Mormon may provide evidence for helping to restore the original reading.*

There are a number of Isaiah passages that are quoted more than once in the Book of Mormon:

Isaiah 11:4–9	2 Nephi 21:4–9 / 2 Nephi 30:9,11–15
Isaiah 49:22–26	1 Nephi 21:22–26 / 2 Nephi 6:6–7,16–18
Isaiah 52:1–2	2 Nephi 8:24–25 / 3 Nephi 20:36–37
Isaiah 52:7	Mosiah 12:21 / 3 Nephi 20:40
Isaiah 52:8	Mosiah 12:22 / Mosiah 15:29 /
	Nephi 16:18 / 3 Nephi 20:32

Isaiah 52:9–10	Mosiah 12:23–24 / Mosiah 15:30–31 /
	3 Nephi 16:19–20 / 3 Nephi 20:34–35
Isaiah 52:15	3 Nephi 20:45 / 3 Nephi 21:8
Isaiah 53:7	Mosiah 14:7 / Mosiah 15:6

As an example of where comparison suggests possible emendation of the text, consider two quotations from Isaiah 49:

1 Nephi 21:25–26 / 2 Nephi 6:17–18 / / Isaiah 49:25–26

BM1	for	I will contend with **him**
BM2	for **thus saith the Lord**	I will contend with **them**
KJV	for	I will contend with **him**
JST	for **thus saith the Lord**	I will contend with **them**

BM1	that **contendeth** with thee **and I will save thy**
BM2	that **contendeth** with thee
KJV	that **contendeth** with thee **and I will save thy**
JST	that **contend** with thee **and I will save thy**

BM1	**children** and I will feed them that oppress thee with
BM2	and I will feed them that oppress thee with
KJV	children and I will feed them that oppress thee with
JST	children and I will feed them that oppress thee with

BM1	their own flesh
BM2	their own flesh
KJV	their own flesh
JST	their own flesh

The first line in this collation (BM1) gives the original text from 1 Nephi 21; the second line (BM2) gives the original text from 2 Nephi 6. Note that the first text is identical to the King James text. But the second text may have originally been closer to the King James text than it currently is. We only have the printer's manuscript for the second text and two of the differences could be errors:

- First, evidence from immediate corrections in the manuscripts shows that Oliver Cowdery frequently had difficulty in distinguishing between Joseph Smith's pronunciation of *them* and *him*, since in normal speech both these pronouns are pronounced identically—as *'em*.[17] So the pronoun *them* in 2 Nephi 6:17 may have actually been *him*. Nonetheless, the pronoun *them* may well be correct; it could represent an attempt to make the pronoun agree with the *them* that occurs in the following clause ("and I will feed them").

- Second, the phrase "and I will save thy children" could have been accidentally lost in copying since this clause and the next one both begin with the same words ("and I will").

Despite these possibilities, there is probably not enough evidence to actually emend the text in 2 Nephi 6.

Eighth Finding: *Joseph Smith's "New Translation" of the Bible used the 1830 edition of the Book of Mormon as a source for changing some of the corresponding biblical text in Isaiah.*

The Joseph Smith Translation (or JST, for short) shows that Joseph Smith sometimes used the Book of Mormon text to make changes in the Isaiah text of the Bible.[18] For instance, the JST of Isaiah 29 follows the Book of Mormon text, including the much longer paraphrastic section from 2 Nephi 27:6–24 that deals with reading a sealed book. The identity is word-for-word except for two minor changes (*that* instead of *which* in verse 10 and a deleted *if* in verse 13).

In fact, we can show that the base text for making these changes in Isaiah is the 1830 edition of the Book of Mormon. The Joseph Smith Translation, when it follows the Book of Mormon text, agrees with the 1830 edition, as in 2 Nephi 27:5, for which the 1830 edition contains a unique reading:

2 Nephi 27:5 // Isaiah 29:10

BM*	and the seers hath he covered **because of your iniquity**
1830	and the seers hath he covered **because of your iniquities**
BMc	and the seers hath he covered **because of your iniquity**
KJV	the seers hath he covered
JST	and the seers hath he covered **because of your iniquities**

The printer's manuscript and all Book of Mormon editions from 1837 on have *iniquity*. Only the 1830 edition has the plural *iniquities*.

It is not surprising that Joseph Smith viewed the Book of Mormon as an inspired text and thus felt free to use the Book of Mormon in altering the biblical text for Isaiah. But apparently he did not realize the extent to which his copy text, the 1830 edition, contained textual errors; as a consequence, these errors were carried over into the JST. This transmission of textual errors, as well as the specific use of the 1830 edition, was first discovered by Don Bradley, Scott Grover, and Keith Clayton, three students in my 1994 class on textual criticism of the Book of Mormon.[19] The most striking examples of errors being transmitted come from the Wilford Wood fragment for 2 Nephi 7, where Oliver Cowdery accidentally introduced a number of changes into the printer's manuscript:

2 Nephi 7:2, 4, 5 // Isaiah 50:2, 4, 5

> BM* I make **the** rivers a wilderness **and** their fish **to stink**
> 1830 I make **their** rivers a wilderness **and** their fish **to stink**
> BMc I make **their** rivers a wilderness **and** their fish **to stink**
> KJV I make **the** rivers a wilderness their fish **stinketh**
> JST I make **their** rivers a wilderness **and** their fish **to stink**

> BM* he **wakeneth** morning by morning he **wakeneth** mine
> 1830 he **waketh** morning by morning he **waketh** mine
> BMc he **waketh** morning by morning he **waketh** mine
> KJV he **wakeneth** morning by morning he **wakeneth** mine
> JST he **waketh** morning by morning he **waketh** mine

> BM* ear the Lord God hath **opened** mine **ear**
> 1830 ear the Lord God hath **appointed** mine **ear**
> BMc ear the Lord God hath **opened** mine **ear**
> KJV ear the Lord GOD hath **opened** mine **ear**
> JST ear the Lord God hath **appointed** mine **ears**

Textual errors such as *their* for *the* (in verse 2), *waketh* for *wakeneth* (two times in verse 4), and *appointed* for *opened* (in verse 5) were copied over into the JST.

Conclusion

This brief summary of work on the Isaiah quotations in the Book of Mormon shows how complex the whole subject can be. Not only does textual criticism provide insight into possible changes in the Book of Mormon text, but it can also help us see how the text was revealed to the Prophet Joseph Smith and then transmitted and preserved in printed editions down to our own time. The changes in the text are minor and not too frequent—and they never prevent us from understanding the spiritual message of the Book of Mormon.

Notes

1. Joseph Smith Jr., *The Holy Scriptures, Inspired Version, Containing the Old and New Testaments: An Inspired Revision of the Authorized Edition* (Independence, Missouri: Herald House, Reorganized Church of Jesus Christ of Latter Day Saints, 1974).

2. David Daniell, *Tyndale's New Testament* (New Haven: Yale University Press, 1989), vii–xiv.

3. F. F. Bruce, *The English Bible: A History of Translations from the earliest English Versions to the New English Bible* (New York: Oxford English Press, 1970), 86–92.

4. Daniell, *Tyndale's New Testament*, vii–xiv.

5. Jon Nielson, "Authorship of the King James Version of The Bible" (master's thesis, Brigham Young University, 1994), 93.

6. Andrew Stewart, "KJV as a Source for the Biblical Quotations in the Book of Mormon" (unpublished research paper for Royal Skousen's course on textual criticism of the Book of Mormon, Brigham Young University, 1991), 1.

7. Stewart, "KJV as a Source," 5–6.

8. Stan Larson, "The Historicity of the Matthean Sermon on the Mount in 3 Nephi," in *New Approaches to the Book of Mormon: Explorations in Critical Methodology,* ed. Brent Lee Metcalfe, 115–63 (Salt Lake City: Signature Books, 1993), 116.

9. Royal Skousen, "Towards a Critical Edition of the Book of Mormon," *BYU Studies* 30/1 (1990): 51–2, 55.

10. M. H. Black, "The Printed Bible," in *The Cambridge History of the Bible: The West from the Reformation to the Present Day,* ed. S. L. Greenslade (Cambridge: Cambridge University Press, 1963), 419.

11. For color and ultraviolet black-and-white photographs of this fragment, see Skousen, "Piecing Together the Original Manuscript," *BYU Today* 46/3 (1992): 22.

12. Larson, "Historicity," 129–30.

13. Ibid., 130–1.

14. Royal Skousen, "Critical Methodology and the Text of the Book of Mormon," *Review of Books on the Book of Mormon* 6/1 (1994): 127–8.

15. William Calhoun, "Isaiah, Italics, and the Book of Mormon"; Margaret Robbins, "King James Version as a Source for the Biblical Passages Quoted in the Book of Mormon" (unpublished research papers for Royal Skousen's course on textual criticism of the Book of Mormon, Brigham Young University, 1991).

16. Larson, "Historicity," 129–30.

17. For examples, see Skousen, "Translating the Book of Mormon: Evidence from the Original Manuscript," in *Book of Mormon Authorship Revisited: The Evidence for Ancient Origins,* ed. Noel B. Reynolds (Provo: FARMS, 1997), 61–93.

18. For a summary of how often Joseph Smith used the Book of Mormon in his revision of Isaiah in the JST, see Richard P. Howard, *Restoration Scriptures: A Study of Their Textual Development,* 2nd ed. (Independence, Missouri: Herald House, 1995), 102–3, 106.

19. Don Bradley and Scott Grover, "Textual Fingerprinting: Examining Joseph Smith's Use of the Book of Mormon in His 'New Translation' of the Bible"; Keith Clayton, "Translation, Transmission, and Transcription: The Book of Mormon Isaiah Variants and the JST" (unpublished research papers for Royal Skousen's course on textual criticism of the Book of Mormon, Brigham Young University, 1994).

Isaiah in America, 1700–1830

Andrew H. Hedges

Although commentators and ministers in America made use of all parts of the Bible, they did not cite Isaiah as extensively or in the same ways as did the writers of the Book of Mormon.

The Nephite record in the Book of Mormon provides great knowledge about Isaiah and his messages. This chapter discusses the use of Isaiah in the Book of Mormon as compared with eighteenth- and early-nineteenth-century American use and understanding of the writings of this biblical prophet. Many of the early ministers and theologians clearly loved the Bible and succeeded in some ways in both understanding and living its teachings, but the book of Isaiah was perhaps still quite difficult for them to understand. The Prophet Joseph's translation of the ancient Nephite record was a unique, valuable, and timely resource for understanding the gospel in general and Isaiah's teachings in particular. In the record, several prophets, and even Christ himself, quote Isaiah extensively and give lengthy and detailed discussions of this ancient prophet's writings. The publication of the Book of Mormon in early-nineteenth-century America thus provided a wealth of insight into Isaiah's message.

Knowing how the Bible as a whole was used in America during the first decades of the 1800s and in earlier centuries provides a better understanding of how the book of Isaiah was used by ministers in Joseph Smith's time. Although early America was home to a number of Christian denominations, most seventeenth- and eighteenth-century Americans, especially those living in the North, were heirs to the early Puritan emphasis on the Old Testament. The Puritans were devout Christians, some of whom settled New England in the 1600s in hopes of reestablishing the "covenant society" that existed between God and the ancient Israelites. With such an agenda, the Puritans looked to the Old Testament for insights on the workings of the ancient covenant, as well as for the laws upon which they based their society; indeed, many of the Massachusetts Bay Colony's early laws were quoted directly from the legal sections of the books of Exodus and Leviticus. These laws prohibited many of the same practices that were prohibited in the Old Testament and prescribed some of the same punishments for transgressing laws that the Lord delivered to Israel through Moses.[1] The emphasis on the legalism of the Old Testament slowly subsided during the colonial period because the founding Puritans' vision failed to reproduce itself in succeeding generations, but as more people arrived in America from various parts of Europe, the larger Old Testament idea of America as a "covenant" nation lived on, and subsequent generations of American colonists, in true Puritan fashion, persisted in looking to the Old Testament to help them explain, interpret, and understand everything from natural disasters to military setbacks in terms of this covenant.[2]

As tensions mounted between the American colonies and England in the late 1700s, Americans continued to view the stories comprising Israel's epic history as types for their own experiences.[3] Many preachers and ministers of the period found the parallels between the Americans' plight under British rule and that of the ancient Israelites under Egyptian rule so compelling that they explicitly identified the colonies' cause against the king of England with captive Israel's cause against the pharaoh of Egypt.[4] This identification became so complete and pervasive in American society during the Revolutionary era that many civic leaders promoted it. The patriot and dignitary Benjamin Franklin, for example, suggested that the national seal be adorned with the image of Moses leading the Israelites to safety through the midst of the Red Sea; Thomas Jefferson proposed for this same seal a picture of Israel being led through the wilderness by pillars of cloud and fire.[5]

Old Testament themes continued to permeate American culture for half a century after the Revolution—so much so that according to one historian, scholars "have as much difficulty taking cognizance of [them] as of the air the people breathed."[6] At the same time, however, because the threat from Indians and foreign nations was subsiding, American clergymen were able to turn their attention away from the idea of a national covenant relationship—which was in their eyes clearly being fulfilled—and focus their energies on an aspect of the new nation's religious life that most felt needed much improvement and that did not seem to be taking care of itself—that is, on individual spirituality and conversion. This was not the first time in America's history that large numbers of preachers and laymen became concerned with their own and others' spirituality. Because of the efforts of such theologians as Jonathan Edwards and itinerant preachers like George Whitefield, America underwent a series of religious revivals in the late 1730s and early 1740s known as the First Great Awakening, in which large numbers of people recommitted themselves to religion. Although widespread and emotional, the First Great Awakening was much shorter than the Second Great Awakening, which lasted for the first half of the nineteenth century.[7] Ministers and laymen of this period in a sense rediscovered the New Testament and all its treasures; religions that had formerly focused mainly on the Old Testament now turned to the four Gospels and to Paul's letters. The new orientation was drastic enough that some well-established conservatives accused members of the rising generation of preachers, like Alexander Campbell, of "throwing away the Old Testament."[8] Although the Old Testament was far from forgotten in American culture during this time, churchgoers heard much less of it during the 1820s, the period when Joseph Smith was translating the plates, than had their parents and grandparents.[9]

How was the book of Isaiah used throughout all this religious excitement? Surprisingly enough, despite its own emphases on Israel's covenant with God and the importance of living the spirit of the law, the book of Isaiah played a relatively humble role in early America's religious history. Ministers quoted it far less frequently than they quoted other biblical texts. Clerics of the 1600s and 1700s who were concerned about the developing nation's covenant relationship with God found the stories of Abraham, Jacob, Noah, and Moses better suited to their needs and tastes than the prophecies contained in the prophetic books.[10] This trend continued into the 1800s, when preachers who quoted the Old Testament—notwithstanding the renewed interest in conversion and Christ's teachings—quoted more from these grand narratives than from other portions of the Bible, such as Isaiah.[11] Parley P. Pratt, who as a boy attended Baptist, Presbyterian, and Methodist meetings in New York during the early 1800s, began his study of the scriptures by reading lessons on Joseph in Egypt, Saul, Samuel, and David.[12] With all the religious instruction Pratt received, however, and despite this future apostle's interest in religious matters and his insatiable appetite for reading, he was twenty-three years old before he delved into the Old Testament prophets—something he was apparently forced to do on his own. It was an exercise that left him "astonished," he wrote, "at the darkness of myself and mankind on these subjects."[13]

Although their use was not widespread, the Old Testament prophets, and specifically Isaiah, were used by early American clergy. Ministers of the colonial and early national periods used Isaiah and other books of both the Old and New Testaments in two rather similar ways. Ministers often used several verses from a book of scripture as the text of their sermons, essentially as an introduction to the topic they wished to address. These topics included everything from national politics to the dynamics of conversion. Ministers also frequently quoted a passage of scripture, or several passages from a number of different books in the Bible, to illustrate a particular point. While virtually all sermons included these so-called demonstrations to some degree, theologians like Jonathan Edwards were frequently embroiled in theological controversies and dug deeper into gospel principles than most, pulling references from virtually every book in the Bible as they sought to clarify their points and to silence the opposition. Just as the sermons covered a wide variety of subjects, so the theological treatises addressed all of Christianity's big questions, including topics still being debated today: ethics, virtue, the need for baptism, and the requirements for conversion.

While it was quoted less frequently at that time than other books in the Bible, Isaiah was nevertheless quoted and discussed by ministers and theologians alike in early America on some occasions. It is clear, however, that these churchmen were more concerned with establishing and maintaining positions on contemporary religious issues than they were with understanding the issues that weighed heavily on Isaiah's mind, for despite extensive coverage of virtually every subject of concern to Americans, no one ever systematically developed and consolidated the themes of Isaiah's writings. Ministers found Isaiah's messianic prophecies most valuable as they discussed such subjects as the nature of Christ and real humility. And some, notably a number of early missionaries to the Indians, made tentative suggestions about how the colonists' efforts to convert the Indians—identified as members of the lost tribes of Israel by some and as Gentiles by others—fit into the historical scheme outlined by Isaiah.[14] But these early ministers and missionaries often based their ideas about Christ and the restoration of Israel on their reading of a very few, almost standard verses, and they made no attempt to look at the book as a whole or to integrate these and the book's other themes so that "both Jew and Gentile," "black and white, bond and free, male and female, and . . . the heathen" (2 Nephi 26:33) could understand their respective roles in history and the nature and extent of the salvation that is offered them through the atonement of Christ.

Jonathan Edwards, perhaps the most famous of all the colonial theologians and author of scores of discourses, quoted Isaiah extensively in his discourse "Concerning the End for Which God Created the World," in which he argued that the ultimate purpose of the creation of the world is to glorify God. Edwards quoted many of the same Isaiah passages that the Nephite prophets found remarkable and useful, including verses from Isaiah 48 and 49. True to form, however, Edwards used these verses out of the context in which the prophet wrote them and simply used them, along with numerous passages from other books of scripture, to back up his ideas about the purpose of the creation.[15] Such a method leaves readers well versed in scriptural passages that attest that the Lord created this earth for a purpose but leaves them completely uninformed about the full message of Isaiah. In stark contrast to this approach, the prophet Nephi reads Isaiah 48 and 49 (see 1 Nephi 20–21) to his brothers before contextualizing and clarifying the full range of significance, "both temporal and spiritual," that these scriptures hold for "all the kindreds of the earth" (1 Nephi 22:3, 9).

George Whitefield, one of Edwards' contemporaries who was as influential as Edwards, also used passages from Isaiah, especially as texts for his famous sermons. For example, Whitefield turned to Isaiah 54:5 and 48:10 to introduce masterful sermons on what it means to have Jesus Christ as a "husband" and to be "chosen . . . in the furnace of affliction," but Whitefield went no further with Isaiah's overall message than to summarize briefly the surrounding verses in an attempt to familiarize his listeners with Israel's predicament at Isaiah's time.[16] Again, such use of these Isaiah verses, however well it may have awakened some of the more irreligious people in colonial America to a sense of their religious duties, contrasts sharply with how the same verses are used in the Book of Mormon. During his visit to the Nephites, Christ closes his sweeping discussion of the fulness of the Gentiles, the coming forth of the Book of Mormon, and the restoration of Israel by quoting Isaiah 54 (see 3 Nephi 22), which addresses these themes. Nephi finds many of the same themes in Isaiah 48, which he quotes to his brothers in an effort to "more fully persuade them to believe in the Lord their Redeemer" (1 Nephi 19:23).

The sermons and writings of these and other colonial clergymen influenced later generations of Americans, and their style of using Isaiah in particular and the scriptures in general continued into the nineteenth century.[17] Nowhere is this more apparent than in the works of Charles Grandison Finney, one of the Prophet Joseph's most famous contemporaries and a fellow upstate New Yorker. Like his predecessors and most other nineteenth-century ministers, Finney studied and preached from all parts of the Bible, especially the New Testament, to help sinners identify themselves, renounce their sins, and become Christians. For all his familiarity with the Bible, however, this popular revivalist and talented theologian limited his use of Isaiah almost solely to those portions that discuss the nature of Christ and the Holy Spirit.[18] Finney was much less concerned than Whitefield or even Edwards with placing the passages he used in their historical and scriptural contexts, and accordingly, the lessons Finney draws from the verses he used are much more narrow in scope than those drawn by the Nephite prophets, who also turned to Isaiah for insight on the Savior. For example, Finney's partial quotation of Isaiah 53 to prove only that Christ had a "human soul"[19] draws far less about Christ from this text than does the Nephite prophet Abinadi's treatment, which expounds the same chapter in what are some of the most beautiful and enlightening chapters in the Book of Mormon about the Savior and his relationship with his Heavenly Father (see Mosiah 14–15). Of course, in his interpretation of these and the other Isaiah passages he quoted, Finney was not wrong or misguided, but when one compares his use of the book with that of the Nephite prophets, one sees that the ancient prophets found Isaiah's message far more meaningful than did the modern minister.

The nineteenth-century minister who perhaps came the closest to using Isaiah to the same extent and to drawing similar conclusions as the Nephites was Ethan Smith, a contemporary of the Prophet Joseph and pastor of the Congregational Church in Poultney, Vermont. Using parallels between some Native American religious beliefs and certain Old Testament teachings as his guide, Smith argued that the American Indians were nothing less than the lost ten tribes. Smith drew heavily on Old and New Testament sources, including Isaiah, to show that the gospel would be completely restored to these tribes, as was foretold in the scriptures. He then turned to Isaiah 18 for evidence that this restoration was to take place through the people of the United States of America.[20] Despite his insight, however, Smith used Isaiah and other texts to promote his own agenda rather than to illuminate the fine points of Isaiah's teachings.

Virtually every minister who turned to the book of Isaiah in the seventeenth, eighteenth, and early nineteenth centuries—with the notable exception of Joseph Smith, as Ann Madsen has shown[21]—used it as the text of a sermon or to illustrate a particular point. But despite the emphasis early Americans placed on reading the Bible, they used Isaiah almost exclusively as a good quote book. The Nephites, on the other hand, who quoted Isaiah extensively and who took time to develop fully his teachings about Christ, the Lord's covenants with his people, and the future restoration of Israel, used it as a primary source for learning about the history of what the Lord had done for the salvation and redemption of mankind.

The only people in early America who made any real attempt to understand Isaiah as a whole were the biblical commentators of the time, most of whom, like their counterparts today, systematically examined the contents of every chapter and book in the Bible and provided readers with their findings. Two biblical commentaries commonly used by American ministers, scholars, and churchgoers in the 1830s were the multivolume sets by Thomas Scott and Adam Clarke. Both works are masterpieces of scholarship. Clarke used several Hebrew, Greek, Latin, and Syriac versions of various passages of scripture and other manuscripts in order to clarify many scriptural passages, and both authors, in their attempts to present the most up-to-date interpretation possible of the scriptures' true meaning, drew on the insights of earlier commentators and ministers. Both tackled Isaiah with gusto, and serious students of the Bible no doubt found their discussions of various topics as helpful as we find good commentaries today. By their own admittance, however (see below), portions of Isaiah remained shrouded in mystery and obscurity for these commentators—portions which, interestingly enough, are highly developed in the Book of Mormon.

Both these scholars—especially Scott, who was much more concerned with historical interpretation than was Clarke—understood some of the concepts and verses that the Nephite prophets found particularly noteworthy. For example, the restoration of the Jews in the last days is one of the most important ideas in Isaiah. Scott argued that such phrases as "the branch of the Lord" and "them that are escaped of Israel" (Isaiah 4:2) specifically "point at the conversion of the Jews in the latter times of the world."[22] He believed that the restoration of which Isaiah speaks is to be a literal one.[23] How and through whom this restoration was to be effected, however, was unclear to Scott, who made it clear to his readers that his commentary was in no way an attempt "to *prophesy* from the *prophecies*."[24] Scott found enough evidence in Isaiah 14:1–2 and 49:24–26 to suggest that Israel's restoration would follow the destruction of Rome and the Catholic Church,[25] but he cautioned his readers "not [to] judge of what [he] said upon these obscure subjects, as so many positive assertions, but only as probable conjectures."[26]

The Nephite prophets, on the other hand, who had themselves "escaped of Israel," saw Isaiah 14 and the restoration of the Jews in an entirely different light. Blessed with several resources Scott did not have—personal familiarity with Jewish prophecy, the authority to expound revelation under inspiration of the Holy Ghost, prophecies about the patriarch Joseph's descendants, and a visit by Christ himself—the writers of the Book of Mormon understood that those who had fled Jerusalem would become Isaiah's branch (see 2 Nephi 3:4–5), and through the fulness of the gospel that would be restored to the Gentiles, their writings would be instrumental in bringing the house of Israel to a knowledge of the Savior (see 1 Nephi 13:34–35; 19:18–19; 2 Nephi 3:12; 3 Nephi 16:4). The workings of this restoration are discussed throughout the Book of Mormon: Nephi, using Isaiah as his guide, presents the whole plan in the first two books of that ancient record, and prophets like Lehi, Enos, Mormon, and Christ himself flesh out the details. Not only is the finished product a much clearer explanation of how "the Lord will set his hand again the second time to restore his people" (2 Nephi 25:17) than Scott and other commentators—who were entirely unaware of ancient America's prophets, their origins, and their faith—could have hoped for, but it is also an explanation that involves far more historical figures than early commentators ever imagined.

Nineteenth-century American biblical commentators also saw much less in Isaiah 29 than did the prophet Nephi. Both Scott and Clarke found this chapter to be largely a generalized account of the various destructions awaiting Jerusalem and the Jews. They viewed the sieges foretold in verse 3 as refering in turn to the Assyrians, Babylonians, and Romans;[27] the "speech . . . low out of the dust" (verse 4) as the Jews' "timid and servile intreaties, and doleful complaints" to their "haughty conquerors";[28] the sealed book's "vision of all" (verse 11) and its deliverance to both the learned and the unlearned as describing the Jews' inability to understand their own prophecies, which lack of knowledge led them to crucify "their promised and long expected Messiah";[29] and the "marvellous work and a wonder" (verse 14) as the Lord's leaving the shortsighted Jews "to their ruin."[30] Except for the last few verses in Isaiah 29, which promise that "they . . . that erred in spirit shall come to understanding," (verse 24) this whole chapter, according to Scott and Clarke, is little more than a detailed pronouncement of woe upon the Lord's ancient covenant people.[31]

How different in both content and tone are such commentaries from the prophet Nephi's writings on this chapter. For Nephi, this revelation is a vision of hope for Jews and Gentiles alike, describing the coming forth of the Book of Mormon, its early reception among the Gentiles, and its utility in righting the wrongs of generations (see 2 Nephi 26–27). A commonly held belief in America during the 1800s, and one that these commentators apparently endorsed, was that, in the words of the Reverend Leonard Woods, "no command or promise, either of the Old Testament or the New, was particularly addressed by the writers to any individual now living."[32] Scott and his colleagues thus believed that the references to individuals in Isaiah 29 foretold events that had been fulfilled long before the early nineteenth century. Nephi, however, who was familiar with "the manner of prophesying among the Jews" (2 Nephi 25:1), saw through inspiration that this chapter described the momentous sequence of dialogues that was to take place between three individuals of the early nineteenth century: Joseph Smith, Martin Harris, and Charles Anthon.

Although the commentators of Joseph Smith's time seem to have addressed more of Isaiah's themes than did those who confined themselves to writing sermons and theological treatises, it is clear that neither group used the ancient prophet's writings as extensively as they are used in the Book of Mormon. Neither did any early Americans use Isaiah's words with the same interpretive slant that we find in the Nephite record. This is not to suggest, of course, that we have all the answers; many Latter-day Saints would probably agree with Scott that despite the "elegance and sublimity of [Isaiah's] style and imagery, . . . [and] the profoundness of his thoughts, . . . the Lord seems purposefully to cast an obscurity on [his writings], as a trial of our humility."[33] It does suggest, however, that the Latter-day Saints have, among other insights in the Book of Mormon, a wonderful and unique commentary on a biblical book that few people over the centuries seem to have appreciated or fully understood. That we will employ this resource in our study of Isaiah and the gospel is my humble prayer.

Notes

1. See, for example, *Abstract of the Lawes of New England as They Are Now Established* (London: Coules and Ley, 1641), reprinted in Peter Force, comp., *Tracts and Other Papers Relating Principally to the Origin, Settlement, and Progress of the Colonies in North America, from the Discovery of the Country to the Year 1776*, vol. 3 (Gloucester: Peter Smith, 1947). One early minister suggested that New Englanders do away with kings, governors, and magistrates altogether in an effort to pattern their government after that given in the Pentateuch (see John Eliot, *The Christian Commonwealth: or, The Civil Policy of the Rising Kingdom of Jesus Christ* [London: Livewell Chapman, 1660], reprinted in *Collections of the Massachusetts Historical Society*, 3rd ser., 9 (1846): 127–64.

2. Perry Miller, "The Old Testament in Colonial America," in *Historical Viewpoints*, ed. John A Garraty (New York: Harper and Row, 1970), 1:96–9; Richard L. Bushman, *From Puritan to Yankee: Character and the Social Order in Connecticut, 1690–1765* (New York: Norton, 1967). For examples of sermons preached on natural and military disasters, see Samuel Davies, *Sermons on Important Subjects* (New York: J. and J. Harper, 1828), 3:132–44, 160–73.

3. Mark A. Noll, "The Image of the United States as a Biblical Nation," in *The Bible in America: Essays in Cultural History*, ed. Nathan O. Hatch and Mark A. Noll (New York: Oxford University Press, 1982), 43.

4. Ibid., 40–4

5. Ibid., 40.

6. Miller, "The Old Testament," 95.

7. The Second Great Awakening was nowhere more intense than in upstate New York in the 1820s, where Methodists and Presbyterians held so many revival meetings that ministers began to refer to that region as the "burned-over district."

8. Ibid., 100.

9. Ibid., 95–6, 99–101.

10. Ibid., 98.

11. Noll, "The Image of the United States," 44–5.

12. Parley P. Pratt, ed., *Autobiography of Parley P. Pratt* (Salt Lake City: Deseret Book, 1985), 1–2.

13. Ibid., 14.

14. For examples, see, "Tracts Relating to the Attempts to Convert to Christianity the Indians of New England," in *Collections of the Massachusetts Historical Society*, 3rd ser., 4 (1834): 25, 29, 72–4, 119–20, 155–7, 197; Daniel Gookin, "Historical Collections of the Indians in New England [1674]," in *Collections of the Massachusetts Historical Society*, 1st ser., 1 (1859): 141, 143–6, 154, 160, 223; and Ethan Smith, *View of the Hebrews; or The Tribes of Israel in America* (Poultney, Vt.: Smith and Shute, 1825), republished as Charles D. Tate Jr., ed., *View of the Hebrews by Ethan Smith* (Provo, Utah: BYU Religious Studies Center, 1996). I am indebted to both Kent Jackson and John Welch for directing me to Smith's work.

15. Jonathan Edwards, *Ethical Writings*, vol. 8 of *The Works of Jonathan Edwards*, ed. John E. Smith (New Haven: Yale University Press, 1989), 475–502.

16. George Whitefield, *Sermons on Important Subjects* (London: Thomas Tegg, 1829), 151–3, 687–8.

17. Leonard Woods, *Lectures on the Inspiration of the Scriptures* (Andover, Mass.: Mark Newman, 1829), 49. Many of the sermons and writings of such influential men as Edwards, Whitefield, and Samuel Davies were common fare for early-nineteenth-century preachers, revivalists, and laymen. Major works of all three of these men were published or republished during Joseph Smith's lifetime. For example, Davies, one-time president of Andover Col-

lege, was author of sermons so popular with Americans that they
went through at least four editions.

18. Charles Finney, *The Heart of Truth: Finney's Lectures on Theology* (Minneapolis: Bethany, 1976), 137, 139–40, 142–4, 148.

19. Ibid., 139.

20. Smith, *View of the Hebrews.* A number of anti-Mormon
writers have suggested that Joseph Smith borrowed heavily from
Ethan Smith's work when he "wrote" the Book of Mormon. For a
summary of their arguments and Mormon refutations, see Tate,
View of the Hebrews by Ethan Smith, vii–xxii.

21. See Ann Madsen, "Joseph Smith and the Words of Isaiah,"
in this volume.

22. Thomas Scott, *The Holy Bible . . . Containing the Old and
New Testaments: With Original Notes, Practical Observations, and
Copious Marginal References* (Philadelphia: William W. Woodward,
1826), 3:95–6.

23. Ibid., 3:128.

24. Ibid.

25. Ibid., 3:134, 254.

26. Ibid., 3:81.

27. Ibid., 3:178.

28. Ibid.

29. Ibid., 3:179.

30. Ibid., 3:180.

31. Ibid., 3:178–81; Adam Clarke, *The Holy Bible . . . Containing the Old and New Testaments: With a Commentary and Critical Notes*
(New York: J. Emory and B. Waugh, 1831), 3:774–7.

32. Woods, *Lectures*, 56.

33. Scott, *The Holy Bible . . . with Original Notes*, 3:81.

PART FOUR

Words Ancient and Modern

Notes on Vocabulary
in Isaiah 2–11, 13–14, 29, 48–54

Donald W. Parry and Janet L. Garrard Willis

This glossary explains the archaic or perhaps unfamiliar English words or usages found in the English translation of the Isaiah texts in the Book of Mormon.

Isaiah 2

2   *mountain of the Lord's house* = the temple
4   *plowshares* = blades for plows
    pruninghooks = blades on long handles used for pruning
        trees
6   *be replenished from the east* = take wisdom from apostate
        religious systems from the East
    soothsayers = persons who attempt to predict the future
    please themselves = shake hands with, make a covenant with
9   *mean man* = a common man
11 *haughtiness* = pride
15 *fenced wall* = a wall around a city
16 *Tarshish* = place unknown, "ships of Tarshish" may rep-
        resent wealth and economic prosperity
18 *abolish* = destroy
20 *moles* = blind rodents that live underground
21 *clefts of the rocks* = crevices or caves
22 *cease ye from man* = stop depending on mortal man
    wherein is he to be accounted of? = how much is he worth?

Isaiah 3

1   *the stay* = HEB: the protector
    the staff = HEB: support, walking stick
    the whole stay of bread and the whole stay of water = in con-
        text probably refers to the whole quantity of physical
        support, as well as spiritual support

whole stay of bread and whole stay of water = (?) in context,
    probably refers to the whole quantity of physical
    support, as well as the spiritual support mentioned
    earlier in the verse.
2 *prudent* = wise
    ancient = elderly
3 *captain of fifty* = military commander
    cunning artificer = skilled craftsman
    eloquent orator = person gifted with public speaking
        ability
5 *proudly* = disrespectfully
    base = vile, vulgar
9 *shew of their countenance* = the look on their face
10 *eat the fruit of their doings* = enjoy the consequences of
        their righteous living
11 *the reward of his hands shall be given him* = he will suffer
        the consequences of his actions
14 *spoil of the poor* = property taken from the poor
16 *wanton* = flirtatious, seductive
    mincing = taking short rapid steps (to make their ankle
        jewelry tinkle)
17 *discover their secret parts* = expose them, put them to
        shame
18 *cauls* = HEB: headbands
    round tires = jewelry or ornaments shaped like a crescent
        moon
    mufflers = HEB: veils
19 *mufflers* = HEB: veils
22 *mantles* = loose, sleeveless piece of clothing worn over
        hair and other clothes
    wimples = cloaks
    crisping pins = purses
23 *glasses* = see-through garments
    vails = shawls
24 *rent* = a torn rag (Alma 46 also uses this word to mean a
        torn piece of cloth)
    stomacher = a robe

sackcloth = coarse cloth

burning = branding (a mark of slavery)

26 *lament* = cry or mourn

desolate = empty or cleaned out; specifically a reference to Jerusalem

Isaiah 4

1 *reproach* = disgrace, stigma of being unmarried and childless

2 *branch of the Lord* = the Lord's people

5 *cloud and smoke by day* = elements connected with the presence of God

shining of flaming fire by night = presence of God

defence = protection

6 *tabernacle* = in historical context, a holy yet temporary place of shelter, often a tent

covert = shelter

Isaiah 5

2 *fenced it* = put a wall around

winepress = machine used to press grapes into wine

3 *betwixt* = between

5 *eaten up* = animals will graze on it

trodden down = trampled

6 *digged* = hoed or weeded

briers = thorny plants

7 *judgment* = justice

a cry = a cry of distress

8 *join house to house* = to want and to steal other people's property (Micah 2:2) or to obtain property through legal but unethical means

10 *bath* = Hebrew unit for measuring liquid

homer = Hebrew unit of capacity; about 11.5 bushels or 100 gallons

ephah = Hebrew unit for measuring dry goods; just over a bushel

12 *viol* = lyre
    tabret = tambourine
    pipe = a flute
13 *famished* = starving
14 *pomp* = extravagance, noise, uproar
17 *waste places* = ruins
    strangers = foreigners
18 *draw iniquity with cords of vanity* = are too proud to cut
        themselves loose from their sins
    draw . . . sin as it were with a cart rope = pull around large
        burdens of sin as animals pull a loaded cart (com-
        pare 2 Nephi 28:22, awful chains)
19 *counsel* = advice
23 *justify the wicked for reward* = acquit the guilty man for a
        bribe
    take away the righteousness of the righteous = take away the
        good man's legal rights, cheat him
24 *fire devoureth the stubble* = fire destroys the wicked as if
        they were dry stalks left over after the harvest
    chaff = the worthless material left over after harvesting
        wheat
25 *carcases* = dead bodies; variation of carcasses
26 *ensign* = a banner, a flag
    hiss = whistle
27 *girdle of their loins* = HEB: waistcloth
    latchet of their shoes = shoe fastener
28 *bows bent* = bows strung and ready
    hoofs . . . like flint = hard hooves
    wheels like a whirlwind = wheels spinning around like a
        tornado

Isaiah 6

1   *train* = the hem or skirt of his garment
2   *seraphims* = angelic beings that serve in Jehovah's heav-
        enly court
    twain = two

4 *posts of the door moved* = HEB: foundations of the thresh-
    olds trembled
5 *undone* = HEB: cut off; become overwhelmed with the
    immensity of one's personal sins
  purged = removed through washing
10 *make the heart of this people fat* = harden their hearts
13 *teil tree* = linden tree; tree of fine, white grain
  substance = stump

Isaiah 7

2 *confederate* = united in league with
  Ephraim = here this refers to all of the northern Israel
3 *conduit* = canal or tunnel
  in the highway of the fuller's field = by way of the launderer's
    field near the stream below the pool of Siloam
4 *tails of these smoking firebrands* = the two kings have little
    fire left; smoldering stumps of firebrands (smolder-
    ing wood)
6 *vex* = disturb
  breach = make a hole in by continual attacks
8 *threescore and five years* = 65 years
12 *tempt* = test or try
14 *virgin* = pure young woman
16 *abhorrest* = hate
18 *hiss for the fly* = whistle up a tormentor; that is, signal the
    opposing forces
20 *shave with a razor that is hired* = the land will be depopu-
    lated by a foreign invader
21 *nourish a young cow, and two sheep* = only a few self-
    sustaining survivors will remain
23 *silverlings* = small piece of silver
25 *mattock* = a tool used for chopping and digging, a hoe

Isaiah 8

1 *Maher-shalal-hash-baz* = Isaiah's son, whose name means
  "speedy-spoil-quick-booty"

3   *the prophetess* = Isaiah's wife
4   *spoil* = riches taken in war, booty
6   *waters of Shiloah* = a spring of water in Jerusalem which
        symbolizes Jesus Christ
    Rezin and Remaliah's son = the kings of Syria and Israel,
        who are united against Judah
9   *associate yourselves* = form alliances
    gird yourselves = arm yourselves, prepare for war
10 *nought* = nothing; variation of naught
11 *with a strong hand* = with power
13 *let him be your fear* = be reverent and humble before God
14 *sanctuary* = temple
    stone of stumbling, rock of offence = dismay and suffering
        for unbelievers
    gin = trap
    snare = trap
16 *bind up the testimony* = tie the scroll and seal it with wax
18 *are for signs* = their names are symbolic; his sons' names
        mean "God is with us" (Immanuel), "speedy-spoil-
        quick-booty" (Maher-shalal-hash-baz) and "a remnant
        shall return" (Shear-jashub)
19 *them that have familiar spirits* = sorcerers who commune
        with the dead
    wizards that peep and mutter = sorcerers
    for the living to the dead = for the living on behalf of the
        dead
20 *law* = scripture
    testimony = value of the scripture
21 *hardly bestead* = hard pressed, beset by troubles or ene-
        mies, in a plight
    fret = worry

Isaiah 9

1   *vexation* = trouble, or period of distress
2   *darkness* = apostasy and captivity
    great light = Christ

they that dwell in the land of the shadow of death = those who have disbelieved

4   *yoke of his burden* = weight of his troubles
    staff of his shoulder = taskmaster's staff used to smite slaves—a symbol of oppression
    rod of his oppressor = bondage

7   *zeal* = impassioned eagerness

8   *lighted upon* = come to, fallen on

10 *hewn stones* = stones shaped with a tool
    sycomores = fig trees
    cedars = generally denotes cedar trees of Lebanon

12 *before* = in the east
    behind = in the west

14 *rush* = stiff, grass-like plant

17 *hypocrite* = someone who claims to believe a certain set of beliefs, but does not follow them
    folly = foolishness

18 *thickets* = dense groups of shrubs, small trees, or brush

Isaiah 10

1   *grievousness* = oppressive decrees

3   *day of visitation* = day of judgment

5   *indignation* = extreme anger

6   *tread* = to stomp or walk upon
    mire = filth or refuse or deep mud

10 *idols* = object of worship
    graven images = artistic representation of an animate creature, such as a painting or statue

13 *prudent* = wise, having good judgment
    bounds = boundaries, frontiers

16 *fat ones* = those with abundance

18 *standardbearer* = a person that carries a banner; frequently the banner is political in nature and carried during warfare

20 *remnant* = portion that remains
    smote = struck

stay upon = remain faithful to

22 *consumption* = destruction

26 *scourge* = a devastating disease or event

27 *anointing* = refers to the coming of the Savior; HEB: oil

33 *lop the bough* = cut off large branches of a tree that may be fit for use but are pruned so that the rest of the tree will be healthy

haughty = proud and overbearing

Isaiah 11

1 *rod* = new growth or shoot of a plant

3 *reprove* = correct others

4 *rod of his mouth* = his (just) word

5 *girdle* = innermost piece of clothing

reins = waist

8 *hole of the asp* = home of a poisonous snake

cockatrice = poisonous snake

10 *ensign* = banner, flag

13 *vex* = irritate or bother greatly

14 *fly upon* = come down on; attack the western slopes that were Philistine territory

spoil = plunder

15 *tongue of the Egyptian sea* = narrow strip of land extending into the Red Sea

seven streams = the Lord will split the river into seven parts

dryshod = without getting their shoes wet

Isaiah 13

3 *sanctified ones* = "sanctified ones" and "saints" are synonymously translated from either of two Hebrew words in the Old Testament

4 *tumultuous* = full of commotion or uproar

mustereth = gathers together, calls up for military duty

8 *a woman that travaileth* = a woman in childbirth

9 *wrath* = extreme anger

11 *arrogancy* = pride
   haughtiness of the terrible = HEB: pride of the tyrants or oppressors
12 *a man* = a mortal
14 *chased roe* = hunted deer
   sheep that no man taketh up = unshepherded, abandoned sheep
15 *thrust* = pierced or stabbed
16 *dashed* = smashed by hurling against something hard, destroyed
   spoiled = plundered
   ravished = raped, defiled
18 *fruit of the womb* = children
20 *make their fold* = enclose and tend sheep during the night
21 *doleful creature* = HEB: wild beasts that live in the desert
   satyrs = HEB: he-goats, or demons
22 *houses* = HEB: palaces, meaning the abandoned palaces of destroyed Babylon
   wild beasts of the islands = hyenas
   dragons = jackals or wild dogs

Isaiah 14

1 *strangers* = non-Israelites
   joined with = will be preached to, be converted
   cleave = join with
4 *proverb* = a satirical song
   golden = HEB: proud
5 *sceptre* = one of the symbols of a king's power
6 *a continual stroke* = constant blows
   hindereth = slows or stops
8 *fir* = HEB: cypress tree
   laid down = in death
   feller = tree cutter
11 *pomp* = vanity
   viols = fiddles or violin-like instruments
13 *sides of the north* = in the farthest north

16 *narrowly look upon thee* = HEB: squint at you
18 *his own house* = his family tomb
19 *an abominable branch* = a rejected branch
    raiment = clothing
    the stones of the pit = the very bottom
    trodden = walked upon
20 *renowned* = remembered by future generations
23 *bittern* = nocturnal wading bird, heron
    besom = broom
24 *purposed* = intended
27 *disannul* = cancel or destroy
29 *out of the serpent's root shall come forth a cockatrice* = from a
        less-poisonous or nonpoisonous snake will come a
        poisonous snake
    serpent's root = HEB: the bottom of a snake
        cockatrice = venomous snake
        (Or, from a less or nonpoisonous snake comes a poi-
        sonous snake)
30 *root* = posterity
31 *dissolved* = destroyed

Isaiah 29

1 *Ariel* = hearth of God or the temple; another name for
        Jerusalem
3 *camp against thee round about* = surround you
4 *thy speech shall whisper out of the dust* = your testimony
        will come to the living after you are dead (compare
        Moroni 10:27)
    familiar spirit = ghost
5 *chaff* = the worthless material left over after harvesting
        wheat
6 *tempest* = storm
7 *munition* = something that serves as a defense
    as a dream of a night vision = passing vision or dream
10 *closed your eyes* = given you spiritual blindness
13 *people draw near . . . removed their heart far from me* = the
        people claim to love God, but their actions show

that they do not
fear = regard or reverence for
14 *perish* = die out
prudent = wise
15 *seek deep* = try with much effort
works are in the dark = they hide their actions
16 *shall be esteemed . . . he had no understanding?* = their
works will testify of who made them
17 *esteemed* = valued, regarded
18 *the blind shall see out of obscurity* = will lose their spiritual
blindness
19 *meek* = humble before God
21 *snare* = trap
the gate = place of public transactions
a thing of nought = something that has no worth
22 *wax* = grow, become
23 *fear* = regard or reverence for
24 *erred* = made mistakes

Isaiah 48

2 *holy city* = Jerusalem, HEB: consecrated city
stay themselves = rely upon, HEB: are sustained by
3 *shewed* = showed, HEB: made them understand
4 *obstinate* = stubborn
thy neck is an iron sinew = you are stiff-necked or proud
brow brass = metaphor for pride
5 *molten image* = metal idol used for worship
graven image = carved idol
8 *treacherously* = unfaithfully, or in a dishonest manner
transgressor = HEB: apostate or rebel
9 *defer mine anger* = hold back or put off anger
10 *refined thee* = HEB: made [you] pure, purged you
furnace of affliction = purifying heat of trial
11 *polluted* = HEB: defiled, stained
13 *spanned* = stretched across the whole of, spread out
14 *do his pleasure* = Cyrus will do his desire, or wish

18 *then had thy peace been as a river* = HEB: your welfare or
   peace would have flowed and prospered
   thy righteousness as the waves of the sea = [implied] your
   righteousness would have been constant
19 *Thy seed also had been as the sand* = you would have had
   many descendants
   offspring of thy bowels = your descendants
20 *utter* = HEB: proclaim

Isaiah 49

2 *shaft* = body of an arrow
   quiver = container used for carrying arrows
4 *for nought* = for nothing, in vain
6 *give thee for a light to the Gentiles* = use you for an
   example or missionary to the foreigners
7 *abhorreth* = hate or despise
8 *inherit the desolate heritages* = built up that which has
   been wasted (compare Isaiah 61:4)
   an acceptable time = a favorable time
9 *feed in the ways* = sheep grazing along the way
   high places = barren hills
10 *smite* = strike, destroy
15 *sucking child* = a nursing baby
16 *walls* = HEB: walls of protection
   graven = carved, engraved
19 *swallowed thee up* = conquered you
20 *strait* = tight or narrow
25 *terrible* = HEB: tyrant, unrighteous leader

Isaiah 50

1 *bill* = HEB: scroll or evidence of
   iniquities = sins
2 *shortened* = impaired
   rebuke = HEB: chiding, reprimand
4 *in season* = at an appropriate time

6 *smiters* = HEB: strikers, people who hit
7 *confounded* = disgraced
8 *contend* = fight
9 *wax old* = grow old, decay
11 *kindle* = build, start
    compass yourselves about = are surrounded by

Isaiah 51

1 *Hearken* = hear and follow
   whence ye are hewn = from which you are cut
6 *vanish away* = HEB: be dispersed
   wax old = decay
   abolished = done away with, destroyed
7 *revilings* = insults
10 *ransomed* = HEB: redeemed or delivered
17 *dregs* = sediment remaining at the bottom of a cup of
      wine; last remaining, unwanted part of something

Isaiah 52

2 *arise, and sit down* = arise from the dust and sit down in
      dignity, being redeemed
   bands of thy neck = bonds, chains, or fetters used to re-
      strain a captive
4 *sojourn* = HEB: reside
7 *tidings* = news
   publisheth = HEB: makes heard
8 *bring again Zion* = HEB: return to Zion, or restore Zion
10 *made bare* = show strength
11 *unclean* = unholy
    vessels = HEB: instruments
12 *your rereward* = your rear guard, person guarding your
      back
13 *prudently* = wisely
    extolled = HEB: uplifted, glorified
14 *astonied* = astonished

visage = face, appearance

marred = HEB: disfigured

15 *so shall he sprinkle many nations* = so shall many nations marvel at him

Isaiah 53

2 *comeliness* = HEB: glory or beauty

3 *acquainted with grief* = familiar with grief

esteemed = HEB: valued

4 *borne* = HEB: carried

5 *chastisement of our peace* = punishment that brings us peace

stripes = wounds caused by a whip or similar object

7 *dumb* = silent

8 *declare his generation* = speak concerning his descendants

10 *pleased* = HEB: had a purpose for

11 *see of the travail of* = HEB: see the fruit of his pain

12 *intercession* = an act in behalf of

Isaiah 54

1 *barren* = women who cannot have children

travail with child = experience childbirth

2 *habitations* = homes

4 *confounded* = perplexed, confused

reproach = HEB: shame

6 *when thou wast refused* = HEB: because you were despised

9 *wroth* = angry

11 *stones* = HEB: building stones

12 *carbuncles* = red precious stones

16 *waster* = destroyer

Authorship of the Book of Isaiah in Light of the Book of Mormon

John W. Welch

*While questions remain about exactly when some Isaiah
passages were written or assembled, the Book of Mormon shows
that its Isaiah passages took their final form before 600 B.C.*

Over the years, biblical scholars have raised questions about the authorship of the book of Isaiah, often viewing it as a compilation of scripture written by more than one author. In the opinion of many text-critical scholars, the disputed chapters (mainly chapters 40–66) were written or edited after the time Lehi and Nephi left Jerusalem, after the Babylonian destruction and the resulting deportation of Judah to Babylon in the sixth century B.C.[1] Because most of Isaiah 48–54 is quoted in the Book of Mormon with specific attribution to the prophet Isaiah, biblical scholarship and the Book of Mormon diverge in this regard. Although many fundamentalist anti-Mormons do not raise this point as an issue against the Book of Mormon because they accept the literal integrity of the Bible and hence the single authorship of Isaiah, this discrepancy has been noted by several liberal critics of the Book of Mormon.[2] This chapter briefly outlines and documents the basic nature of the so-called Isaiah question regarding the Book of Mormon and describes the answers given by Latter-day Saints in respect to this matter.

Affirmative Arguments by Latter-day Saints in Favor of Single Authorship

Most Latter-day Saint writers ultimately resolve the Isaiah authorship question by accepting the scriptures at face value.[3] The Book of Mormon clearly attributes to Isaiah the authorship of the Isaiah chapters quoted by the Nephite prophets, and from this fact most LDS readers strongly infer that Isaiah was the author of all sixty-six chapters. Several Latter-day Saint scholars have also pursued the linguistic and historical critiques in greater depth and have responded in various ways to the idea of late authorship for Isaiah 40–66. These Latter-day Saint writers often advance arguments based on the internal unities that run through all sixty-six chapters of Isaiah.[4] The presence of internal consistencies in such stylistic elements as parallelism, psalmody, imagery, repetition, paronomasia, and certain distinctive expressions support Isaiah's unity.[5] In this line of reasoning, Latter-day Saint scholars have essentially joined sympathies with a strong contemporary school of Isaiah scholarship that has actually left the question of Isaiah authorship and simply undertaken the study of the many unifying characteristics that are indeed demonstrable in the book of Isaiah as it is found in the Bible.[6]

While these unifying characteristics provide evidence of single authorship, at least to the extent that one would usually expect to find commonalities throughout any book written by a single author, these unities do not necessarily establish authorship, though they are most easily explained as the result of a single hand. In other words, while all the writings now found in the book of Isaiah could have been produced by multiple authors who shared common vocabularies, idioms, philosophies, ideologies, and stylistic features, or while the observable unities in the resultant text could have been fashioned by a final editor or compiler, it is hard to imagine how and when all that collaborative or consolidating work could have been accomplished. It is easier to believe that all those unities were there from the beginning.

Moreover, LDS writers have pointed out that New Testament authors and Christ himself are recorded as having quoted later chapters of Isaiah, using the name of Isaiah (in

Greek, Esaias) and no other.[7] Critical scholars, however, do not feel that this settles the historical authorship question. Perhaps Christ and the New Testament writers simply used the name and person of the prophet Isaiah to identify the quote as coming from "the book of Isaiah," without necessarily certifying whether the textual history of each part of the Isaiah scroll dates to before or after 600 B.C. Thus, these New Testament references are helpful but do not settle the question of authorship.

Arguments against Multiple Authorship: Issues of Form, Content, and Prophetic Foreknowledge

Other Latter-day Saint studies have pointed out weaknesses in the arguments presented by critical biblical writers. The main arguments can be separated into three areas: (1) the form of the prophecies, (2) the content of the prophecies, and (3) the ability of a prophet to foretell the future.

Form

Some scholars feel that the differences in form are so varied (some structures vanishing, others appearing, even when the subject matter remains the same) that their diversity establishes multiple authorship.[8] However, diversity in form is still inconclusive in resolving the problem of Isaiah authorship. Isaiah was active as a prophet and apparently as a writer for at least forty years. Any author, working as Isaiah did over a long lifetime, might well produce an eclectic book that contains a disparate collection of his own poems, prophecies, and narratives. Certain stylistic differences, either deriving from the writer's association with new ideas or alternately due to increased seclusion are not only possible, but are probably to be expected in writings coming from different times in a long lifespan of an author. Hebrew poetry and Isaiah's abilities and style (praised as "genius") allow for a range of creative differences. As a prophet, Isaiah could either speak as himself or for God—using God's own "literary style" in addition to his own. Moreover, it is evident that the various sections and chapters of the book of Isaiah were drafted originally as independent prophecies or separate oracles that were eventually gathered together on a single scroll. Isaiah did not sit down one day and write all sixty-six chapters systematically. Thus, many reasons may account for the various forms of writing found in the book of Isaiah.

For Latter-day Saints, the compositional variety in the book of Doctrine and Covenants might come to mind as a possible comparison. The revelations of the Doctrine and Covenants were not written at one time: Doctrine and Covenants 1 was not the first but the sixty-sixth section written, as a preface to the 1833 Book of Commandments; many sections are not printed in their chronological order; a few sections are aggregates of separate revelations; while Joseph Smith was solely instrumental in most of the revelations, one revelation to Joseph Smith was jointly received with Sidney Rigdon (section 76), a few others were drafted by Oliver Cowdery (sections 20, 134), and two were written by Brigham Young (section 136) or John Taylor (section 135) after Joseph Smith's death. A similar amount of complexity may have been involved in the creation of the book of Isaiah. Indeed, it seems likely that Isaiah 1, like Doctrine and Covenants 1, was written as a preface to an initial collection of Isaiah's prophecies. Stylistically, a high degree of repetitive language is found throughout the Doctrine and Covenants, but changes in style, emphasis, and themes also occur over time. The same can be said of the book of Isaiah. If a person 2,600 years from now did not know the history of the Doctrine and Covenants, that person might conclude that there was a deutero-Joseph, a tertio-Joseph, and perhaps would even suggest that section 87 must have been written after the outbreak of the Civil War.

Moreover, some of the stylistic differences between the various parts of Isaiah might be the result of the work of a scribe or collector. Although we have no evidence of this one way or the other, it is not out of the question that Isaiah sometimes used a scribe (as did Jeremiah, Paul, and Joseph Smith), or that a prophet who succeeded Isaiah and knew him well compiled or abridged Isaiah's writings and in indeterminable ways influenced the final form of Isaiah's texts. Two Latter-day Saint examples show the possibility of such subsequent assistance: Mormon collected and abridged the various Nephite texts, and Joseph Fielding Smith compiled and edited the teachings of the Prophet Joseph Smith. If such compiling or editing is accomplished by a skilled person duly called and inspired to prepare the final text, the Latter-day Saint view is not troubled by the prospect of such subsequent involvement. So long as such work was completed fairly soon after Isaiah's lifetime and was clearly attributed to Isaiah before 600 B.C., this prospect would also raise no particular difficulty for the Book of Mormon. Indeed, the Book of Mormon does not require all of the Isaiah material found in the Book of Mormon to have been written by a single individual—only that the content and final form of those chapters were authoritatively attributed to Isaiah prior to 600 B.C. But, of course, we cannot conclusively determine whether anything like these possible scenarios actually occurred in the case of the book of Isaiah.

Content

The content of the book of Isaiah embraces a vast field—too many subjects, some analysts feel, to have been written by one person.[9] LDS and other scholars, however, have countered that, as Isaiah came to understand more about the future during his lengthy prophetic ministry, he naturally adapted his theological ideas to different needs, insights, and circumstances.[10]

Many critics believe that if the theological ideas in chapters 1–39 are typical of the earliest historical Isaiah, then the shift to much larger and fuller ideas in the following chapters are not his and must have been written later:[11] the first thirty-nine chapters warn and rebuke; while the last twenty-seven are full of comfort, deliverance, and redemption. But LDS writers have responded that this development could have been deliberate—other books feature the same progression from doom to hope. Over time, as Isaiah received more understanding, changing circumstances could have brought him to shift the content and emphasis of his messages.[12]

Moreover, one may well argue that the differences between the first and second halves of Isaiah are not as great as the critics have asserted. Warnings, rebukes, promises, and blessings are found throughout the entire book, as has been shown in many of the recent studies of unities in Isaiah. It has also been suggested that errors in the transmission and translation of some biblical texts may stand behind certain difficulties that have been detected by critical scholars in studying the words of Isaiah.[13] In light of these eventualities, it seems that the critical scholars may have correctly and adeptly identified certain inconsistencies or disunities in the ancient biblical texts, but they may not always be so adroit at proposing explanations for those discrepancies.

Prophetic Foreknowledge

Ultimately, the main problem turns on the nature of prophecy. In many ways, the argument against Isaiah being the sole author of all sixty-six chapters is an argument against the possibility of divine, prophetic inspiration about future historical developments. Some scholars believe that Israelite prophets spoke only to and about their contemporaries.[14] Prophetic messages, they believe, were intimately related to the circumstances of the time and that their messages were focused solely on their particular age. To avoid futuristic interpretations, many scholars have offered the following alternatives: some have changed the time the prophecy was made or the time to which the prophecy refers; some have interpreted the prophecy so that the prediction disappears, or have understood the prophecy as a literary device used by a contemporary to give the effect of foretelling; and others insist that later editors must have added the section.[15] Other scholars, including Latter-day Saints, however, believe that prophets are not restricted to foretell only a certain portion of the immediate future. God may see fit to reveal much more information to his servants than we realize or presently understand.

Similar arguments against single authorship are also advanced by scholars who deny the possibility of revelation in the precise sense of detailed foreknowledge of future names and specific events. If such foreknowledge is impossible, then an alternative explanation must be given for future prophecies in Isaiah about the destruction of the temple or the return of the Jews to Jerusalem. One of the main problems is a result of the prophecy about Cyrus found in Isaiah 45; how could Isaiah have known the name of this Persian king over 250 years before Cyrus lived?

The LDS response to such a question and its related problems affirms that ancient prophets had detailed foreknowledge of future names and specific events. The Book of Mormon contains several specific revelations recorded by Nephi, Jacob, Benjamin and others, disclosing the names of Jesus, John, and Mary, as well as particulars about the life and ministry of Christ. Latter-day Saints also cite evidence in the book of Moses, which testifies that future details of the eternal plan of salvation were revealed to Adam, Enoch, and others in antiquity.

When Were the Plates of Brass Written?

Another issue that might bear on the Isaiah authorship problem in connection with the Book of Mormon arises from the uncertainty over when the plates of brass were written. If that date were better known, it would establish the latest possible date for the final composition of the version of Isaiah found on the plates. While the Book of Mormon gets us very close to the original text of Isaiah himself, it takes us only as close as the version found on the plates of brass. In other words, if the plates of brass were not made and inscribed until around 620–610 B.C., this would allow time for possible collecting, editing, redacting, or supplementing to have been done to the writings of Isaiah after his death, around 700 B.C., and for that work to have already entered the standard version of the biblical text before the Isaiah texts were written on the plates of brass. In other words, in certain respects the critical biblical scholars may be right: it is possible that the book of Isaiah did not take its final form until sometime after Isaiah's death. On the other hand, the Book of Mormon rules out a late date for most of that process, establishing a *terminus post quem*, after which at least the Isaiah texts quoted in the Book of Mormon could not have been written and finalized.

Although earlier dates for the making of the plates of brass are possible, it makes sense to view them as a royal record compiled and inscribed around 620–610 B.C. by King Josiah, who reigned from 640–609 B.C. The plates contained the book of Deuteronomy (1 Nephi 5:10), and that scroll was most likely the book of the law that was not discovered by Josiah until 625 B.C. That discovery made Josiah and others in Jerusalem acutely aware of the fact that books of scripture could get lost, which would have motivated them to do everything in their power to create a permanent archive and a durable copy of their most sacred records to prevent any loss of scripture from happening again. Moreover, Deuteronomy 17 requires the king to have a copy of the law and to read in it all the days of his life. The rediscovery of the forgotten book of Deuteronomy that contained this particular scripture could have prompted Josiah to see record keeping as a royal function and to make records that would not wear out or become illegible through extensive use. In addition, the plates of brass were in Laban's custody in a treasury. The text simply says, "Laban hath the record" (1 Nephi 3:3), not that he necessarily owned them. Because he commanded a garrison of fifty soldiers inside the walls of Jerusalem, Laban may have been the captain of the king's guard or a high-ranking military officer. His treasury could have held public as well as personal records. While the plates of brass contained important genealogies, it is not likely that records of this quality would have been "family records" alone. Perhaps the genealogies served several royal purposes, such as settling disputes over marriage, inheritance, property, or other legal claims based on family status. Finally, dating the plates of brass to the end of the seventh century is consistent with the fact that they included information down to the commencement of the reign of

Zedekiah and many prophecies of Jeremiah, who began to prophesy in 628 B.C.

Of course, other possible dates and scenarios can be imagined. Perhaps the plates of brass were a sacred record that had been kept up to date all along by prophets who preceded Lehi. Perhaps Laban had confiscated this book, making it property of the state, when one of those prophets was put to death for prophesying against Jerusalem and the king. But without knowing when the plates of brass were inscribed, it is not possible to say whether the writings of Isaiah underwent any modifications between his day and Lehi's lifetime, which changes may have caused some of the results that puzzle the scholars today.

How Much of Isaiah Was on the Plates of Brass?

We may also wonder how much of Isaiah the plates of brass contained. Because the Book of Mormon does not absolutely require any part of the book of Isaiah to have been written before 600 B.C. except for those chapters or passages that are quoted or otherwise used in the Book of Mormon itself, it is possible that some parts of Isaiah were missing from the plates of brass.

For example, because Nephi begins quoting Isaiah in 2 Nephi 12 at Isaiah 2:1 instead of at Isaiah 1:1, it is possible that Isaiah 1 was not on the plates of brass. If it had been, one might have expected Alma the Younger to have quoted Isaiah 1:18 about "though your sins be as scarlet, they shall be as white as snow." In addition, the Cyrus information in Isaiah 45 is not quoted in the Book of Mormon. Although one may well believe that Isaiah 45 was original with Isaiah, nothing in the Book of Mormon precludes the possibility that all or part of that chapter was written after Lehi left Jerusalem and, hence, was not on the plates of brass. Likewise, chapters 56–66, the so-called Third Isaiah, which scholars have argued most strongly to be post-exilic, do not appear in the Book of Mormon. Were these chapters not on the plates of brass?

Isaiah 54 presents a particularly interesting case. Did the Nephites have this text before Jesus quoted it to them in 3 Nephi 22? In the same speech, Jesus quoted Malachi 3–4, and it is eveident that those chapters were not on the plates of brass (3 Nephi 26:2). While the answer to this question about Isaiah 54 is uncertain, we have a number of clues: (1) In 3 Nephi 22:1, Jesus introduced Isaiah 54 by saying, "And then shall that which is *written* come to pass." On another occasion when Jesus quoted from texts already possessed by the Nephites, he said: "ye have heard that it hath been said by them of old time, and it is also *written before you*" (3 Nephi 12:21). Does the absence of the words "before you" in 3 Nephi 22:1 imply that the Nephites did not previously have Isaiah 54, or is this omission insignificant? (2) After quoting Isaiah 54, Jesus said: "And now, behold, I say unto you, that ye ought to search these things. Yea, a commandment I give unto you that ye search these things diligently." Is this a new commandment to search these things because they are new, or is it an instruction to search the old records more diligently? (3) In 3 Nephi 23:6, when Jesus is about to give the Nephites Malachi 3–4, he said: "Behold *other* scriptures I would that ye should write, that ye have not." (23:6). Does the word "other" imply that he has already given them one other scripture, namely Isaiah 54, that they did not previously have, or does the phrase "that ye have not" introduce only Malachi 3–4? (4) After giving Malachi 3–4, and following same pattern as with Isaiah 54, Jesus "expounded" that text "unto the multitude." In each case, Jesus gave the text, explained it, and commanded the people to record and teach it. Does this pattern imply that Isaiah 54 was just as new to the Nephites as was Malachi 3–4? When Jesus said,

"These scriptures, which ye had not with you, the Father commanded that I should give unto you" (3 Nephi 26:2), was he referring only to Malachi 3–4 or also to Isaiah 54?

Conclusion

It is interesting to think about the issue of Isaiah authorship in light of the Book of Mormon. Although several puzzles remain unsolved, there is no question in my mind that Isaiah wrote everything attributed to him in the Book of Mormon and that strong presumptions and reasonable arguments can be mounted in support of Isaiah's authorship of the entire book that bears his name. I do not believe that a record created around 600 B.C. could ever have passed off as an original Isaiah text something that everyone knew had been written only a few days earlier. But, if it should somehow, hypothetically, turn out that some of the Isaiah texts that are found in the Book of Mormon were written or edited between 700 and 600 B.C., the Book of Mormon itself does not rule this out as a possibility. In the meantime, the Book of Mormon gives direct evidence that the plates of brass contained Isaiah chapters 2–14, 28–29, 40, 43, 48–53, perhaps 54, and 55:1–2. Because these sections are widely scattered throughout much of the book of Isaiah, one may infer that all of Isaiah was on the plates of brass. Indeed, if the Book of Mormon is accepted on other sufficient grounds as a true historical account, then this record in turn adds new evidence concerning the perplexing issues of Isaiah authorship that has not been not available to or considered by the scholarly world.[16]

In the final analysis, in response to all the criticisms and questions concerning Isaiah authorship, most Latter-day Saints simply ascribed greater authority to the Book of Mormon than to critical biblical scholarship. Because the

Book of Mormon expressly indicates that Isaiah wrote Isaiah 2–14 and 48–54, few additional questions about the authorship of those chapters need to be asked in LDS circles. Moreover, even in scholarly terms, any bearing that the questions of Isaiah authorship might have on the Book of Mormon must be begin and end with the acknowledgment that we probably lack sufficient evidence to answer all those questions conclusively. For Latter-day Saints, this ultimately leaves the question of the truthfulness of the Book of Mormon, as it has always been, in the realm of faith and as a matter of personal testimony.

Notes

1. See Walter Brueggemann, "Unity and Dynamic in the Isaiah Tradition," *JSOT* 29 (June 1984): 89–107; David Carr, "Reaching for Unity in Isaiah," *JSOT* 57 (March 1993): 61–80; Brevard S. Childs, *Introduction to the Old Testament as Scripture* (Philadelphia: Fortress Press, 1979): 316–25; 325–38; Ronald E. Clements, "Beyond Tradition-History: Deutero-Isaianic Development of First Isaiah's Themes," *JSOT* 31 (February 1985): 95–113; Ronald E. Clements, "The Unity of the Book of Isaiah," *Interpretation* 36 (1982): 117–29; Richard J. Clifford, "The Unity of the Book of Isaiah and Its Cosmogonic Language," *CBQ* 55 (1993): 1–17; Craig A. Evans, "On the Unity and Parallel Structure of Isaiah" *VT* 38 (1988) 129–47; and John L. McKenzie, *Second Isaiah*, vol. 20 of the Anchor Bible Series (Garden City, New York: Doubleday, 1964): xv–xxiii.

2. See Wayne Ham, "Problems in Interpreting the Book of Mormon as History," in *Courage: A Journal of History, Thought and Action* 1 (1970–71): 19–20; George D. Smith, "Isaiah Updated," *Dialogue: A Journal of Mormon Thought* 16 (summer 1983): 41, 47–51; reprinted in Dan Vogel, ed., *The Word of God: Essays on Mormon Scripture* (Salt Lake: Signature Books, 1990): 114–5, 123–4.

3. See, for example, LaMar L. Adams, "Isaiah: Disciple and Witness of Christ," in *A Witness of Jesus Christ: The 1989 Sperry Symposium on the Old Testament*, ed. Richard D. Draper (Salt Lake

City: Deseret Book, 1989), 1–17; Keith H. Meservy, "Isaiah 53: The Richest Prophecy on Christ's Atonement in the Old Testament," in *A Witness of Jesus Christ*, ed. Draper, 155–77; Cleon W. Skousen, *Isaiah Speaks to Modern Man* (Salt Lake City: Ensign Publishing, 1984), and many others.

4. See such works as Avraham Gileadi, "The Holistic Structure of the Book of Isaiah" (Provo: Brigham Young University, Ph.D. diss., 1981); Victor L. Ludlow, *Isaiah: Prophet, Seer, and Poet* (Salt Lake City: Deseret Book, 1982), 547; Sidney B. Sperry, *Answers to Book of Mormon Questions* (Salt Lake City: Bookcraft, 1967), 88–91.

5. Ludlow, *Isaiah: Prophet, Seer, and Poet*, 547–8. Of course, the earliest Bible manuscripts from the Dead Sea Scrolls (about 100 B.C.) present Isaiah as one complete book. No one doubts, however, that the book of Isaiah took its final form any later than the fifth century B.C., well before the time when the earliest known Bible manuscripts were copied. Thus, this evidence does not go back far enough to be of much use to the Book of Mormon. More useful information would need to demonstrate that Isaiah chapters 48–54 were written before the sixth century B.C.

6. See works such as, Oswald T. Allis, *The Unity of Isaiah: A Study in Prophecy* (Philadelphia: Presbyterian and Reformed Publishing, 1950); David Carr, "Reaching for Unity in Isaiah," *JSOT* 57 (March 1993): 98–107; Ronald E. Clements, "The Unity of the Book of Isaiah," *Interpretation* 36 (April 1982): 117–29; Richard J. Clifford, "The Unity of the Book of Isaiah and Its Cosmogonic Language," *CBQ* 55 (Jan. 1993): 1–17; Craig A. Evans, "On the Unity and Parallel Structure of Isaiah," *VT* 38 (April 1988): 129–47; Letitia D. Jeffreys, *The Unity of the Book of Isaiah* (Cambridge: Deighton Bell, 1899); Rolf Rendtorff, "The Book of Isaiah: A Complex Unity: Synchronic and Diachronic Reading," *SBL 1991 Seminar Papers* (Atlanta: Scholars Press, 1991), 8–20.

7. Ludlow, *Isaiah: Prophet, Seer, and Poet*, 543; Roberts, "Higher Criticism and the Book of Mormon," 778–80; Sperry, *Answers to Book of Mormon Questions*, 86; James E. Talmage in *Conference Report* (April 1929): 45–9.

8. S. R. Driver, *An Introduction to the Literature of the Old Testament* (New York: Charles Scribner's Sons, 1923), 238; McKenzie, *Second Isaiah*, xvi.

9. Richard J. Clifford, "The Unity of the Book of Isaiah and Its Cosmogonic Language," *CBQ* 55 (January 1993): 1–17. Clifford suggests three themes in Isaiah 40–55 that do not coincide even with a redactional unity: Zion as the destination of the Exodus and land-taking; creation; and Cyrus as Yahweh's king. McKenzie, *Second Isaiah*, xv–xxiii. On the basis of vocabulary, style, thought, knowing the name of Cyrus, and having a different world of discourse than First Isaiah, along with numerous other details, McKenzie holds to a multiple authorship of Isaiah.

10. Kent P. Jackson, "The Authorship of the Book of Isaiah," *1 Kings to Malachi*, vol. 4 in *Studies in Scripture* (Salt Lake City: Deseret Book, 1993), 80; Ludlow, *Isaiah: Prophet, Seer, and Poet*, 544.

11. Driver, *An Introduction to the Literature of the Old Testament*, 242.

12. Jackson, "Authorship of the Book of Isaiah," 81–3; Ludlow, *Isaiah: Prophet, Seer, and Poet*, 544.

13. Sperry, *Answers to Book of Mormon Questions*, 91–7.

14. See, for example, works concerning Isaiah by Karl Marti, Heinrich F. Hackmann, Bernhard Duhm, and Thomas K. Cheyne See also McKenzie, *Second Isaiah*, xvi. The nature of prophecy is also discussed by Jackson, "Authorship of the Book of Isaiah," 82; Ludlow, *Isaiah: Prophet, Seer, and Poet*, 543; Roberts, "Higher Criticism and the Book of Mormon," 774; Sperry, *Answers to Book of Mormon Questions*, 77.

15. See Ludlow, *Isaiah: Prophet, Seer, and Poet*, 542.

16. Jackson, "Authorship of the Book of Isaiah," 84.

Wordprinting Isaiah
and the Book of Mormon

John L. Hilton

*Measuring peculiar characteristics of Book of Mormon authors has
produced interesting findings, but external constraints in Isaiah's
texts preclude statistically conclusive wordprints.*

The use of a tool of statistical analysis called wordprinting gives us some limited but interesting information about the authorship of the writings of Isaiah found in both the King James Version (KJV) of the Old Testament and the Book of Mormon. Comparing wordprints of these Isaiah texts with wordprints of some other texts in the Bible and Book of Mormon also reveals some interesting information.

Wordprinting is based on what appears to be a normal human phenomenon.[1] Without being consciously aware of it, when we speak freely or write each of us uses a different set of noncontextual words, such as *and, the, of, in, that, with,* and so on. The rest of our vocabulary is heavily influenced by context—by the subject under discussion, by the size and nature of our audience, and by many other such contextual factors. But our use of these noncontextual words remains relatively constant as long as we are not constrained by other factors, such as the need to quote another person or to fit our words into a formal structure like poetry. These personal free flow writing patterns of using noncontextual words tend to be stable throughout a person's life.

Wordprinting can be used to determine whether a particular author wrote a particular block of text. This is done by comparing the wordprint of the unascribed text with wordprints from other texts known to have been written by the suspected author and with wordprints of texts known to have been written by various other authors.[2] If the word-print for the unascribed text differs from the wordprints of texts known to have been written by the suspected author more than the wordprints of the other known texts vary among themselves, then this suspected author did not likely write the unascribed text. But if the use of noncontextual words varies the same or less between the known and un-known texts as that use varies among the known texts, then the author of the known texts is a good candidate for the author of the unascribed text. That author becomes an even better candidate if the wordprints of his known texts match the wordprint of the unknown text better than do the word-prints of the writings of other possible authors.

Wordprint Comparisons between Old Testament and Book of Mormon Texts

One technique used in wordprinting, called text calibra-tion, provides a useful measure of how alike texts are that have been translated from another language into English. If the original texts were written in the same language at about the same time and if the translation process is quite literal, wordprinting their English translations will produce text-calibration values that will form a recognizable pattern. Other texts from the same original language and time that are translated literally will consistently produce the same pattern.[3]

Using text calibration to compare KJV Old Testament English texts translated from the biblical Hebrew with texts from the English Book of Mormon produces some interest-ing conclusions. The first generation of Book of Mormon record keepers wrote about 95 percent of the small plates. The text-calibration values of their writings align very closely with the values from the KJV English prose of Jeremiah, 2 Kings, and 2 Chronicles, whose authors wrote in Hebrew around 600 B.C., the time when that first generation of Book of Mormon writers are described as leaving Jerusalem. On the other hand, the values from texts of later writers such as Alma, Mormon, and Moroni do not align at all with the values from Jeremiah and the other biblical texts. These Book of Mormon text-calibration measurements are consistent with the supposition that the original language in which the first generation's small plate authors wrote was the same as Jeremiah's Hebrew, while the original languages of Alma, Mormon, and Moroni were something different (see Mormon 9:32).[4]

Wordprinting Isaiah

Some Bible scholars have argued that most of the words in the first forty chapters of Isaiah may have come from Isaiah—the son of Amoz who lived in the eighth century B.C. before the Babylonian exile—but they argue that the remaining twenty-six chapters must have been written after the exile by a second writer or by some combination of writers. Unfortunately, all present wordprinting tests cannot provide conclusive answers on the question of whether there was one or more than one writer for the book of Isaiah because of the surprisingly small amount of that book that was apparently written free from external constraints.

Most of the Isaiah text is written in poetry, which forced the author to change his noncontextual words and word order to fit the poetic form. Naturally, the wordprint of the poetic sections should not measure the same as the prose sections. Writing that has a poetic cadence can still be wordprinted with some success, however, if one compares the wordprint of the poetic section only to the wordprints of similar poetic texts by known authors. Nevertheless, word-print testing of texts written under such constraints is less sensitive in distinguishing different authors.

For example, when Shakespeare's poetic plays are tested with wordprint procedures, all his major plays are consistent within themselves and to each other, but they are clearly independent from all the other known playwrights of his day, including Ben Jonson and Christopher Marlowe, who have left similar poem plays to compare against. However, as these lengthy plays were tested, it was found that, because of their poetic nature, the sensitivity of the wordprints for distinguishing between authors was only about one-half of the sensitivity for wordprint testing between the texts of free-flow prose writers using the same sixteenth- or seventeenth-century Elizabethan English.

Not only do Isaiah's writings contain a large amount of poetry, they also contain extensive quotations from the word of the Lord. Once again this constraint on the writer's free choice of words presumably weakens the pattern of non-contextual word choices that usually creates a recognizable personal wordprint. Together, the quotations and poetry constitute nearly 85 percent of the book of Isaiah, making successful wordprinting difficult.

The present wordprints of the biblical text of Isaiah indicate a slight distinction between the first and second halves of the text. However, the small but measurable shift in pattern is not the change expected by proponents of multiple authorship for Isaiah, since it occurs much earlier—ten chapters earlier—than is expected by their theory. The shift does make it seem likely that at some time during the text's transmission, more than one editor, or nonliteral translator, or poet, or additional writer contributed to the extant text. But at the present time, we cannot say more than that, based on the wordprinting evidence.

Notes

1. For a more detailed and technical explanation of word-printing and of the findings summarized here, and a discussion of the development of much of the wordprint procedures, see John L. Hilton, "An Update of Wordprinting on the English Isaiah Texts and the Book of Mormon" (Provo, Utah: FARMS, 1996), originally presented at the FARMS conference on "Isaiah and the Book of Mormon," 20 May 1995; and John L. Hilton and Kenneth D. Jenkins "On Maximizing Author Identification by Measuring 5000 Word Texts" (Provo, Utah: FARMS, 1987).

2. For example, see the discussion of Samuel Johnson as the author of Rev. Dodds' prison sermon in Hilton and Jenkins, "Maximizing," 21, 23–4; see also Noel B. Reynolds and John L. Hilton, "Thomas Hobbes and Authorship of the Horae Subsecivae," *History of Political Thought* 14/3 (1993); and Noel B. Reynolds and John L. Hilton, "Wordprinting Francis Bacon," *1995 Joint International Conference ACH/ALLC,* University of California, Santa Barbara, 11–15 July 1995.

3. See Hilton, "An Update," for a more detailed and technical discussion of this technique.

4. For a report of wordprinting tests that examine Book of Mormon authorship questions more extensively, see John L. Hilton, "On Verifying Wordprint Studies: Book of Mormon Authorship," *BYU Studies* 30/3 (1990); and Hilton, "An Update."

Isaiah and the Latter-day Saints
A Bibliographic Survey

John S. Thompson and Eric Smith

This annotated bibliography introduces to general readers the many books and articles by modern LDS scholars about Isaiah, with emphasis on Isaiah in the Book of Mormon.

One of the great challenges of both the Bible and the Book of Mormon is understanding the writings of Isaiah. The archaic idioms and symbolic language that Isaiah employs, the historical figures and events that provide the background to his writings, and the poetic forms that structure his words are formidable barriers that can discourage and bewilder the reader. To help overcome these barriers, many LDS authors have come forward offering notes and commentary. Some of these authors have degrees in such fields as ancient Near Eastern studies, biblical studies, and history, and they use tools such as philology, historical criticism, and literary criticism to help the reader uncover the meaning of Isaiah's words. Others rely exclusively on a deep, abiding love for Isaiah's message, uncovering the meaning of his words through concentrated study of the English scriptures. However, all approach Isaiah's writings with a testimony of the restored gospel of Jesus Christ and the added insight that modern revelation provides.

This bibliographic survey's primary purpose is to inform readers about many of the LDS articles and books on Isaiah—particularly on some of the more famous Isaiah passages (e.g., the mountain of the Lord's house [Isaiah 2:2–3], the Immanuel prophecy [Isaiah 7:10–16], the rod and stem of Jesse [Isaiah 11:1, 10], and the sealed book [Isaiah 29]—that are available for study. The survey will give the reference and a summary of the work, focusing on each author's interpretations of Isaiah and often noting similarities and differences between writers' interpretations, so that readers can be aware of the various schools of thought surrounding Isaiah's writings.

Because so many LDS authors have written about Isaiah or have included references to his writings in their works, this survey is limited to published books or articles that deal extensively with Isaiah. The works included are arranged in a general chronological order from earliest to most recent so that the reader can see the influences that earlier writers may have had on later writers and discern the development of various schools of thought. An addendum at the end of this survey focuses on LDS writings about the suffering servant song in Isaiah 53.

Pratt, Orson. "The Ancient Prophecies." *Journal of Discourses* (7 January 1855), 2:284.[1]

Some of the earliest published works in the LDS corpus of literature that deal extensively with Isaiah address the famous "sealed book" prophecy in Isaiah 29. Orson Pratt, in a discourse given on 7 January 1855, is one of the first on record to comment on Isaiah 29 and the role of the Book of Mormon in fulfilling that prophecy.[2] Though his discourse was intended to treat the subject of the fulfillment of ancient prophecies in general, Pratt chooses to narrow his topic to those prophecies dealing with the Book of Mormon, with the bulk of his message dealing with Isaiah 29. Pratt discusses the careful phraseology given in this chapter, noting, for example, that Isaiah mentions that "the 'words of the book,' not the book itself, were sent to the learned" (p. 288). Pratt comments that if Martin Harris had taken the actual gold plates to Charles Anthon, then this prophecy would not have been fulfilled to the letter.

Given the literalness of Pratt's interpretation of Isaiah 29, it is clear that he feels the Book of Mormon is indeed the book mentioned in this chapter. There is no mention of the prophecy being allegorical for the people of Isaiah's day or for the state of apostasy in general, thus making the Book of Mormon only one of many ways to apply or "liken" the prophecy. Further, it is uncertain whether Pratt simply saw the correlation between the events surrounding the coming forth of the Book of Mormon and Isaiah 29 and thus interpreted the prophecy accordingly, or whether he was influenced by Nephi's use of Isaiah 29 in 2 Nephi 27. In either case, Pratt certainly felt that Isaiah wrote directly concerning the Book of Mormon and those events surrounding its coming forth.

Smith, John Henry. "A Marvelous Work and a Wonder." *Millennial Star* 45 (8 October 1883): 648–52.

This editorial provides another early commentary on Isaiah 29. This commentary focuses on the Great Apostasy (the "deep sleep" of Isaiah 29:10) and the restoration as a whole (the "marvelous work and a wonder" of Isaiah 29:14) being the fulfillment of Isaiah's words. In the tradition of Orson Pratt, the role of the Book of Mormon in fulfilling this prophecy is also briefly mentioned; however, the bulk of Smith's work is a review of Church history, emphasizing that the enemies to the work of God constantly find that the "wisdom of their wise men shall perish" (Isaiah 29:14). Again it is assumed that Isaiah wrote pointedly concerning the Book of Mormon and the last days; there is no mention of Isaiah possibly giving this prophecy for his own day or for the condition of apostasy in general.

Roberts, B. H. "The Difficulty of Passages from Isaiah Being Quoted by Nephite Writers, that Modern Bible Criticism (Higher Criticism) Holds Were Not Written until the Time of the Babylonian Captivity—586–538 B.C., and Not Written by Isaiah at All." In *New Witnesses for God*. Vol. 3. Salt Lake City: Deseret News, 1909. Reprinted as "An Objection to the Book of Mormon Answered." *Improvement Era* (July 1909): 681–9.

————. "Higher Criticism and the Book of Mormon." *Improvement Era* (June 1911): 665–77; (July 1911): 774–86.

Some of the other earlier works concerning Isaiah were prompted by the higher critics' claims that Isaiah did not author much of the Old Testament book attributed to him.[3] In one chapter of his book *New Witnesses for God, Vol. 3* and two years later in a published speech, B. H. Roberts sought to familiarize his audience with the higher critics' claims about Isaiah and to discuss the relationship between those claims and the authenticity of the Book of Mormon. If the critics are right and chapters 40–66 of Isaiah were written during or after the period of Babylonian captivity (beginning ca. 587 B.C.), then the Book of Mormon may be in error in attributing texts to Isaiah that were written not by him but by one or more authors living over twenty years after Lehi and his family left Jerusalem with the brass plates. In both his works, Roberts suggests many arguments to counter the higher critics' claims about Isaiah:

- Isaiah 40 does not begin with a separate heading, and it is thematically connected with Isaiah 39.

- According to Jewish historian Josephus, Cyrus King of Persia was influenced by Isaiah's prophecy that God would choose Cyrus to allow Israel to return to their own land and build the temple.

- Luke records that Christ read Isaiah 61:1–2 and claimed that he was its fulfillment without any mention of Isaiah 61 being authored by someone else.

- Much of the difference in literary style between different sections of Isaiah can be attributed to Isaiah's poetical genius, the grandeur of Isaiah's message, and the passage of time between Isaiah's early and late writings.

- A testimony of the truthfulness of the Book of Mormon is itself proof that Isaiah was the sole author of the book attributed to him.

Jenson, Nephi. "Isaiah 29." *Improvement Era* (April 1910): 512–5.

Another treatise on Isaiah 29 comes from a small article written by Nephi Jenson in the *Improvement Era.* Like Orson Pratt and John H. Smith, Jenson argues that the Book of Mormon is indeed the "book" to which Isaiah refers. He shows that the character of the book Isaiah describes matches the characteristics of the Book of Mormon—i.e., the Book of Mormon contains a "vision" of a nation that is "brought down" and will "speak out of the ground," and it contains material about Christ's ministry, since the book Isaiah describes will make the "meek rejoice in the Holy One of Israel."

Further, Jenson interprets the "marvelous work and a wonder" that shall make the "wisdom of their wise men [to] perish" as being fulfilled in the lives of young missionaries who take the message of the Book of Mormon and the restored gospel into the world and "without difficulty" are able to "defend this restored gospel against the most skillful attacks of the most scholarly theologians" (p. 514).

Isaiah's book is also described by Jenson as having an affect on people such that "the meek should increase their joy in the Lord." Jenson feels that the testimony and devotion

of those saints who suffered for the gospel is answer enough
to point to the Book of Mormon as the book spoken of in
Isaiah 29.

Talmage, James E. *Conference Report* (April 1929): 44–9.

In April general conference 1929, James E. Talmage gave
an address on the need for a testimony born of the Spirit
rather than being influenced by technicalities such as geography and higher criticism, which, if overstated, can cause
some to be "led away into the jungle of error" (p. 45). For
example, Isaiah's authorship problem and its relation to the
Book of Mormon should not be an issue if one is first
grounded in a testimony of the truthfulness of the Book of
Mormon. The need to put the Lord's revelations (including
the Book of Mormon) above the theories of men is emphasized. Since the Book of Mormon quotes from all parts of
Isaiah, as far as Talmage is concerned, the issue is settled.
Talmage concludes his speech by addressing the ways scholars divide the book of Isaiah into various sections, including by prophecy and literary style. Concerning this latter
point, Talmage refers to Milton's poems "L'Allegro" and "Il
Penseroso," showing that these two poems support the idea
that an author can adapt style to theme; and therefore Isaiah's
supposed dual authorship can also be explained as differences in style based on theme.

Sperry, Sidney B. "The 'Isaiah Problem' in the Book
of Mormon." *Improvement Era* (September 1939): 524–
5, 564–9; (October 1939): 594, 634, 636–7. Reprinted
in *Our Book of Mormon*. Salt Lake City: Stevens and
Wallis, 1947, 155–77. Reprinted again in *The Problems
of the Book of Mormon*. Salt Lake City: Bookcraft, 1964,
73–97 (this book was published later under the title
Answers to the Book of Mormon, 1967). Reprinted again
in *Book of Mormon Compendium*. Salt Lake City:

Bookcraft, 1968, 493–512. Reprinted once more in *Journal of Book of Mormon Studies* 4/1 (1995): 129–52.

Like B. H. Roberts and James Talmage, Sidney B. Sperry, in this *Improvement Era* article, addresses the scholarly claim that the book of Isaiah was written by more than one author. He addresses the relationship between those claims and the authenticity of the Book of Mormon. Sperry first responds to this problem by demonstrating that although many scholars doubt that Isaiah actually wrote much of the work attributed to him, many other scholars support the unity of Isaiah's writings. Higher critics have not proven beyond reasonable doubt that Isaiah did not author the book of Isaiah. Sperry outlines several factors that have influenced scholars to support the unity of Isaiah, including:

- The Septuagint and other ancient versions of Isaiah do not hint at multiple authorship of Isaiah.

- Christ and many of his apostles quote extensively from all parts of Isaiah's writings and often attribute these passages to Isaiah.

- Expressions peculiar to Isaiah, such as "the Holy One of Israel," are found in all the sections disputed by the scholars.

Sperry finishes his article by comparing the Isaiah texts in the 1920 edition of the Book of Mormon with the Hebrew, Greek, Syriac, and Latin versions of Isaiah. He argues that in some instances when the Book of Mormon departs from the Hebrew reading of Isaiah (as reflected in the King James Version), those variants agree with one of the other ancient versions of Isaiah, giving validity to some of the Book of Mormon's variant Isaiah quotations as being ancient in origin and not Joseph Smith's own inspired revisions.

Sperry, Sidney B. *The Spirit of the Old Testament*. Salt
Lake City: LDS Department of Education, 1940.

One of the earliest general treatments of Isaiah is found
in Sidney Sperry's book *The Spirit of the Old Testament*.
Containing two chapters on Isaiah (pp. 156–78), this book
introduces the reader to the ancient prophet by giving overviews of his personal history, the time period of his ministry, and his prophecies. It also provides a verse-by-verse commentary on Isaiah 1, which "forms an excellent preface to
the book because it contains a summary of certain characteristic and essential teachings of Isaiah" (p. 161).

The second Isaiah chapter of Sperry's book focuses on
various topics that Isaiah addresses, including the "mountain of the Lord's house" (Isaiah 2:2), which he avoids relating to any specific modern LDS temples, but rather associates it to the general gathering of latter-day Zion. Sperry
also discusses the recovery of Israel's remnant, the redemption of Israel, and predictions of the Messiah's coming. While
commenting on these Messianic predictions, Sperry points
out several Isaiah passages that are traditionally associated with Christ but notes that in some cases, the context
of the quoted verse suggests an alternative fulfillment.
For example, he explains that while most Christians associate the Immanuel prophecy in Isaiah 7:14 with Christ, some
scholars suggest that the context of that verse is not so easily interpreted. Sperry makes no attempt to solve this di-
lemma; he merely introduces the problem, leaving the reader
to wonder at his viewpoint and interpretive approach to
some of Isaiah's more difficult passages.

Sperry, Sidney B. "The Eleventh Chapter of Isaiah."
Instructor 79 (July 1944): 332–4.

Four years after publishing his book *The Spirit of the Old
Testament*, Sperry published an article in the *Instructor*

interpreting the meaning of some of the more famous verses in Isaiah 11. His remarks in this article reveal a little more about the approach Sperry takes in interpreting Isaiah. Using Doctrine and Covenants 113, Sperry indicates that the "stem of Jesse" (v. 1) is Christ, and based on the Doctrine and Covenant's description concerning the "rod" (v. 1) and "root of Jesse" (v. 10), Sperry concludes that these both refer to the Prophet Joseph Smith. According to Sperry, this is one reason Moroni quoted this chapter to Joseph Smith, saying it was about to be fulfilled. Sperry believes that the prophecies in this chapter deal exclusively with the last days. For example, he reasons that the mention of nations by their names known in Isaiah's day were simply there because his people would not recognize the names of modern nations from whence parts of scattered Israel would be gathered. Sperry does not entertain the notion that this prophecy may indeed have a fulfillment in Isaiah's own day. In other words, rather than allowing for the possibility of interpreting these verses in the context of Isaiah's day, Sperry interprets the prophecies all within the context of the last days. Hence, he seems to reject the idea of dual fulfillment of Isaiah's prophecies.

Sperry, Sidney B. *The Voice of Israel's Prophets: A Latter-day Saint Interpretation of the Major and Minor Prophets of the Old Testament.* Salt Lake City: Deseret Book, 1952. Republished as *The Old Testament Prophets.* Salt Lake City: Deseret Sunday School Union, 1965.

In chapters 2–10 of his book *The Voice of Israel's Prophets*, Sperry expands on his earlier works "The 'Isaiah Problem' in the Book of Mormon" and *The Spirit of the Old Testament*, providing more background detail on Isaiah and his world, discussing the Isaiah authorship problem, and systematically dividing the entire Isaiah text into various topical sections with commentaries.

Because this work treats Isaiah in far more depth than do his earlier works, the reader gets a clearer view of Sperry's approach to interpreting Isaiah. As mentioned earlier, when faced with possibilities of multiple fulfillment in an Isaiah passage, Sperry chooses rather to interpret the utterance within a single historical context. For example, he asks, "Is it [the Immanuel prophecy] to be taken as representing an event of the immediate future[?] . . . Or, on the other hand, is the sign the prophet's way of telling a truth about an event in the distant future which the unspiritual Ahaz would not fully understand?" (pp. 29–30). He then quotes Matthew 1:23, which identifies Jesus Christ as the fulfillment of the sign, stating, "I believe that Matthew's interpretation is the correct one" (p. 30). He does not explain why. Unlike other scholars, he does not feel that Isaiah's prophecy was fulfilled in Isaiah's own day.

Taking the approach that each prophecy has only one fulfillment allows Sperry to explain each section of Isaiah in a single chronological context. He seems to choose the traditional LDS interpretation of Isaiah's prophecies: he, like Orson Pratt and others, views the prophecy of Isaiah 29 as being fulfilled in the restoration and the coming forth of the Book of Mormon, not as an allegory for the people of Isaiah's own day.

Reynolds, George, and Janne M. Sjodahl. *Commentary on the Book of Mormon.* Vol. 1. Salt Lake City: Deseret Book, 1955.

Reynolds and Sjodahl's book provides a verse by verse commentary of the entire Book of Mormon text, including the Isaiah quotations. The remarks provided give insight into the authors' approach to interpreting the Isaiah passages. Like Sperry, the authors' views are basically conservative. For example, the authors interpret the prophecy of the "mountain of the Lord's house" (2 Nephi 12:2, parallel to

Isaiah 2:2) as referring to the "Church of God" that will grow until it becomes as a mountain, filling the whole earth. There is no mention of this prophecy being fulfilled in specific LDS temples of the last days. Unlike Sperry, however, the authors are more willing to accept the idea of multiple fulfillment of Isaiah's prophecies. For instance, when interpreting the Immanuel prophecy, the authors declare that this prophecy was fulfilled in Ahaz's day but quickly add that it had another fulfillment in Christ as well. However, they do not specify if any other elements in the prophecy beyond the virgin and child have a correspondence with Christ's day (e.g., they don't address whether the Ephraim and Syria of Ahaz's day mentioned in the Immanuel prophecy have a prophetic parallel in Christ's day).

In contrast to Sperry, Reynolds and Sjodahl simply state in their comments on 2 Nephi 21 (parallel to Isaiah 11) that "rod out of the stem of Jesse" is the Messiah. It appears that no use of Doctrine and Covenants 113 is made to interpret the text, for it identifies the Messiah as the "stem of Jesse," leaving out the question of who the "rod" may represent.

Reynolds and Sjodahl's comments on 2 Nephi 27 (parallel to Isaiah 29) are interesting in light of the traditional views espoused by earlier writers. Breaking away from traditional interpretations of Isaiah 29, Reynolds and Sjodahl are careful to emphasize that it was Nephi, not Isaiah, who saw in vision the Book of Mormon coming forth in the last days. Indeed they assert, "Nephi, in these paragraphs, describes the Book of Mormon and its coming forth in the latter days *in the language of the Prophet Isaiah*" (p. 396, emphasis added). The authors depart from the traditional view that Isaiah himself was speaking of the Book of Mormon and suggest that Nephi borrowed from the words of Isaiah and likened them to the vision of the Book of Mormon which he, Nephi, had seen. Note also Reynolds and Sjodahl's interpretation of the "marvelous work and wonder":

> Isaiah says that the Lord, because of the emptiness of the worship, would perform a "marvelous work and wonder," by means of which the wisdom of their wise and the understanding of their prudent would perish and be hid; and *Nephi applies this language* to the coming forth of the Book of Mormon, as the beginning of *a* [not "the"] marvelous work and wonder. (399)

Again the authors stress that Nephi likened the words of Isaiah to his own prophetic view of the future; however, since they do not interpret Isaiah's writings directly, Reynolds and Sjodahl's views on Isaiah's original message are unknown.

Rasmussen, Ellis T. "Isaiah: A Messenger of God." *Instructor* (February 1962): center insert.

———. "How Isaiah Warned His People . . . and Us." *Instructor* (February 1964): 64–5.

From 1955 to 1966, little published material was devoted specifically to Isaiah. Ellis Rasmussen published two short devotional-type articles that discuss some of the major teachings of Isaiah and explain how they are relevant to modern-day readers.

Palmer, Spencer J., and William L. Knecht. "View of the Hebrews: Substitute for Inspiration?" *BYU Studies* 5/2 (1964): 105–13.

Spencer J. Palmer and William L. Knecht's article carefully compares the Book of Mormon Isaiah text with that in Protestant clergyman Ethan Smith's 1823 *View of the Hebrews*, showing that most of the Isaiah passages in the Book of Mormon are different from those used by Ethan Smith. This point lends credence to the view that Joseph Smith did not draw on *View of the Hebrews* for the story of the Book of Mormon, as some critics have claimed.

Crowther, Duane S. *Prophets and Prophecies of the Old Testament.* Bountiful, Utah: Horizon, 1966.

Duane S. Crowther wrote this book in 1966 to facilitate the study of scripture by outlining and analyzing each of the prophetic books in the Old Testament and also providing charts and historical timelines. When discussing Isaiah, Crowther systematically assigns each chapter of Isaiah to one of four periods of prophetic fulfillment: (1) the days of Israel, Judah, and Assyria; (2) the days of Judah, Babylon, and the captivity; (3) the days of Christ's ministry; and (4) the last days. This systematic approach lends itself to interpretation similar to that of Sperry, for Crowther assigns each prophecy a single fulfillment in time. However, unlike Sperry, Crowther does not mention the other interpretations that scholars have suggested. For example, when he states that the Isaiah's Immanuel prophecy in chapter seven "concerned an event [i.e., the birth of Jesus Christ] which was to take place more than seven centuries later," (p. 337) he does not mention that other scholars have interpreted this prophecy differently.

When interpreting chapters of Isaiah that he believes pertain to the last days, Crowther often refers to the Book of Mormon's usage of Isaiah. For example, he uses 2 Nephi 26 and 27 extensively to interpret Isaiah 29, concluding in agreement with the traditional interpretation that Isaiah was himself writing about the Book of Mormon. Isaiah 29 is a chapter that Crowther believes "would be one of the most difficult of all the prophecies of the Bible, if it were not for the aid of a passage from the Book of Mormon which clarifies it and gives it the necessary interpretation" (p. 348). Crowther also discusses the Book of Mormon in his short discussion of the Isaiah authorship problem (see pp. 377–80).

Skousen, W. Cleon. *The Fourth Thousand Years*. Salt Lake City: Bookcraft, 1966.

Also in 1966 W. Cleon Skousen devoted a significant number of pages in his *The Fourth Thousand Years* to Isaiah. After discussing some reasons Isaiah is difficult to read—for example, Isaiah's writings are poetic, he uses complex literary expressions, and he deliberately wrote in obscurity to veil his words from the faithless—Skousen focuses mainly on the Book of Mormon's relationship to Isaiah's writings. He emphatically states that the Book of Mormon settles the question of the Isaiah authorship problem because it quotes from the Isaiah sections that scholars have attributed to later dates. He also draws parallels between the writings of Nephi and Isaiah, concluding that both prophets foretell the same events after experiencing nearly identical visions.

This conclusion leads him to interpret Isaiah primarily through the eyes of Nephi—that is, Skousen uses Nephi's writings to discuss the meaning of Isaiah's prophecies that pertain to the ministry of Christ, the latter-day restoration (including the coming forth of the Book of Mormon), and the second coming. He uses 1 Nephi 11:13 to make a straightforward association of the Immanuel prophecy with Christ and refers frequently to the later chapters of 2 Nephi to identify twenty prophecies in Isaiah 29 that he believes were fulfilled by the coming forth of the Book of Mormon. Like Sperry, Skousen interprets Isaiah's prophecies as having a single fulfillment, and judging from the numerous references to Sperry's works, Skousen was heavily influenced by Sperry. However, like Crowther, Skousen is quick to reach conclusions without addressing or even mentioning the questions and conflicts surrounding the interpretations he uses.

> Sperry, Sidney B. "How to Read Isaiah." *Instructor* 101 (March 1966): 96–7, 99.

Also in 1966 Sidney B. Sperry published two small articles. The first, "How to Read Isaiah," is a general help for understanding Isaiah. Sperry suggests dividing Isaiah's book into seven topical divisions with outlines, and concludes his article with a detailed analysis of Isaiah 2. Consistent with his earlier interpretations of the phrase "mountain of the Lord's house," Sperry suggests that the phrase "seems to be a place where God may be at home with his people" (p. 97) but quickly adds in the next paragraph that in light of Isaiah 11:9, which suggests that the whole world will be the holy mountain during the millennium, and Doctrine and Covenants 133:13, the phrase apparently "has a more extended application than we have been accustomed to give it" (Ibid.)

Sperry's approach to interpreting Isaiah's prophecies as having a single fulfillment is furthered by a comment he gives on Isaiah 11:11–22. Rather than viewing the judgments of Israel mentioned in these verses as occurring at other times in Israel's history, Sperry states that "this day of judgment will be at or about the time of our Lord's Second Advent" (ibid.). He supports this idea through a clause that appears in verses 11 and 17 stating that the "Lord alone" will be exalted at that day. Sperry feels that the only time in history that the Lord alone will be exalted is at his second coming.

> Sperry, Sidney B. "The Problem of the 'Rod' and 'the Root of Jesse' in Isaiah 11." *Improvement Era* 69 (October 1966): 868–9, 914–7. Reprinted in *Answers to Book of Mormon Questions*. Salt Lake City: Bookcraft, 1967, 247–53.

The second article Sperry published in 1966, "The Problem of the 'Rod' and 'Root of Jesse' in Isaiah 11," gives more detail concerning Sperry's views on Joseph Smith being the fulfillment of this prophecy. He responds to concerns that Joseph Smith is described by Brigham Young as being a "pure Ephraimite" but Doctrine and Covenants 113:4 describes the "rod" as partly a descendent of Jesse and partly Ephraim. He also responds to the notion that the context of this prophecy is millennial, suggesting that the "root of Jesse" should be a leader of that future day.

Matthews, Robert J. "The Message of Isaiah." *Instructor* (October 1968): 410–1.

In 1968 Robert J. Matthews published a short article entitled "The Message of Isaiah" that contained a potpourri of items concerning Isaiah. Matthews lists numerous well-known phrases in society that come from the writings of Isaiah. He notes that the "Holy One of Israel" is a phrase used almost excusively by Isaiah; hence, Book of Mormon authors may have become familiar with this phrase through him. Matthews also argues that the Messiah prophecies are the central message of Isaiah, pointing out that Isaiah is the Old Testament prophet quoted most frequently in the New Testament. He also suggests that a familiarity with modern scripture can aid in understanding Isaiah, since sections of the Doctrine and Covenants have close linguistic and subject matter parallels to Isaiah (e.g., D&C 133 and Isaiah 63–4; D&C 113 and Isaiah 11, 52).

Sperry, Sidney B. *Book of Mormon Compendium.* Salt Lake City: Bookcraft, 1968.

Sperry's *Book of Mormon Compendium,* like Reynolds and Sjodahl's *Commentary on the Book of Mormon,* provides Book of Mormon commentary that includes remarks on the Isaiah quotations. In fact, Sperry states in the preface of his work that "the greatest contribution of this volume is probably to be found in my explanations of the meaning of the Isaiah chapters in the Book of Mormon."[4] As seen in his earlier works, Sperry's approach to the Isaiah passages in this volume is conservative. For Sperry, a major aspect of understanding the Isaiah texts comes from knowing what time period Isaiah is considering in each passage. Assuming that each verse or group of verses addresses a single time period in history allows Sperry to avoid speculating about multiple fulfillments of Isaiah's prophecies. For example, his comments on 2 Nephi 23 (parallel to Isaiah 13) do not allow verses 1–13 to be applied to ancient Babylon and the modern figurative Babylon; instead, he applies these verses only to modern times, and he applies verses 14–22 only to ancient times, giving no rationale for the shift in interpretation.

Sperry's avoidance of dual-fulfillment ideology can again be seen in his discussion of the Immanuel prophecy. Rather than entertain the idea that Isaiah's prophecy has more than one fulfillment, Sperry agrees with Matthews's interpretation of the prophecy in spite of the difficulties in dating that Isaiah 7:15–16 introduces. However, unlike his earlier comments, or lack thereof, in *The Voice of Israel's Prophets*, Sperry offers a solution to the difficulties:

> Offhand, they [the verses in question] seem to demand an interpretation of the sign which looks to the near future for its fulfillment rather than to the time of Christ. . . . Personally, I am inclined to accept Immanuel as a reference to the Savior, and especially in the light of [Isaiah 8:8], where Judah is referred to as Immanuel's land. The allusion to Immanuel suggests that the land of Judah (about which Ahaz was concerned) had a great destiny to fulfill, and hence that it was not about to be destroyed by Syria and Ephraim. Verses 15 and 16 of [Isaiah 7] simply make our Lord's infancy *a symbolic representation of the short-lived nature of the threat to Judah.* (p. 199, emphasis added)

Sperry offers a viable solution to this problem, but he does not seem altogether convinced by his own argument, as evidenced by the question mark he places next to the word *Immanuel* when he associates the name with the Lord in the paragraph following this quotation (see p. 200).

McConkie, Bruce R. "Ten Keys to Understanding Isaiah." *Ensign* (October 1973): 78–83.

In this article Bruce R. McConkie uses Book of Mormon passages that refer to Isaiah to teach his readers that a personal understanding of Isaiah's teachings is essential to salvation and that God will reveal the meaning of those teachings to the diligent and receptive, just as he revealed it to Nephi. McConkie then gives his readers ten guidelines for enhancing their understanding of Isaiah. One of the most important guidelines, according to McConkie, is to study the Book of Mormon version of Isaiah and the interpretations of Isaiah given by Book of Mormon prophets. He declares that no one can understand Isaiah's teachings without first acquiring a testimony of the Book of Mormon and that "the Book of Mormon is the world's greatest commentary on the book of Isaiah" (p. 81). He closes by giving a brief chapter-by-chapter outline of Isaiah.

Adams, L. LaMar, and Alvin C. Rencher. "A Computer Analysis of the Isaiah Authorship Problem." *BYU Studies* 15/1 (1974): 95–102.[5]

Based on a computer-aided statistical analysis of various stylistic features of the book of Isaiah and 11 other Old Testament books, L. LaMar Adams and Alvin C. Rencher address the authorship problem of the book of Isaiah. The authors pinpoint a number of stylistic elements of Hebrew that, much like a fingerprint, normally vary from author to author but remain consistent within the works of one author.

Using the Hebrew text, they determine the frequency of these elements in Isaiah and other Old Testament books. They analyze these frequencies and conclude that "the statistical results in this study do not support the divisionist claim that little or no evidence exists for unity of the book of Isaiah.... The two parts of Isaiah most often claimed to have been written by different authors, chapters 1–39 and 40–66, were found to be more similar to each other in style than to any of the control group of eleven other Old Testament books. The book of Isaiah also exhibits greater internal consistency than any of the other eleven books" (p. 102).

Ludlow, Daniel H. *A Companion to Your Study of the Book of Mormon.* Salt Lake City: Deseret Book, 1976.

Ludlow's book is a collection of verse-by-verse commentaries and various quotes and insights concerning selected verses in the Book of Mormon. Ludlow presents a wide variety of other interpretations, generally without any personal remarks (for example, see his reporting of D&C 113). Ludlow's preference, when he offers his opinions, seems to be for the traditional views.

Nibley, Hugh W. "Great Are the Words of Isaiah." In *The Sixth Annual Sidney B. Sperry Symposium.* Provo, Utah: Brigham Young University, 1978. Reprinted in *Old Testament and Related Studies,* ed. John W. Welch, Gary P. Gillum, and Don E. Norton. Salt Lake City: Deseret Book and FARMS, 1985, 215–37.

In this address Hugh Nibley discusses the various methods people use to dilute the prophet's message. For instance, some claim that Isaiah moralizes rather than preaches doctrine. Others try to show that Isaiah's God is vengeful and savage. Still others affirm that there were several Isaiahs who all said different things. Following these remarks, Nibley summarizes the first chapter of the book of Isaiah in layman's terms. His comments at this point are interesting in light of the many arguments put forth by previous LDS scholars concerning the Isaiah authorship problem and its relation to the Book of Mormon (see, for example, the writings of B. H. Roberts, James E. Talmage, and Sidney B. Sperry). Nibley notes that most secular scholars believe that chapter one is a summary of Isaiah's writings written by a later disciple, and he remarks that the Book of Mormon never quotes from Isaiah 1, inferring that perhaps the scholars are right concerning the later dating of this chapter. For Nibley, there may still be unanswered questions concerning the authorship of Isaiah and what was actually recorded on the brass plates. Nibley finishes his speech by focusing on the human qualities Isaiah describes as either favored or despised by God.

Nyman, Monte S. *Great Are the Words of Isaiah: An Understandable Guide to Isaiah's Monumental Message.* Salt Lake City: Bookcraft, 1980.

Nyman's work is the first LDS verse-by-verse commentary devoted specifically to Isaiah. Because it emphasizes how modern prophets and the Book of Mormon interpret the words of Isaiah, this book is a great resource for LDS interpretations of each verse in the book of Isaiah. This approach is also evident in appendices B–F, in which Nyman identifies specific chapters and verses in Isaiah that are quoted or alluded to in other scriptures and in comments made by general authorities of the LDS Church, including all references found in *Teachings of the Prophet Joseph Smith.*[6]

Nyman structures his book on the assumption that Isaiah 1–35 is a compilation of Isaiah's revelations, chapters 40–66 compose the "vision of Isaiah" mentioned in 2 Chronicles 32:32, and chapters 36–39 constitute a historical account that was inserted between these two separate sections when the whole was compiled (see pp. 16–7). He breaks each of these three major sections into chapter groupings that are related in content and form. He then summarizes each grouping and gives notes and comments on each verse, relying heavily on scripture and the interpretations of modern prophets.

Nyman avoids tying Isaiah's prophecies to more than one time period. His intent is to elucidate the original meaning of the text as it applies to a single time period, but some of his comments within the first few chapters indicate that he recognizes that "some prophecies were *originally intended* to apply to two or more different times, places, or situations" (p. 12, emphasis added). Although he professes belief in the dual fulfillment of Isaiah's prophecies, Nyman does not point out which prophecies are subject to dual fulfillment. For instance, one expects Isaiah's Immanuel prophecy to appear in this category, but Nyman simply suggests that the child mentioned in verses 14 and 15 of chapter 7 is Jesus Christ, while the child in verse 16 could be any child. In other words, when Isaiah tells Ahaz of the sign, he shifts his prophetic vision from the distant future to the immediate future, giving two different prophecies consecutively rather than a single prophecy with dual fulfillment.

Nyman, while commenting on Nephi's use of the word *liken*, cautions to his readers that "to 'liken' a scripture to a different situation than that in which it originated is not always to learn the original message of that scripture. To correctly interpret a scriptural passage is to learn its original meaning" (p. 12). In other words, he suggests that to liken a scripture is to take it out of context—separate it from its original meaning—and apply it to another situation or time period. Nyman seeks to interpret Isaiah by instead focusing on the original meaning of Isaiah's words. However, in this regard, it is interesting that Nyman does not view Isaiah 29 as being "likened" by Nephi while Isaiah himself had a different "original meaning," as others (such as Reynolds and Sjodahl) have suggested. Rather, Nyman interprets Isaiah 29 as being a direct reference to the Book of Mormon.

Matthews, Robert J. ""Why do the Book of Mormon selections from Isaiah sometimes parallel the King James Version and not the older—and thus presumably more accurate—Dead Sea Scrolls text." I Have a Question. *Ensign* (March 1980): 40.

In this article Robert J. Matthews addresses the question, "Why do the Book of Mormon selections from Isaiah sometimes parallel the King James Version and not the older—and thus presumably more accurate—Dead Sea Scrolls text of why the Book of Mormon Isaiah passages are generally more like the Isaiah passages in the King James Version than those in the Dead Sea Scrolls text?" He argues that the Dead Sea Scrolls show evidence of poor transcription (differing considerably from the Greek Septuagint text), and that even though they are older than the King James Version, they are not necessarily more accurate. He also argues that the Book of Mormon may not always reflect a detailed analysis of every word on the gold plates. Therefore, Joseph Smith may have used the King James Version in the tranlation process not to copy from, but as a "vehicle to express the general sense of what was on the Gold Plates."

Adams, L. LaMar. *The Living Message of Isaiah.* Salt Lake City: Deseret Book, 1981.

A year after Nyman published *"Great Are the Words of Isaiah,"* L. LaMar Adams published his book, which is intended to inspire LDS readers to study the words of Isaiah for modern application. The bulk of the book provides spiritual and academic keys to help the reader understand Isaiah's message, especially focusing on the Book of Mormon versions and interpretations of Isaiah. Several chapters focus on topics in the book of Isaiah that deal primarily with the last days, but these are written mainly to inspire the reader to follow what Adams feels is Isaiah's main directive to the Latter-day Saints: "to come unto Christ in a more determined manner" (p. 86).

Adams adopts the perspective that Isaiah's prophecies may find fulfillment in more than one time period, concluding that because Isaiah was addressing a stubborn people, his prophecies are more for Latter-day Saints than for the people of Isaiah's own day. "Thus," explains Adams, "Isaiah's prophecies are either of the last days or can usually be applied to *both Isaiah's days and the last days*" (p. 30, emphasis added). Appendix A demonstrates this assertion by outlining the major prophecies of Isaiah and pointing out that the prophecies first fulfilled in Isaiah's day are often paralleled by latter-day events.

The final section of Adams's book, appendix B, is a revised translation of the apocryphal *Ascension of Isaiah*. Basing his revised translation on work done by R. H. Charles,[7] Adams "reverse translates" passages where he believes Charles was confused or had mistranslated. He first translates Charles's English version into Hebrew, and then he translates it back into English.

Petersen, Mark E. *Isaiah for Today.* Salt Lake City: Deseret Book, 1981.

Each chapter of this book is devoted to a specific historical or doctrinal topic: "Predictions of Christ," "The Marvelous Work," "The Unlearned Man," "One That Is Learned," and "The Old Jerusalem." Petersen discusses topics that he feels specifically address the last days or are relevant to the last days, such as the prophecies concerning Christ. Petersen sees no value in the historical events mentioned in Isaiah except as the history helps us understand our times: "Isaiah is definitely for today. His dealings with the ancient kings of Judah and his confrontations with them over the attacks of the Assyrians and the Babylonians are all in the past. Reference to them is strictly historical and has little relevance for us" (p. 8).

Petersen unhesitatingly claims that Isaiah saw the events of the last days and identifies specific instances of fulfillment. For example, he believes that the "mountain of the Lord's house" in Isaiah 2:2 refers specifically to the Salt Lake Temple. In analyzing the prophecies of Isaiah 29, Petersen quotes and discusses almost every verse in 2 Nephi 27 (see pp. 77–97). He interprets the "sealed book" in the traditional manner—that is, as the Book of Mormon—and like McConkie in "Ten Keys," Petersen feels that a testimony of the Book of Mormon and a familiarity with its treatment of Isaiah are essential to understanding Isaiah: "To understand Isaiah, people need to understand the Latter-day Saint point of view. They cannot and never will understand him otherwise" (p. 6).

Ludlow, Daniel H. *A Companion to Your Study of the Old Testament*. Salt Lake City: Deseret Book, 1981.

Like his earlier work, Daniel H. Ludlow provides little direct personal commentary on Isaiah in this book but offers quotes and cross-references to aid in scripture study. He also often mentions the various interpretations put forth by other scholars but leaves it to the reader to decide their plausibility. For example, in his discussion on Isaiah 2:1–3, which contains the phrase "mountain of the Lord's house," Ludlow remarks that "some LDS students of the scriptures have noted the possibility of dual fulfillment" (i.e., the Salt Lake Temple and future Jerusalem temple. p. 283).

Gileadi, Avraham. *Apocalyptic Book of Isaiah: A New Translation with Interpretative Key.* Provo, Utah: Hebraeus Press, 1982. [8]

Avraham Gileadi was one of the first LDS scholars to adopt fully the idea of dual or multiple fulfillment as a method for interpreting Isaiah's words. Taking an extreme approach, Gileadi assumes that every event and entity in the writings of Isaiah provides a typological pattern for the last days. In his *Apocalyptic Book of Isaiah,* Gileadi gives his own new translation of the book of Isaiah, and he concludes with various approaches that can be used to study and understand Isaiah. The first approach, which forms the foundation for his other methods, is to analyze the structure of Isaiah. Gileadi identifies several types of structures that span the whole book of Isaiah, including some that are found in other ancient Near Eastern literature. For instance, the threefold narrative plot—(1) trouble at home, (2) exile abroad, and (3) happy homecoming—found in Egyptian literature, such as in the story of *Sinuhe,* is also found in the book of Isaiah: chapters 1–39 portray the trouble at home, chapters 40–54 describe exile, and chapters 55–66 predict a happy homecoming.

Another structure, which Gileadi calls the "Bifid" structure (see p. 172), breaks the book of Isaiah into two halves, chapters 1–33 and 34–66, which parallel each other in theme and word usage and are ordered chiastically. According to Gileadi, this literary structure conveys to Isaiah's readers the message that events and entities in history are types for the future. Based on these and other structures, Gileadi argues for the unity of Isaiah because if any part of Isaiah was missing from the whole, the structures could not exist.

Gileadi's structures form the basis for two other methodologies that he calls "Synthesis of Events" and "Entity Synthesis" (see pp. 189–205), in which various events or figures throughout Isaiah's text are synthesized into one archetype that becomes the basis for interpreting the future. For example, Gileadi feels that all covenants that God made with individuals and with Israel as a whole are synthesized into one "New Covenant" (see pp. 205–6). Synthesizing parallel past events and looking at the combination of traits and events thus becomes the interpretive key to understanding Isaiah's message about the last days, teaches Gileadi.

One of the more interesting interpretations that Gileadi provides concerns the identity of the "rod" and "root of Jesse" in Isaiah 11. Based on word studies and parallel structures, Gileadi concludes that the person spoken of in these verses is a latter-day Davidic king, not Joseph Smith and not the Messiah (for he is the "*stem* of Jesse"). This king will be instrumental in the salvation of Israel and in the events surrounding the ushering in of the millennium.

Ludlow, Victor L. *Isaiah: Prophet, Seer, and Poet.* Salt Lake City: Deseret Book, 1982. [9]

This book remains one of the most comprehensive LDS commentaries on Isaiah. Ludlow provides the reader with a verse-by-verse commentary of Isaiah that includes structural analysis, a comparison of textual versions, clarifications of word meanings, cultural and historical background, and references to modern interpretations given by various biblical scholars and LDS general authorities. He also includes the Book of Mormon's variant Isaiah texts in his analysis and provides a short section explaining how and why Isaiah was used in the Book of Mormon (see pp. 93–8).

Ludlow does not shy away from difficult passages and provides the reader with the various scholarly opinions about the text in question. The balanced nature of his work (he gives many interpretations and viewpoints in addition to his own) allows for such speculation without affecting the quality of his work.

Ludlow does not hesitate to speculate on how certain of Isaiah's prophecies have been fulfilled. For example, he interprets Isaiah 19:5–10 as possibly being fulfilled by the Aswan Dam (see pp. 212–6). Ludlow embraces the idea of more than one fulfillment of various prophecies, and he lists and explores many possible fulfillments of Isaiah's prophecies. For example, his commentary gives his own interpretations and the interpretations of scholars concerning the Immanuel prophecy and how it might have been fulfilled in Ahaz's day (though he never suggests the precise identity of the virgin). Ludlow then states that "given this brief background, it seems that this sign, or prophecy, can find fulfillment *as a call to faith* on three levels": (1) in Ahaz's day "a son was to be born and named Immanuel as a sign of the Lord's power of deliverance"; (2) "to the people at the time of the birth of Christ, it was as a sign to know that Jesus Christ . . . was to come"; and (3) in the last days, the "memorial" of Christ's birth is a sign of God's promise that in the end of the world, against all odds, the Lord will bring about Zion (see pp. 144–5; emphases added).

In his comments on Isaiah 29, Ludlow again provides multiple explanations for the "sealed book" prophecy rather than stating emphatically that it refers to the Book of Mormon. His various interpretations are as follows:

- Isaiah was only talking to the Jews of Jerusalem about the Bible and other records.

- Isaiah was talking to the Nephites. Nephi recognized this and expanded or restored parts of Isaiah 29.

- Isaiah was addressing the Jews, but Nephi used this as a transition point to talk about his own record (i.e., he "likened" Isaiah's words to his own circumstances).

- Isaiah was talking to the last days about any number of records.

Having given the above possible interpretations, Ludlow does seem to favor the idea that Isaiah was speaking specifically about the Book of Mormon. He bases this preference on the fact that the Joseph Smith Translation seems to correspond more closely with the Book of Mormon version of Isaiah 29 than with the King James Version.

Ludlow's views on Isaiah 11 is another point of interest, especially in light of other authors views on the "rod" and "root of Jesse." Ludlow, like Gileadi, breaks with traditional views that the person(s) in these verses represent Joseph Smith and through a simple concordance word study analysis, puts forth the idea that the "rod" and "branch" of the first verse refers to a great Jewish leader of the last days who will be called David. This cannot be Christ, Ludlow affirms, since Doctrine and Covenants 113 identifies the "stem of Jesse," not the "rod," as Christ.[10]

Martin, Loren D. *Isaiah: An Ensign to the Nations.* Salt Lake City: Valiant, 1982.

The main purpose of Martin's book is to analyze and provide a verse-by-verse commentary of the first five chapters of Isaiah. He provides in-depth studies of these selected chapters, relying heavily on Near Eastern culture and variant meanings of the Hebrew to illuminate textual inferences and to define certain terms. Martin speculates on specific instances in history that might fulfill certain prophecies (for example, he interprets Isaiah 2:21 as referring to the mass suicide at Masada [see pp. 69–71]), and he feels that Isaiah's words often have a double meaning, "intentionally leaving major portions of a complete picture unclear or entirely missing. Such gaps and ambiguities were left to be filled in by modern scripture, revelation, prophetic interpretation and historical events" (p. 2).

Smith, George D., Jr. "Isaiah Updated." *Dialogue* 16/2 (1983): 37–51. Reprinted in *The Word of God: Essays on Mormon Scripture*, ed. Dan Vogel. Salt Lake City: Signature Books, 1990.[11]

In response to the traditional Christian and Mormon interpretations applied to Isaiah, George D. Smith "examines Isaiah's prophecies in their historical context and compares their meaning as a message for his time with the expanded meaning that Christians and specifically Mormons have since applied to them thousands of years later" (p. 37). Relying heavily on modern biblical scholarship and the interpretations of non-LDS scholars, Smith declares that the events of Isaiah 7:14 and Isaiah 29 are contemporary to Isaiah himself—single prophecies of single events fulfilled in Isaiah's day.

Smith argues that Christians (specifically Matthew) apply the Immanuel prophecy to Christ when in fact Isaiah did not have Christ in mind when he gave it. He believes that a similar mistake is present in interpretations of Isaiah 29, contending that Isaiah wrote this chapter only to the people of his day. He describes the "unwillingness of the people and their leaders . . . to understand the word of Yahweh. The leaders read, but do not understand. . . . The masses, on the other hand, cannot even read the law, for they do not know how" (p. 45). He asserts that Latter-day Saint tradition, which is based on Nephi's likening the text to his own people's future, changes or "updates" the interpretation of the verses in this chapter to refer to the restoration and the coming forth of the Book of Mormon, with the Charles Anthon story playing a significant role in the fulfillment of Isaiah's words. On the basis of these conclusions, Smith rhetorically argues, "Can the substitution of new meaning be justified as a dual message hidden in Isaiah's original words?" (p. 51). He believes that many people force dual or multiple fulfillment on Isaiah's prophecies by reinterpreting the original message of Isaiah—which was actually intended only for Isaiah's contemporaries—in the context of other historical time periods and then applying these new interpretations to the original text.

Lundquist, John M. "Temple Symbolism in Isaiah." *Isaiah and the Prophets: Inspired Voices from the Old Testament.* Ed. Monte S. Nyman. Provo, Utah: BYU Religious Studies Center, 1984, 33–55.

Lundquist focuses on the central role of the temple in Isaiah's writings. Lundquist outlines a comparative study in ancient Near Eastern temple typology and discusses many verses in the writings of Isaiah that reflect this same typology, specifically those dealing with the cosmic mountain, communal meals, covenant making, and the waters of life.

Gileadi, Avraham. "Isaiah: Four Latter-day Keys to an Ancient Book." *Isaiah and the Prophets: Inspired Voices from the Old Testament.* Ed. Monte S. Nyman. Provo, Utah: BYU Religious Studies Center, 1984, 119–37.

In this article Avraham Gileadi identifies four Book of Mormon keys that enable the reader to understand Isaiah better. The first two keys, found in 2 Nephi 25:4–5, are identified as the spirit and the letter of prophecy: reading under the influence of the Holy Ghost and with a testimony that Jesus is the Christ provides the spirit key, and understanding the literary methods the Jews used to convey the word of the Lord provides the letter key. Gileadi elaborates on this second key, giving examples of literary methods (such as parallelisms and metaphors) and cultural elements (such as Near Eastern suzerain-vassal relationships). He then gives the implications of these elements and methods on understanding covenant theology in Isaiah. The third and fourth keys Gileadi identifies are the Savior's command in 3 Nephi 23:1 to "search" Isaiah's words and the Savior's statement in 3 Nephi 23:3 that all of Isaiah's words "have been and shall be." Gileadi interprets this last phrase literally, arguing that every prophecy of Isaiah is a type of things to come and thus can have dual purpose and fulfillment.

Adams, L. LaMar. "A Scientific Analysis of Isaiah Authorship." *Isaiah and the Prophets: Inspired Voices from the Old Testament.* Ed. Monte S. Nyman. Provo, Utah: BYU Religious Studies Center, 1984, 151–63.

LaMar Adams's piece is essentially the same article he coauthored with Rencher in 1974 for *BYU Studies* but directed more toward the lay reader.

Tvedtnes, John A. "Isaiah Variants in the Book of Mormon." *Isaiah and the Prophets: Inspired Voices from the Old Testament.* Ed. Monte S. Nyman. Provo, Utah: BYU Religious Studies Center, 1984, 165–77.

Tvedtnes discusses many of the Isaiah verses in the Book of Mormon that vary from their corresponding verses in the King James Version of the Bible.[12] Tvedtnes shows numerous examples of how the variants in the Book of Mormon are supported by other ancient texts, such as the Septuagint, the Vulgate, and 1QIsa (the Isaiah Scroll from Cave 1 at

Qumran), and how the variants enhance or complete the poetic structure of the verses in question.

Skousen, W. Cleon. *Isaiah Speaks to Modern Times*. Salt Lake City: Ensign, 1984.

This book gives a verse-by-verse commentary of the entire book of Isaiah and also presents Isaiah and his world by topic. The topical chapters generally expand on information in Skousen's *The Fourth Thousand Years*, but the verse-by-verse commentary makes up the bulk of the book. As a whole, the comments are Skousen's own thoughts and interpretations. Occasionally he refers to other scripture, particularly the Book of Mormon, which he uses primarily to identify the "correct" reading of various passages of Isaiah. He seldom refers to the works of others, although he claims in the preface that an "attempt has been made to bring together some of the finest work of many scholars both past and present" (p. iv). As in his earlier works, he tends to smooth over difficult verses, providing his own interpretation and avoiding any mention of conflict surrounding the text. Again, he interprets Isaiah's prophecies as each having only one fulfillment, relying on traditional interpretations rather than considering the possibility of variant interpretations or multiple fulfillment.

Adams, L. LaMar. "Jesus' Commandment to Search the Words of Isaiah." *The Old Testament and the Latter-day Saints: Sperry Symposium 1986*. Orem, Utah: Randall Book, 1986, 177–92.

In this address LaMar Adams discusses the need to study and apply the words of Isaiah. He focuses more on inspiring his readers than on providing commentary and draws on Isaiah's words to urge readers to prepare spiritually for the second coming through repentance and endurance.

Taking the traditional approach, Adams emphasizes that Isaiah prophesied the restoration. He uses Isaiah 29 and the coming forth of the Book of Mormon as an example of how prophecies have been fulfilled in the last days.

> Hoskisson, Paul Y. "A Latter-day Saint Reading of Isaiah in the Twentieth Century: The Example of Isaiah 6." *The Old Testament and the Latter-day Saints: Sperry Symposium 1986.* Orem, Utah: Randall Book, 1986, 193–210.

In this chapter, Paul Y. Hoskisson identifies six reasons that Isaiah may be difficult to read: (1) Isaiah wrote in poetry, (2) he wrote in an elevated Hebrew literary style, (3) he is culturally removed from today, (4) he is chronologically removed from today, (5) he draws heavily on scripture and doctrine outside his own time and place, and (6) he spoke prophetically. Hoskisson then shows that these potential obstacles can actually be used as tools for understanding Isaiah by analyzing Isaiah 6 using his knowledge of Isaiah's style and cultural milieu.

> Jackson, Kent P. "Nephi and Isaiah." In *1 Nephi to Alma 29.* Vol. 7 of *Studies in Scripture.* Ed. Kent P. Jackson. Salt Lake City: Deseret Book, 1987.

The main purpose of Kent P. Jackson's article is to introduce the reader to the major Isaiah section in the Book of Mormon (2 Nephi 12–24) and to comment on the nature of Isaiah's writings and Nephi's stated purpose for quoting Isaiah. Jackson provides no commentary on the Isaiah section itself, but gives an outline that divides each chapter into groups of related verses, briefly summarizing each group. Jackson cautions, "Readers should not assume that every statement of an ancient prophet must have a specific meaning in the latter-day setting" (p. 132). In other words, readers should not think that every utterance was originally intended to be fulfilled twice. Rather, like Nephi and Jacob, they should focus on applying the *"principles* contained in Isaiah's words to their own circumstances" (p. 132). This seems to be more a statement on avoiding extremism than denying the possibility of dual fulfillment.

> Ludlow, Victor L. "Isaiah as Taught by the New Testament Apostles." In *The New Testament and the Latter-day Saints,* ed. H. Dean Garrett. Orem, Utah: Randall Book, 1987.

Victor Ludlow here provides a literary analysis of the Isaiah passages quoted in the New Testament. Rather than providing his own interpretation of Isaiah, the main purpose of Ludlow's article is to focus on how each New Testament writer used and interpreted Isaiah. Ludlow notes parallel Isaiah passages in the four Gospels and comments on the distinct ways in which the various writers use the Isaiah passages; however, he does not interpret the reasons for the differences or similarities between the gospel accounts. In other words, he does not discuss *why* Isaiah's writings were used the way they were but simply discusses *how* they were used.

> McConkie, Joseph Fielding, and Robert L. Millet. *First and Second Nephi.* Vol. 1 of *Doctrinal Commentary on the Book of Mormon.* Salt Lake City: Bookcraft, 1987.[13]

McConkie and Millet's book paraphrases and comments lightly on each chapter of the Isaiah block in 2 Nephi. It also includes a short introduction to the Isaiah section, explaining why the Nephites quoted Isaiah and giving tips to understand his words better (see pp. 273–7).

McConkie and Millet state that Isaiah's prophecies have "multiple fulfillments and repeated applications" (p. 282). For example, they interpret Isaiah 13–14 as referring to both the conquest of the historical Babylon and the future destruction of the wicked at the second coming (see p. 282). Further, they find fulfillment of the Immanuel prophecy both in Isaiah's day and in the birth of Christ—though as is frequently the case in this book, they do not explain how they reached their conclusion (see p. 280). In spite of these two examples, the authors generally do not explore all possible fulfillments of Isaiah's words; rather, they focus on those fulfillments that pertain to the restoration. For example, the authors suggest that Isaiah 49 (parallel to 1 Nephi 21) may be applied either to Isaiah himself or to ancient Israel but that such applications should not "obscure [the chapter's] greater meaning as it applies to Christ and Joseph Smith" (p. 157). The authors then go on to interpret the chapter as referring to Joseph Smith and Christ without discussing in any detail the other possible fulfillments. For example, when discussing the "rod" and "root of Jesse," the authors simply adopt the traditional view espoused by Sperry that this is Joseph Smith without mention of a possible latter-day Davidic king interpretation, as Ludlow and Gileadi have suggested.

Their discussion of 2 Nephi 27 (parallel to Isaiah 29) is similar to Reynolds and Sjodahl's, emphasizing that Nephi, not Isaiah, saw in vision the Book of Mormon. McConkie and Millet avoid any reference to what they feel Isaiah's perspective was. Commenting on Nephi's use of Isaiah, McConkie and Millet state, "Nephi expands to all the nations of the earth Isaiah's prophecy relative to the plight of Judah. His [Nephi's] is a vision of universal apostasy" (p. 313).

Gileadi, Avraham. *The Book of Isaiah: A New Translation with Interpretive Keys from the Book of Mormon.* Salt Lake City: Deseret Book, 1988.[14]

Gileadi's second book is largely a revision of his first book, now aimed at an LDS audience. Gileadi integrates into the introduction his article from *Isaiah and the Prophets* concerning the four latter-day keys for understanding Isaiah. He also discusses general structural patterns in Isaiah's work. However, Gileadi's interpretations of Isaiah prophecies seem to focus on the topic of the mortal latter-day Davidic king. Gileadi is sure that the main thrust and message of Isaiah is to prophecy of the role of this Davidic king in the temporal salvation of Israel, as opposed to the spiritual salvation made possible by Christ. Hence, most of Isaiah's prophecies that have been typically attributed to Christ are seen by Gileadi as referring to this Davidic king, including the Immanuel prophecy and the prophecy in Isaiah 9 that inspired Handel's "For Unto Us a Child is Born."

Because this book addresses an LDS audience, Gileadi freely uses Doctrine and Covenants 113 in his interpretation of the "rod," "stem of Jesse," "branch," and "root of Jesse" in Isaiah 11. His interpretation again focuses on the role of this latter-day Davidic king. Gileadi interprets the "stem of Jesse" as Christ, that is, the trunk of the tree. The "rod," or "watersprout," as Gileadi calls it, represents Joseph Smith or the Latter-day Saints in general (i.e., comparable to the wild branches, the gentile nations, in Jacob's olive tree allegory). Gileadi emphasizes that this "rod" will not of itself bear fruit, but that a "branch" or "root [Gileadi translates this as "sprig"] of Jesse" will be grafted into it, and it (the branch) will bring forth fruit. The branch, according to Gileadi, represents the Davidic king and the natural branches of Israel, which will bear fruit in the day of judgment when they are redeemed through the ministry of this mortal Davidic king. The role of this Davidic king, according to Gileadi, was fulfilled by Hezekiah in Isaiah's day, but as a dual fulfillment another would rise primarily from the house of Judah in the last days.

Ludlow, Victor L. *Jesus' "Covenant People Discourse" in 3 Nephi: With Old Testament Background and Modern Application.* Provo, Utah: BYU Religious Studies Center, 1988.

Victor Ludlow's address explains that a major purpose of the Book of Mormon is to teach Israel about its covenant relationship with God. Many references to covenant relationships appear in the Isaiah quotations in 1 Nephi, 2 Nephi, and 3 Nephi. Nephi quotes Isaiah because, as Christ taught, Isaiah's writings contain the full covenant relationship between God and the house of Israel. In 3 Nephi 20–25, Jesus delivers what Ludlow calls the "Covenant People Discourse," teaching the people to read the words of Isaiah, which include a checklist of items that point to the fulfillment of the covenant between God and the house of Israel. The Savior quotes Isaiah 52 and 54 and concludes his discourse by admonishing the people to search the words of Isaiah, which contain the important promises given to Israel.

Parsons, Robert E. "The Prophecies of the Prophets." *First Nephi: The Doctrinal Foundation,* ed. by Monte S. Nyman and Charles D. Tate Jr. (Provo: BYU Religious Studies Center, 1988): 271–81.

This article discusses various prophecies concerning Jesus Christ that Nephi quotes from the lost Old Testament prophets Neum, Zenock, and Zenos. The majority of the article, however, focuses on the prophecies of Isaiah in 1 Nephi 20–21 (parallel Isaiah 48–49). In considering that Nephi states that he quotes Isaiah in order to more fully persuade his brethren to believe in Christ (see 1 Nephi 19:23), Parsons notes that most of Isaiah 48–49 does not deal with Christ directly, so he concludes that perhaps "a belief in Christ comes not only through what the scriptures say of him per se, but also by understanding the covenants he has made with Israel and how they will be fulfilled" (p. 275).

Focusing on 1 Nephi 21 (parallel Isaiah 49), Parsons notes that verses 1–3 deal with a "servant" of God and that this servant is typically argued by scholars to be either the Messiah or Isaiah himself. Parsons solves the problem by adopting the multiple fulfillment approach to Isaiah's prophecies, saying, "I believe *servant* has a dual meaning, namely Christ and Israel" (p. 276). He then outlines how both Christ and Israel (particularly Ephraim) fulfill the prophecies in verses 5–9.

Farley, Brent. "Nephi, Isaiah, and the Latter-Day Restoration." *The Book of Mormon: Second Nephi, the Doctrinal Structure.* Ed. Monte S. Nyman and Charles D. Tate Jr. Provo, Utah: BYU Religious Studies Center, 1989, 227–39.

Farley's piece primarily identifies and explores the Isaiah sections in Nephi's writings that point specifically to the restoration. Farley follows traditional LDS views but allows for both specific and general interpretations. For example, drawing chiefly on the writings and sermons of Church leaders, he interprets the prophecy in 2 Nephi 12:2–3 (parallel to Isaiah 2:2–3) as referring specifically to the Salt Lake Temple and generally to temples around the world. He interprets the phrase "out of Zion shall go forth the law" (2 Nephi 12:3, parallel to Isaiah 2:3) as being specifically fulfilled by LDS Church general conferences and generally fulfilled by the establishment of America. Farley views 2 Nephi 27 (parallel to Isaiah 29) as referring to the Book of Mormon, a book of scripture that aids in the missionary labors that Isaiah alludes to in 2 Nephi 15:26–30 (parallel to Isaiah 5:26–30). The tone of his article implies that he thinks Isaiah originally intended the same interpretations as those Nephi gives to Isaiah's words.

Gentry, Leland. "God Will Fulfill His Covenants with the House of Israel." *The Book of Mormon: Second Nephi, the Doctrinal Structure.* Ed. Monte S. Nyman and Charles D. Tate Jr. Provo, Utah: BYU Religious Studies Center, 1989, 159–76.

This article interprets the sections of Isaiah quoted by Jacob in 2 Nephi 6–8 (parallel to Isaiah 49:22–52:2), relying heavily on Jacob's Isaiah commentary in 2 Nephi 6, 9, and 10. Gentry gives his view on Isaiah's prophecies by stating that "Isaiah uses events of his own day to transport us far into the prophetic future" (p. 159).

Gentry interprets Isaiah's words in this section of the Book of Mormon by applying the prophecies in the larger history of Israel but offers striking possible fulfillments for many of the prophecies. For example, Gentry suggests that Egypt "licked the dust of the feet of God's chosen people" (p. 165) when the Egyptians fled from Sinai during the Six-day War (see Isaiah 49:23). He also notes that 2 Nephi 6:6–7 (parallel Isaiah 49:22–23) could be seen fulfilled in the Indian Placement Program and the missionary labors among the Lamanites. He doesn't mention of how the aforementioned prophecies might have been fulfilled in Isaiah's day; however, when commenting on 2 Nephi 7:11 (parallel Isaiah 50:11), he notes that "such was the folly of ancient Israel! Such is the folly of many today as we prepare for his Second Coming" (p. 168).

Adams, LaMar. "Isaiah: Disciple and Witness of Christ." *A Witness of Jesus Christ: The 1989 Sperry Symposium on the Old Testament.* Ed. Richard D. Draper. Salt Lake City: Deseret Book, 1990, 1–17.

In this piece Adams discusses why Christ turned to Isaiah for a witness of his own ministry. He suggests that Isaiah wrote more concerning Christ's first coming, atonement, second coming, and millennial reign than did any other prophet. He also suggests that Isaiah wrote more majestically, poetically, and melodically than other prophets and that Isaiah's prophecies treated such broad subjects as premortal councils, the creation, the history of the world, Christ's ministry, the last days, and the millennium. Adams also believes that because Isaiah is esoteric, he is understood by those who are spiritually prepared. Isaiah's own life is a witness of Christ.

Meservy, Keith. "Isaiah 53: The Richest Prophecy on Christ's Atonement in the Old Testament." *A Witness of Jesus Christ: The 1989 Sperry Symposium on the Old Testament.* Ed. Richard D. Draper. Salt Lake City: Deseret Book, 1990, 155–77.

In this piece Meservy argues that the modern biblical scholars' rejection of the idea of prophecy limits their ability to interpret Isaiah because they must identify someone else as the subject of the passages that Christians interpret as prophecies about Christ. Using Isaiah 53 as a model, Meservy shows numerous specific parallels between this prophecy and the life of Christ. He rhetorically asks, "How many specific details in Isaiah's prophecy have to be consistent with Jesus' life before we conclude that it is statistically impossible for Isaiah to have known such details without having had any foreknowledge of Christ?" (p. 156). His arguments seem to imply that Isaiah's words are fulfilled only in Christ. He argues against the possibility of fulfillment in other entities.

Gileadi, Avraham. "Isaiah—Key to the Book of Mormon." In *Rediscovering the Book of Mormon,* ed. John L. Sorenson and Melvin J. Thorne. Salt Lake City: Deseret Book and FARMS, 1991.

Since Isaiah is so often quoted and alluded to in the Book of Mormon, Gileadi suggests using Isaiah to interpret the

Book of Mormon. In accordance with his approach to interpreting Isaiah seen in his earlier works, Gileadi notes that Isaiah's prophecies are based on Old Testament archetypes—specifically the Passover, the Exodus, wandering in the wilderness, and conquest of the promised land—and that these patterns also provide a key to the prophetic future as well. Gileadi suggests that since Book of Mormon authors relied so much on Isaiah's words, they also chose events in their lives that typified these patterns. Hence, there are many allusions to the Exodus motif in the Lehite exodus from Jerusalem, Alma's exodus from King Noah, and the Jaredite exodus from the tower of Babel. Gileadi suggests that Nephi quoted so often from Isaiah to make sure his readers would pick up on the pattern in the latter days so they would make a latter-day exodus out of Babylon.

Nyman, Monte S. "Abinadi's Commentary on Isaiah." In *The Book of Mormon: Mosiah, Salvation Only through Christ*, ed. Monte S. Nyman and Charles D. Tate Jr. Provo, Utah: BYU Religious Studies Center, 1991.[15]

In the tradition of the various scholarly suggestions concerning the identity of the "suffering servant" in many of Isaiah's chapters, Nyman suggests that Abinadi's commentary in Mosiah 15 on the words of Isaiah in Mosiah 14 (parallel Isaiah 53) proves that Jesus is the sufferer referred to in Isaiah's writings. Little of Nyman's own interpretations of Isaiah are explored in this article, since the main purpose is to identify what Abinadi did with Isaiah's writings.

Ridges, David J. *Isaiah Made Easier.* Springville, Utah: Copies Plus, 1991.[16]

For each verse of Isaiah, this book gives parenthetical inserts and explanations taken from elsewhere in the scriptures and from other Isaiah commentaries. Because Ridges's interpretation comes from a variety of sources, it is difficult to identify exactly how Ridges interprets Isaiah. In any case, according to his foreword, he is more interested in suggesting possible fulfillments of Isaiah and in showing Church members that Isaiah's prophecies can be understood and enjoyed more than he is in providing a definitive analysis and interpretation of Isaiah's prophecies.

Jackson, Kent P. "Authorship of the Book of Isaiah." *1 Kings to Malachi.* Vol. 4 of *Studies in Scripture.* Ed. Kent P. Jackson. Salt Lake City: Deseret Book, 1993, 80–5.

Jackson's article describes reasons that some biblical scholars attribute the book of Isaiah to multiple authors. Jackson sees the denial of prophetic foresight as the fundamental supposition guiding these scholars. Although he admits there are many differences between the various sections of Isaiah, he feels that these differences can be ascribed to, among other causes, differences in emphasis. Isaiah 1–39, for example, emphasizes judgment, whereas chapters 40–66 emphasize reconciliation. Jackson also argues that the most important piece of evidence for Isaiah's authorship of the later chapters is the inclusion of many of the later chapters in the Book of Mormon (see p. 84).

Meservy, Keith. "God Is with Us (Isaiah 1–17)." *1 Kings to Malachi.* Vol. 4 of *Studies in Scripture.* Ed. Kent P. Jackson. Salt Lake City: Deseret Book, 1993, 86–107.

Meservy's article gives a chapter-by-chapter commentary on Isaiah 1–17. Although he makes no attempt to show any common theme in these chapters, his introductory statement hints that what he believes to be the overarching messages of these chapters are that rising generations would know from reading Isaiah's prophecies the reason they had been separated from their land, and why the rising generations must not stop hoping for the blessings that God promised their forefathers. Meservy generally does not give a specific time for the fulfillment of Isaiah's prophecies, preferring instead to interpret Isaiah in the larger context of the plan of salvation. For instance, his comments on Isaiah 2:1–3 simply suggest that the Lord will again "sanctify [Jerusalem] and establish his residence once more in his holy mountain" (p. 91). He does not try to tie these verses to any specific temple in the last days.

Meservy views the Immanuel prophecy as being fulfilled in Isaiah's own time by the birth of Isaiah's son, an event described in Isaiah 8:3–4. He reasons that God often uses deliverance from specific earthly threats to signify the ultimate deliverance of humankind through his Son; thus "there should be no problem in seeing how God used the birth of a baby in Isaiah's time to foretell deliverance for that generation, while focusing attention on the birth of another baby, through whom all the world will be delivered" (p. 97). In other words, Isaiah's son is a type for Christ. Meservy accepts the idea of dual fulfillment on a typological basis but focuses on the broader situational parallels rather than finding parallels with every entity in the prophecy.

Seely, David Rolph. "The Lord is Our Judge and Our King (Isaiah 18–33)." *1 Kings to Malachi*. Vol. 4 of *Studies in Scripture*. Ed. Kent P. Jackson. Salt Lake City: Deseret Book, 1993, 108–27.

Seely also provides a chapter-by-chapter commentary on Isaiah, dividing chapters 18–33 into three distinct units: chapters 18–23 are part of Isaiah's Oracles against Foreign Nations (found in chapters 13–23), chapters 24–27 make up a last-days vision that is commonly called the Apocalypse of Isaiah, and chapters 28–33 are a collection of loosely connected prophecies of the judgment and the restoration. Seely feels that what unifies chapters 18–33 is the image of the Lord as lawgiver and judge who sends judgments on disobedient Israel and other nations.

Seely assigns single fulfillments to many of Isaiah's prophecies but seems willing to embrace the possibility of multiple fulfillments. For instance, he indicates that the destruction spoken of in Isaiah 29:1–14 occurred when Jerusalem was destroyed in 587 B.C. and A.D. 70, but he also notes that Nephi applied the same prophecy of destruction to his own people; however, Seely does not state whether he believes that Isaiah originally intended the prophecy to apply to Nephi's people.

Jackson, Kent P. "Comfort My People (Isaiah 34–50)." *1 Kings to Malachi*. Vol. 4 of *Studies in Scripture*. Ed. Kent P. Jackson. Salt Lake City: Deseret Book, 1993, 128–45.

Jackson comments on virtually every verse in chapters 34–50 and outlines some of the significant features of this section: Israel's unity as a single nation no longer divided into two separate kingdoms (Judah and Ephraim); God's reconciliation with his people, emphasized by prophecies of millennial conditions; God's power to foretell the future (Jackson points out that, ironically, this is the very point that causes many to say that Isaiah did not author the book attributed to him); and the work of God's servant. This last feature reveals Jackson's views about dual fulfillment. He states that "the servant's identity is not made clear. Perhaps more than one interpretation is valid" (p. 136), an assertion that seems to indicate that Jackson accepts the possibility of multiple fulfillments. He contends that the servant can be interpreted to be Israel as a people, the prophets, or Jesus Christ, explaining that "because all good things and all good people are types of Christ and reflect his nature, perhaps we can identify the servant of whom Isaiah wrote on different levels, depending on the information provided" (p. 137).

Seely, David Rolph. "The Lord Will Bring Salvation (Isaiah 51–66)." *1 Kings to Malachi*. Vol. 4 of *Studies in Scripture*. Ed. Kent P. Jackson. Salt Lake City: Deseret Book, 1993, 146–64.

Seely provides a chapter-by-chapter commentary on Isaiah. Seely maintains that the main theme of Isaiah 51–66 is salvation, a concept that includes the first coming of the Messiah, the gathering of Israel, and the second coming with its accompanying establishment of the millennial kingdom. He remarks that Isaiah's prophecies "do not always delineate precisely between what was to be fulfilled in Christ's first coming and what would be fulfilled by his second coming. Hence we speak of the 'dual nature' of prophecy, meaning that a prophecy will be partially fulfilled in the meridian of time but not completely until the Messiah returns in glory" (p. 159). This is a slightly different definition of *dual fulfillment* than those given by other authors surveyed in this bibliography. Seely teaches that the first part of Isaiah 9:6 ("unto us a child is born, unto us a son is given") was fulfilled at the birth of Christ, but the rest of the verse ("and the government will be upon his shoulder") will be fulfilled at his second coming. This interpretation views Isaiah as giving two different consecutive prophecies rather than a single prophecy that could be fulfilled in various ways.

The only indication that Seely entertains the idea that one prophecy might be fulfilled in several ways is found in his commentary on the servant image in Isaiah. In addition to identifying the servant as Christ, he remarks, "Servant imagery is developed throughout Isaiah in many passages where the servant is a type that can be variously applied to Israel, Cyrus, Isaiah, and all of the servants of the Lord as they participate in bringing salvation" (p. 151). It is unclear whether he views all these applications of the servant type as part of the original meaning of Isaiah's prophecies or whether he thinks we can simply liken the fulfillment of these prophecies to various individuals.

Rasmussen, Ellis T. *A Latter-day Saint Commentary on the Old Testament*. Salt Lake City: Deseret Book, 1993.

In this single–volume Old Testament commentary, Rasmussen divides the verses up into small blocks on which he then comments. Rasmussen, like other conservative scholars, tends to view Isaiah's prophecies as having a singular fulfillment; however, he feels that Isaiah "integrated" past, present, and future prophecies in the same block of scripture and that Isaiah's prophecies of immediate situations often had future "applications" (see p. 503).

Rasmussen remarks that the passages in Isaiah 2 concerning the "mountain of the Lord's house" were fulfilled when the true religion and church was restored as a gathering place in Zion, taking a conservative approach like Sperry's in this regard. Further, Rasmussen emphasizes, like Reynolds and Sjodahl, that it was Nephi who saw that the elements of Isaiah 29 would be fulfilled in the lives of his own people.

Gileadi, Avraham. *The Literary Message of Isaiah*. New York: Hebraeus Press, 1994.[17]

Avraham Gileadi's most recent book is mostly a collection, revision, and expansion of all his previous works, including his doctoral dissertation.[18] This book contains the new translation of Isaiah and the discussion of the four keys to understanding Isaiah that is included in Gileadi's earlier works. It also adds a comprehensive concordance to his translation and a lengthy and meticulous analysis of the Bifid structure of Isaiah (the structure is introduced in far less detail in Gileadi's earlier work *The Apocalyptic Book of Isaiah*). Because the work is directed toward a non-LDS audience, it cites the Book of Mormon only once (see p. 2, n. 3), but LDS readers will discern restoration influences throughout the work.

Gileadi identifies his approach to analyzing Isaiah in three ways: "first, structural analysis, which examines prophetic meanings embedded in the manner of organizing the material; second, rhetorical analysis, which examines the meanings of individual terms and expressions, particularly as they connect different parts of the text; and third, typological analysis, which examines events out of the past that may foreshadow the future" (p. 10). As is seen in his earlier works, typology is particularly important to Gileadi's interpretation of Isaiah. In summarizing his understanding of prophecy in Isaiah, he says:

> Isaiah consistently uses episodes out of Israel's past as types on which to frame prophecies of the future. Having seen the end from the beginning in a great cosmic vision, he was able to view both Israel's ancient history (particularly his own day) and also the last days, the time of the end. He thus carefully frames his words in such a way as to capture both time periods in a single prophecy. (p. 27)

Again, multiple fulfillment is the approach that Gileadi takes in interpreting Isaiah.

One of the major scholarly positions defended by Gileadi in this work is the unity of Isaiah. His detailed analysis of the Bifid structure of Isaiah suggests that the whole book was one literary masterpiece rather than a collection of documents from various authors throughout various periods of history.

Ball, Terry. "Isaiah's Imagery of Plants and Planting."
In *Thy People Shall Be My People and Thy God My God:
The 22nd Annual Sidney B. Sperry Symposium*, ed. Paul Y.
Hoskisson. Salt Lake City: Deseret Book, 1994.

Terry Ball's article discusses the imagery of plants and planting in the prophetic message of Isaiah. Ball explains that the
book of Isaiah refers to plants or their parts more than three
hundred times. Isaiah used plants as metaphors to teach his
people about "their relationship to God, their need for repentance, their future according to His plan, and the ministry of
their Messiah" (pp. 17–8).

Gorton, H. Clay. *The Legacy of the Brass Plates of Laban: A
Comparison of Biblical and Book of Mormon Isaiah Texts*.
Bountiful, Utah: Horizon, 1994.[19]

This book compares the Isaiah texts of the Book of Mormon with those in the King James Version, the Douay-Rheims
(an English version of the Latin Vulgate), an unidentified English version of the Septuagint, and the Pontifical University of
Salamanca's 1947 translation of the Hebrew Old Testament. The
last publication is included because the author states that "in
all probability [it is] a translation of the Masoretic Hebrew dating from the ninth century" (p. 13). Gorton notes how the various biblical versions differ from the 1981 Book of Mormon version and discusses how the changes in the text reveal that "plain
and precious" truths were being removed or altered in order to
cast apostate Israel in a more favorable light and to lessen the
judgments of God that Isaiah made known to them.

Brewster, Hoyt W., Jr. *Isaiah, Plain and Simple: The
Message of Isaiah in the Book of Mormon*. Salt Lake City:
Deseret Book, 1995.

Hoyt Brewster's book is the most recent LDS work that
concentrates exclusively on Isaiah. It reproduces all the

significant Isaiah quotations in the Book of Mormon—including the Isaiah portions quoted in 1 Nephi 20 and 21, 2 Nephi 6–8, Mosiah 14 and 15, and 3 Nephi 20 and 22—along side of the parallel verses from the Bible. Verse-by-verse commentary is also provided. The comments clarify or paraphrase difficult wording, identify and explain differences between Book of Mormon and biblical Isaiah versions, give historical or cultural context to the passages, sometimes explore the Hebrew or Greek meanings of certain terms, suggest interpretations for prophecies, and often include statements from other scriptures or from LDS Church leaders about topics suggested by the verse in question. In addition to the verse-by-verse commentary, Brewster provides a brief introduction to the study of Isaiah and gives overviews for each chapter and group of verses he analyzes.

For some of the more difficult Isaiah passages, Brewster does not shy away from mentioning alternative arguments but typically will defend the traditional LDS viewpoint. Some of the arguments for a particular interpretation originate in Brewster himself, while many come from the host of other LDS commentators—particularly Nyman, Ludlow, and Sperry—whom Brewster catalogs in his work. In interpreting the Immanuel prophecy, Brewster makes clear his belief that Immanuel is Jesus Christ by citing biblical and Book of Mormon passages about the birth of Christ and by quoting a portion of Sperry's interpretation of the prophecy. However, Brewster also mentions that biblical scholars typically assign the fulfillment of this prophecy to Isaiah's day (see pp. 69–70). Brewster's discussion of the "rod" and "root of Jesse" in Isaiah 11 also favors the traditional LDS view that these prophecies refer to Joseph Smith. He mentions Ludlow's interpretation of this as a latter-day Davidic king but states that "this interpretation is not consistent with the view generally held by Latter-day Saints" (p.109). Brewster often mentions opposing views to typical LDS interpretations but rarely takes issue with the arguments for those opposing views.

Conclusions

As can be seen in the above survey, many different interpretations of Isaiah's prophecies exist among LDS scholars. Some simply tackle each prophecy in a single historical context, while others see prophetic fulfillment on many levels and in multiple time periods. Some maintain traditional interpretations—especially those dealing with Christ, the Book of Mormon, and the restoration—while others propose that Isaiah's prophecies have much to do with his own day, viewing people of latter ages as simply likening these prophecies to their own events and circumstances.

Who is right? Can any one method of interpretation be applied to all of Isaiah's prophecies? Perhaps the best answer is that prophecy and its interpretation are the domain of prophets, and as Latter-day Saints believe, when God needs to clarify a matter, he will do so through his living oracles. The question of who is ultimately correct may never be settled until the mouthpiece of the Lord speaks. In the meantime, however, we can examine differing viewpoints and try to determine the meaning behind Isaiah's words. By using the new insights gained in study and in the spirit of prayer, reverence, and the pursuit of knowledge, we can be inspired to a greater determination to live the principles, doctrines, and commandments that God has given us through his prophet Isaiah.

Modern LDS Comments
on Isaiah 53

Not only was Isaiah 53 understood messianically by Abinadi and Nephite prophets before him, but also it has been similarly read and expounded by latter-day prophets and scholars. In his personal exposition on this chapter, Elder Jeffrey R. Holland emphasizes the events and feelings in the mortal experience of Jesus Christ that fulfilled both the exquisite letter and the empassioned spirit of Isaiah's prophecy.[20] Elder Holland, along with several other LDS commentators, interprets various phrases in Isaiah 53 as they refer to events in the passion of the Savior or to attributes of his divine character. The following survey of LDS literature on Isaiah 53, which supplements the annotated bibliography at the end of this volume, shows the frequency with which this text has been cited by LDS commentators. Although a few differences of opinion exist in these explications, they all operate within a general framework that is consistent with the definitive interpretation offered by Abinadi.

Isaiah 53:1

Most LDS scholars interpret the two questions in this verse, in some way, to refer to how the messages of the prophets concerning Christ are ignored or misunderstood. Meservy, however, interprets the first question to mean that Christ's words themselves will be rejected: "When Christ comes to earth, who will believe His words (report)?," and Meservy cites New Testament references in which Christ himself raises these same questions with the Jews (for example, John 8:43: "Why do ye not understand my speech? even because he cannot hear my word").[21] Reynolds and Sjodahl would translate this verse, "Who hath believed our words of Him in whom the power and authority of God is made known?," saying that the verse is better translated as containing only one query, not two, focusing more directly on Christ as the subject of this chapter. The answer to this question is "no one."[22]

The second question is often interpreted to mean that the arm of the Lord is revealed in the being of the mortal Messiah,[23] and Ludlow cites numerous ancient and modern prophets who have identified the "arm of the Lord" as Christ.[24] Other LDS scholars believe the second question asks, "To whom has God revealed his priesthood, his gospel?" and also affirm that all knowledge of God must come from revelation,[25] whereas Ridges and Sperry understand this question to read, "Who sees God's hand in things?" or "To whom is the power or might of the Lord revealed?"[26]

Isaiah 53:2

Verse two reveals details of Christ's mortal life—despite predominantly unrighteous surroundings, he will be nurtured by the Lord.[27] Nearly every LDS writer agrees that Christ's divine knowledge and character did not manifest itself in such a way as to draw attention to himself.[28]

Isaiah 53:3

Speaking of the rejection of Christ, Brewster and Seely point out that he was rejected by those of his own country (see Matthew 13:57; Luke 4:24; Mark 6:1–6),[29] and Meservy and McConkie and Millet understand this to refer to Christ's popularity with the masses, who followed him for healing and teaching, but when initial needs were satisfied, they left him, particularly after his "bread of life" sermon in John 6.[30] Millet feels that no one can understand the sorrow and loneliness of Christ, and, according to Reynolds and Sjodahl, people looked the other way when they saw Christ, just as two of the three men in the Good Samaritan story turned from the injured man.[31] Seely compares John 1:5 (the light shines in darkness, but the darkness comprehends it not) and John 1:11 (he came to his own, but they received him not), and Sperry interprets "grief" as "sickness."[32]

The phrase "and we esteemed him not" is commonly understood to mean that people generally, either living at Christ's time or in the present day, are preoccupied by wickedness and adultery, and resent and despise Christ for intruding into their selfish, lustful way of living.[33] McConkie and Millet add that "our esteem of Christ is measured by our obedience to his commandments."[34]

Isaiah 53:4

Speaking of the lines beginning in verse four, Ludlow finds Isaiah's most important concepts about Christ's role.[35] Ludlow expounds on the laws of mercy and justice, explaining why there must be an opposition in all things, and applies these laws to Christ's atonement, adding that justice made the atonement "necessary" and mercy made the atonement "possible," and that Christ had to be both capable and willing to perform the atonement.[36] Some scholars emphasize the irony,[37] the gravity, and the reality of the weight of the sins of the world that Christ bore,[38]while others, such as Ludlow and Millet emphasize the understanding and forgiving nature of Christ.[39]

The phrase, "we did esteem him stricken, smitten of God, and afflicted," refers to the mistaken idea that the suffering of the servant was a punishment from God. But the reality is, as is explained in verse five, "he was wounded for our transgressions." Meservy observes that Isaiah emphasizes eleven times in this chapter the vicarious nature of Christ's atonement.[40]

Isaiah 53:5

The concept of peace sustains many interpretations. Brewster sees in this verse the idea that peace of mind is available after repentance, which has been made possible by the Savior's suffering (chastisement).[41] Meservy elaborates that we deserve chastisement because of our guilt, which is suffered by Christ, bringing us peace. *Shalom*, meaning "peace," derives from the Hebrew verb *shillem*, meaning "to reconcile." Thus, Christ's peace is not a friendly greeting, but a gift of the Spirit, a wholeness of being, a oneness with God.[42] Ridges and Reynolds and Sjodahl agree that Christ was punished so that we could have peace, and "chastisement" here may be interpreted as "burden" or "burden of establishing"; all peace must come from righteousness, and the burden of Christ was to once again bring peace to Judah, which had wandered in sin.[43] Sperry interprets "chastisement of our peace" as "chastisement that led to our salvation."[44] Many LDS commentators point out that, although everyone makes mistakes, we often turn from Christ, thinking that we know how to find true happiness better than he does, and that because we are more interested in our own fancies and whims, we indulge in our own appetites and desires.[45]

Isaiah 53:6

In the phrase, "and the LORD hath laid on him the iniquity of us all," Meservy and Ridges interpret "LORD" ("Jehovah" in Hebrew), as referring to the Father (the Father laid on Christ our iniquity), whereas Rasmussen and Skousen interpret

"LORD" here, and in verse ten, to refer to Jehovah himself, since the Lord is the Savior—Christ let himself be persecuted.[46]

Isaiah 53:7

The description of Christ's sufferings continues in verse seven, and though most interpret "oppressed" and "afflicted" in a general sense of persecution, Reynolds and Sjodahl specify that "oppressed" means he was trampled down by the abuse of power and authority vested in the Jewish hierarchy, and "afflicted" refers to his physical sufferings at trial.[47] They continue, saying that "he opened not his mouth," not only in his trial, but also during his entire ministry, where he offered no excuses or apologies for his teachings.[48]

Isaiah 53:8

Scholars have offered many interpretations of "who shall declare his generation? for he was cut off out of the land of the living." Most believe Isaiah is saying that Christ was "cut off from land of living" because he died without offspring; nevertheless, the righteous are Christ's seed (Mosiah 15:10–13).[49] Elder McConkie says that the question, "Who shall declare his generation?" means "Who shall give the genealogy of the Messiah? Who shall tell the Source whence he sprang? Who can name his ancestors and tell the progenitors who preceded him? What of his Father and mother, his grandparents? Who shall declare his beginning, his genesis, his generation?" and points out that both Luke and Matthew give the genealogy of Christ at the beginning of their records.[50] McConkie and Millet state that "declare his generation" means, "Who shall declare his genesis, his roots, his origin?" believing that the only ones who

can testify today about Christ's true origin are those who
have an understanding of his mortal and immortal attributes,
derived from his mortal mother and immortal Father.[51]
Sperry recognizes that "Who shall declare his generation?"
is often taken to mean "Among his contemporaries who was
concerned?" but he thinks "generation" means the same
thing as "seed" (spirit posterity or believers), and thus renders this verse, "And who will be concerned with his true
believers?"[52]

Isaiah 53:8

Meservy, Reynolds and Sjodahl, Skousen, and Sperry all
note that "stricken" in the Greek Septuagint reads "smitten
to death," and according to Skousen, this helps us understand that this chapter refers to a single person, not to the
nation of Israel, as some have insisted.[53]

Isaiah 53:9

For most scholars, making "his grave with the wicked"
refers to Christ's crucifixion between two thieves, and "with
the rich in his death" was directly fulfilled when Christ was
buried in the tomb of the wealthy Joseph of Arimathea.
Brewster continues, saying that the word "because" should
read "although" (Christ was put to death, *although* he had
done no violence), and cites 1 Peter 2:22 ("Who did no sin,
neither was guile found in his mouth").[54] Ridges adds that
in the German version "violence" reads "wrong"—Christ
was perfect.[55]

Isaiah 53:10

How should we understand the idea that "it pleased
the Lord to bruise him"? Elder Melvin J. Ballard has been
influential for many, whose words express thanks that the
Father did not intervene and spare the Son, and who says

that the Father hid in a distant corner of the universe during the Gethsemane ordeal.[56] Sperry and Brewster suggest that the word *Lord* was improperly copied onto the brass plates and into other Bible sources, for it should read "Elohim bruised Jehovah."[57] Others say that "Lord" may validly refer to either Elohim or Jehovah: Elohim was pleased to bruise Christ, as verified in John 3:16 ("For God so loved the world"), but one could also say that Jehovah was pleased to bruise himself.[58] Sperry discusses at length the apparent difficulty here, and says that Abinadi seems to think that the "Lord" was Elohim (Mosiah 15:7–8); in any case, he adds, Christ is the Father in a special sense, and he also discusses this Father-Son status.[59] Most other scholars simply interpret verse ten to read that since the atonement was absolutely essential to the plan of salvation, it pleased the Father that Christ would volunteer for this assignment, and the Father was pleased with Christ's suffering for others and his obedience, but not for the wickedness of mortals.[60]

"Seed," in verse ten, also has a range of interpretations. Several quote Elder McConkie, saying that the word "seed" includes the righteous that Christ visited in the spirit world during the three days of entombment, and also those who are adopted into Christ's family by obedience.[61] Others agree, saying "seed" are those who become spiritually adopted children of Christ by taking his name and living his commandments;[62] "loyal followers,"[63] or "seed" are those who accept the gospel, and by accepting it, become Christ's children, and thereby he is not cut off from land of living.[64]

Verse ten continues, "he shall prolong his days, and the pleasure of the Lord shall prosper in his hand." Elder McConkie writes that if this prophecy were meant to be fulfilled in Christ's day, it failed, but in the resurrection, the pleasure of the Lord is perfected, for when spirit and element are inseparably connected, God and man can receive fullness of joy (see D&C 93:33).[65] Brewster similarly explains that only in the resurrection of Christ was this prophecy fulfilled, because in mortality his days were shortened and in death he could not enjoy a fullness of joy.[66] Sperry seems to understand that "the seed shall have length of days (unending life)," and that "the pleasure of the Lord" refers to "the will of the Lord" which shall be accomplished through Christ.[67]

Isaiah 53:11

Christ and the Father will both be satisfied with results of the atonement (see Matthew 3:17, "in whom I am well pleased").[68] In the next phrase, scholars have interpreted "knowledge" to be the Father's knowledge that "It is finished,"[69] or "the knowledge he brings,"[70] or knowledge Jesus had of how to save.[71] With this knowledge and through the atonement, we will be justified, or declared righteous and pronounced innocent before God.[72] Meservy adds that the phrase "justify many" describes the exact nature of Christ's atonement, for though the atonement is available to all, many, but not all, will choose to accept it.[73] Nyman agrees that even though Christ suffered the pains of all humanity, only those who follow him will receive the full benefit (see 2 Nephi 9:21).[74]

Isaiah 53:12

The last verse deals with how Christ, because he willingly laid down his life, will share the victory with the Father. It refers to Christ's death among transgressors, and reveals that Christ knows by his experience what it is like to suffer pain and affliction (see Alma 7:11).[75]

Notes

1. See also *Orson Pratt's Works*, 23–9.

2. It is interesting to note here that Orson Pratt mentions that "Mr. [Joseph] Smith did not know anything about this prophecy at that time, for he was unacquainted with the contents of the Bible; he was brought up to work" (288). Hence, there appears to be no record of the Prophet ever equating the "sealed book" of Isaiah 29 with the Book of Mormon.

3. For a more recent synopsis of the Isaiah problem, see the *Anchor Bible Dictionary*, s.v. "Isaiah, Book of (Second Isaiah)."

4. Sperry's explanations of the meanings of Isaiah 2–14 (parallel to 2 Nephi 12–24) can also be found in his *The Isaiah Quotation: 2 Nephi 12–24* (Provo, Utah: FARMS, 1984); reprinted in *The Journal of Book of Mormon Studies* 4/1 (1995): 192–208. Sperry's analysis is consistent with his analysis in *Book of Mormon Compendium*, which is to focus more on clarifying or restating Isaiah than on scrupulously interpreting him.

5. The findings presented in this article are discussed more generally in "I Have a Question," *Ensign* (October 1984): 29, and are more specifically described in L. LaMar Adams, *The Living Message of Isaiah* (Salt Lake City: Deseret Book, 1981), 22–6, which is discussed in this bibliography (see p. 23).

6. Joseph Fielding Smith, comp., *Teachings of the Prophet Joseph Smith* (Salt Lake City: Deseret Book, 1976).

7. R. H. Charles, trans., *Ascension of Isaiah* (London: Black, 1900).

8. *Apocalyptic Book* is briefly and favorably reviewed in *Dialogue* 17/4 (1984): 144 by Gene Sessions, who calls the work a "masterpiece of scholarship."

9. Ludlow's work is reviewed by Paul Y. Hoskisson in *BYU Studies* 23/4 (1983): 503–8. Hoskisson calls the work an "important achievement" (p. 508) and a source of "reputable scholarship" and "informed discussion" (p. 503). He praises the work more

specifically for its "happy balance" (p. 504) of various source materials and for providing alternative interpretations (instead of dogmatic ones) for numerous passages. However, Hoskisson disapproves of certain features of the work, including Ludlow's infrequent references to the Dead Sea Scrolls, his belief that the Hebrew *elohim* always refers to God the Father, and his use of the word *irreligious* to refer to Palestinian Jews.

10. Brief summaries of Ludlow's interpretations on Isaiah 11 and 29 can also be seen in his *Unlocking the Old Testament* (Salt Lake City: Deseret Book, 1981), 145–76.

11. See William Hamblin's response to this article, entitled "'Isaiah Updated' Challenged," *Dialogue* 17/1 (1984): 4–7.

12. This article is an abridgment of an article of the same name, which Tvedtnes published through FARMS in 1981. The full 140-page article examines and classifies every Isaiah passage in the Book of Mormon that differs from the King James Version.

13. The first and second volumes of *Doctrinal Commentary* are reviewed by Louis Midgley in *Review of Books on the Book of Mormon* 1 (1989): 92–113, and by J. Frederic Voros Jr. in *BYU Studies* 29/2 (1989): 121–5. Midgley vigorously attacks the very plan or structure of the books, arguing that to McConkie and Millet, the Book of Mormon text "merely becomes the occasion for moralizing, platitudes, admonitions, while the actual meaning of the text may be ignored" (p. 105). Voros identifies numerous passages in the work that he finds "puzzling" (p. 124), "troubling" (p. 125), and even "uncharitable" (p. 125).

14. Gileadi's *New Translation* is reviewed by Alfred E. Krause in *Sunstone* 12/5 (1988): 44–5, Donald W. Parry in *Review of Books on the Book of Mormon* 4 (1992): 52–62, Bruce D. Porter in *Review of Books on the Book of Mormon* 4 (1992): 40–51, and Royal Skousen in *BYU Studies* 28/3 (1988): 124–7. Krause and Skousen are generally positive in their reviews, praising Gileadi's translation and introduction for making Isaiah comprehensible to a lay Latter-day Saint audience while at the same time appealing to biblical scholars from various other faiths. Although Porter is favorable in his assessment of Gileadi's translation, he heavily criticizes Gileadi's introduction for its "insistence on the dominance

within Isaiah of prophecies pertaining to the mission of the latter-day Davidic king" (p. 43). Parry also disapproves of Gileadi's introduction and extends it to Gileadi's translation, finally concluding that students of Isaiah would be better off not reading Gileadi's book (p. 62).

15. Though Nyman has not published a major article or book on Isaiah since 1991, he remains one of the most prolific Latter-day Saint Isaiah scholars. His most recent contribution appears to be his brief discussion of the possible fulfillments of the "kings" and "queens" language of Isaiah 49:23 in "What is the meaning or known fulfillment of the prophecy 'Kings shall be thy nursing fathers, and their queens thy nursing mothers'? (1 Ne. 21:23)," I Have a Question, *Ensign* (August 1994): 61. Nyman maintains a conservative approach to Isaiah, suggesting that the "kings" and "queens" are either (1) LDS missionaries who take the gospel to the Lamanite people or (2) the gentile nations—especially Great Britain and the United States—that have helped found the modern state of Israel.

16. Ridges is reviewed briefly by Terrence L. Szink in *Review of Books on the Book of Mormon* 4 (1992): 164–5, who finds minor deficiencies in the work. For example, the notes sometimes attempt to clarify terms that need no clarification. Szink states, however, that the work fulfills its goal of showing that Isaiah is comprehensible.

17. David Rolph Seely partly evaluates but mostly summarizes *Literary Message* in *Review of Books* 8/1 (1996): 69–79.

18. See Avraham Gileadi, "A Holistic Structure of the Book of Isaiah," (Ph.D. Diss. Brigham Young University, 1981).

19. Gorton's work is reviewed by Garold N. Davis and Mark J. Johnson in *Review of Books on the Book of Mormon* 7/1 (1995): 123–9, 130–8. Davis and Johnson both find the book a valuable tool for scholarship because it lays out several Isaiah texts side by side for easy comparison. The reviewers also find valuable Gorton's discussion of the "spiritual nature of the losses of the Isaiah texts" (p. 138), but they also point out deficiencies in the work. For example, Gorton ignores some significant Book of Mormon Isaiah passages, including the Isaiah chapters found in 2 Nephi 21 and 22.

20. See Elder Holland's chapter on this subject earlier in this volume. This addendum, prepared by Eric Smith and John W. Welch, augments the chapter on Isaiah 53 and Mosiah 14 in this volume.

21. Keith H. Meservy, "Isaiah 53: The Richest Prophecy on Christ's Atonement in the Old Testament" in *A Witness of Jesus Christ: The 1989 Sperry Symposium on the Old Testament*, ed. Richard D. Draper (Salt Lake City: Deseret Book, 1990), 156–7. In this volume, Jeffrey Holland discusses Isaiah as a witness for Christ.

22. George Reynolds and Janne M. Sjodahl, *Commentary on the Book of Mormon*, 2 vols. (Salt Lake City: Deseret Book, 1956), 2:154–5.

23. Hoyt W. Brewster Jr., *Isaiah, Plain and Simple: The Message of Isaiah in the Book of Mormon* (Salt Lake City: Deseret Book, 1995), 247.

24. Victor L. Ludlow, *Isaiah: Prophet, Seer, and Poet* (Salt Lake City: Deseret Book, 1982), 447.

25. Joseph Fielding McConkie and Robert L. Millet, *Doctrinal Commentary on the Book of Mormon: Jacob through Mosiah* (Salt Lake City: Bookcraft, 1988), 2:221.

26. David J. Ridges, *Isaiah Made Easier* (Springville, Utah: Copies Plus Printing, 1991), 47; Sidney B. Sperry, *Book of Mormon Compendium* (Salt Lake City: Bookcraft, 1968), 301–2.

27. See Brewster, *Isaiah, Plain and Simple*, 248; Avraham Gileadi, *The Apocalyptic Book of Isaiah: A New Translation with Interpretative Key* (Provo, Utah: Hebraeus Press, 1982), 136; Ludlow, *Isaiah: Prophet, Seer, and Poet*, 447; Bruce R. McConkie, *The Promised Messiah* (Salt Lake City: Deseret Book, 1978), 277–8; McConkie and Millet, *Doctrinal Commentary*, 2:222; Meservy, "Isaiah 53," 158; Robert L. Millet, "Abinadi's Messianic Sermon (Mosiah 12–16)," in *A Symposium on the Book of Mormon* (Salt Lake City: The Church of Jesus Christ of Latter-day Saints, 1986), 99; Monte S. Nyman, "Abinadi's Commentary on Isaiah," in *The Book of Mormon: Mosiah, Salvation Only Through Christ*, ed. Monte S. Nyman and Charles D. Tate Jr. (Provo, Utah: BYU Religious Studies Center, 1991), 165; Monte S. Nyman, *Great Are the Words of Isaiah* (Salt Lake City:

Bookcraft, 1980), 207; Reynolds and Sjodahl, *Commentary on the Book of Mormon*, 2:156; Ridges, *Isaiah Made Easier*, 47; Cleon W. Skousen, *Isaiah Speaks to Modern Times* (Salt Lake City: Ensign Publishing, 1984), 657; Sperry, *Book of Mormon Compendium*, 302.

28. For further similes involving young plants, compare Psalm 1:3; Jeremiah 17:5–8; and tender branches, see Jacob 5:4, 6.

29. Brewster, *Isaiah, Plain and Simple*, 248–9; David Rolph Seely, "The Lord Will Bring Salvation (Isaiah 51–66)," in *Studies in Scripture*, ed. Kent P. Jackson, 8 vols., *1 Kings to Malachi* (Salt Lake City: Deseret Book, 1993), 4:152.

30. Meservy, "Isaiah 53," 159; McConkie and Millet, *Doctrinal Commentary*, 2:222.

31. Millet, "Abinadi's Messianic Sermon," 99; Reynolds and Sjodahl, *Commentary on the Book of Mormon*, 2:157. See also Ridges, *Isaiah Made Easier*, 47.

32. Seely, "The Lord will Bring Salvation," 152; Sperry, *Book of Mormon Compendium*, 302.

33. See Meservy, "Isaiah 53," 159–60.

34. McConkie and Millet, *Doctrinal Commentary*, 2:222–3.

35. Victor L. Ludlow, *Unlocking the Old Testament* (Salt Lake City: Deseret Book, 1981), 169–70.

36. Ludlow, *Isaiah: Prophet, Seer, and Poet*, 449–52.

37. Meservy, "Isaiah 53," 160.

38. Brewster, *Isaiah, Plain and Simple*, 250; Skousen, *Isaiah Speaks*, 658–9; Sperry, *Book of Mormon Compendium*, 302–3; see also Mosiah 14:4.

39. Ludlow, *Isaiah: Prophet, Seer, and Poet*, 452; Millet, "Abinadi's Messianic Sermon," 99.

40. Meservy, "Isaiah 53," 160–2.

41. Brewster, *Isaiah, Plain and Simple*, 252.

42. Meservy, "Isaiah 53," 162.

43. Ridges, *Isaiah Made Easier*, 48; Reynolds and Sjodahl, *Commentary on the Book of Mormon*, 159.

44. Sperry, *Book of Mormon Compendium*, 303.

45. See Meservy, "Isaiah 53," 162–3; Reynolds and Sjodahl, *Commentary on the Book of Mormon*, 2:160; Skousen, *Isaiah Speaks*, 660–1; Sperry, *Book of Mormon Compendium*, 303.

46. Meservy, "Isaiah 53," 163 (and endnote 9); Ridges, *Isaiah Made Easier*, 48; Ellis T. Rasmussen, *A Latter-day Saint Commentary on the Old Testament* (Salt Lake City: Deseret Book, 1993), 532; Cleon W. Skousen, *The Fourth Thousand Years* (Salt Lake City: Bookcraft, 1966), 533.

47. Reynolds and Sjodahl, *Commentary on the Book of Mormon*, 2:160–2.

48. Reynolds and Sjodahl, *Commentary on the Book of Mormon*, 2:161.

49. See Brewster, *Isaiah, Plain and Simple*, 255; Meservy, "Isaiah 53," 165 (and endnote 10); Nyman, "Abinadi's Messianic Commentary," 174–5; Nyman, *Great Are the Words of Isaiah*, 209; Reynolds and Sjodahl, *Commentary on the Book of Mormon*, 2:162; Skousen, *The Fourth Thousand Years*, 533 n. 92.

50. McConkie, *Promised Messiah*, 471; Bruce R. McConkie, "Who Shall Declare His Generation?" *BYU Studies* 16/4 (1976): 553–5.

51. McConkie and Millet, *Doctrinal Commentary*, 2:224.

52. Sperry, *Book of Mormon Compendium*, 304.

53. Meservy, "Isaiah 53," 165; Reynolds and Sjodahl, *Commentary on the Book of Mormon*, 2:162; Skousen, *The Fourth Thousand Years*, 533 n. 93; Skousen, *Isaiah Speaks*, 661–2; Sperry, *Book of Mormon Compendium*, 304.

54. Brewster, *Isaiah, Plain and Simple*, 256.

55. Ridges, *Isaiah Made Easier*, 48.

56. See Church Educational System, *Old Testament: 1 Kings–Malachi*. 2d ed. (Salt Lake City: The Church of Jesus Christ of Latter-day Saints, 1981), 198; Philip J. Schlesinger, *Isaiah and the Book of Mormon* (n.p., 1990), 97; and Millet, "Abinadi's Messianic Sermon," 100.

57. Sperry, *Book of Mormon Compendium*, 305–6; Brewster, *Isaiah, Plain and Simple*, 257.

58. Nyman, "Abinadi's Commentary," 182–3.

59. Sperry, *Book of Mormon Compendium*, 305–9.

60. Skousen, *Isaiah Speaks*, 663; Ludlow, *Prophet, Seer, and Poet*, 456; Meservy, "Isaiah 53," 166.

61. Brewster, *Isaiah, Plain and Simple,* 257; CES, *Old Testament,* 198; McConkie, *Promised Messiah,* 362; McConkie and Millet, *Doctrinal Commentary,* 2:225; Millet, "Abinadi's Messianic Commentary," 100.

62. Ludlow, *Prophet, Seer, and Poet,* 456; see also Nyman, *Great Are the Words of Isaiah,* 210; Sperry, *Book of Mormon Compendium,* 306;

63. Ridges, *Isaiah Made Easier,* 48.

64. Skousen, *Isaiah Speaks,* 663.

65. McConkie, *Promised Messiah,* 362; see also Millet, "Abinadi's Messianic Commentary," 100–1

66. Brewster, *Isaiah, Plain and Simple,* 258.

67. Sperry, *Book of Mormon Compendium,* 306.

68. See Brewster, *Isaiah, Plain and Simple,* 258; Gileadi, *Apocalyptic Book,* 137; Meservy, "Isaiah 53," 167; Nyman, "Abinadi's Commentary," 184; Ridges, *Isaiah Made Easier,* 48; Schlesinger, *Isaiah and the Book of Mormon,* 94; Skousen, *Isaiah Speaks,* 663; Sperry, *Book of Mormon Compendium,* 306.

69. Meservy, "Isaiah 53," 168–9 (and endnotes 12–4).

70. Ridges, *Isaiah Made Easier,* 48.

71. Skousen, *Isaiah Speaks,* 663–4.

72. Brewster, *Isaiah, Plain and Simple,* 258.

73. Meservy, "Isaiah 53," 168.

74. Nyman, *Great Are the Words of Isaiah,* 184–5.

75. Ibid., 210–1.

Scripture Citation Index

1 Nephi (*continued*)

21:18, p. 332
21:18–25, p. 75
21:19, p. 326
21:21, pp. 326, 384
21:22, pp. 25, 117
21:22–3, pp. 110, 113, 326
21:22–6, p. 69
21:23, p. 505
21:24, p. 385
21:25–6, p. 386
21:26, p. 26, 83
22, pp. 25–6, 80, 116, 151
22:2, p. 56
22:3, p. 151
22:3, 9, p. 397
22:6, p. 80
22:7, pp. 110, 112
22:7–14, pp. 110, 111
22:8, pp. 112, 191
22:8, 9, 12, p. 111
22:9, p. 112
22:11, p. 80
22:14, p. 342
22:17, p. 115
22:22, p. 348n. 28
22:23, p. 165
22:24–5, p. 25
22:26, p. 25

2 Nephi

1:1, pp. 104, 118
1:4, pp. 104, 238n. 24
1:5–7, p. 207
1:10–1, p. 239
1:13, 14, 21, 23, p. 286n. 2
1:24, p. 187
2:8, p. 307
3, p. 107
3:3, p. 122n. 10
3:4–5, p. 401

3:7–9, 14–5, p. 107
3:12, p. 401
3:19–20, p. 211
4:34, p. 167
5, pp. 123, 144–5n. 2
5:28, 34, p. 145n. 2
5:30, p. 121n. 6
6, pp. 27, 77–83, 123, 145n. 2, 386, 387
6, 9, 10, p. 483
6:1–4, pp. 125–6
6:2, p. 125
6:3, p. 131
6:4, pp. 67, 69, 132
6:5, p. 191
6:5–9:22, p. 126
6:6, p. 26
6:6, 17, p. 69
6:6–7, pp. 139, 483
6:6–8:25, p. 69
6:6–18, p. 79
6:8, p. 238n. 24
6:8–11, p. 139
6:9, p. 26
6:10, pp. 26, 129
6:11–3, p. 27
6:14, p. 240n. 33
6:14–5, p. 27
6:17, p. 387
6:17–8, p. 386
6–8, pp. 77, 483, 493
6–10, pp. 24, 26–8, 30, 123–50, 152, 166
7, pp. 379, 384
7:1, p. 69
7:1–2, p. 11
7:2, pp. 27, 141, 384
7:2, 4, 5, pp. 380, 388
7:6, pp. 141, 333
7:7–8, p. 141
7:9, p. 27
7:10, p. 27
7:11, pp. 27, 483
7–9, p. 32
8:2, p. 126

8:2–3, p. 318
8:3, pp. 141, 142
8:4, pp. 27, 129, 136
8:4–5, p. 142
8:5, p. 129
8:7, pp. 136, 142, 327
8:9, p. 27
8:9–10, p. 141
8:10, p. 146n. 7
8:11, p. 27
8:12, p. 142
8:13, pp. 27, 131, 329
8:15, p. 132
8:16, p. 142
8:21, p. 236n. 11
8:22, p. 69
8:22–3, p. 142
8:24, pp. 52, 132
8:24, 25, p. 272
9, p. 305
9:1, pp. 124, 144n. 2
9:2, pp. 27, 306
9:3, p. 307
9:3–4, p. 138
9:4–22, p. 133
9:4–5, p. 143
9:5–6, p. 131
9:6–7, p. 133
9:7, p. 129
9:14, p. 132
9:15, p. 129
9:17, p. 136
9:21, p. 502
9:22, p. 129
9:23, p. 132
9:23–6, p. 126
9:24, p. 132
9:25, p. 136
9:25–7, p. 133
9:27, p. 136
9:27–38, p. 126
9:27–43, pp. 126–7
9:28, p. 166
9:30, p. 166
9:39, pp. 126, 130

Subject Index

atonement *(continued)*
  imagery of 10, 16–8, 316
  Jerusalem location of 60
  applied to house of Israel 98,
    203
  between man and god 301
  prophet teachings about
    262, 293, 358
  results of Jesus Christ's 7,
    20, 133
  salvation through Christ 7,
    20, 133, 341, 497–8, 502
  the word 148n. 22
  See also under Jesus Christ
Atonement, Day of 128, 131–4,
  148n. 22
authorship of Isaiah 149n. 33,
  423–35, 439–43, 450, 451, 457,
  458, 462–3, 464, 486, 491
autumn festivals, Israelite
  123–50

Babylon
captivity of Israel by 198, 200,
  203, 256, 274–5, 401, 457, 461,
  478, 485
  as enemy 149n. 32, 236n. 9
  destruction of 73, 158, 168,
    203
  Israel delivered from 62,
    102–3, 154, 252, 461, 478
  symbolism of 73–4, 155, 171
Babylon, king of 101, 198–9
Ball, Terry 492
Ballard, Melvin J. 500
baptism for the dead 281
barren woman 314–36, 340, 344,
  345, 346, 347n. 12
beautiful 258–9, 261, 274, 288
Begrich, J. 137

Benjamin 289n. 25, 312n. 6
Benson, Ezra Taft 114, 116
Bible 56, 104–5, 171, 177, 215,
  223, 226, 233, 245, 246, 282,
  354, 359, 371, 391–403, 423,
  424, 439, 445, 472
  compared to Book of
    Mormon 56, 246n. 77,
    369–90, 391–405, 439, 472
  evidences Book of
    Mormon's truthfulness
    226
  integrity of Isaiah in 423–4
  Joseph Smith's understand-
    ing of 91n. 21
  and the Joseph Smith
    Translation 227–33, 245n.
    66, 472
  teachings from 282, 391–405
  on watchmen 255–9
  See also Joseph Smith
    Translation (JST); King
    James Version of the Bible
    (KJV); New Testament;
    Old Testament
bill of divorcement 11
Bloom, Harold 91n. 21
Blowing of the Trumpets 128
book, heavenly 172, 181–2,
  184, 186, 190n. 14
Book of Commandments 426
Book of Mormon 97, 485
  as the sealed book 209, 211,
    220, 224, 230, 446–7, 449–
    50, 471–2, 503n. 2
  authenticity of 226, 448, 451,
    456–7
  restoration of 62, 109, 159,
    191, 210–1, 216, 222, 361, 364,
    365, 402, 455–6, 458, 474

Nephi's own 24; 26; 28; 159;
161; 168; 201–6; 202; 204–5;
213; 214–5; 216; 217; 219;
229; 238nn. 21, 22; 239
See also multiple fulfillment
of prophecy.
prophecy, spirit of 32, 47, 56–8,
63, 64n. 8, 118, 474
prophet(s) 3, 32, 48, 57, 64n.
13, 107, 187–8, 195, 199, 205,
262, 272, 275, 283, 288, 303,
320, 329, 364, 425, 495
call/commission of 172, 353
call narratives of 172–89
prophetic speech forms 48,
54–65
prophetic worldview 19–33,
305, 308
prophets, false 64n. 6
prophets, Nephite 68, 75–83,
86, 396, 398, 400, 423
psalm of Nephi 167
Puritans 391–2

Qumran 277, 278, 291n. 37,
476
qeḏuššāh. See song of praise

Rachel 347n. 11
Rad, Gerhard von 127
rainbow 339
Rasmussen, Ellis T. 359, 490,
498
Rebekah 347n. 11
Redeemer 97, 99, 111, 153, 264,
272, 293, 322, 329–31. *See also*
Jesus Christ
redemption 95, 99, 103–4, 105,
107, 110, 117, 118, 119, 120, 208,
264, 266, 272, 298, 305, 399
of Israel. *See also* Israel:
restoration of

rejection of Christ 496–7
Rencher, Alvin C. 462–3
Reorganized Church of Jesus
Christ of Latter Day Saints
372
repentance 133–5, 213, 321,
498
representative of God 125
restoration 12, 13, 62, 100, 107,
113, 119, 186, 187, 198, 203,
216, 273, 353, 356, 357, 360,
447
of the gospel 107, 109, 113,
115, 116, 117, 118, 119, 156,
215, 217, 222, 261, 398, 401,
445, 449–50, 479, 482, 490,
494
of Israel 25, 28, 31, 84, 104,
139, 168, 185, 397, 458, 487.
See also Israel: gathering of
of the Jews 205, 400
of the Nephites 143
resurrection 20, 27, 129, 264–5,
299, 304, 307, 341, 501
resurrection of the dead 305,
307
revelation 49, 51, 54–5, 56, 57–
8, 108, 237n. 12, 426
Revelation, book of 171–2,
178, 186
Reynolds, George 454–6, 496,
497, 498, 499, 500
Ricks, Stephen D. 171–90
Ridges, David J. 485–6, 496,
498, 500, 505
Rigdon, Sidney 229, 231, 246n.
74, 426
righteousness, verification of
340–2
Robbins, Margaret 382
Roberts, B. H. 448–9

List of Contributors

Robert A. Cloward is an institute instructor in Cedar City, Utah, for the Church Educational System.

John Gee is currently a Ph.D. candidate in Egyptology at Yale University.

Cynthia L. Hallen is associate professor of linguistics at Brigham Young University.

Andrew H. Hedges is visiting assistant professor of Church history and doctrine at Brigham Young University.

John L. Hilton is adjunct professor of statistics at Brigham Young University.

Jeffrey R. Holland is a member of the Quorum of the Twelve Apostles of The Church of Jesus Christ of Latter-day Saints.

Ann N. Madsen is senior lecturer of ancient scripture at Brigham Young University.

Donald W. Parry is assistant professor of Hebrew language and literature at Brigham Young University.

Dana M. Pike is assistant professor of ancient scripture at Brigham Young University.

Stephen D. Ricks is professor of Hebrew and Semitic languages at Brigham Young University.

David Rolph Seely is associate professor of ancient scripture at Brigham Young University.

Andrew C. Skinner is associate professor of ancient scripture at Brigham Young University.

Royal Skousen is professor of English at Brigham Young University and since 1988 has served as the editor of the Book of Mormon critical text project.

Eric Smith is a Brigham Young University graduate who is currently studying law at the University of Utah.

John S. Thompson is currently coordinating the seminary and institute programs in the Philadelphia area for the Church Educational System.

John W. Welch is Robert K. Thomas Professor of Law at Brigham Young University and serves as editor-in-chief of *BYU Studies.*

Janet L. Garrard Willis is a Brigham Young University graduate who worked as an editorial assistant for *BYU Studies* and taught high school English.